Roads to Saratoga

John Trumball
The Surrender of General Burgoyne at Saratoga, 16 October 1777 (detail)
Yale University art Gallery
Trumbull Collection

Roads to Saratoga

THE CONTINUING SAGA
ABOUT THE SETTLEMENT AND DEFENSE
OF NEW YORK'S MOHAWK VALLEY
DURING THE 1700S

Gil Herkimer

Alfa Publishers
715 Upper South Broadway, Suite 1002
Corpus Christi, Texas 78401

Dedicated to my Palatine ancestors

OTHER BOOKS BY GIL HERKIMER

Roads to Oriskany
Roads to Niagara (to be published in 2000)

The author thanks the Yale University Art Gallery for the rights and reproduction permission to reprint *The Surrender of General Burgoyne at Saratoga, 16 October 1777* by John Trumball.

Alfa Publishers, Corpus Christi, Texas
Copyright © 1999 by Allen G. Herkimer, Jr.
All rights reserved. Published 1999.
Printed in the United States of America

ISBN 0-9651170-1-4

CONTENTS

ACKNOWLEDGMENTS

I never imagined my original book, *Roads to Oriskany,* which dealt with the German Palatines' early 1700 emmigration to the New York Colony as the British indentured servants would evolve into a trilogy. As the author researched the subject, he discovered more stones that needed to be uncovered and explored. This book, *Roads to Saratoga,* overlaps the period just after the Battle of Oriskany and continues through the time when the British general, Gentleman Johnny Burgoyne, surrenders to the American general, Horatio Gates at Saratoga. As in the Oriskany book, the author interweaves the lives and activities of the fictitious Palatine Heindrick family and their friend, who live in New Palatine, a fictious settlement located in the Mohawk Valley's western frontier.

My first acknowledgement is to my ancestors who emigrated from Germany's Palatine area during the very early 1700s, worked as British indentured servants in their futile effort to manufacture naval supplies, especially pine tar and masts, for the growing British naval armada; then these newcomers settled in New York's Mohawk Valley, surviving its inclement weather and other adversities associated with life in the colony's western most frontier and its primitive forests.

One individual to whom I am greatly indebted is Walter Rose, a longtime friend who helped me comb through numerous books and libraries for factual information about the Palatines, General John Burgoyne, General Philip Schuyler, their associates, and accompanying me on some of my hikes through the Mohawk Valley.

A very special thanks to Suzanne Warned and the Yale University Art Gallery for allowing me to use the reproduction of John R. Trumbull's, *The Surrender of General John Burgoyne at Saratoga,* 16 Oct 1777, on the book's cover. Also, another special thanks to Todd Sanders of the Publishing Services Group for his help in the design and the layout of the book, to Thelma Mennem for her editing skills, and to Scott Player for his research and fine work on the maps.

Finally, I am extremely grateful to my wife, Fay Page, for her editing assistance, her constant encouragement and love to finish this portion of the planned trilogy.

G.H.
Corpus Christi, Texas
September 22, 1999

INTRODUCTION
Facts or Fiction?

This book is the sequel to *Roads to Oriskany* which was about the emigration of the fictional Heindrick family from Germany's Palatine region. The family came to America as indentured servants in the British experiment to manufacture naval supplies in the southern part of the New York colony. The book accurately described the Palatines' trials and tribulations as they settled and defended New York's Mohawk Valley, and ended with the bloody Battle of Oriskany.

Roads to Saratoga continues the Heindrick's saga with their friends and neighbors, and their interactivities with factual historical characters and events, accurately describing occurrences that happened after the Battle of Oriskany, subsequently leading to the defeat of the British at the Battle of Saratoga. I have used fictional characters as either participants in or as storytellers of historical events; these have been thoroughly researched and recorded. In writing the dialogues between historical principals, such as Generals Gates and Arnold, I have exercised my imagination. These dialogues are based upon research of the characters' attitudes and the situation being discussed.

The following is an attempt to clarify fact from fiction. I hope you find this helpful.

ONE   Before and After

This chapter is intended to give you an accurate, historical perspective of New York's Mohawk Valley, hereafter referred to as the *valley,* and its early inhabitants; all are factual individuals except the Heindrick family.

TWO   The End Has Just Started

I have identified the Battle of Lexington as the *beginning of the end* of the ancient, ancestral ties among the Iroquois Indian tribes, as well as the division of the white settlers in the valley; leading, eventually, to freedom from the king of England.

THREE   Southward Ho!

Felix and Fanny Loescher, the *unpowdered* woman, are historical individuals who accompanied Burgoyne while he implemented his "Thoughts" on the separation and capture of the American colonies. This author and other historians owe a debt of gratitude to Major-General von Riedesel's wife, Madame Fredrika von Riedesel, for her faithful recording of Burgoyne's expedition.

FOUR   The Day After

After the Battle of Oriskany, General Philip Schuyler did order General Benedict Arnold to recruit militia from the valley for the eastern front, as described.

FIVE   Two Brothers

The demographic information of slavery and blacks in New York is reported as researched, as is the story of Hon Yost as told by Sergeant George Jefferson.

SIX   Act of Providence

The term, "Act of Providence," has been frequently used by historians in describing the horrific thunderstorm, which fortunately for the rebels, fell during the Battle of Oriskany. The thirteen-year-old, Jan Van Eps and the fifteen-year-old Oneida Indian Chief's daughter are factual, as is Dr. Petri, General Herkimer's personal physician.

SEVEN   Targeted Fortress

Benedict Arnold and Ethan Allen's capture of Fort Ticonderoga is recorded as researched, as is Arnold's meeting with Washington, and Henry Knox's expedition to Boston.

EIGHT   **Southward Bound**

Burgoyne's selected generals and their backgrounds are identified as researched. Using fictional residents of New Palatine, I have created possible reactions of the Palatines, rebel and loyalist alike, to the call for enlistments to the Tryon County Militia.

NINE   **Escape and Triumph**

This chapter describes how St. Clair led the American retreat from Fort Ticonderoga, and the fort's eventual capture by the British.

TEN   **In Hot Pursuit**

The story as told by fictional character, Helena Kerchner, about Mrs. Samuel Campbell, her sister, Mrs. Cannon, and the Buxtons is factual as related and researched by the author. Colonel Philip Skene, a loyalist leader, is a factual individual who selfishly advised Burgoyne; Skeneborough or Skeneboro, was named after him. The Battle of Hubbardon has been reported as accurately as possible.

ELEVEN   **Interlude**

The story about the three young girls attacked by Indians while picking raspberries outside Fort Stanwix is factual, as is the report of the material and construction of the first Continental flag to be flown over a battle; there is some controversy as to the exact time and place when the flag was first raised on a battle site.

TWELVE   **Decisions, Decisions**

Arnold's reflections concerning the Battle of Quebec accurately depict the facts of the battle. Arnold and Washington actually did spend four days together in reviewing Quebec; afterwards, Washington ordered Arnold to construct a naval fleet on Lake Champlain.

THIRTEEN   **Lull Before the Storm**

The scalping and murder of Jane McCrae, which resulted in a grand rush of volunteers to join the rebel army, is factual.

FOURTEEN   After Oriskany

The story of General Herkimer's death is factual.

FIFTEEN   Double Trouble

The often mentioned date, November 12, 1757, was the actual date the valley experienced a most disastrous raid by the French and Indians. White Tail is the fictional Mohawk nephew of Chief Joseph Brant who befriended Walter Heindrick and Helena Kerchner; to the author's best knowledge, Chief Brant, who is a factual and historical character, did *not* obstruct any assistance to his former neighbor, General Herkimer.

SIXTEEN   Engagement

Gates's incessant rivalry and jealousy of Philip Schuyler and Benedict Arnold is well documented.

SEVENTEEN   To Arms

Through dialogue, I have tried to accurately describe the Battle of Bennington as researched. Kateri Tekakwitha, a Mohawk candidate for sainthood, was actually the first Indian nun.

EIGHTEEN   The Other Shoe

Thanks to Colonel Daniel Morgan and his Virginia riflemen, the Kentucky rifle, as described, was truly one of the rebels' secret weapons.

NINETEEN   Preparedness

Again, Madame von Riedesel's diary has masterfully documented Burgoyne and his troops' activities.

TWENTY   The Crisis Is Near

The story of Arnold's departure, and Poor's petition are factual, as is Morgan's wild turkey call to reassemble his troops.

TWENTY ONE   Down on the Farm

The *crisis is near* warning of Colonel Colburn to General Gates was a forewarning of the inevitable demise of traditional European warfare used by Burgoyne and the acceptance of the rebel's guerilla fighting as executed by Arnold and Morgan; meanwhile Gates preferred to keep his distance from Bemis Heights.

TWENTY TWO   Interlude

The story, as told by Sergeant George Jefferson, about the sixteen-year-old Lieutenant Hervey of the British 62nd Regiment is factual, as is the account of the captured British soldier carrying a message in a swallowed musketball. Gates actually did tell Arnold, "As far as I'm concerned your services are inconsequential to the army."

TWENTY THREE   Begin the Game

Assisted by first-hand reports from artillery officer Ebeneazer Matton and Madame von Riedesel, I have faithfully described the Battle of Saratoga, including Arnold's role.

TWENTY FOUR   Aftermath

Burgoyne, actually honored Simon's burial request as described. The story of the soldier's wife volunteering to bring water back from the river is factual.

TWENTY FIVE   Negotiations

The recorded dialogues among the British and American officers accurately reflect the negotiation process and the prevailing attitudes of the American soldiers.

TWENTY SIX   Ground Their Arms

Burgoyne, while *house guest* of General Philip Schuyler, actually did visit Arnold at a hospital in Albany, New York, after the convention process was completed.

TWENTY SEVEN Homeward

Walter Heindrick's and Benjamin Jefferson's stories about their families are based upon similar, researched real-life stories, as is Ole Folks's description of transportation on the Mohawk River. Blood Creek was named as described.

TWENTY EIGHT At Last!

The report of Seneca Chief Sayenquerahta's statement concerning Indian food shortages is factual, as were the reports of Chief Brant's and Major John Butler's Rangers threats to continue raids throughout the valley. White Tail's Aunt Mary story is based upon a real person named Mary Jemison. Walter's description of the ambush at Oriskany and Herkimer's wounding is factual.

TWENTY NINE The Parting

While staying with General Schuyler in his home, Burgoyne did, in fact, apologize for the destruction of Schuyler's original Saratoga mansion. "That's the fate of war . . . let's say no more about it," was Schuyler's response. As for Gates's farewell, the speech included here gives an accurate account of Gates's *message* to his troops.

MAPS

CANADA AND THE NORTHERN CAMPAIGN

NORTHERN CAMPAIGN ENLARGEMENT

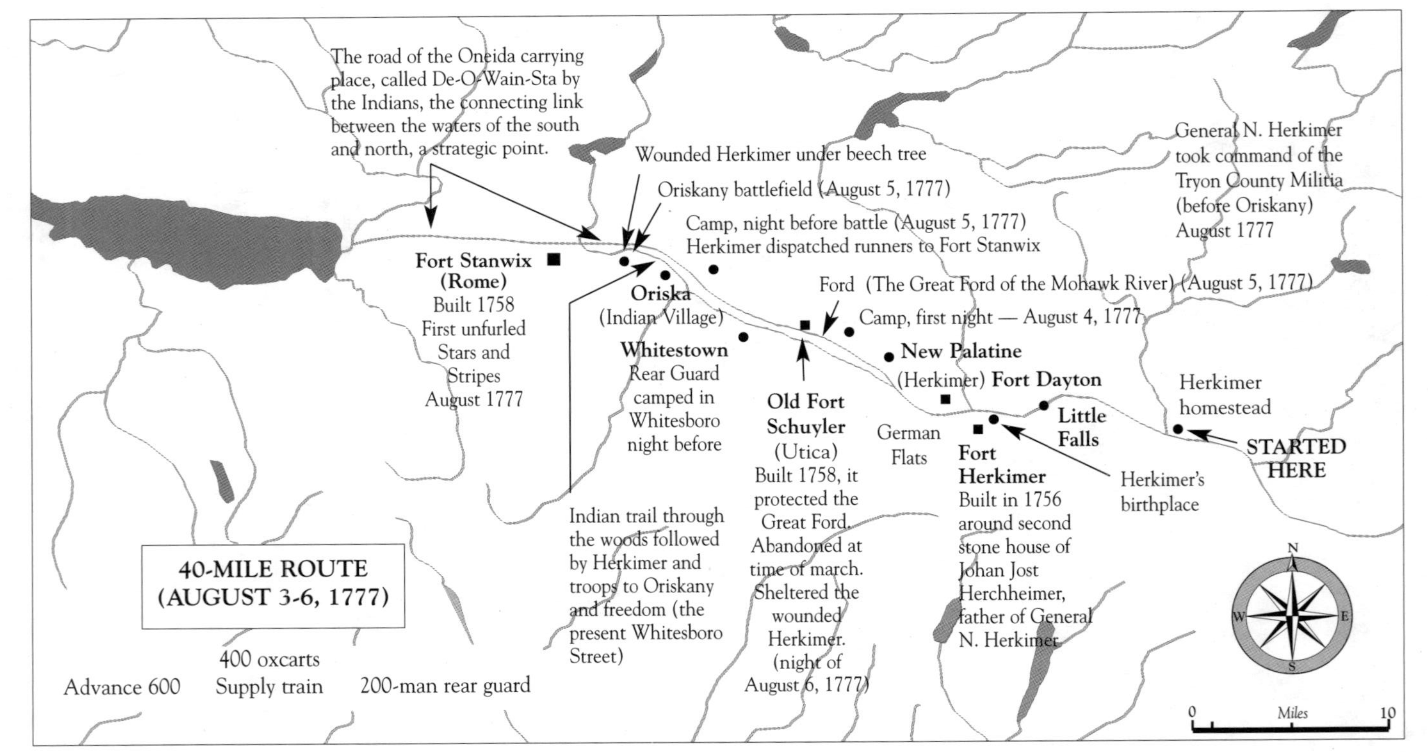

THE BATTLE OF FREEMAN'S FARM
SEPTEMBER 19TH, 1777

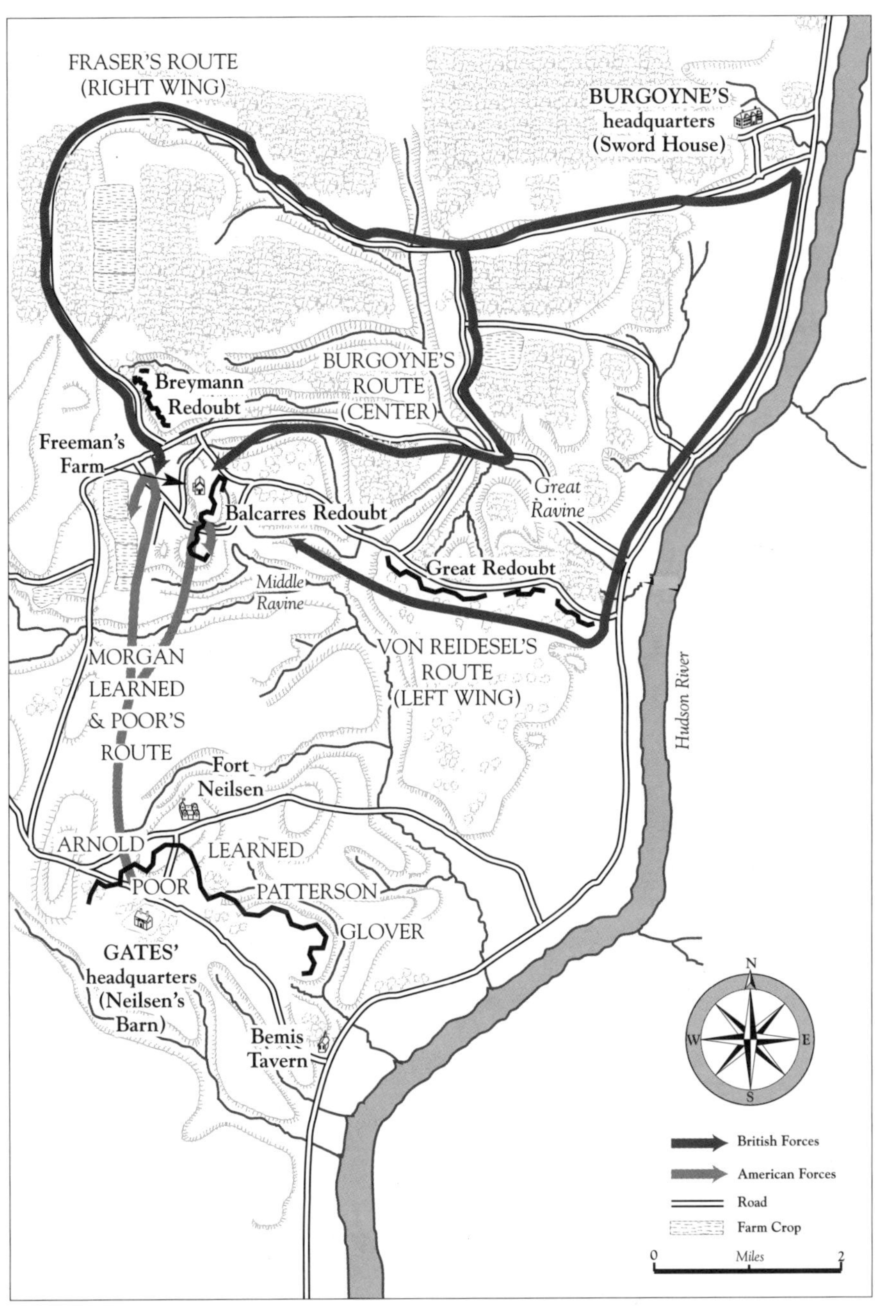

THE BATTLE OF BEMIS HEIGHTS
OCTOBER 7TH, 1777

FAMILY CHARTS

HEINDRICK

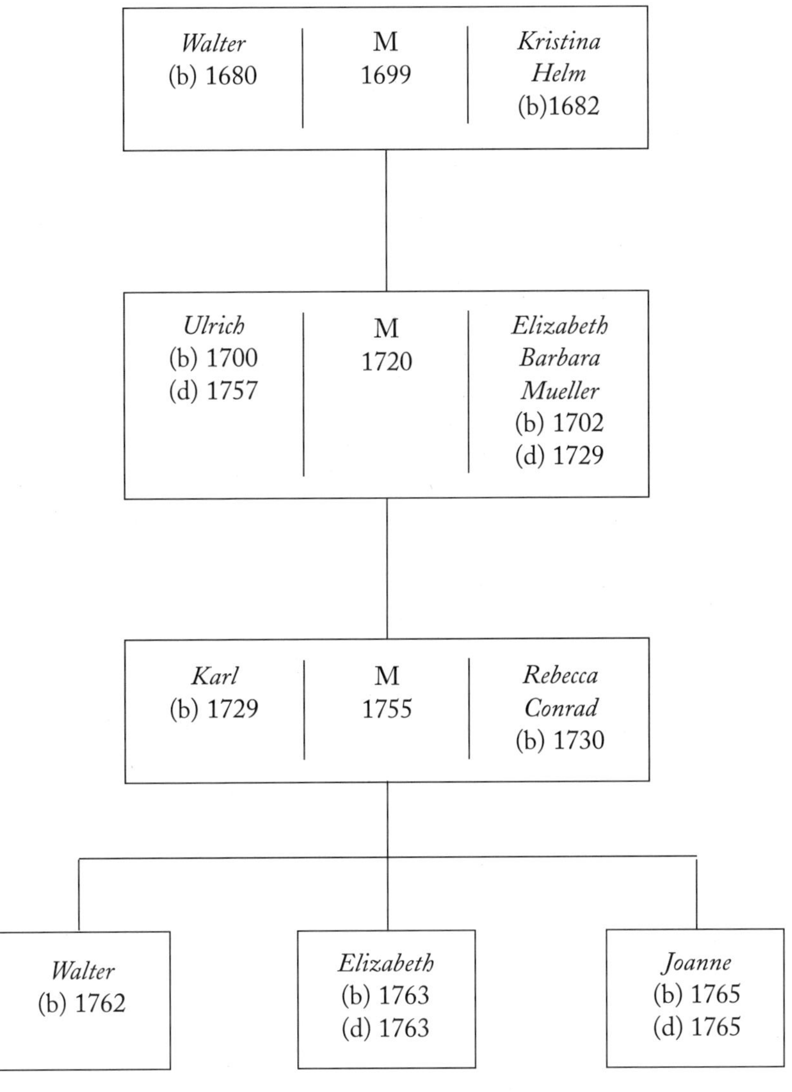

KERCHNER

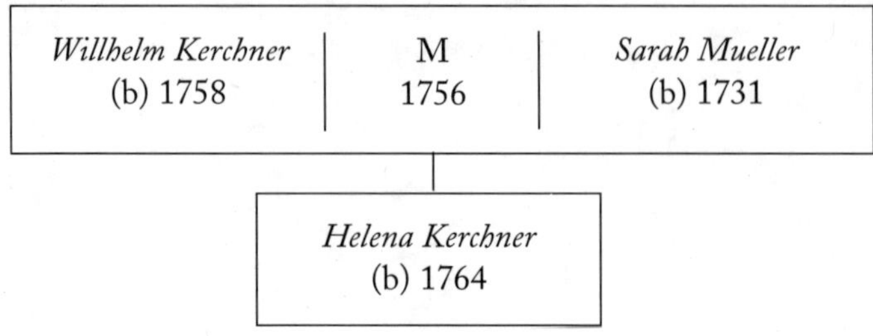

STOUFFER

JEFFERSON
(former Slaves of Herr Schuyler)

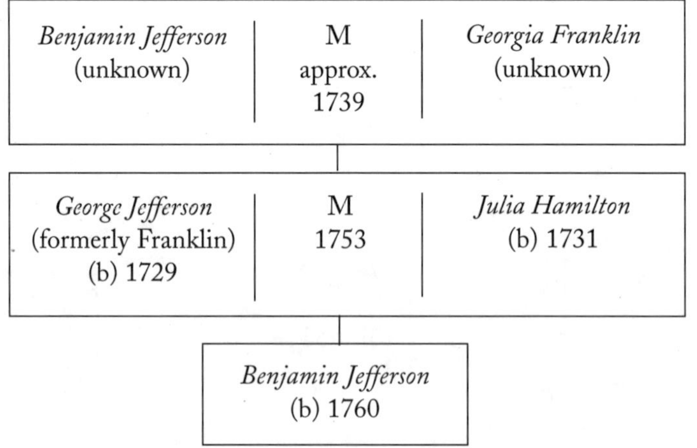

PROLOGUE

Wednesday, August 6, 1777, was the day of infamy for all British loyalists (Tories), rebels, and Indians living in New York's Mohawk Valley.

The years of pent-up rage and hatred were all disastrously brought together on that day during the Battle of Oriskany that ended with many British, Tories, rebels, and Indians entangled in a death grip with each other wherever they fell, many never to be found or buried.

Everyone in the valley knew that peace could never be reached until both rebels and Tories were conclusively free from the domination of King Charles III of England or the British completely defeated the rebels and returned them as subjects of the Royal Crown. Even if the latter was to occur, the absolute defeat of the British and their Tory supporters could be the only acceptable and ultimate solution.

There will always be controversy about who won the gouging and slashing in the Battle of Oriskany. General Nicholas Herkimer's force of 800 Tryon County Militia failed to relieve Fort Stanwix, the isolated fortress in the wilderness that protected the western entrance of the valley. Most importantly, British Brigadier General Barry St. Leger's forces of regulars, Tories, French, and Indians never reached their assigned destination, Albany, New York. And luckily for the rebels, all of St. Leger's forces left the battle site while the rebels were still in possession. The royalists, undoubtedly, did so knowing that the rebels were too badly mauled (later estimated at 200 killed, 250 wounded and 200 militia taken prisoners) to follow them. The remaining able-bodied colonists were able to leave the scene of battle, taking their wounded with them and claiming to have beaten off the enemy. This would seem to indicate that they left the field without hindrance.

The greatest tragedy of this battle was that most of the rebel forces, which included most of German Flats's Committee of Safety, were killed. According to the Committee of Safety, the "flower of our militia are either killed or wounded except one hundred and fifty of the original eight hundred who had left Fort Dayton en route to Fort Stanwix who stood the field and forced the enemy to retreat." General Herkimer himself was fatally wounded. With the exception of the "*dastardly rear guard (approximately two hundred) which retreated at the first fire,*" the militia suffered terribly.

Historians have agreed that despite the relatively small number of men engaged, the encounter resulted in what was *one of the bloodiest and most bitterly fought battles of the American Revolution.* Hardly a single family—rebel, Tory or Indian—in the valley did not suffer a wounded member or a death.

This day of infamy was not the end; it was just the beginning of the end.

BEFORE AND AFTER

EARLY 1700'S

NEW YORK'S MOHAWK RIVER VALLEY

Before white settlers even set foot in the domain, the Mohawk Valley had an interesting history.

For centuries it had been inhabited by numerous Indian tribes, the most important of which was the powerful Five Nations Confederacy or the League of the Iroquois. The league was originally comprised of the ancestors of the Mohawk, Oneida, Onondaga, Cayuga, and Seneca and were joined eventually by the Tuscarora tribe. For them, the valley had been the nearest place to paradise.

One of the valley's earliest white explorers, Arendt Van Curler, viewing the cool, clear valley streams flowing through and around narrow, jagged cataracts, was completely overwhelmed by the valley's stark beauty and its potential resources. These streams plunged down and over waterfalls, deepening the gorges before they joined the valley's mighty Mohawk River, which flowed east-west between Lake Ontario and the Hudson River. Van Curler had often seen the native Indians using the river and its tributaries as their primary means of transportation for the region.

In 1642, Van Curler reported to the Dutch patroon, Van Rensselaer, who had commissioned him to explore the valley, that the valley was "the most beautiful land that eyes of man ever beheld."

During the early 1600's and into the 1700's the white population of the New World consisted primarily of transplanted Europeans, initially led by the Dutch, French, and English. Eventually, many English settlers migrated westward along the Mohawk Valley, and gradually these became the dominant political force in the colony. Consequently, the Iroquois had, for over a century, believed that the English were friendly, and that they were the progeny of the "Great White Father" on the other side of the sea.

This situation became increasingly unsettled during the early 1700's. It was then that a group of cantankerous lovers of freedom, stubbornly independent thinkers known as the *Palatines* arrived in the valley from Germany via England.

The Palatines were from an area which encompassed both sides of the Rhine River and its tributaries, the Main and Neckar rivers. The Palatine extended roughly from the junction of the Moselle and the Rhine south to Basel, Switzerland, alongside the Lorraine region, and as far west along the Main as Bayreuth, bordering the Upper (or Bavarian) Palatinate.

During May 1707, the French unexpectedly crossed the Rhine River terrorizing and plundering the Palatinate, Baden, and Swabian Circle of southwestern Germany. That September, the French forces retired across the Rhine, having, in the words of an angry French colonel, ". . . over-run the lazy and sleepy Empire and not only maintained a great army in it all the year, but sent contributions and money back into France to help the King's other affairs." From a military point of view, this invasion had been unnecessary. It was also a political blunder, as it united German resistance against France's King Louis XIV.

For the people living in the Palatine war zone, the devastation from these invasions, together with heavy taxation and religious quarrels, wiped out the fruits of many of their new and promising ventures, and discouraged many of them from striving for better living conditions in the their devastated home land.

Near the end of 1708, nature added to the Palatines' misery. During October, an unprecedented cold settled and stayed to curse the region. The cold was so intense that, by November, firewood would not burn in the open air. In January 1709 wine and spirits froze into solid blocks of ice. Birds on the wing fell dead, and saliva congealed as it fell from mouth to ground.

One blustery night, a group of Palatines congregated in Walter and Christina Heindrick's home in Heidelberg, Germany, together with their nine-year-old son, Ulrich, and others of their cold, shivering, hungry friends and neighbors. Everyone huddled together on the straw-covered dirt floor of the Heindricks farmhouse. That night they unanimously accepted the "golden promises" offered by England's Queen Anne which extolled the benefits of settling in Her Majesty's Plantations in America to manufacture and harvest naval supplies for Her Majesty's Navy. The golden promises, partially penned by Lutheran minister Rev. Josus Kocherthal, helped to create the impression that all persons willing to emigrate to America could expect the same help, support, and land grants from the British government as he, the good Reverend, and his followers had received.

After much discussion, postponements, and prayers, the Heindricks and their friends began the long, frustrating, and exhausting journey that would lead them through the Netherlands, England, and eventually to the valley.

A three week journey down the Rhine and its tributaries led a great number of Palatines to The Hague and Rotterdam. Queen Anne dispatched transport ships to Rotterdam and ordered the ship captains to return to England with the Palatines.

In late April 1709 four transports carrying 852 Palatines left Rotterdam and arrived in London in early May. This was the first of eight similar transports that eventually brought 13,146 Palatine emigrants from Germany to England. The last emigration was on October 11, 1709, when 1,082 Palatines left Rotterdam and arrived in London on October 18th. Palatines were literally flooding London.

Queen Anne, however, suddenly decided to save only "poor German Protestants." The Roman Catholic Palatines in London and in Rotterdam awaiting transportation were given the choice of becoming "poor Protestants" to be saved by the Queen or to return to their homes along the Rhine. Many of the Palatines were followers of Martin Luther, others were devout Roman Catholics; still some found it necessary to change their religion.

Their misery had not stopped when they arrived in England. Poverty. Death. Starvation. Disease. Quarrels. Crowded quarters.

Heat and rain. Cold and snow. These and many other adversities had not discouraged the Palatines. In fact, their determination to leave this cursed misery once and for all was strengthened.

It was not until April 10, 1710 that ten ships finally pulled anchor from Portsmouth, England and set sail for New York. On June 13, 1710 the *Lyon* entered New York harbor. Another ship, the *Herbert*, was wrecked on the eastern shore of Long Island on July 7. The last ship of the convoy did not reach New York until August 2, 1710. The miserable traveling conditions caused great numbers of young children to die. The last letters before the journey began from Portsmouth in April reported 80 deaths on one ship and 100 sick on another. Thomas Benson, a surgeon, reported that on his ship alone, 330 persons had been seriously sick at one time.

Soon after they arrived in the New York Colony they discovered why the British had been so generous with their promises. To their surprise and dismay, the Palatines learned that they had been brought to New York Colony as *indentured servants*. They were settled north of New York City in Livingston Manor to work in an experiment to produce naval supplies (masts, yard arms, etc.) and tar for the British sailing vessels. The Palatines understanding of the promise given was that upon arriving in America, the British would assign each of them forty acres of land. According to contracts written in the English language (most could read only German), the British controlled the prices they charged the Palatines for food, tools, and whatever other services they used. These charges were to be added to overall costs for each Palatine. Thus, the total cost of transport, relocation, staples, and other supplies was totally controlled by the British. To the stunned Palatines, their terms of servitude seemed to be a never-ending process. Nevertheless, they continued to work, albeit intermittently, and they did not try to hide their disgust with the system or the situation.

By September 1712 the entire naval supply venture to which they had been assigned was an economic disaster. The unwillingness of the labor supply to work under frontier conditions, poor project management, and inexperienced instruction in the tar-making methods all contributed to the failure of the naval-stores project. On September 6,1712, New York Governor Robert Hunter ordered the Palatines to be informed that henceforth they would have to provide for themselves. The last day of the Crown's governmental support was September 12, 1712; only a few helpless widows and orphans were taken care of until September 23rd.

Autumn had barely arrived yet they had already experienced the bleak and freezing weather of upstate New York. Many were attracted to Pennsylvania by William Penn's intensive marketing campaign; some returned to New York City while others migrated north to the Albany and Mohawk Valley area. From the time they had settled in the fertile Mohawk Valley the Palatines were generally prosperous and had built strong and substantial homes, forts, and settlements.

On November 12, 1757, a military force composed of 300 Indians, French, and Canadians came up the Black River Valley, emerged from the mountain forests, and fell without warning on all the Palatine settlements on the north side of the Mohawk River. They made a clean sweep. Settlers' residents and barns stuffed with harvested crops, stock, horses, cattle, sheep, and swine were burned. Some people were slain and nearly 100 carried off as prisoners. Most of the valley people saved themselves by fleeing across the river and seeking refuge in the fort on the south side while the enemy completed the destruction, taking much booty and many prisoners. By nightfall, it was over; the destruction was complete.

One of the victims was Ulrich Heindrick. The nine-year-old emigrant, who in 1709 had migrated from Germany's Palatine with his parents, was a man now, married and with a grown son, twenty-eight-year-old, Karl. It was Karl, together with his wife Rebecca, who discovered Ulrich's savagely mutilated body, and his wooden farmhouse burned to the ground in the settlement of New Palatine in the Mohawk Valley. Karl and Rebecca vowed revenge and were determined that their next home would be built of stone or brick.

In April 1758 a small band of French marauders and a large body of Indians attacked the Palatine settlements on the south side of the river, but this time the party did not succeed in completely surprising the settlers. Warning had been received in time to allow many of the settlers to congregate in a fort where Captain Nicholas Herkimer, the future general, was in command. The attack failed, but not before the invading force killed thirty of the Palatines and destroyed many of the unprotected farmsteads.

During the following year, French-controlled Quebec fell to the British. This collapse and the following Peace of Paris Treaty in 1763 concluded the French and Indian War and marked the end of France as a power in North America. The colonists then enjoyed a period of peace from the constant fighting caused by the international politics on the colony's western frontier. The Palatines, as well as the other valley settlers and returning captives, were able to resume developing the valley and rebuilding their devastated homes and barns. Prosperity came back again to stay—for a while.

Throughout the French and Indian War, the Palatines were notable for their demonstrated bravery and effectiveness in battle. From the settlements stretching from German Flats to Palatine, a sturdy dependable group of militia, separated into nine companies, was organized by Sir William Johnson, a baronet and Indian Superintendent for all North America; he had depended upon this militia for his measures of defense during the French and Indian War.

The militia was designed to meet critical emergencies or, in less formal operations, to keep control of the country and cut off foragers. The militiamen showed a reluctance to travel to distant parts of America and serve in the formal army; they were more willing to bear arms with the regulars for a limited period of time if the brunt of the conflict was situated in their own region. These men were often less than ideal combat troops, but their proficiency with firearms and their familiarity with the terrain often counterbalanced their lack of formal military training. Turbulence, however, continued throughout the valley, but the tension among the residents did not come from the interference of a foreign nation. The resentment, hatred, and related differences were always simmering, and kept rising among the European settlers in the valley.

The search for religious freedom had been one of the primary reasons why the English had settled in the Americas, especially in the New England colonies. Differences in religious beliefs became a major political controversy among the Colonists and the mother country. The northern members of the Anglican Church of America were eagerly advocating for an episcopate of their own. These actions threatened the New England Congregationalists and the middle Colony Presbyterians who formed into an opposing religious affiliation to counteract the Anglicans. This group feared that the introduction of an episcopate would lead to political powers wielded by American bishops similar to those of the English bishops and result in constraint of the rights of other denominations. These religious differences, together with the Colonists' varying degrees of allegiance to the King, created a powder keg of emotions which would soon ignite.

Those New York colonists who held a strong allegiance for King George III of England were known as "loyalists" or "Tories" and were lead by the New York Colony's wealthiest landowner, Sir William Johnson. Most of those who felt no degree of loyalty toward the King were called "rebels" or "patriots" and were not members of the Anglican Church of America; the majority of Palatines were members of the Dutch Reformed Church. Their greatest and foremost wish was to obtain more freedom from the mother country. Indeed, the more radical desired complete freedom from the King.

Another issue seldom mentioned was slavery. The existence of slavery in colonial New York is an accepted historical fact. Ironically, one historian has written, "while the Palatines cherished their freedom, their value of it did not extend to the darker race."

In 1771 nine to ten percent of the population of Albany County was black; of a population of 40,000 there were 4,000 blacks. It is interesting to note that in that year, shortly before the revolution began, slave ownership in the area remained largely confined to the old Dutch and German families. By the second half of the eighteenth century, slave ownership in New York and New England was on the decline, partly for economic reasons and partly because of growing abolitionist sentiment. During the Revolution, *manumission* was made an incentive for blacks living in New York to join the colony's militia.

These differences and other related discords pitted families against neighbors, siblings against siblings, and even parents against their children.

Meanwhile, the British were aggressively persuading the Iroquois Confederacy to honor their ancient alliance with the King and to join him in subduing his mutinous subjects. The British and Tories pursued every tribe, enticing them with bundles of novelties and trinkets which delighted the Indians for they had never seen such marvels. The British heaped the Indians with countless thousands of beads, ostrich feathers, small jingling bells to adorn the women, and a flood of rum for the warriors.

During this period, the Oneidas and Tuscaroras tried to remain neutral but through efforts of Mohawk chieftain Joseph Brant and Loyalist Major John Butler, the other tribes of the Iroquois Confederacy were convinced that the King needed their help. Both Brant and Butler, however, knew too well the changeable nature of the Indian.

Soon there was a major split in political and religious sentiment among the white settlers and the unity of the League of Iroquois Nations. The Great Peace, which had been created by the ancients to preserve all of the tribes, was beginning to unravel. The temptations of a dauntless, conniving manipulator at the valley's "eastern door," and the rum and knickknacks at the valley's "western door" were weakening the valley's alliance. Volatile emotions were building up to a grand crescendo not only in the Mohawk Valley, but throughout all thirteen colonies, especially in New England.

On the evening of April 18, 1775, everything climaxed.

❋{ 2 }❋

THE END HAS JUST BEGUN

SPRING 1775

———

NEW ENGLAND COLONIES

On the evening of April 18, 1775, Massachusetts Bay Colony Governor Gage ordered British Major John Pitcairn to quell unrest in Lexington, one of the colony's trouble spots. Pitcairn marched his Redcoats all night to his assigned destination. In the morning, the British troops arrived at Lexington and were greeted by a stubborn collection of ill-equipped men and boys who had assembled on the village common, parallel to the long line of exhausted Redcoats. All stood their ground.

Major Pitcairn was appalled at the sight of this conglomeration of rag-tag farmers, clerks, craftsmen, and juveniles. His immediate thought was how dare this upstart collection of renegades challenge the King of England's superbly trained armed forces. He quickly commanded the Patriots to "Disperse, ye Rebels, disperse!"

To this day nobody knows who fired a shot from behind a stone wall—*the shot heard around the world.* It signalled the beginning of a war that was to continue for eight long years.

Shooting became widespread. Finally, the rebels dispersed, leaving eight of their comrades dead on the green grass of the village's common. Major Pitcairn proceeded to march his Redcoats toward Concord—*victoriously.* The end has just begun, he thought, but the rat-tag group of Patriots were saying the same among themselves; each group anticipating ultimate victory.

After the British encounters with the rebels at Lexington and Concord in April 1775, the Americans were stubbornly clinging to Fort Ticonderoga, their *Gibraltar of the American Revolution,* and the south end of Lake Champlain. Simultaneously, the British were reinforcing New York City with the evacuated British Army from Boston.

During this time, the Iroquois realized that many white families were still faithful to England, while others desired their freedom from the King. This required the Indians to make some major adjustments in their relationships. Over the years they had become very dependent upon the colonists for tools, food stuffs, and other commodities such as rum.

As Chief of the Mohawk, Joseph Brant had needed very little persuasion to convince his people to join the British cause; the Cayuga and the Seneca joined with less enthusiasm. Missionary Samuel Kirkland, Brant knew, would persuade the Oneida and Tuscarora to join forces with the rebels. Neither side was able to convince the Onondaga toward anything but *neutrality.* Thus, the once strong confederacy, built upon ancestral ties, was about to face its most serious crisis because of the white settlers' political and military differences.

King George III and his generals desperately tried to quell the fighting and to bring the colonists back into the Empire's fold. The King and his advisors believed that New Englanders instigated all the turmoil and, if that section of the colonies was separated from the others, the unrest would eventually disappear. While assisting General Sir William Howe in the defense of Boston, British Major General John Burgoyne conceived a brilliant strategy designed to achieve this goal.

In late December 1776 King George III received his friend Major General John Burgoyne in audience. Burgoyne had been writing what he called "Thoughts for Conducting the War from the Side of Canada." His "Thoughts," as he fondly referred to his work was ready for presentation to the King.

Burgoyne's strategy required organizing three major expeditions that would ultimately meet in Albany, New York. According to his plan, the first expedition, under his leadership, would separate the colonies and hasten their ultimate surrender. This force, comprised of 8,000 veteran British, German, and Canadian troops, was supported by a train of field guns, several powerful ships on Lake Champlain, and a formidable Indian force.

The second expedition was into the heart of the *colonies' breadbasket*. Its goal was to separate the northern part of the New York Colony from the other colonies. The expedition, under the command of Lieutenant Colonel Barry St. Leger, a forty-year-old veteran officer who had accompanied General Wolfe at Quebec during the French and Indian War, left Montreal shortly after Burgoyne's departure. St. Leger's forces were made up of British, Highlanders, Hessians, Tories, French-Canadian woodsmen, and about 700 Indians, most of them Senecas. They had been ordered to get themselves and their equipment up the Oswego River, over Oneida Lake, and capture Fort Stanwix. From this fort in the wilderness, St. Leger's forces would continue east and meet with General Burgoyne at Albany. Thus, Burgoyne's overall goal of effectively isolating New England and northern New York from the rest of the colonies would be achieved.

General Sir William Howe, commanding the third expedition, was to head north from New York City with a strong army fortified by a fleet of ships. They were to proceed up the Hudson River reducing the fortifications along the way and finally converging with the Burgoyne and St. Leger forces at Albany.

Successful completion of the expeditions would eliminate colonial communications and transport lines thus separating New England and the Mohawk Valley from the southern colonies. It would also isolate the Continental Army from its vital breadbasket.

After more than a generation of quarrels and disputes, on Wednesday morning, August 6, 1777, the Battle of Oriskany eliminated any thoughts of successfully completing Burgoyne's second expedition through the Mohawk Valley. The battle occurred in a narrow, swampy ravine approximately two miles west of Oriskany, the target and end of many of the valley's quarrels.

If Arendt Van Curler, who in 1642 called the Mohawk Valley "the most beautiful land that eyes of man ever beheld," were alive that day, August 6, 1777, he doubtlessly would still be overwhelmed with the valley's beauty and its resources. What Van Curler would not have foreseen was the ever-growing, invisible schism between the peoples of the valley.

On this day of infamy, the cool, clear valley streams still continued to flow through and around narrow, jagged cataracts. Water still plunged down and over the falls, deepening the gorges before reaching the Mohawk River, then joining the great Hudson River near Albany, and eventually entering the Atlantic Ocean. The Indians and the valley's white settlers used the Mohawk River and its tributaries as their primary source of transportation. In fact, the Mohawk Valley, due to its fertile river bottom and excellent navigation system, was rapidly becoming the nation's breadbasket.

The able-bodied valley farmers, together with their wives and children, returned from the Oriskany battlefield to haying the fields, cutting the corn, and assisting their neighbors with the chores required to prepare for the colony's harsh winter. Merchants opened their shops and craftsmen resumed using their skills. At this time, too, others were either burying their dead or caring for their wounded.

❋{ 3 }❋

SOUTHWARD, HO!

JUNE, 1777

CUMBERLAND HEAD, NORTH OF VALCOUR ISLAND, CANADA

Standing with his support officers and resplendent in his full dress uniform with its scarlet, shiny brass buttoned military jacket, General Burgoyne was an impressive and magnificent figure. Squinting through the early morning fog with his spyglass, the general saw the last of Brigadier General Barry St. Leger's formidable force vanish into the morning's mist as it paddled and rowed its way down the St. Lawrence River toward the western expedition's ultimate goal—Albany, New York.

After being appointed commander of the Army of the North, General Burgoyne left England on March 20, 1777. He was carrying a copy of Lord George Germain's orders to Sir Guy Carleton, the Governor-General of Canada. His ship made a moderately fast crossing of the Atlantic and dropped anchor in the magnificent fjord-like reaches of the St. Lawrence between the cliffs of Levis and the awesome rock-mass of Quebec on May 6, 1777. While disembarking he noticed that the snows were melting and the St. Lawrence River's ice was breaking up. Twelve days later he arrived in Montreal and immediately immersed himself into organizing the Army of the North. This campaign would be the most important and meaningful of his military career.

Shivering from the damp fog's penetration of his wool jacket, Burgoyne knew that his expedition leader, St. Leger, was feeling the same exhilaration and excitement. Seeing the grand assembly of military forces, various thoughts raced through his mind: directing the advancement toward the enemy; visualizing the coming battle; anticipating the victory; even the thought of a possible defeat served him and St. Leger. The next day Burgoyne scheduled his forces, consisting of nearly 8,000 British, German, and Canadian troops, embarkation at Saint Johns on the Richelieu River.

He was very satisfied with his selection of St. Leger to command the Mohawk Valley expedition. St. Leger consciously modeled himself after the Burgoyne, so it was small wonder that the two men established an immediate rapport. A cavalryman like the general, the young St. Leger was handsome, personable, dashing, and had a keen eye for beauty in the opposite sex. He wore his uniforms with an air, had been reckless in combat as a junior officer, and had even traveled through the North American wilderness with his own private larder and portable wine cellar.

St. Leger had never held an independent command, had only a vague grasp of the principles of strategy, and knew literally nothing about the sharp differences between Old World fighting and the battle techniques used in the vast, uncivilized interior of North America.

The general and St. Leger were perhaps alike in showing their military excitement, but here their similarities ended. Burgoyne was aware that his nonmilitary side equally excited him. Also in the back of his mind, remained the lingering warning his friend Charles James Fox had kept whispering. He remembered the previous year's Christmas Day at the Brook's Club when he had wagered Fox fifty guineas that he would be home victorious by Christmas 1777; the general calculated that he had only six months until Christmas Day. Now he was reminded of Fox's parting remark, "A bit of warning to you; be not overly sanguine in your expectations. I believe when next you return to England you will be a prisoner on parole." Burgoyne needed to dismiss these pessimistic thoughts. Now, he needed a quiet time—to be alone—to escape for an hour or two.

St. Leger's route would take him across Lake Ontario to Oswego. From there the army would travel up the Oswego River, over Oneida Lake, proceed along the Mohawk River and capture Fort Stanwix. His ultimate destination was to join the General at Albany, New York. Neither general knew very much about the terrain, but the dapper, middle-aged General Burgoyne was so confident of the success of St. Leger's expedition and that he decided to take most of St. Leger's equipment and supplies from Canada, along with his own, down the Lake Champlain route to Albany.

But before St. Leger was ready to embark, Burgoyne was faced with a major ordinance problem. The colonel who was his designated commissary-general became seriously ill with ague. Since no other commissioned officer was experienced in the art of transporting large quantities of supplies, munitions, and all the other gear required for a large military force to have readily available, he pondered whether he should hire a civilian.

He considered himself fortunate when he found a Quebec man, Felix Loescher, who had been the proprietor of a general store near New York's Fort Ticonderoga while the British garrison had been stationed there. In addition, Loescher was familiar with the upper New York wilderness area thus making the moving of the bulky goods easier and faster. While Fort "Ti," as it was fondly referred to, was under British control, Loescher became wealthy selling various items to the officers and their families. After the Americans captured Fort Ticonderoga, he stuffed his cash in a small cart and fled to Quebec, leaving most of his other earthly possessions behind.

Fueled by his burning desire to get even with the Americans, Loescher jumped at the opportunity the British general offered him. But there was one problem that needed to be resolved before he could accept the position. He was afraid that his flighty, part-Indian wife, Fanny, who was less than half his age, would get into trouble if he left her in Quebec. He agreed, therefore, to accept the position on the condition that Fanny would travel with him. Burgoyne knew that he was on weak ground to refuse such a reasonable request at this time, so he agreed to the terms. Loescher's wife would accompany him on the long trek through the northern New York wilderness to Albany.

Burgoyne was not one to forget the nicer amenities of life. On the evening of May 24, the general hosted a dinner party in the log fort he was using as his Montreal headquarters. All the ladies who would accompany the expedition were present. Baroness Frederica von Riedesel, a shrewd observer and compulsive letter-writer, was seated on the host's right and the wife of a Major Sir John Acland was on his left. Gentleman Johnny, as he was fondly referred to by his friends, did not let the pressures of a military campaign allow him to forget that the Major's wife was the daughter of an English earl. No record of this wilderness dinner's menu has been kept, but it is known that eight separate courses were served and consumed along with ample quantities of champagne, among other beverages. All of the ladies had powdered their hair except one; Fanny Loescher proudly displayed her flowing, blue-black tresses. According to Baroness von Riedesel, "The Army [had] suffered its first casualty, the General having fallen victim to the charms of Mme. Loescher. She is animated and has a certain charm, but she lacks the poise and grace of many of our ladies, so several of us were surprised that the General spent so long a time in her company." Apparently the ladies were also envious when, after dinner, the General spent more than a half-hour chatting with an *unpowdered* lady. Perhaps he even shared one of his most important concerns with her, that a number of the Canadians who had enlisted were already deserting the ranks. In the main, however, he was in high spirits regarding his great campaign, and generally, his troops were in good health and eager for the operation to begin.

Lord George Germain's letter dated March 26, 1777, directed Governor Carleton to provide sufficient troops to protect Canada, and to employ the remainder of the army to Burgoyne's two expeditions. After naming Burgoyne the commanding general of the Army of the North, the letter instructed both expeditions to proceed with all possible haste to join General Sir William Howe in Albany, New York where Burgoyne and St. Leger were to place themselves under Howe's command. Germain also told Carleton, "I shall write to Sir William from hence by the packet." Unknown to Burgoyne, while he was on the high seas, Germain received a letter from General Sir William Howe making it clear beyond any reasonable doubt that the general of the Army of the North could expect little help from Howe.

Burgoyne politely excused himself from his support officers, General William Phillips who would act as second-in-command of the expedition, Major General Baron Friedrich Adolph von Riedesel commander of the German mercenary contingent, and Brigadier Simon Fraser, the combat-hardened Scotsman the general had selected as infantry commander. They all knew that Burgoyne needed his quiet time. As they watched the handsome, fiftyish general in his scarlet jacket disappear into his tent of doubled layers of oiled silk, which served as the expedition's temporary headquarters, each in his own way silently asked for guidance for him and their quest.

Burgoyne knew that his officers commonly referred to him as "Gentleman Johnny," although never to his face. He knew also that his February 4, 1723 birth to the former Anna Maria Burnestone and her husband, John, had caused many Londoners' tongues to gossip, especially when Lord Bingley was named as his godfather. The general was aware, too, that many were amused by his personal habits, talking about them and writing about him at length.

Burgoyne paced his tent and thought fondly of his wife of nearly thirty years, the Lady Charlotte Stanley. After an extended illness she had died a few days after he had set sail from Quebec to England. He had landed at Southampton in late November 1776 and hurried to London, where his worst fears were confirmed. He had prepared himself for this tragedy, but its anticipation did not soften the impact. He had visited his wife's grave in a driving rainstorm, which severely aggravated his own condition, and for the only time in his adult life he was seen to weep in public.

Coming back to reality he strolled directly toward an oak chest in the tent, lifted the top, and surveyed his cache of French champagne submerged in crushed ice. "At least the French can do something right," he smiled to himself as he selected a chilled bottle from the chest.

For years he had made a ritual of opening a bottle of champagne. First, immediately following the popping of the cork, he ceremoniously placed his nose over the top of the bottle in order to capture the essence of its fruity bouquet, which had long waited to escape from its prison. Next, he selected a wide-mouth, hollow-stemmed, crystal champagne glass, which had been chilled in the same ice as the champagne. After pouring the bubbling, amber contents into the crystal, he raised the glass and placed it just below the tip of his nose so he could continue to experience the champagne's bouquet while the bubbles occasionally bounced from the surface of the clear, chilled beverage to land on his nose as if saying, "Here I am, General, enjoy the moment." Finally, he took a healthy sip, and refilled the glass. He pushed his chair back just enough so he could enjoy the sight of his favorite beverage; he liked to watch the bubbles racing to the top. At times, he had likened the bubbles to his troops always striving to get to the top of his command—to excel—to bring glory to themselves and the British Empire.

"Enough of these military thoughts," he decided. "This is my quiet time." After taking another swallow of champagne, he replaced the bubbling glass on his desk.

His thoughts roamed back to his Lady Charlotte.

This day reminded him of the time shortly after they had married, when he had volunteered to accompany the expedition to capture Belle-Ile, off Saint-Nazaire. His volunteering for this dangerous service led to considerable protest from his young bride. He remembered the flowery verse he had composed to help soothe her troubled heart and spirits. Poetry, as well as his play-writing, had always been for the General the kind of diversion he needed to escape the demanding pressures of the military. With quill in hand, he dipped the tip in the ink well and proceeded to rewrite his verse to Lady Charlotte.

> *The power that formed my Charlotte's heart,*
> *Thus tender, thus sincere,*
> *Shall bless each wish that love can start,*
> *Or absence foster there.*
> *Safe in the shadow of that Power,*
> *I'll tread the hostile ground;*
> *Though fiery deaths in tempest shower,*
> *And thousands fall around.*

His thoughts drifted back to when he was still handsome in his mid-forties, without the double chin that had recently appeared. Then he had been attentive to the ladies and flirted mildly at dinner parties and other functions, but had remained stubbornly loyal to his wife. While Charlotte's health continued to deteriorate, and she looked older than her years, he had refused to take advantage of the offers of romance which came his way. Some of his opponents for membership to the House of Commons even tried to make issue of his failure to practice monogamy, suggesting that he engaged in playing around on the sly. But, all attempts, even into the late 1770s, claiming to prove he had cheated on his wife, were total failures. The general conceded to all who listened that "Gentleman Johnny" had acquired his reputation as a ladies man before his marriage. But, once he married, he was committed to his wife. His belief was unyielding; a man of honor should keep his marriage vows, no matter what the behavior of his contemporaries, under any and all circumstances.

He poured the last of the champagne from the bottle, caressed the glass, and with a flare, drank the last of the sparkling beverage. He then replaced the glass on the desk and continued his quiet time on his bed, which was always with him on his campaigns.

The bed was not the only piece of personal furniture that he always carted with him; others included a desk and a padded work chair with legs that could be collapsed. His chests of clothing were filled with several complete changes of uniforms. One of the duties of the commissary-general and three orderlies was to maintain the extensive supply for his larder, which included no less than fourteen different kinds of fresh, smoked, and pickled meats and fish, numerous vegetables and fruits, as well as flour so that his cook-orderly could bake bread. The orderlies were also responsible for equipping two carts with special springs that reduced their jolting motion and which carried his wines and furniture. He usually traveled with two aides-de-camp, three orderlies, and a groom; the aides were served by their own orderlies.

He was referred as an *enlightened* general.

His personality did not always fit well with most eighteenth century generals, yet it was partly responsible for his popularity. Most could learn from Gentleman Johnny because he practiced what he preached. Rarely did he dine alone at the end of a long day's march. Eager to be invited to his dinners were subordinate generals and senior colonels, but Burgoyne made it a point to invite captains, lieutenants, and cornets who had distinguished themselves in one way or another. Gentleman Johnny discouraged military talk and encouraged the types of conversation reminiscent of London gentlemen's clubs.

Shortly after midday, one of the general's orderlies awakened him with the news that the cook would be serving luncheon for all remaining senior and junior officers within the half-hour. It would be similar to the one that had been served the previous day before St. Leger and his forces embarked up the St. Lawrence.

He emerged from his tent and squinted against the high-noon sun's bright light. Standing at attention, watching the drummers and fifers as they practiced on the parade field, he fully believed that he had masterminded a flawless strategy that would bring victory to England and glory to himself.

Burgoyne immediately dismissed all such thoughts and thanked the master planner for the ability to impress his personality on his soldiers and win their confidence and affection. The troops were good; the officers were of as high a caliber as any to be found in any army in the world at the time; and they were plentifully supplied with artillery. He remembered Lieutenant Thomas Anburey's observation: "If good discipline, joined to health and spirit among the men being led by General Burgoyne, who is universally esteemed and respected, can ensure success. It may be expected." Confidently, General John Burgoyne stood proudly before his highly disciplined troops. He, as well as Governor Sir Guy Carleton, had serious reservations about the wisdom of employing Indians in any capacity other than as scouts or guides. However, Lord Germain had insisted that Indians and Negroes be procured to force the colonists into submission

⧖

The following day Burgoyne with an army of 7,900 men embarked at Saint Johns, on the Richelieu River headed for Albany. He believed that his and St. Leger's forces would join together under General Howe, thus splitting the colonies. His officers had urged the troops to leave their leggings and blanket coats in Canada to reduce the amount of supplies to be carried. Since the Canadians had been unsuccessful in acquiring the initial number of horses needed, oxen were pressed into service to ease the severe shortage of transport. This was not helped by the fact that many carriages, hastily constructed of unseasoned timber, fell apart on the rough track from Chambly to

Saint Johns, even before the expedition had arrived at the place of embarkation. Nevertheless, Burgoyne, in the full-dress uniform of a British general, was determined to get the expedition started. His first objectives were Crown Point and Fort Ticonderoga.

On July 25, fifty-three days after embarking from Montreal, St. Leger's expedition arrived at Oswego. Twelve days later, he and his forces would be embroiled with the Mohawk Valley rebels at Oriskany.

✳ { 4 } ✳

THE DAY AFTER

EARLY, THE MORNING OF AUGUST 7, 1777

———

NEW PALATINE SETTLEMENT IN THE MOHAWK VALLEY

It was not until late in the evening of the 6th of August that the settlers of New Palatine heard about the bloody ambush at Oriskany from a messenger. He informed the settlers that the survivors were on their way back home, but Rebecca Heindrick and Helena Kerchner, after hearing the report, agreed that they were not content to wait for the return of the militia. Helena had been living with the Heindricks in their stone farmhouse after she had evaded her parents and the other Loyalists who were en route to Canada.

After a restless attempt to sleep, the women arose at the crack of dawn to one of the valley's usual early morning fogs. Without eating breakfast, they packed some cheese, apples, johnny cake, and beer in a knapsack and started their half-mile trek down the narrow wagon lane which joined the King's Highway. The dew on the tall grass along the farm lane brushed against their bare legs reminding them of their mission's urgency. They dodged, straddled, even walked through and around mud puddles and mired ruts to reach the junction. Turning right and heading west toward Oriskany and Fort Stanwix on the King's Highway, the road was more treacherous than usual because of the previous day's thunderstorm.

Not knowing whether their loved ones and friends were dead or alive, they trudged along hand-in-hand. The hemlock branches bowed and dripped over them while the early fall colors of maple and oak trees peeked at the two women. Each silently prayed that God would return their men; Rebecca's husband Karl, and their son

Walter. Helena prayed to the Lord for her parents, Wilhelm and Sarah Kerchner, who had joined the loyalists in Canada. She prayed that she had made the appropriate decision when she escaped from the Canadian camp and returned to New Palatine and the Heindricks. The fog, which enveloped and chilled them through their woolen dresses, seemed to embrace and reassure them that their prayers would be answered. They concluded their prayers with "His will be done."

After having been on the road nearly two hours, they heard the faint, monotonous, somber sound of a distant drum. Looking through the fog toward the horizon, they saw the crest of a hill and out of the fog emerged staggering images looking as if they were coming out the mouth of a huge cave. Each image struggled along the rutted and mired road. Some fell and tried to stand and walk again while others seemed content to stay down.

As Helena and Rebecca drew closer, they saw that the "images" were men. Some were trying to balance themselves on crude crutches, others were being carried on makeshift litters of green boughs or rifles, while still others were lying in the few remaining ox-drawn carts. Many with their heads bandaged, were being lead by guides, and many more seemed to be wandering and following like blind sheep.

The somber, distant sound of the drum continued and became louder. They knew that General Herkimer had selected only one drummer boy, the fifteen-year-old Walter Heindrick, Rebecca and Karl Heindrick's son and Helena's boyfriend. They also knew not to look for General Herkimer's white mare. The messenger had told the settlers that after Herkimer's mare was killed and the general's leg severely injured, he had ordered his saddle to be removed from the mare and placed beneath a beech tree located on a knoll so that he could continue to direct the battle. According to the messenger, it was from this site that Herkimer stated, "I will face the enemy."

As Rebecca and Helena were frantically searching for Karl and Walter, they were approached by a large, muscular colored man with his head partially bandaged hiding his left eye, and his left arm in a sling. Looking directly at Rebecca he asked, "Ma'am, did I hear you ladies asking for a Mister Karl Heindrick?"

"Yes, sir," Rebecca smilingly replied. It was her first smile of the day. "He's my husband," she proudly assured him. "Why do you ask about Karl?"

"I have come all the way from Albany, New York in hopes to find him. My former master permitted my father and me to use manumission for our freedom. When I arrived at Fort Dayton, I was immediately assigned to the Tryon County Militia," he proudly stated. "I had heard that Mr. Heindrick was ahead with General Herkimer. I've been ordered by Major General Philip Schuyler to see General Herkimer. Unfortunately, I was not able to catch up with Herkimer on the march, and I fell in with the rear guard." He apologetically added, "We were lucky!"

"What is your name and why are you looking for Karl?" asked Karl's puzzled wife. "This is my," she hesitated and corrected herself, "Our, prospective daughter-in-law, Helena Kerchner," Helena smiled and nodded acknowledgement.

"My name is George Jefferson. Karl will remember me as George Franklin," he replied with a broad smile, and excused himself as he was bumped into by other searching women. "At one time, nearly fifty years ago, we were like brothers with his father, Ulrich, and my mother Georgia Franklin."

"Yes. Yes," acknowledged Rebecca as she smiled, "I remember Karl fondly telling me about how you two used to hike the hills and swim in Wood Creek."

"He did speak of me?" a delighted George asked. "I was hoping that he would remember me." He bowed his head and apologetically admitted, "That was one of my saddest days when my mother and I left Karl's father. But my father had already been granted some degree of freedom, and he came to take my mother and me back to Albany." He sensed the women's urgency to find Karl. "I must complete my work with the rearguard and see General Herkimer. Are you still living in the same house off the King's Highway in New Palatine?"

"Same location, but our home is now made of stone," Rebecca said. "On your way back to Albany, please stop by and see us. By that time Karl and our son, Walter, will be there." She silently prayed that this would be true. With both hands he clasped Rebecca's outstretched hand, "Please tell Karl that I'll stop by to see him before I return to Albany next Sunday." Rebecca saw tears in his eyes as George turned and strolled toward his guard unit.

"Mr. Jefferson," called Rebecca, "why not plan to attend church services with us at the Heidelberg Tavern next Sunday. I know that Karl would love to see you and have you as our guest. Please meet us at our home Sunday morning or even better Saturday evening, whichever is most convenient for you."

"That sounds like a great idea. Thank you, Mrs. Heindrick. I look forward to being with you," George replied as he slipped his left foot in the stirrup, swung his right leg over his chestnut gelding, and headed west along the rutted way.

As the sound of the drum became louder, the women immediately broke into a run hoping to find their men. The militia drew closer and it seemed that the fog slowly rose to welcome them. Rebecca and Helena mingled among the battered and empty-eyed men. By this time, other women and children had joined them, and the sound of the drum became *louder and louder and louder*. But they were still unable to see the drummer through the fog. Rebecca and Helena anxiously raced among the wounded toward the sound of the drum. They saw no orderly column of militia. There was nothing but mass confusion as men, women, and children frantically screamed and raced about with their arms raised and opened. Periodically, these open arms closed around a discovered loved one. Other arms never opened for an embrace as their owner's eyes continued to search for someone who would never return.

On the crest of the next hill, Helena spied the drummer boy. Her heart leaped with joy as she recognized Walter and the drum he had made out of white birch bark. Along side him were two men carrying a litter. A dreadful sinking feeling suddenly over came Rebecca. She knew something terrible had happened, and she raced toward the litter. The wounded soldier on it was not her Karl. It was General Herkimer.

His left leg was bandaged and he was sitting upright on a litter made of boughs and coats, smoking his clay pipe. They were to learn later that three Indians had jumped out to claim this most coveted scalp of all, but fell at the general's feet under musket fire. The bullets that killed them were the last fired that day. Behind Herkimer's litter Rebecca and Helena watched while the Heindricks' neighbors, Calbert Swartz and George Raab, embraced their wives. As soon as the men saw Rebecca, they grabbed her hand and led her to a group of crude litters. Her heart sank. She saw bandaged heads. Legs and arms in splints. Wounded staring empty-eyed toward the rising noon sun. Her friends guided her toward a litter. On it was a wounded militiaman lying on his stomach. Rebecca immediately recognized the back of Karl's head. He was still wearing the red scarf which she had knitted for him; his good luck charm he always used to tell her. Awakened, Karl turned his face toward the commotion and through the foggy sunlight recognized Rebecca leaning over him.

"Oh, my dearest, Karl," she cried as she hugged him and smothered him with kisses. She knelt beside him filled with joy and wept as never before. "Oh, my blessed one, we're together again." Karl's leg wound did not appear to be as serious as the general's, but it was a bloody mess. Rebecca was told that the calf of his right leg had been hit with a musket ball but that no bones appeared to have been broken.

During all of this, Helena had reached Walter, and joyfully grabbed one of his drumsticks and started to beat the drumhead while Walter took the other stick and playfully tapped the top of Helena's head. Then they both dropped their sticks. He set his drum to one side. Oblivious to other joyous reunions, and the frustrated searches of other women and children hunting for loved ones, Helena and Walter embraced while the battle-worn militia continued on its way home. Rebecca and Helena would wait for the appropriate opportunity to tell Karl about his brother.

The results of the battle were sure to be discussed and debated by rebels, Tories, British, and Indians alike. As for the for the Heindrick family, they silently thanked God for bringing their men back alive from their ghastly experience. History would record this as *one of the bloodiest and most bitterly fought battles of the American Revolution.*

One far-reaching result of the battle was its emotional impact on the Indians. Their losses at Oriskany, which included five Seneca chiefs, hurt them and for a long time they hesitated to fight for the British again. After a short time and many jugs of rum, the memories of their experiences convinced them to seek retaliation against the rebels and to carry on the war together with their British allies.

❊ 5 ❊

TWO BROTHERS

HEINDRICK'S NEW PALATINE FARM

It had been slightly over forty years when he had last walked hand-in-hand between his mother, Georgia Franklin, and father down this same narrow, half-mile lane that connected the Heindrick's farmhouse to the King's Highway. That day was one of the saddest of his ten-year-old life. Without any warning, this strange man and his mother were compelling him to leave Karl, the only "brother" he had ever known. He and his mother had lived with Ulrich Heindrick ever since his wife, Beth, had died giving birth to Karl. It was then that Ulrich's neighbors, Herman Schultz and his wife Louisa, had volunteered Georgia's services as Karl's wet-nurse and Ulrich's housekeeper for as long as he needed them.

On that day in 1739, the lane was a narrow, grassy path on which the Heindrick's one horse pulled the two-wheel cart to and from the farm and the settlement of New Palatine. George Jefferson guided his chestnut gelding down the same, but now wider lane, and around its fresh mud puddles from the previous night's thunderstorm.

Sizable maple trees lined both sides of the rutted byway. He could remember these mature maple trees being tapped for sap during the early springs of past years. He virtually could smell the *sugaring*, as the natives called it, and taste the final product, the valley's main sweeteners—maple sugar, maple cream, or maple syrup.

It had not been until after he and his parents had arrived in Albany that he learned why he had left the Heindrick home.

"Slavery" was a new word to him. He soon learned that slavery was common in colonial New York. The one thing he knew was that his skin color was slightly darker than Karl's, but Karl and Ulrich had always treated him as family. Simply, George and Karl had always considered themselves brothers. Therefore, he was relatively ignorant of the term slavery. This was what had made him so sad when his parents would not let him say goodbye to Karl and his father.

After leaving the Heindrick's home, he and his parents had headed straight for Johan Jost Herkimer's stone house in German Flats. This served as a trading post for the Palatines and Indians as well as a freighting center for transporting goods to and from Albany. From there, they were able to work their way back to his father's home in Albany.

His father, Benjamin Jefferson, had been one of the fortunate few young slaves who were purchased by a very generous and opportunistic Dutchman named Hans Schuyler. Herr Schuyler owned and operated a successful livery stable in Albany city. After observing how efficiently the young, muscular teenager could handle the smithy works, as well as his natural talent with horses, Herr Schuyler was ready to begin grooming the young black for an apprentice position, since he had no children of his own.

It was common for slave owners in the small towns and on the farms in the New York Colony and the Mohawk Valley, who had a few slaves, to use them as domestic servants or to train them in the occupation of their owner. Generally, slave owners in New York and New England developed a more personal relationship which was not as easily possible on a plantation employing hundreds of hands; land and slave ownership in the North was modest in comparison to the Southern plantations.

In 1737, the black population of Albany County, including all of the Mohawk Valley, exceeded fifteen percent, ninety-five percent of whom were slaves. Just six years ago in 1771, nine to ten percent of Albany County's forty thousand population was black. After George had become more familiar with the slave issue, it became apparent that slave ownership in New York and New England was declining due partly to economic reasons and partly because of growing abolitionist sentiment in the North. After the revolution began, especially in New York, manumission was made an incentive for blacks to join the state's patriot forces. During the French and Indian War, Herr Schuyler allowed George and his father to take advantage of manumission and join the Albany County militia.

Shortly after being acquired by Herr Schuyler, Benjamin Jefferson had met his future bride, Georgia Franklin. They used to meet in secret. Eventually, she became pregnant, but both knew that Herr Schuyler would not accept a child out of wedlock. One night Georgia stole away from Albany and headed west toward the less populated frontier. Eventually, she became employed as a domestic by Ulrich Heindrick's neighbors, Herman and Louisa Schultz. Before she had left Benjamin, he had promised her that once he had completed his apprenticeship, and was to allowed to operate as a freeman, he would come and bring Georgia and their child back to Albany. It had taken Benjamin over ten years to keep his promise. Soon after they returned to Albany, Herr Schuyler requested that Benjamin and Georgia be officially married, and that young George be baptized. These requests were complied with within a week by the minister of the Albany Dutch Reformed Church. It took another additional four weeks for Benjamin to officially change George's last name from Franklin to Jefferson.

This was all in his past, now both his parents were dead. He was grateful for the sound family traditions and work ethic his parents had instilled in him. Because of these and Herr Schuyler's appreciation of fine value sets, he now was part owner in operating one of Albany's three most thriving livery stables under the name of Schuyler and Jefferson's Livery. It was through his father's owner, Hans Schuyler, that George was introduced to Hans's cousin, Major General Philip Schuyler. General Schuyler had sent George on an assignment to ask General Nicholas Herkimer to recruit and transfer, after the Fort Stanwix mission, additional troops for the campaign being waged by Major General John Burgoyne along Lake Champlain and eastern front.

Upon learning that General Herkimer had been seriously wounded, he had been notified that he was to meet with General Benedict Arnold at Fort Dayton to assist in recruiting volunteers for the campaign against Burgoyne. After spending most of the week with Arnold, George was looking forward to seeing Karl and his family. However, before he left the valley he wanted to stop and give his regards to General Herkimer.

He was lost in thought when he was brought back to reality by the sound of a barking dog. It was then that he realized he was approaching the familiar setting, only now the house was completely surrounded by a stone wall. He tied his horse to the hitching post near a huge wooden gate, and entered the inter *keep*. The new stone house was nearly double the size of the wooden farmhouse he once knew as home. The front of the house still overlooked the Mohawk River, but the wall obstructed the view of the river. Sheep were lackadaisically grazing the keep. As he walked toward the front porch, he recognized the lady who had opened the porch door as Karl's wife, Rebecca. She waved a greeting to him.

"Welcome, Mr. Jefferson," Rebecca greeted him. "Why don't you bring your horse into the keep and let him graze and drink with the sheep. I'm sure that they'll get along real fine."

"Thank you, ma'am," said George as he brought the chestnut with the bouncing and tail-wagging dog trailing them into the keep.

"We're so pleased that you were able to arrive here Saturday evening. Again, Mr. Jefferson, welcome to our home," she smiled as she opened the door leading into the farmhouse's living room. As he entered the living room, George saw a man about his own age sitting in a rocking chair with one leg bandaged and propped upon a high step stool. Immediately, each man recognized the other. Broad smiles flashed upon their faces as George swiftly went to Karl's chair. They embraced sweeping away the many lost years, each cultivating many questions to be asked of the other. As Helena entered the room with Walter, Rebecca introduced them to their visitor. The ladies excused themselves to the kitchen giving the men an opportunity to discuss the past week, Karl's wound, Walter's experience with General Herkimer, and the Oriskany battle in general.

Shortly, Rebecca and Helena came in carrying a steaming pot of spiced cider and a plate of freshly baked maple sugar cookies. During the next couple of hours, and with another pot of spiced cider, they compared experiences during the past forty years while the fire in the huge stone fireplace took off the evening's chill.

As George was about to leave for Fort Dayton, and stop on the way to visit General Herkimer, Rebecca reminded him of the special church service at the Heidelburg Tavern. She and Karl invited him to stay over night and to join them as their guest.

"I'd be honored to stay with you," he replied.

"Remember one thing, George," Karl smiled. "You and I are brothers." Again, they embraced, bridging the lost years.

During the evening meal, the Heindricks wanted to learn more about George's assignment to the valley.

"It was through my father's owner, Hans Schuyler, that I was first introduced to Major General Philip Schuyler. In fact he always used to request my services attending to his horses. That's before I exercised my manumission rights and joined the Albany County Militia. Once in the militia, General Schuyler assigned me as one of his aides.

"A little over a week ago, the general was complaining to me that he wasn't sure from one day to the next whether he or Major General Horatio Gates commanded the Army of the North. He knew that he had to send a force to relieve the siege of Fort Stanwix. That, of course, had been the responsibility of General Herkimer and the Tryon County Militia, but General Schuyler wanted reinforcements to assure that St. Leger and his troops did not make it to Albany. When the general asked for volunteers among his staff of brigadier generals, the silence was frightening. Then the general and I heard a raspy voice loudly saying, "I'll take it." Believe it or not, it was not a brigadier volunteering, but a major general, the second-in-command of the Army, Benedict Arnold. General Schuyler was delighted and promptly issued Arnold orders to lead a detachment of troops and assist in the relief of Fort Stanwix.

"Arnold knew that he would have to recruit volunteers along the way if he was to match St. Leger's superior force. He had no illusions about the difficulty of relieving Fort Stanwix. He knew that the farmers were in the middle of their haying, but he was still disappointed with the low turnout of militia recruits. Counting the Oneida, the Tuscarora, and the regular army, Arnold estimated that his troops did not exceed one thousand. Meanwhile, his scouts reported that St. Leger's forces were nearly twice as many.

"When we arrived at German Flats, Arnold delivered a daring order to St. Leger's command, stating flatly that if their arms were not laid down within days, he would *show no mercy—take no quarter.* Ignoring his officers' reluctance to move before receiving reinforcements, Arnold ordered his troops to begin their march toward Fort Stanwix.

"While we were en route, Arnold heard a rumor that St. Leger was squeezing the fort, and had placed it under siege. Not knowing the result of General Herkimer's intervention, Major General Arnold suspected that relieving the fort was now an emergency. He devised a daring plot," George chuckled, "to disperse the enemy."

"We have heard something about the plot," remarked Karl. "Didn't John Joost Schuyler have something to do with it?" asked Rebecca.

"That's correct, Mrs. Heindrick," George responded.

"Now let's stop right here," Rebecca demanded. "Let's remember we're all family. If I can call you George, you can call me Rebecca," she smiled and looked into George's ebony face as it reflected the flame of the fireplace.

As Walter placed another log on the fire, Karl asked George, "Isn't this John Joost Schuyler also known locally as Hon Yost?"

"That's correct, General Herkimer's nephew. He's the son of Herkimer's sister, Maria."

"Please tell us, George," inquired Helena, "what the daring plot was?"

"Well it seems," continued George, "that Colonel Weston, commander of the Massachusetts troops at Fort Dayton, learned that a Tory meeting was being planned at the home or a tarvern owned by a Mr. Shoemaker, two miles distant; Weston sent a detail of troops to round them up. Shoemaker had been a justice of the peace under commission from the king and was a man of prominence in the neighborhood. For some time Walter Butler had been hoping to attract more recruits for St. Leger, and knowing Shoemaker to be loyal to the king, Butler had urged him to call a meeting with other Tories. Butler himself, along with fourteen soldiers and fourteen

Indians, went down from St. Leger's encampment near Fort Stanwix to help in the recruitment process."

"That Walter Butler is a cousin to Martha Butler's husband, Jerome," added Rebecca. "She is the lady who owns the Heidelberg Tavern where we will be going to church tomorrow."

"Yes, those Butlers are all a bunch of Tories," Walter commented, "especially that Colonel John Butler and his son Walter. Although Martha firmly denies that she is related *to that Tory bastard* as she calls him."

"What did Arnold do after learning about the meeting at Shoemaker's home?" asked Helena as she poured cider from the china tea pot.

George took another sip of warm spiced cider, he wiped the perspiration from his brow with a handkerchief, and continued, "Arnold ordered the capture and court-martial of all involved. I remember the surprised looks on their faces when the Major General walked into the house. I was right at General Arnold's side while our troops circled the house so that no one could escape. As you probably have heard, Walter was found guilty as a spy and sentenced to die the following morning by the acting judge, Lieutenant Colonel Marinus Willet, who had been appointed by Arnold.

"John Joost Schuyler was one of those we rounded up and jailed."

"As I have mentioned earlier, locally he's better known as Hon Yost," Karl commented. "He is considered a half-wit, but perhaps he was not quite as crazy as some of his neighbors believed."

"Yes, he's crazy like a fox," commented Walter. "It's common knowledge here in the valley, that he was well known among the Indians, and that they consider idiots the special favorites of the gods."

"That belief," added Rebecca, "was often shared by many medieval European Christians."

"Well, Hon Yost's parents and brother promptly appeared at Fort Dayton to plead his case. Arnold told them that if Hon Yost faithfully executes the mission to which he was going to assign him, he would personally assure the entire family's safety to their home near the "little falls of the Mohawk." All readily nodded agreement.

"This is going to be no picnic Arnold warned," George continued, "because if Hon Yost fouls up, not only will he be a dead duck, but the rest of you will be placed in jail forever or else hanged as spies.

"His family knew that Hon was basically a trustworthy individual, and that he usually did whatever was asked of him, especially if it had anything to do with Indians. His mother offered to stay as a hostage, but Arnold would not agree with that. He finally accepted Nicholas Schuyler's offer to remain in the jail at Fort Dayton until his brother had completed his mission.

"I remember that meeting at Fort Dayton with General Arnold and a few of his trusted officers. We met with Hon Yost and one of the Oneida sachems, who was a friend of our troops and of Hon Yost. The sachem happily agreed because he wanted to have a hand in defeating the British and making the Senecas and Canadian Indians look foolish.

"As Arnold detailed his plan, Hon Yost and the sachem became more and more excited about this new mission. Finally, the scheme which they (we) concocted was designed to frighten the enemy, especially the Indians," smiled George as he recalled the jubilation displayed by Hon Yost. Arnold gambled that once the Indians learned of the great number of rebel forces advancing toward them and the British, the Indians would become totally disillusioned with the British and would soon mutiny and desert.

"It was after this part of plan was agreed upon, that Hon Yost suggested that we make him look like an escapee. Arnold nodded and ordered Yost to take off his ragged clothes and throw them on the dusty ground. He then order the officers to take their rifles and fire a few musket shots into them. All hoped that this disguise would make the Indians believe that Yost had narrowly escaped. Arnold ordered Hon Yost to go directly to the Indian camp, grossly exaggerate the size of the advancing rebel troops, and incite as much panic as possible. Afterwards he instructed the sachem to take a circuitous route to Fort Stanwix and allow himself to be captured in the enemy camp.

"What were the Indians doing and where were they?" Helena asked excitedly. "How about the British?" Secretly she was thinking of her parents who were off somewhere in the western wilderness with other Loyalists and Tories.

"You must remember that all of this was happening after the Battle of Oriskany, while the British and the Indians were half-heartedly attacking Fort Stanwix," reminded George. "When Hon Yost, in his muddy, ragged clothes, suddenly came bursting into the lodge where the Indians were holding a pow-pow. The Indians were startled and at first did not recognize their friend. They were dumbfounded. Here was someone they had known for many moons and faithfully trusted, looking almost dead and frightened to the point of hysteria."

"I know Hon Yost," remarked Karl. "I can visualize him staging this scene and giving the Indians a real tall tale."

"Well, he certainly must have given them a real good show," commented George, "because they started asking him many questions. Pointing to his riddled clothes, he told about his near brush with death while he was escaping from those damn Yankee bastards. Then he began telling the sachems about the size of the advancing Rebel forces. When they asked him for the number of foreign troops, he shook his head mysteriously, shrugged his shoulders, pointed upward toward the leaves on the trees, raised his arms high, and made a huge circle before bringing them down at his side. The Indians were astounded and fearful of the approaching menace. Yost's news spread like wildfire through the Indian camps.

"Ultimately, the news reached General St. Leger. Immediately, he demanded Hon Yost be brought to his command tent. St. Leger's officers had accused him of lack of energy and had often suspected him of being intoxicated during most of the time they were besieging Fort Stanwix. But on this day, there was no doubt that he had full command of his senses. When St. Leger, with a few of his trusted officers and Indian leaders, asked Yost about the number of advancing troops, he reported that there are at least two thousand, and they were so near to this location that they should be here within twenty-four hours. In addition he told them his pitiful tale about his capture, trial, and sentence to death. He reported, too, that Shoemaker and Butler were to be hung that day. St. Leger immediately started planning an ambush against Arnold's troops, similar to the one he had staged against Herkimer."

"From what we've heard," Karl commented, "the Indians knew General Benedict Arnold as the *Dark Eagle,* the name given him by the Abenaki chief, Natanis; they knew that he was a fighter who would not easily be ambushed."

"That's right, Karl," agreed George. "Even Hon Yost knew that, and as soon as he had finished telling St. Leger about Arnold and his troops, he burst from the command tent and ran through the camps screaming about Arnold's advancing forces.

"Meanwhile, the ingenious Oneida sachem had intentionally fallen in with several friendly Indians as they were making their way back to camp. Quickly, he spread the alarming news among his fellow Iroquois, that the valley was swarming with rebel troops, at least three thousand men. To make the story even more frightening, he added that Burgoyne had been cut to pieces. Shocked, the Indians raced around their campgrounds spreading the news with the Oneida sachem among them. The sachem offered a wampum belt and confirmed to the Indians all that Hon Yost had reported, with a few added embellishments. He also reaffirmed that the Americans had no desire to injure the Indians. Their only wish, he told them, was to attack and defeat the British troops and the Tory Rangers.

"I could go on forever about the Hon Yost story," George concluded, "but I'll quickly bring it to an end. The chiefs agreed unanimously that they were no longer going to fight for St. Leger and that he and his troops should retreat to Oswego. Shortly after that, the Indians notified St. Leger of their decision, knowing that without Indian support, his forces could not capture Fort Stanwix. That afternoon, August 22, St. Leger ordered his troops to strike their tents and pack up. As St. Leger and Sir John Johnson rode toward Oswego, each trying to blame the other for the failure of their mission, two of the Indian chiefs instructed a young warrior to lag behind until these officers approached a bog of clay and mud. He was told to run out in front of them as if alarmed and yell, "They are coming! They are coming!""

"According to what we've heard here," stated Walter, "Benedict Arnold's name alone had caused the rout of the British."

"I guess we'll have to add Hon Yost's name to that list," smiled Rebecca.

"One might say," added Helena, "that General Arnold wrote the play script and Hon Yost convincingly performed his role."

"The Mohawk Valley owes its freedom to Arnold and Yost," commented Walter.

"The valley owes much to all of you who took the brunt of the British and Indian ambush at Oriskany," George said as he bowed his head in silent prayer.

"Those who really held the fort here in the valley were our wives, sweethearts, and children. They gave all of us the incentive to stand up and fight, and made it all worth fighting for," remarked Karl.

"We're so proud of all our men," beamed Rebecca, as she started picking up the empty cider cups, and placing them in the iron kitchen sink.

"It saddens us, too," added Helena, "when we think of those who will not return to their families and homes. We've been very blessed."

"Come, Helena," said Rebecca, "let the men folks finish talking while you and I prepare a bed for our guest in Walter's room."

The flames in the fireplace were virtually nonexistent as the three men huddled around the hearth and stared at the glowing embers.

George yearned to be with his wife in Albany, but he knew that his mission here was to recruit volunteers for General Arnold. He remembered that the General Schuyler had especially asked him to recruit a drummerboy. He knew, too, that Walter had been serving Herkimer's Tryon County Militia as its drummer. He asked Walter, "What did you think of being Herkimer's drummer?"

"It was exciting," was his immediate response. "What I especially liked was the fact that General Herkimer wanted me right near his side. I'll never forget the time when he and I saw a Tory and an Indian racing toward the beech tree where the general was propped on his saddle. The Indian had a tomahawk in his raised right hand, and the Tory was aiming his musket straight at the general. Suddenly, I recognized that the Indian was my 'blood brother,' White Tail. I stood, raised my hand and hollered his name. He recognized me. At that moment, White Tail was really put to a test. The Tory had his musket raised and was taking aim at the wounded general. Thank the Lord, that White Tail made his decision quickly. He lowered his tomahawk and crashed it into the Tory's skull. None of us knew that while this was happening, Chief Joseph Brant, White Tail's uncle, was closely watching from a distance. As soon as, White Tail had killed the Tory, Brant raised his rifle, aimed toward his nephew, and fired. White Tail didn't know who had shot him. He was my blood brother. Just like you and my father are blood brothers." Walter looked toward his father as he grasped one of George's hands and raised it with his toward the ceiling.

"Amen," each agreed.

"I really don't know why I told you that story about White Tail," Walter admitted as he bowed his head, closed his eyes, and wiped a tear. As he looked toward his father and George he added, "I guess I have unfinished business with some Redcoats and Indians."

"You don't mean that you want to join George and General Arnold do you," asked his shocked father. "What about Helena? Remember that Harvey Perry and George Raab told us that they knew how her father was killed. We'll all need you at the cheese plant and with the farm chores here."

At this moment, George believed that silence was best, and he exercised it. He was going to let his blood brother and his son resolve this discussion. Just then Rebecca appeared and informed the men that the morning would soon appear. They bade each other a good night and carried their unresolved decision to bed.

❊ 6 ❊

ACT OF
PROVIDENCE

11:00 A.M., AUGUST 10, 1777

THE HEIDELBERG TAVERN, NEW PALATINE

"I tell you it was an act of Providence," declared the Valley's only circuit-rider preacher, Reverend Johan Stouffer, as he stroked his salt-and-pepper beard and held his worn, leather-bound Bible close to his breast.

Until the residents of New Palatine completed the construction of the hamlet's new church, Martha Butler, the proprietor of the Heidelberg Tavern, New Palatine's only stone building, made the tarvern available for church services. Promptly at midnight she would stop selling all alcoholic beverages in preparation for the tavern's transformation into New Palatine's Dutch Reformed Mission. It was a community ritual to walk to the tavern for morning worship every Sunday, or ride a horse, or hitch a ride with a neighbor. After tethering their live stock in either the village's livery stable or at one of its various hitching rails or posts, families with children, lovers with their companions, and occasionally the settlement's drunk would wend their way to the tavern to listen to Preacher Stouffer. After the service, the congregation would take their lunches and go to the site of the new church to eat, drink, and continue the construction.

The settlement of New Palatine did not acquire its official identity as a hamlet until the early sixties; prior to that it served as a crossroad and meeting place between Albany, New York on the most developed eastern frontier, Oswego on Lake Ontario, and the

41

wildness of the western frontier. The first building to go up was The Heidelberg Tavern; it served as a convenient meeting place for the journeymen of the day. It also had sleeping quarters in a huge attic that was hot during the summer and mighty cold during the winter. There was always fresh straw on which to sleep, but no facilities for bathing unless the guests chose to take a quick dip in the creek that flowed along the southern border of the tavern. Between the tavern and the creek was a young apple orchard planted by Martha Butler's husband; "that's just about all he's good for—planting trees" was Martha's remark when asked about her husband.

The tavern was on the south side of a six-acre plot of land known as the *common;* it was initially used as a common pasture for the community's sheep and goats. Recently the common was used as the drill field for the Tryon County Militia. Around the common was a dirt road that was sufficiently wide enough to allow a team of horses pulling a four-wheel buggy to turn around. This road, or trail, circled the entire common area. Directly opposite the tavern on the north side of the common was the site where the community was slowing but surely constructing their new Dutch Reformed Church.

A few yards west of the tavern was Wilhelm Kerchner's general store and about a half-mile from the store Karl Heindrick and his family had built a creamery specializing in making the best cheddar cheese in the Mohawk Valley; its speciality was "Rebecca's Limburger," which was in great demand.

Immediately south of the tavern and set back nearly one hundred feet from the main road was a livery stable for the community's inhabitants; they used it to leave their horses while they shopped in the store, drank in the tavern, or attended church services on Sundays and holidays. Just behind the livery stable George Raab had his black-smith shop. Further east about a mile was the Swackhammer's grist mill and directly opposite the smithy shop on the north side of the common was the one-room public school that Calbert Swartz's nephew had started.

About the only characteristic Preacher Stouffer and Martha Butler had in common was that each one was a third-generation Palatine.

The flaxen-haired, voluptuous, middle-aged widow, Martha Butler, served not only as the tavern's sole proprietor, but also as its bartender, part-time cook, part-time waitress, and full-time bouncer. She experienced very little activity, however, as a bouncer; very few of her customers could match her ability to carry two filled one-quart steins in each hand and dance the polka at the same time.

Approximately five years ago, Martha had been caught in one of her few weak moments. After being totally captivated by a dashing, cavalier and first-generation Scot Highlander, Jerome Butler, she soon married him. A few months later she discovered that her idol had more than a roving eye, he had clay feet. She learned that a young, pregnant Scot immigrant was pursuing him and he allowed himself to be caught. Soon after this eye-opener, her Tory-leaning husband decided that it would be safer and more advisable for him to join his cousin, Colonel John Butler, and his Tory Rangers rather than face his enraged wife's mouth, hot temper, and ability to follow through on her threats. Secretly, Martha was hoping that some rebel or Indian would do her a favor and ambush him so as to end her frustrations and their marriage.

Despite Martha's appearance, she was a very deep and sincere individual, a listener, and said only what she knew should and could be said. She was almost always in control of situations, and one of the valley's most enterprising entrepreneurs. It was not unusual for Tories and rebels to gather in her tavern to debate anything from the best way to breed a cow, whose wife was cavorting with whom or visa versa, what kind of fish are biting on what in the Mohawk River or Wood Creek, how to deal with the King and his taxes, or the last battle General George Washington had lost. Through these friendly and casual conversations, Martha was able to gather information which she would convey to Preacher Stouffer. He, in turn, would make sure that the Tryon County Committee of Safety was informed in a timely and appropriate way.

Reverend Johan Stouffer was more at home in the saddle as he traveled from one valley settlement to another, spreading the word of the Lord and any other tidbit he felt needed to be divulged to the proper individuals. He was a people person who enjoyed meeting people, all kinds of people. His stout body and his silvery hair gave him a much older appearance than his thirty-nine years. Dust was usually clinging to his threadbare pant legs, obscuring the original color of the fabric. His knee-high boots appeared to have had little care, little attention had been given to removing the outside layer of dust or mud. Yet, despite his unimpressive appearance, most of the people of the Valley loved and respected the jovial, rotund man in the worn, dark wool, homespun suit.

Preacher Stouffer shared a small, log farmhouse with Red Bird a middle-aged Mohawk princess who served as his mistress, farmhand, mother, and most importantly, his friend. Even though they were deeply devoted to each other they were in no great rush to locate a local preacher who would be willing to marry them; in any case, four years ago they had been married *Indian fashion*. That did not mean that he did not allow his eyes to wander here and there while on the long, wilderness circuit. But Red Bird knew her man; her man was always faithful when she was about. She knew, too, the "Reverend," as she preferred to address him in public, appreciated her help in making his sometimes monotonous profession exciting. He knew that he had never been sexually attractive to the white women of the settlement. They were all just excellent friends who needed each other. Preaching was not his first choice of occupation. His first love was the theater. After many long hours of discussions, which occasionally erupted into all out arguments, his parents had persuaded young Johan to enter the ministry. He had been told that he couldn't make a living being an actor. Their most persuasive argument came when they asked him, "What do you think the neighbors will say when they find out that you're goin' to be an actor?" He had frequently thought about that question since his parents had asked it. That was many years ago; he had restrained his anger and frustration and yielded to their demands. He wished to hell that he had told them what he really felt and wanted. Regardless, Preacher Stouffer had been relatively successful in combining his gospel preaching with his passion for the theater. He knew that he had actor's blood flowing throughout his veins. Each time he stood in or near a church pulpit he envisioned himself on a stage as one of William Shakespeare's characters with the congregation as his audience. As he delivered his message to his audience he could ham-it up to his heart's delight, and most of the time the congregation loved it. This morning, as on every Sunday morning in New Palatine, the Heidelberg Tavern's huge fireplace and hearth served as an attractive background and stage for the good-hearted minister's message.

Imagining himself as Moses, God's servant, parting the Red Sea, the Revered John Stouffer raised both arms toward the tavern's ceiling and strolled among his congregation. With one hand still clutching his Bible and his other hand's forefinger pointing toward heaven, he repeated, "I tell you it was an act of Providence."

"It certainly was an act of Providence," thought Karl Heindrick as he equated the preacher's message to his own experience. Even though his wounded leg still required the assistance of a crutch and pained him horribly, he, Rebecca, Walter and Helena Kerchner were determined to attend the church service and to give their thanks to the Lord for bringing them safely together again after the ambush at Oriskany. He was especially thankful and happy to have found his lost brother, George Jefferson, and that he had consented to join them in worship.

Also in the congregation was Harvey Perry and wife, Hazel. Harvey was still having nightmares hearing and seeing his musket fire bursting in the face of the on-rushing Tory. Seconds later he realized that he had killed his former employer and Helena's father, Wilhelm Kerchner. Today, as during that fateful afternoon, his buddy the hamlet's smithy, George Raab, was by his side.

"Let there be no doubt that the good Lord was watching over our men and boys as they gallantly marched into that valley. What I'm telling you now may seem very difficult for some of you to believe, especially for those who have lost members of your family. Our duty now is to carry on their mission—freedom from the king and his tyranny. Less than a week ago, many sacrificed their lives willingly at Oriskany. Now it's our duty to follow through with their commitment; to rid this valley of the King, his taxes, and his allies once and for all.

Walter clutching Helena's hand gave it a gentle squeeze as they smiled toward one another. The Raabs and Perrys were nodding their heads in agreement, while Karl and Rebecca silently prayed for peace in the valley.

"Into that valley of death's shadow, our loved ones marched fearlessly, never doubting that the Lord was with them." He stopped. There was silence while all watched their preacher massage his beard. He looked about the congregation trying to calculate if it was appropriate to go on. Then, staring sternly about, he continued, "But the dastardly and cowardly British, Tories, and Indians hid behind rocks and trees until most of our militia were caught in this swampy, narrow, wooded trap. Then with musket fire, hatchets, knives, bayonets, and gun butts they set about to wound, scalp, and butcher our men. Our Lord looked aghast upon this horrible scene. At His will, He combined the morning's intolerable heat with its black-thunder clouds and created a monumental thunder storm that enveloped the deep ravine in complete darkness."

With his hands above his head and his fingers imitating rain falling he resumed his dramatic description of the scene. "The rain came down in torrents. Gusts of wind howled through tree-tops, and sheets of lightening flashed in quick succession, with a continuous clash of thunder that drowned out other noises. When wet rifles could no longer be fired, all decided to cease further attempts to do battle and regroup.

"I tell you this was an act of Providence," he declared as he theatrically moved before the fireplace. The congregation was spellbound.

He stroked his beard; then, leaning toward his parishioners and whispering as if he had a secret to tell, he continued. "During that storm, which raged for about three-quarters of an hour, General Herkimer had directed the militia to form a large, irregular circle, each man facing outward, and ordered that there be two men behind each tree, so that one was ready to shoot a charging enemy while the other reloaded. When the storm was over the enemy came charging as before, expecting to find a lone rebel behind each tree or rock. But this time, there was another rebel ready with a loaded rifle, firing at the charger."

Hearing the preacher's description of the change in battle strategy, Harvey Perry leaned forward and glanced toward George Raab. Each smiled and made the sign of the cross as the preacher continued.

"Most of these Indian attackers had been drunk in the morning and began to feel reaction the their liquor. As soon as they discovered the rebel's new strategy, they started to believe the rumor that had been circulated. This whole affair they whispered to each other was a white man's plot to destroy them, and so they began firing into their Tory allies, and loudly shouted their word for retreat, *Oonah! Oonah!* and began to withdraw from the ambush."

Again a dramatic moment of silence as Preacher Stouffer returned to the center of the fireplace. Raising his face toward the ceiling, he closed his eyes, and placed his hands together as if in prayer. Everyone was wondering what he would say next. After a while he resumed, "Yes, we have much to be thankful for. General St. Leger and his forces have been stopped and sent retreating back to Canada. And most importantly, they will not be able to juncture with General Burgoyne in Albany as they had planned.

"During this savage battle we were fortunate to have a number of persons who deserve our gratitude; without their selfless contribution the end may have been different. First, there is our thirteen-year-old neighbor lad, Jan Van Eps, who walked all the way from Schenectady, and who had hidden himself among the ranks of the militia. Then, during the height of the battle, he and our own Walter Heindrick helped to lift the wounded general and carry him to cover. At the general's direction, they set him down on his horse's saddle with his back against the trunk of a large beech tree."

Helena smiled and squeezed Walter's hand as his proud face beamed with a scarlet glow. "Another story you may not have heard," the preacher continued, "but one I'd like to share with you is that of a fifteen-year-old Indian princess. She is the daughter of an Oneida chief who fought side by side with her father's warriors and the Tryon County Militia, firing her musket and shouting her war cries with the rest of her tribe. These young people symbolize the heroism and trust that is needed to build and protect our future, the diversity of our valley, and how and why we must all learn to live together if we are to have lasting peace.

"The famous Greek orator, Horace who lived from 65 to 8 B.C., once stated that whatever prosperous hour Providence bestows upon you, receive it with a thankful hand; and defer not the enjoyment of the comfort of life."

Preacher Stouffer lowered his shaggy head and surveyed the congregation, "Again," he reminded them, "Providence chose that hour to shine upon our militia that day of infamy and there were others who gave their . . ." He stopped his sermon when his attention was diverted as he recognized Dr. Petrie, General Herkimer's own medical advisor, had discreetly entered the tavern and silently closed the door.

Heads turned toward the back of the room as the preacher asked, "Do you, Dr. Petrie, have any good news to give us regarding the General?"

Lowering his head and with both hands clasped together, as if in prayer, the middle-aged physician walked slowly through the gathering toward the tavern's fireplace. Solemnly, the kindly physician raised his face and surveyed his audience. He recognized many of his own patients of past years, and saw in their eyes anticipation of some good news concerning the wounded general. "My good friends," he began, "I do have good news about General Herkimer. As you know he has returned to his home near Little Falls, and is resting as comfortably as possible. I might add that he is able to smoke his clay pipe." The congregation responded with a slight chuckle for most of them had never seen the general without his pipe. "The bad news is that Dr. Robert Johnson, a young French surgeon in the army of Colonel Benedict Arnold, has agreed to perform the amputation of his wounded leg. Dr. Johnson believes that the dismemberment is necessary to save his life. Personally, I believe that his wound would have healed in due time without the amputation. However, I will keep Reverend Johan Stouffer appraised of the general's condition as soon as there is any information which I'm certain that you will be interested in knowing." He reverently bowed his head and left the tavern as silently as he had entered.

If there had been a mouse in the tavern, everyone would have heard it move; the silence was deafening.

For once in his life Preacher Stouffer was speechless. He solemnly surveyed the blank faces staring at him. With hands locked together, he raised them and he asked each one present to say a silent prayer to the Lord and thank Him for all their blessings, and to help them share these blessings with those less fortunate. *And please include, Lord, our enemies as well as our friends,* he added to himself.

He separated his clasped hands and formed a fist. "You see this fist?" he asked as he held up his right hand. "A community is like a fist. As long as the fingers are held together the fist is a powerful weapon; but just pull one finger from the fist and it becomes almost useless and weak. We must all pray to the Lord for His help so as to build upon the Valley's strengths and its diversity, and not upon our differences."

At that moment Karl Heindrick stood up and stated, "Talking about diversity and working together, as well as the recent blessings which Providence has bestowed upon us, I have been fortunate to have found my lost blood brother shortly after the ambush at Oriskany. I am very proud to introduce Sergeant George Jefferson of Albany, New York . . . my blood brother." He bowed toward George to encourage him to stand. As he stood beside his brother, Karl put his hand on George's shoulders and continued, "General Philip Schuyler has assigned George to General Benedict Arnold's force. He did arrive toward the end of the ambush; time enough, however, to injure his right eye, and to catch an Indian's slash on his right arm. George's primary mission is to recruit volunteers to join General Arnold's forces as they head back to Albany. As many of you may know, General John Burgoyne has been advancing south from Montreal. Burgoyne has already captured Fort Ticonderoga. From what we gather, he is scheduled to meet General Howe who is advancing north from New York City. St. Leger was to have merged with them after he had captured Fort Stanwix and the Mohawk Valley, but we defeated that part of their plan."

"Welcome, George," said the smiling preacher, as he came and shook his free left hand. "We are proud to have you here, and we share our blessings with you and the Heindricks. After the service, I know that George would be very willing to talk with any of you who would like to learn more about the volunteer service for Generals Schuyler and Arnold."

"Thank you, Reverend," George responded. "I'm very proud to be here and to have the opportunity to meet you all."

Every head was bowed. Some were kneeling beside their chairs; others were holding hands. Each praying for peace to come to the valley.

With perspiration rolling from his brow, Preacher Stouffer reverently walked through the congregation, stopped at the tavern's entrance, raised his hand, and said "Go in peace to love and serve the Lord." As he crossed himself, the assembly responded "Thanks be to God." As the parishioners slowly began to exit, each was greeted by name, with a warm handshake or a bear hug, and interested questions about missing members of their family, and a sincere "God bless you and yours."

Even though Preacher Stouffer was a resident in nearby German Flats, a community closer to Albany, he was very much a fixture of the New Palatine hamlet.

As the Perrys and the Raabs walked out of the service, George Raab told them that he had heard something alarming from Harry Hunter. Knowing full well that the hamlet's drunk was always full of stories and rumors, they stared toward the short, muscular smithy whose iron-handed grip had defeated most of the Valley's arm wrestlers. They waited impatiently to hear what their close friend was going to tell them. Harvey Perry, with his ruddy complexion and modest paunch fashionably protruding over a handsome leather belt, was escorting his cheerful and jovial wife, Hazel, who was also adequately prepared for a long, cold winter. Looking towards the middle-aged couple, George Raab brushed back his blonde, wavy hair and began by bluntly announcing, "There is a rumor that Mrs. Sarah Kerchner is coming back to New Palatine and is planning to reclaim her husband's general store."

The sudden shock took the redness from Harvey Perry's face and for the first time that day Hazel Perry's face lost its smile. Instantly, Harvey recalled the time when he and George were a part of Herkimer's *circle of death*. They had just finished reloading their muskets when they realized that they were facing another onslaught. This time they were almost face-to-face, eyeball-to-eyeball, with two Tories who had their muskets pointed straight at them. Harvey was the first to shoot. A split second later George's musket burst straight into the other Tory's face, blowing his brains to the winds. A moment later Harvey exclaimed to George, "My God, look who the hell I just killed . . . it's Kerchner, my boss!"

Astonished, Hazel Perry said, "That can't be. Everybody knows that the Kerchners left for Canada. Even when their daughter,

Helena, came back, she said that they were on their way to Canada, and that she did not want go to Canada, because she did not believe as the Tories believed."

Embarrassed, Harvey Perry looked at his wife, "Honey, there's something that neither George nor I have told anyone." He cleared his throat, and seeing George's approving nod Harvey went on. "It all happened so quickly during the battle." Harvey stopped trying to think how to tell their wives, he just burst out saying, "I killed Wilhelm Kerchner!" The shocked women were speechless. Wilhelm Kerchner and his wife had always treated them fairly, and the Perry's dearly loved Helena. But Wilhelm's politics were so dogmatically in favor of the king that many of the hamlet's residents stopped shopping in his general store. Since the Kerchners fled to Canada, the Perry's had continued to manage the store and the residents were slowing returning as shoppers. Meanwhile, the Perrys had kept Helena apprised of the operations, regularity depositing receipts in the area's financial institution, paying the bills, drawing their usual salary, as well as subsidizing the Heindricks for Helena's maintenance. Now, it was a whole new set of circumstances. There would be no easy solutions.

As the Perrys and the Raabs headed toward the livery to reclaim their horses and carriages, across the street a pair of soft blue eyes, partially hidden by blond bangs and a dark brown woolen scarf, enviously peered between the separated slats of a second floor hayloft over the livery. The eyes watched as the Perrys and Raabs disappeared into the stable. Then the eyes quickly switched to watching Helena's every step as she approached the group of men and boys circled around George Jefferson and Walter Heindrick; Helena was anxious to learn more about General Schuyler and General Arnold's call for volunteer recruits. Helena and Walter had spent two lonely hours discussing whether or not he should join Arnold's forces. After Walter had expressed his feelings about losing White Tail, Helena reluctantly agreed so long as the period of volunteerism did not extend more than three months. When this condition was presented to George Jefferson, he assured Helena that he would personally guarantee Walter's return to New Palatine.

{ 7 }

TARGETED
FORTRESS

ON LAKE CHAMPLAIN, NEW YORK DURING THE MID-1700S

No fort in the world has a history quite like that of Fort
Ticonderoga. Fort Ti, as it was frequently referred to fondly, initially
built by the French far out in the wilderness, was in close proximity
to the majestic and scenic Adirondack Mountains along the western
shore of New York's Lake Champlain. The end of the French and
Indian War saw the fall of Montreal, and Canada become a part of
the ever expanding British Empire.

The British military strategists believed that there was little, if
any, need for forts on the Lake Champlain waterway. The king, however, decided to hold and maintain Fort Ti and Crown Point, a
smaller fort directly north of Fort Ti. Crown Point was a strategically
located British supply base.

Early in August 1758 the bulk of the British army, under the
command of Major General Jeffery Amherst, moved into Fort
Ticonderoga in what seemed a lazy, indifferent operation, but which
had been thoughtfully designed, planned, and almost flawlessly executed; the British had seized Fort Ti with a minimum of loss of life.
Before evacuating the fort, the retreating French attempted to destroy
it with fire. Fortunately for the British only the woodwork of the fort,
the barrack floors, the roof timbers, and the wooden facings of the
outer walls were burned; although the fire continued to smolder for
nearly a month. After examining the fort, however, Amherst discov-

ered that the structure had incredibly suffered little permanent damage. Amherst, not always trusting his own engineers, ordered them to repair the fort under close supervision immediately, using the same plan as the French had used to build it. At the same time, the destruction resulting from the explosion of the magazine was repaired and some, if not all, of the wooden walls were replaced with stone.

But then, Amherst suddenly discovered four little French warships on Lake Champlain and, in order to gain control of the lake, he knew they would have to be destroyed. Consequently, he ordered part of his army to start constructing England's own naval fleet at Crown Point and assigned the rest of his troops to continuing the repairs on Fort Ti.

He would spare no cost to achieve his goal of repairing the dilapidated old fort into a mighty fortress that would ultimately cost the British a huge amount of money, yet, in return serve relatively little purpose. By the late summer of 1759 life in Fort Crown Point and Fort Ticonderoga was very monotonous unless one was a fisherman or a swimmer. Historians report that military life was so boring that the commanding officer of Fort Crown Point ran a farm as the commander at Fort Ti probably did.

As diligent as Amherst was in his insistence for competent work, the fort's repaired walls were only thin stone facings covering steep banks of earth and clay. With each bitter winter the frost crept in a little deeper behind the stonework and exerted its destructive force on the rebuilt masonry. After Amherst completed the original repairs, there was little or no preventative maintenance and Fort Ti steadily fell into decay.

By 1770 most of the walls had collapsed in places; the parapets that sheltered the cannon on the ramparts had disintegrated into a mass of dirt and rotten wood, and the stone barracks that once held a garrison of 400 troops were now in a sad state of repair.

In the spring of 1773, Fort Crown Point was almost entirely destroyed. During the spring of 1775, Captain William Delaplace of the 26th Regiment was placed in command of Fort Ticonderoga, with only one officer, Lieutenant Jocelyn Feltham, to assist him. The garrison was comprised of forty-two men; half of these were *old, wore out, and unserviceable* or otherwise incapacitated. In addition, there were two dozen women and children.

Over one hundred miles east of Fort Ti, on April 19, 1775, the pum-
melled British troops, under the command of Lord Percy, retreated
from Concord and Lexington through the Massachusetts countryside and were eventually transported via ferries to the City of
Boston, while rebel Minute Men from the villages north and west of
Boston harried them every step of the way. The Minute Men were
soon reinforced with volunteers from eastern New England and were
able to surround Boston. There, the British command under Sir
General William Howe, who had relieved General Thomas Gage,
was desperately trying to hold this valuable peninsula that was connected to the mainland by an extremely narrow neck of land.
Fortunately for the rebels, the British were unaware that the rebel
forces lacked the artillery, especially heavy artillery, crucial to either
the capture of Boston or to driving the British from their stronghold
on Cape Cod.

Five days after the fight at Concord, Captain Benedict Arnold,
now of the Governor's Footguards of New Haven, was leading his
company to Cambridge. While on the road between Boston and
Connecticut, Arnold met Colonel Samuel Parsons who was returning
to Connecticut from British held Boston. At this time, Parsons told
Arnold of the rebels desperate need for artillery so as to capture
Boston. Arnold, who as a boy had run away from home near the end
of the French and Indian War, had seen a great deal of cannon and
related artillery at Fort Ticonderoga. Remembering this, he told
Colonel Parsons of the artillery pieces at Fort Ti, there for anyone
who had the courage and the energy to capture them. As a result of
this fortunate meeting, two strategic plans against Fort Ti were
immediately developed. Parsons gathered a small but powerful group
in Hartford, Connecticut, while Arnold worked with the patriot
authorities in Cambridge, Massachusetts. On April 30, 1775 Arnold
met with the Committee of Safety, which was responsible for the
area's security, and told them of the great cache of artillery at Fort
Ticonderoga. He estimated that there were at least eighty iron cannon and twenty of brass, from four to eighteen pounders in size, as
well as a dozen large mortars. This embellished estimate was indeed

on the conservative side when the ordnance from Fort Crown Point was added to the booty. After a brief discussion, the committee expressed great interest in Arnold's plan. On that same day, the committee wrote to New York's Committee of Safety about Arnold's proposal to capture Fort Ti, but that it hesitated to encroach on territory in New York without that state's approval.

Earlier in February 1775, a young Pittsfield, Massachusetts lawyer, John Brown, while returning from a trip to Canada to survey the Canadians' opinions toward the Americans, had learned that Americans were not held in high esteem. During his trip, he too, examined the conditions at Fort Ticonderoga. Immediately upon his return, Brown convinced a group of "people on the N. Hampshire Grants"—the Green Mountain Boys, whose leader was Ethan Allen, originally from Connecticut, subdue the British and capture the fort. Brown insisted that the fort be seized at once and hostilities between Britain and the colonies be commenced. Allen and his boys were referred to by the New York authorities as the "Bennington Mob," because the settlement of Bennington served as their capital, and they only followed their own leaders. In fact, the Green Mountain Boys were a few hundred lawless frontiersmen, roaming and subsisting in the region between Lake Champlain and the Connecticut River. They were lead by the boastful, egotistical Ethan Allen, full of impulsive, and explosive energy, who intensively loathed the New Yorkers who claimed some of the lands in the Green Mountains.

By May 1, 1775, the old French fort, Ticonderoga, about which British General Gage's senior engineer, Captain Montresor reported "It's ruinous situation is such that it would require more to repair it than the constructing of a new fort. In many places there are very capital breaches," had three groups targeting it for seizure. Besides the unruly Green Mountain Boys, there was the unofficial but still powerful Connecticut group led by Colonel Parsons and Captain Edward Mott, and the Massachusetts Committee of Safety. A number of official and unofficial meetings were held in various locations regarding the correct strategies to engage Fort Ti. However, the Massachusetts Committee of Safety had its own method of dealing with the subject. They secretly commissioned Colonel *(by their grace)* Benedict Arnold, to seize Fort Ti with an initial party of sixteen plus a contingent of some forty Massachusetts men John Brown had been able to enlist.

Meanwhile, Allen and his Green Mountain Boys were gathered at the Catamount Tavern in Bennington still defiant and planning their strategy. Before the day was over, they were joined by the Connecticut group. The two groups agreed to continue their planning at the farmhouse of Richard Bently in Castleton, a hamlet further north and nearer to the fort. After the meeting, Ethan Allen ventured out to spy out the fort and its surroundings, while another small group went a short distance south to Skenesboro to capture Major Philip Skene, the eminent Tory landholder of the region, and if possible, to seize boats with which to cross Lake Champlain. Late that evening of May 8, 1775, Benedict Arnold, dressed in his sparkling military officer's coat and white breeches, crashed into the farmhouse and demanded command of the expedition, apparently ignoring the recruitment of his authorized four hundred. His insistence was ignored, and the independent frontiersmen guffawed, but they consented to permit him to join his forces with theirs. Resolved to make the most of the situation, Arnold decided to join the assembled groups and bide his time. Allen knew that he, himself, had no official authority to conduct this expedition. He also knew that Arnold had an official commission from the Massachusetts Provincial Congress, which was at the moment the supreme authority in the area. Yet the stubborn Allen still refused to give up formal command to Arnold.

"Now, Mr. Allen," said Arnold addressing the stubborn Vermont woodsman, "you remember when we were fighting side by side last year, when we joined forces with General Montgomery to invade Canada?"

"Sure I remember that time," responded the haughty leader of the Green Mountain Boys. "And we captured Montreal, didn't we?" he added with a spit of disdain.

Arnold continued, "It was shortly after we captured Montreal that we attacked Quebec. It was also at Quebec that I was shot in my leg midway between my knee and ankle; the bullet then lodged in my heel."

"All that stuff is so much bullshit," snarled back the gigantic Green Mountain leader. "All that stuff was over a year ago.

Montgomery got killed. I got captured, and Dan Morgan came in to save your skin. Still the bloody British beat our asses. I'm going to command this expedition, come hell or high water."

"Alright, now calm yourself," Arnold said. "Let's admit that both of us are stubborn, ambitious, and high-spirited, but let's put all of this in the past and concentrate on capturing Fort Ti," he finished, offering his right hand. He believed that Allen would eventually clarify his position of authority. Allen shook hands quickly with Arnold and immediately turned to join his troops.

Late on the evening of May 9 in a place called Hand's Cove on the shore of Lake Champlain, a ragtag gang of about two hundred men assembled. It was composed mostly of Green Mountain Boys, approximately forty of them from Massachusetts and a few from Connecticut. The group was on the lake's eastern shore; it needed to be on the western shore. Daybreak was near and the anticipated boats had not arrived. Fortunately, a couple of flat-bottomed boats were discovered and quickly put to use to ferry the men across the lake. By daybreak, some eighty men had been successfully transported to the western shore; it was now too late to wait for the others.

No one will ever know just what kind of agreement was made between Arnold and Allen after they began their trek to Fort Ti. It is known, however, that Arnold again demanded command of the force, as well as to be the first to set foot in the fortress. These requests Allen denied, but Arnold claims that Allen did agree to share joint authority, and the two would march into the fort side-by-side.

Through their scouting reports, the rebels had learned of a small portal that led into a tunnel. They entered the portal and following the tunnel eventually came into the basement of the eastern barrack building. There they stormed up a flight of stone steps that led them onto the parade ground. Seeing the intruders, the sentry at the entrance pointed his musket toward the group's leader and pulled the trigger, but the gun jammed. The sentry immediately fled into the bombproof shelter on the north side of the parade ground. The invading group, meanwhile, rushed up the steps, through doors, up the walls, and into the barracks where most of the garrison was sound asleep. They were overpowered with ease while still in their bunks and the invaders quickly started plundering.

Arnold, Allen, and a few supporters rushed across the courtyard where they encountered a second sentry who with his bayonet jabbed and slightly wounded one of Allen's Green Mountain Boys. Immediately, Allen struck the sentry down with his sword, demanding to be directed to the fort's commanding officer. Filled with fear and completely shocked, the intimidated sentry pointed toward a staircase that led up to the second floor of the western barrack. Leaving the stunned sentry, the excited Allen, with Arnold close behind, rushed the stairs.

"Come out, you old rat," Allen demanded.

Within seconds, the lone figure of British officer Lieutenant Feltham appeared at the top of the stairs. Captain Delaplace's only officer, Feltham was literally caught with his pants down. He was fully dressed except for his breeches which he carried over one arm. Allen and Arnold stared and began to laugh at the humorous sight. The desperate officer, hoping that his garrison would come to his rescue, tried to delay any further action from the two rebel officers. He did not know that the garrison had been completely vanquished.

With his sword, the impetuous Allen threatened to exercise *no quarter,* and demanded that Feltham surrender the fort to his joint command with Benedict Arnold, under orders of Connecticut and Massachusetts. Arnold was apparently willing to permit Allen to do most of the talking while he tried to restrain Allen's fury. The situation became increasingly more strained and menacing. In the courtyard, the Green Mountain Boys were taunting and mocking Feltham. Finally in the doorway at the head of the stairs, Commanding Officer Delaplace appeared in full dress. His first statement was a question, "Under what authority are you acting?" The slightly more composed Allen proclaimed, "In the name of the Great Jehovah and the Continental Congress."

The startled Delaplace had no alternative but to surrender the fortress to the rebels. Thus, the renowned *Gibraltar of the American Revolution* was captured without bloodshed from the British that evening in May 1775. It could be said that the seizure of Fort Ti was no great military victory. It was, however, the first completely, strategically planned, offensive military campaign of the American

Revolution; while the Lexington and Concord encounters were defensive acts.

One year later, this fortress would become General Burgoyne's initial major target for capture on his way to Albany.

Before daybreak on May 10, Fort Ti was as secured under the joint command of Ethan Allen and Benedict Arnold as it could be. The Green Mountain Boys were their usual uncontrollable selves; plundering, looting the storerooms, and devastating the ammunition magazines. Eventually, the looters were joined by their late arriving compatriots, who not to be cheated out of their share of booty, more than made up for their tardiness. Meanwhile, Arnold, the seasoned veteran of many military campaigns and as commanding officer of a war vessel, tried to minimize the destruction and looting. Predictably, his efforts were in vain; all he accomplished was to further distance himself from Ethan Allen and antagonize the Green Mountain Boys. According to one account, a number of clandestine musket shots were aimed at Arnold, but were wild of their target. At this point of the campaign and in the fort's recorded history, Ethan Allen was indeed the commanding officer.

In the meantime, another detachment of late arrivals from the eastern shore of Lake Champlain under the command of Seth Warner was directed to capture Fort Crown Point. Because of unfavorable winds, this group did not arrive until the following day to capture the impoverished fort's garrison of eleven men and its many cannons. Concurrently, another group of Allen's boys attacked Fort George, located south of Fort Ti near the northern border of Lake George; this fort was seized from the British without any fatal casualties. As a result, the British lost all points of control along the Hudson-Champlain waterway south of St. Jean on the Richelieu River, barely north of the mouth of Lake Champlain.

While Allen's men were capturing the British forts, Benedict Arnold was busy assembling his naval force. On the 13th of May, Skene's schooner dropped anchor near Fort Ti and aboard were the recruits Arnold's officers had enlisted when they returned from

Boston. With these men Arnold now had about 100 who would follow his orders, as well as sail the ships, something of no use to the landlubbers from Vermont, but something of extreme value to an ambitious sailor and soldier such as Benedict Arnold; his military experience contributed to his foresight. He realized and understood the importance of controlling this northern waterway. The British had only one sloop anchored at St. Jean just north of Lake Champlain on the Richelieu River. On May 15th Arnold and his small group of men boarded a batcaux and headed north to capture the British vessel. Fortunately, they encountered and also captured a British bateaux and a British ensign carrying the mail south from Canada. The mail included a current list of the location of all the seven hundred British troops in Canada.

At daybreak on the 18th of May, Arnold and his men were only about half a mile south of St. Jean. He sent a spy ahead to scout out the village and the British sloop. Upon returning, the scout reported that there were only fourteen soldiers in the hamlet, and the sloop's crew consisted of only seven men. As soon as Arnold and his men showed their faces, the British almost instantly surrendered. The British sloop was an exceptional trophy, seventy tons, almost sixty feet in length, and armed with two sizable, brass six-pounder cannons. In time, Arnold would see this vessel renamed the *Enterprise* and armed with twelve guns and a crew of fifty men.

After securing the sloop, Arnold, with his men, used their experience and made necessary arrangements to assure that the British would not have a solitary boat that could float, and that the hamlet of St. Jean would be of minimal use to them. After destroying five bateaux and adding four of the captured bateaux to their fleet, they quickly loaded all the functional supplies, food, and munitions, along with their captives and themselves aboard the vessels and sailed south.

On the voyage south, they were surprised to see Ethan Allen and nearly a hundred of his men headed north in four bateaux. In an effort to outsmart Arnold, and not knowing what he and his men were doing, Allen decided to capture St. Jean. In his haste, he had neglected to carry enough food provisions and by the time Arnold and his men met Allen's, they were desperately famished. While

Arnold's men were transferring some of their provisions to Allen's bateaux, Arnold told Allen, "Holding St. Jean is a *wild impracticable scheme.* Even if it could be could be carried into execution it will be of no consequence, so long as we are masters of the lake. Of that I have no doubt. I am determined to arm the sloop and schooner immediately." Allen ignored Arnold's opinion and continued north.

Allen and the Green Mountain Boys had barely arrived at St. Jean when they learned that a force of British troops was nearing the hamlet. They decided immediately to set an ambush and await their arrival. After waiting for some length of time, Allen's men became fearful, broke camp, and crossed the Richelieu River for a *safe* night's sleep. At daybreak they were awakened with a volley of grapeshot from six British cannon, as well as musket shots. They beat a quick retreat to their bateaux leaving three dead Vermonters behind. In his explanation of this humiliating defeat, Allen wrote the Continental Congress: "Provided I had but 500 men with me at St. Johns, when we took the King's sloop, I would have advanced to Montreal." Apparently this ambiguous excuse did not have any positive effects upon the Congress nor even on his own men. By the end of the month of May, all of the Green Mountains Boys had deserted Ethan Allen and undeniably Benedict Arnold was America's military leader on the Hudson–Lake Champlain waterway.

The thirty-four-year-old Connecticut born captain, Benedict Arnold, had an interesting history. As a successful former apothecary and bookseller, the restless, five foot seven inch Benedict Arnold had invested his earnings into small ships and sailed them along the eastern coast of America buying, selling, and trading cargos of horses and lumber. In the fall of the year he returned with European goods, sugar, molasses, and rum. While in Canada he would purchase horses to be sold in the West Indies and sold the Canadians woolen goods and food. Meanwhile, he was stocking his apothecary shop with books, teas, sugar, powders, watches, jewelry, herbs, spices, prints, stationery, plus anything he thought the public would purchase. He was a confirmed believer in the free enterprise system and was not in any mood to allow the king to rob him of his proper profit. He also entered the business of smuggling together with the wealthy Boston merchant John Hancock, a common profession of the period fraught with the constant danger of seizure by the king's henchmen. Arnold's entrepreneurship transcended from business to the rebel cause for freedom from the king. On May 3, 1775, the Massachusetts Committee of Public Safety appointed him to the rank of colonel with orders to take Fort Ticonderoga.

Although Arnold was successful as a merchant and military person, his marriage to the former Margaret (Peggy) Mansfield, a daughter of one of New Haven's prominent mercantile families, was a near disaster. They promptly had three children, but when Peggy learned that Arnold had contracted venereal disease in the West Indies, she promptly and permanently rejected him from their marital bed. Little else is known of their marriage, except that Arnold resented her for not corresponding with him whenever he spent long months away from home.

In August 1775, George Washington and Benedict Arnold held an unforgettable meeting in Cambridge, Massachusetts during which their affinity was immediate. They conversed about their experiences while living in the wilderness and compared military strategies. Almost instantly they eliminated any further formal talks, with Washington asking what Arnold thought about an invasion of Canada. Both recognized qualities in the other that each wished he, too, possessed. The one area where there seemed to be a major difference between them was that Washington preferred the more traditional European method of warfare, while Arnold was an ardent advocate of the guerrilla type of combat. According to the British military historian, Sir John Fortescue, Arnold:

> In natural military genius neither Washington nor Greene are to my mind comparable with Benedict Arnold. The man . . . possessed all the gifts of a great commander. To boundless energy and enterprise he united insight into a situation, sound strategic instinct, audacity of movement, wealth of resource, a swift and unerring eye in action, great personal daring, and true magic of leadership. . . . He was the most formidable opponent that could be matched against the British in America.

Later that fall Arnold's old nemesis, Ethan Allen, would lead a group of Americans and French Canadians, to whom he had promised pay and booty, on a reckless assault on Montreal. There he was captured and shipped to England, to be later released but never more to participate in the American Revolution.

Meanwhile the Continental Congress ordered Washington's artillery officer, Henry Knox, to survey the cannon in New York City and send any excess to assist in the siege of Boston. From New York City, this gifted, huge man, and like Arnold, a former bookseller, was ordered to proceed to Fort Ticonderoga and to expedite the transfer of all excess artillery to the rebels surrounding Boston. Knox and the other officers identified fifty-nine pieces, including fourteen mortars, two eight-inch howitzers, and forty-three cannons, with a combined weight of sixty tons; all this would have to be conveyed by manpower and oxen over land that had virtually no roads, as well as over a frozen Lake George. In addition to manpower and oxen, Knox was able to utilize barges, bateaux, and sleds. After reaching Fort George on December 17, a month after he had received his initial orders in Cambridge, Knox found a few more guns left there by Benedict Arnold in the spring of 1775. After much toil and struggle, as well as a series of mishaps that included losing a mortar through the frozen lake and surviving a blizzard that left three feet of snow, Knox and his exhausted men, together with all of their artillery pieces except for the one lost in the frozen Mohawk River, were finally in a position to challenge the British forces still trapped in the City of Boston.

❊{ 8 }❊

SOUTHWARD
BOUND

IN MAJOR GENERAL WILLIAM PHILLIPS QUARTERS
ON THE RICHELIEU RIVER

It had been two days since the drums had beat *The General* while sailors and soldiers, under the command of Lieutenant Colonel Barry St. Leger, had hoisted the sides of the longboats amid three boisterous cheers and slowly embarked upon the second expedition of Burgoyne's military plan which he called "Thoughts." The journey down the St. Lawrence River would take the flotilla fifty-three days to arrive, on July 25th, at its first destination, the small village of Oswego located near the western entrance to the Mohawk River Valley. From there, St. Leger was to capture Fort Stanwix and meet Burgoyne in Albany, New York. But, it would not be until August 28th before Burgoyne would learn of St. Leger's disastrous defeat at Oriskany.

On the evening of June 12, 1777, General John Burgoyne requested Major General Baron Friedrich Adolph von Riedesel and General Sir Guy Carleton, the Governor General of Canada to join him for a farewell dinner in Major General William Phillips's quarters. As always, with any meals hosted by Burgoyne, this dinner would be highlighted by generous courses of champagne and other wines.

Burgoyne had selected Phillips, an artilleryman and close friend who had served with him in Spain, to be his second-in-command.

Generally, when considering military tactics and strategies, they consistently arrived at basically identical conclusions whenever weighing a military question. The army had been Phillips's whole life. Unlike his cultured member of Parliament, man about town, and diplomatic mentor, Phillips was very blunt and expressed himself in a soldier's language. He did, however, have drive that his mentor lacked. Phillips also paid little attention to what he ate or drank, limited himself to one aide-de-camp, and willingly slept on the ground during a campaign, rolling himself in a blanket and insisting he was as comfortable as he would have been in a featherbed. He had absolutely no interest whatsoever in theater which was near and dear to Burgoyne's heart. However, the two were more alike than usually appeared to the general public. Honor was equally as important to Phillips as it was to Burgoyne, and like his commander, Phillips always analyzed a situation with long-range strategic results in mind.

General Sir Guy Carleton was responsible for keeping all of the King's Canadian subjects in line. Consequently, he had to keep a tight rein on his domain and found it necessary to hold several regiments of troops in reserve to put down any possible local insurrections. An American invasion, lead by Benedict Arnold and Brigadier General Richard Montgomery, attempting to capture Canada the previous autumn and winter had failed by a narrow margin. But under Sir Guy's regime the principle fort, Ticonderoga, had fallen to the rebels under the joint command of Benedict Arnold and Ethan Allen. Lord George Germain unwittingly had placed Burgoyne and Carleton in difficult positions. Carleton lacked the experience and skills required to execute the three British expeditions designed by Burgoyne yet, he would remain responsible for these functions. Burgoyne, therefore, was not entirely surprised to hear that he was being sent to Canada as second-in-command under Sir Guy. Yet, he was still responsible for the over-all command of the troops in the field. Carleton and Burgoyne did reach an agreement wherein Burgoyne would keep Carleton informed of his activities; thus, indirectly, he would be reporting to the War Office in London.

Major General Baron Friedrich Adolph von Riedesel was the commander of the German mercenary contingent, which included regiments from Hesse as well as units from Brunswick; he was one of the most distinguished military leaders in Europe. Only thirty-nine-years old, von Reidesel had been a professional fighting man since his mid-teens. He knew his business so well that he ordered his troops to put aside their cumbersome, high-crowned brass helmets, which would impede their progress during a wilderness march. He ordered them to substitute either the stocking caps worn by the Canadians or wear the square-crowned fur hats, complete with raccoon tails, that were a favorite of hunters, trappers, and guides. Accustomed to traveling with his family, von Riedesel was expecting his wife and three children to join him soon.

After the aide-de-camp had poured the champagne, the men began discussing the campaign on which they planned to leave the following morning.

Burgoyne asked Carleton why he had been able to recruit only about four hundred Indians for him, while he had, with Chief Joseph Brant's and Indian Superintendent Butler's help successfully recruited over one thousand warriors for St. Leger's campaign.

"I can't explain the reason why we were so unsuccessful in recruiting the Indians for your campaign," responded Carleton as he sipped the last of his champagne. Holding out the empty glass to the aide-de-camp, he continued, "the difficulty is to prevent the number of them to become so many as to cause distress to his Majesty's service. To be honest with you, Johnny, I fear to assign them to your expedition, our principle campaign. If they cause any disturbances during St. Leger's diversionary operation, the impact and the consequences would be less serious."

"What do you mean diversionary operation?" asked Burgoyne. "I did not design St. Leger's operation as any sort of distraction apart from our Canada–Champlain campaign. It is an integrated component of the over-all plan just as is General Howe's segment. We'll all meet in Albany and have the bloody rebels bending and bowing on their knees."

"Let's all drink to that," said Carleton as he raised his hollow-stemmed crystal and touched the other's champagne glasses.

While the aide-de-camp refilled their glasses, Phillips urged Burgoyne and Carleton to construct a chain of supply-garrisons from Montreal to the lakes.

"I remember you had recommended that to me last February," responded Burgoyne. "I liked the idea, William. In fact, I had included that scheme in my February memorandum, but I guess it has been overlooked in our planning process."

"Governor," inquired Phillips, "could you deploy the 31st Regiment at Sorel, Fort Chambly, Saint John's, Isle aux Noix, and Point au Feu?" Before the governor could respond Phillips added, "I think we should strongly consider posting still a third Canadian regular unit at Sorel to enforce such orders for the necessary *corvee* labor required." Again before Carleton could answer, Phillips concluded, "A fourth, perhaps MacLean's, to conduct similar policing of the French–Canadians at Fort Chambly."

Surprisingly Carleton agreed, "I think those are some very good ideas. As soon as you embark tomorrow, I promise to send the necessary soldiers."

Burgoyne smiled, and lead his generals to the dinner table dressed with freshly pressed and starched linen tablecloths and napkins. He raised his chilled glass of champagne; his companions followed suit. "Here's to King George the Third, a successful campaign, and the defeat of those damn Yankee rebels."

"Hear! Hear!" echoed the others.

"There is something that I am extremely anxious about," voiced von Reidesel. There was complete silence except for the tinkling of silver serving spoons on the boned china serving plates. "I have observed flaws in many of our carts and I question whether we have a sufficient number of horses."

"You have identified two of my major concerns," agreed Burgoyne. "On June 6th, I was presented proposals by a local contractor for the procurement of one thousand horses to pull five hundred carts. To save expenses, I reduced the proposal to below what would be adequate, but I chose to trust that these will be sufficient resources to complete the expedition.

"Regarding the carts," Burgoyne continued, "I retained my request for five hundred carts, which I believe will barely carry fourteen days of provisions at a time."

"Unfortunately," voiced Sir Guy, "the contractors not only neglected the supply of horses; they also failed to produce carts in sufficient quantity."

"What really concerns me," stated Phillips, "is that the carts appear to be flawed, as von Riedesel has noted. The first problem I see is that they were constructed primarily of green lumber and I'm certain this will cause us frequent breakdowns and much delay along our route. Let's assume that the green lumber will not give much trouble, but I also observed many other flaws in the shabby workmanship immediately after the carts were supposedly completed."

"I think we are all in accord," expressed Burgoyne. "Obviously, the carts and horses, as well as the artillery, are going to require considerable manpower to operate and maintain them. But what has me most concerned," he continued looking at Sir Guy, "is the fact that our Canadian recruits keep deserting our ranks and the few provincials we have are almost completely worthless."

As Phillips's aide-de-camp was clearing the table, Burgoyne's aide-de-camp was preparing a flaming dessert to be served with a demitasse spiked with a pony of cognac. All were admiring the skills of the two aides-de-camp. Feeling that this might be the appropriate time to bring up another concern, Phillips stated, "As far as I know there has not yet been any arrangement made for marching the field artillery by land."

Looking somewhat embarrassed, Sir Guy acknowledged, "I remember that a couple of weeks ago you requested me to send the 29th Regiment to Fort Saint John for extended garrison duty and to service our troops, but to tell the truth I just haven't been able to complete the task."

Staring directly toward Sir Guy, Burgoyne stated, "We agreed earlier to get these measures completed."

Sir Guy nodded his agreement to Burgoyne as an aide-de-camp refilled their champagne glasses.

Silently, each general was appraising the uneasy status of preparation for the expedition. At best, each believed that the makeshift efforts to gather sufficient carts and horses to move the artillery, food, support supplies, and other personnel baggage, as well as the recruitment of men were adequate for the moment. But the haphazard attempts at the expedition's immediate planning had delayed the preparations for its long-range plans.

At this point, a bit influenced by too much champagne, the governor elected to vent his exasperation at the division of command. Looking at Burgoyne he said, "You're responsible for forwarding the provisions, which shall pass through this province, for your army advances. I will give you give all the assistance in my power."

Carleton's anxiety and frustrations continued as he stared toward Phillips and stated, "I really question your logic for requesting me to post soldiers at Point au Feu. That location is the southeast garrison in the chain, as you call it and the depot for provisions, artillery stores, and rafts for transporting the carts."

Before Burgoyne could respond to Carleton's statement, Phillips quickly replied, "I agree with you that Point au Feu is beyond the latitudinal limits of the province, but it is certainly within the frontier, which I have conceived to extend to Crown Point and Ticonderoga."

"I was led to believe that Lord Germain's orders to me are that I'm to be strictly limited to the province, and not to be responsible for leading an army into New York," said Carleton. "However," he yielded, "I am fully persuaded of the need for such a step, but I shall lay blame, if any be imputed to me for exceeding my orders, upon you, General Burgoyne. In addition, I doubt whether I have any legal jurisdiction over French–Canadians for seizing and court-martialing those who planned to desert or already have deserted." Continuing looking toward Burgoyne, he concluded, "On this matter, I refer you to the attorney general of Montreal for a legal opinion. Personally, I believe that you should deal with the deserters yourself."

Before Burgoyne could respond to Carleton, a messenger from Quebec was ushered in by an aide-de-camp and announced that General von Riedesel's wife and three children had just arrived in Canada from Germany and their long voyage across the Atlantic. Von Riedesel, in his broken English, expressed his delight that his family would be joining him soon; his anticipation and joy was evident. Looking askance, Burgoyne did not share the German general's joy even though he was looking forward to evenings with the commissary officer's wife. The messenger continued his report that 39 transport ships had arrived in Canada from Portsmouth filled with money, clothing, dispatches, eleven British army companies, and 400 French soldiers from Hanau, in addition to 100 recruits from Brunswick.

Burgoyne's immediate response was, "We can't afford to waste any more time. We'll not wait for those men and supplies to arrive here in Montreal." He raised his partially filled glass, the others following his example. "Here's to tomorrow and a successful campaign."

"Hear! Hear!" responded his colleagues. "Long live the King," they all joined in as they departed from Phillips's quarters to their respective berths. Burgoyne looked forward to the rest of the day with the lady "without the powdered wig." Tomorrow he and Carleton would travel to Isle aux Noix. From there, he would commence the southern expedition and Carleton would return to Montreal.

⧗

Unfavorable winds delayed Burgoyne's expedition for two days. Finally, on June 17, 1777, Burgoyne boarded his barge, *Lady Maria,* and sailed from Isle aux Noix to Cumberland Point, north of Alcour Island where the present day city of Plattsburg is located. Burgoyne assembled his complete compliment at Cumberland Point; his purpose was to thank his troops and to remind them that he believed in them and in their shared goals. "Based upon my experience in two campaigns here in America," he began, "I believe that the rebels are infinitely inferior to the King's troops in open space and hardy combat."

"I do caution you," he warned them, "neither the distance of camps, nor the forests and rivers are to be regarded as securities against their attempts." He raised his scarlet uniform's cuff, polished the brass buttons, silently evaluated his forces, then added, "Use the woodland resources to your advantage; seek protection from the trees and boulders. When felling trees, make sure that the tree points outward toward the enemy; this affords our advance scouts added protection from the rebel marksmen."

As he surveyed his troops, he realized he had lost the attention of many. Quickly he stepped down from the platform on which he was speaking, walked up to one of the regulars, and seized his rifle. Lifting it high over his head, he returned to his makeshift podium, and promptly lowered the rifle butt hard against the wooden platform.

Now, he had their complete attention. He posted the rifle to the *present-arms* command position with the end of the rifle slightly above his head. Holding the rifle in his left hand, he pointed his right index finger on the long steel bayonet attached to the gun. "See this bayonet!" he exclaimed. "This is your friend. Use it!. Use it!" he repeated, then faked a bayonet jab. "Men half as strong as our own soldiers may be their match in fighting, but bayonets in the hands of valiant men are irresistible." His troops had heard many stories of Burgoyne's personal valor and courage and he had their admiration. However, he wanted to instill his own unshakable belief and faith in his troops. He reminded them, "It will be our glory and preservation to storm the enemy, when possible. Lastly, I want to remind you that any stragglers and plunderers will meet with reprisal at the hands of our Indian allies. I demand and expect complete order and obedience." He promptly left the platform and returned the rifle to its owner. With drums beating and the bugle blaring, Burgoyne turned and boarded the *Lady Maria* with much pomp and fanfare. The ship's cannon blasted a shot signalling the beginning of the march southward.

Unaware of the progress of St. Leger's expedition, the next day, June 21st, was the same day St. Leger would leave Montreal to begin his journey to Oswego. Burgoyne remembered that he had a meeting with their Indian allies scheduled on the following day at a predetermined location along the River Bouquet. But for the first day of this expedition he was going to enjoy the voyage and he looked forward to spending the evening with the lady who never powdered her hair.

As planned for June 21st, an odd mixture of British military and Indian chiefs and warriors met *in Congress* at a campsite on the River Bouquet. Burgoyne and his staff dressed in their pressed, scarlet, military jackets with their shiny brass buttons, white breeches, and knee high, highly polished black riding boots presented a sharp contrast to the 400 Indian allies adorned in vermilion, black, and green war paint.

From the same wooden platform he had used the previous day Burgoyne, through an interpreter, assured the Indian warriors that he and his officers considered them brothers. He continued, "We brothers must go forth in the might and valor of our cause . . . strike at the disturbers of public order, peace and happiness, destroyers of commerce, enemies of the state." In dramatic fashion, Burgoyne stopped for a moment, as if he were on stage playing the conquering hero, and waited for the appropriate cue to start his most forceful declaration. Raising his head toward the heavens, he silently prayed that these savages would understand at least half of what he was saying. The Indians were silent and impatiently waited for the *white chief* to start speaking.

"I want to remind you to use restraint, and to fight within the rules by which I have urged you to contact the enemy. I have prohibited any unnecessary bloodshed, and strictly forbid the taking of scalps from the wounded or dying.

"However," he qualified this statement, "if any of you do experience any American barbarities such as base, lurking assassins, incendiaries, rangers, and plunderers, I emphasize that the great essential reward, the worthy service of your alliance . . . will be examined and judged upon the test only of your steady and uniform adherence to my orders and counsels."

Suddenly, an ancient Iroquois chief, in full war regalia, stood up from his squatting position among the gathered warriors and declared, "All our warriors have sharpened their emotions upon their hatchets, and are ready to serve their great white father across the water." The warriors jumped up sporadically from their squatting positions and waved their tomahawks and spears in the air. Burgoyne realized there was no way for him to regain their attention and continue his oration. He ordered his staff to break out the rum and allowed the Indians to be regaled with liquor and other refreshments until, at the peak of their revelry, the Indians terminated their festivities with a war dance.

While the Indians were celebrating, Burgoyne was sitting at his field desk aboard the *Lady Maria* writing his third speech, "Proclamation to the American People," which was reproduced and ready for circulation on June 24th. This speech or declaration was the strongest of the three he had developed since leaving Montreal. He addressed this document to the *temperate parts of the Public, and to the breasts of the suffering thousands in the Provinces.*

"I share the sorrow and the dilemma of the Loyalists. I deplore the punishment and abuse which the patriots have inflicted upon the most quiet subjects . . . without distinction of age or sex, for the sole crime of allegiance to the Crown . . . which include arbitrary imprisonment, confiscation of property, persecution and torture, and unprecedented in the inquisitions of the Romanism Church."

He warned the rebels that his troops were in the full power of health, discipline, and valor, and that they were determined to strike when necessary. Further, he warned his troops could strike far and wide.

"I have but to give stretch to the Indian forces under my direction, and they amount to thousands, to overtake the hardened enemies of Great Britain and America, wherever they may lurk. Resistance would be punished, and I promise to evoke the vengeance of the state against wilful outcasts through devastation, famine, and every concomitant horror that a reluctant but indispensable prosecution of military duty must occasion. I do, however, wish to deprecate the countryside and I promise not to disturb the domestick, the industrious, the infirm, and even the timid inhabitants . . . provided," he continued, "they remain quietly at their houses.

"I encourage countryside provincials to bring to me every sort of provision, for which they would be reimbursed in solid coin, and I promise we will assist loyal subjects to rescue their neighbors from patriot dungeons."

After Burgoyne had read, and edited this proclamation he called his aide-de-camp. He directed him to have this document reproduced, circulated throughout the colonies, posted in every town common, and read by every towncrier in the colonies.

In fact, the proclamation was widely distributed on both sides of the Atlantic. Burgoyne did not write the document to estrange its readers, but his haughty manner of writing and his contemptuous point of detail caused many of his readers to respond with anger or laughter. To many rebels, Burgoyne became known as "General Swagger," his proclamation to the American people in which he almost promises to cross America in a hop, step, and a jump. The great Englishman, Edmund Burke, admitted that he "couldn't understand the Burgoynese dialect, no less plain English." Even tears of laughter were said to have rolled down the checks of the Prime Minister Lord Germain, who had approved the expedition.

Burgoyne, however, was not distressed by such reaction. He was castigated more seriously by rebels in New York and Englishmen in London because he was using Indians in his campaign, which they believed to be despicable. Over the next few months his critics would prove themselves correct; Burgoyne would learn that the Indians were virtually useless soldiers because they were unaccustomed to the European concept of military discipline and doing battle. The Indians were, in fact, a greater hindrance to his progress than they were in defeating the rebel cause.

⧗

Walter Heindrick and Helena Kerchner were standing on the common in the center of New Palatine, reading and rereading the notice that had recently been posted on the settlement's public announcement plank. This was a maple tree at the edge of New Palatine's common used not only for public notices, but also for communicating with friends who might come to town infrequently, for invitations to weddings, baptisms, and other communications.

IMPORTANT NOTICE
TO ALL MALE CITIZENS
OF TRYON COUNTY

All 16 to 60 year Men not Presently Members
of the Tryon County Militia are Ordered to Report
to the New Palatine Common at 8:00 a.m. sharp
on May 22, 1777, to Enlist in the Militia.

Walter and Helena had heard General Herkimer announce the order for enlistment during the previous day's church service at the Heidelberg Tavern. Most residents of New Palatine had expected such an announcement and planned to report to the common. Others had chosen to ignore the requested order for enlistment, and refused to volunteer for service in the militia. Among these dissenters was

Wilhelm Kerchner, Helena's father, who now stood among other New Palatine residents denouncing Herkimer's *outlandish* order. In fact, he had voiced his disapproval during the church service. Walter and Helena remembered her father very distinctly when he had shouted in church, "Damn it! You bunch of rabble-rousers, especially you, you fake general! You and that infernal Committee of Safety! The only safety you want is to save your own skin!" Then staring about the congregation, he continued, "All of you, the whole pathetic lot of you, you don't know when you're well off. Our king has given us this wonderful land, and now you are willing to risk losing it all. My wife and I will not have any part of your foolhardy talk. It's treason! That's what it is! It's treason against our king!" After he had delivered his opinion of Herkimer's orders, Wilhelm Kerchner grabbed his wife Sarah's and Helena's hands and pulled them after him from the church and the service. Reflecting upon her father's outburst, Helena felt totally humiliated.

The next day, she had disclosed her feelings about the incident to Walter. "It wasn't so much because of what my father said, because I believe we are all entitled to our opinions. It was the way in which he did it."

"You know that all of my family believe in the rebel cause," confessed Walter.

"Yes, I know you do," responded Helena. "That's the trouble. So do I! It has reached the point where I don't dare to express my opinion at home. In fact, my mother and I have just agreed not to bring the subject up at all in our home, especially when my father is about."

Walter was embarrassed for Helena. He knew that she loved her father, but he also knew that she wished he would keep his thoughts more to himself, especially concerning *those foreigners.* Both knew the Kerchner family would suffer if he did not. Walter changed the subject. "Helena, I know I'm only fifteen years old, but "old Honikol" is going to need a drummerboy. I know that I can learn to beat the drum for the militia. And, if I have to shoot, you know that I can hit a squirrel at one hundred yards."

Fighting back her tears, Helena looked into Walter's eyes and squeezed his hand. He brought her fingers to his lips and kissed them. In silence they walked away from the crowd.

The following morning, the Wilhelm Kerchner family had disappeared. As usual, their clerk, Harvey Perry, opened the general store promptly at 6:30 A.M. He found a note, signed by Wilhelm, stating that Sarah, Helena, and he were traveling north to join Colonel Butler at Fort Niagara; they would return after the Loyalists won the war.

Because of the current state of emergency, General Herkimer had promoted Walter's father, Karl Heindrick, the day after posting the notice to captain of the platoon. Nearly a month later on June 6, 1777, young Walter was beating a steady drum rhythm as the New Palatine Platoon of the Tryon County Militia marched, showing much improvement over their earlier efforts. Everyone agreed that Walter's drumbeat had helped tremendously to improve their marching.

Suddenly the crowd surrounding the drill field grew silent. Walter quickly set his drum on the ground and began running toward a girl with a torn coat and no shoes. She staggered and fell upon the field of the common. By this time Walter was hovering over her as a mother would over her injured child. The girl lay unconscious on the green grass.

"Helena!" Walter cried. "My Helena, what has happened to you? Where have you been? How did you get here?"

But the half-starved, fourteen-year-old was oblivious to her surroundings and to Walter's questioning. The assembled crowd continued to gaze and to mutter to one another in amazement. Noting everyone's concern about the two teenagers, Captain Karl Heindrick dismissed the platoon until the following morning.

ESCAPE AND TRIUMPH

JUNE 24, 1777

CROWN POINT, LAKE CHAMPLAIN

High winds and fog continued to delay Burgoyne's flotilla which reminded many of a miniature armada. Finally, on the afternoon of June 24th, Bourgoyne ordered the gunboats to set sail, again. The oarsmen courageously forged ahead through high and rolling seas, forcing the troops to bail out their boats periodically. While, the thirty-six-year-old, combat-hardened infantry commander, Simon Fraser, and his advance corps pushed ahead and arrived at Crown Point on June 25th. Burgoyne, meanwhile, had ordered the army to prepare to leave for Crown Point when weather permitted. He prayed silently that the dismal weather the expedition had been experiencing was not a grim predictor of the campaign's future. As the British forces approached Crown Point, they realized that the small American garrison had retreated rapidly to Fort Ticonderoga. Burgoyne and the German soldiers established their camp at Chimney Point, just opposite Crown Point, where he immediately ordered them to unload the gun powder, balls, and paper from the magazine ship. Then he directed his men to construct a hospital, to install magazines, and to manufacture cartridges. He advised them to be especially careful and attentive in handling their musketry cartridges, warning them that it might be some time before their supplies could be replaced because it was so difficult to transport supplies across Lake Champlain. Some of his troops transferred cannon, shells, and shot from the bateaux which had been caulked with oakum at Chimmney Point. Others meanwhile were desperately grappling with the dense underbrush and fighting with the swarming mosquitos, deer flies, and pesky gnats so as to clear paths through the almost impenetrable forest. These Adirondack *noxious vermin* fought their usual persistent and consistent battle with any intruder who invaded their territory and the desperate British forces were no exception. To combat this unexpected *enemy,* the exhausted men built large fires to scatter and discourage them.

The troops had been wearing their uniforms since their arrival in America and these were in such bad shape, but replacements were not expected for a long time. In an effort to obtain material for uniform patching, and to make their jackets more useful for operating in the dense woods, the jacket tails of the uniforms were removed. The three-cornered felt hats were trimmed into caps much like those worn by the light infantry, and the tufts of colored hair designated the various regiments and lent a jaunty touch. Eventually, all of the German troops were issued long overalls striped blue and white, similar to bed ticking. Their breeches and leggings were made of a single piece of material, and most of their ungainly boots were replaced by some lighter form of footgear. Every British soldier carried a knapsack, blanket, haversack of provisions, canteen, hatchet, one-fifth of the equipment of a tent, a musket, and sixty rounds all totalling approximately sixty pounds.

By June 30th, Burgoyne's forces had converged at Crown Point. From there, the rebels were within sight and the enemy's watchboats could be seen maneuvering about, but were still beyond the reach of the British guns.

Burgoyne ordered Lieutenant William Digby to lead an advance corps to Three Mile Point, so called because of its position north of Ticonderoga. From their post, according to Digby, the advance troops had a full view of the rebels' worklines, and their flag of liberty displayed on the fort's summit. While the activity at Ticonderoga was being watched by the advance forces, British gunboats were clustered at anchor across the river from Three Mile Point.

Having seen and estimated the rebels' situation and compared it to his own strength and position, Burgoyne decided to attack Fort

Ticonderoga the following day. Without delay, he issued orders to prepare for the attack:

> We are to contend for the King and the Constitution of Great Britain, to vindicate the Law and to relieve the Oppressed, a Cause in which His Majesty's Troops and those of the Princes, his Allies, will feel equal Excitement. The Services required of this particular expedition are critical and conspicuous. During our progress, occasions may occur, in which neither difficulty nor labour nor life are to be regarded.

This Army Must Not Retreat! Thus began the implementation of Burgoyne's "Thoughts," the writings predestined to change the course of the American Revolution and the future presence of the British in America.

In June 1777, Gates forced General Philip Schuyler, the Commander of the American troops in the northern department of the Continental Army, to relinquish the fort's command. Schuyler immediately appointed Major General Arthur St. Clair to take command of Fort Ticonderoga. St. Clair arrived at the fort on June 12th, and Schuyler arrived on June 19th to attend a Council of officers.

St. Clair, an ex-British officer who had served under General William Howe at the taking of Quebec, had settled in America at the end of the French and Indian War, marrying the heiress granddaughter of Governor James Bowdoin of Massachusetts. Schuyler's biggest complaint was that Gates had "done nothing, comparatively speaking" to strengthen Fort Ti. In fact, St. Clair replaced the recently promoted Major General Anthony Wayne, who had been in direct command of the fort, thus enabling Wayne to join General George Washington. Before his departure, Wayne had informed Washington that "all was well at the fort and that it can never be conquered, without much loss of blood." This totally erroneous report further reinforced Washington's belief in Fort Ti's impregnability and its safety from attack. General Horatio Gates, however, did not concur with this assumption. He believed that the British would and could attack the fort, and he hoped that "Providence would conceal from Sir William Howe his true interest and goal." Gates believed the ultimate goal was forming a junction of the two armies on the line of the Hudson.

General Schuyler, however, believed that the British in Canada would advance on Albany by the western route, via the Great Lakes and the Mohawk Valley, rather than by the southern route through Ticonderoga. So as to be prepared for both alternatives, Schuyler ordered the construction of two schooners on Lake George. He also ordered General Nicholas Herkimer to mobilize the Tryon County Militia in the Mohawk Valley.

As late as May 1777, Fort Ticonderoga's command was virtually completely ignorant of Burgoyne's maneuvers and the size of his army. To remedy this, Major Benjamin Whitcomb, the chief scout at Fort Ti, tried to learn the British plans and their troop strength. At first Whitcomb was frustrated when his scouts were driven away by the Indians who formed a screen around the British post of Montreal. But near the end of the month, a British prisoner named William Amsbury was captured on the Onion River. He disclosed that Burgoyne had 10,000 troops in Canada, and that he planned to advance on Albany by way of Ticonderoga, together with a diversionary force, through the Mohawk Valley. It was difficult for Whitcomb and the newly arrived commander, St. Clair, to know whether Amsbury was telling the truth. St. Clair finally decided that Amsbury was a spy and sent him to Schuyler, who relayed St. Clair's opinion to General Washington. On June 13th, Washington replied, "even if Amsbury's information is true, he could not conceive it would be within the power of the enemy to execute it."

When the Council of Officers finally convened, disarray and indecision abounded within the command. Amsbury's *true but suspect* information only served to increase the skepticism and vacillation of Gates, who was still in overall command. To add to the confusion, the recently arrived young Polish volunteer, engineer officer, Thaddeus Kosciuszko, advised that the ascent of Mount Defiance by large guns was practical, once the steep sides had been graded by fatigue parties. But neither Gates nor anyone else commanded enough spare men to garrison the Mount together with Fort Ti, even with the recently arrived reinforcements; 3,000 Colonials and militia, to man the frontage of 2,000 yards. Many of these troops were barefoot, all were ragged, and all knew that the supplies were insufficient to defend the fort against a prolonged siege. In addition to the garrison at Fort Ticonderoga, only 700 men were under arms in the Northern Department. Comparing these troops to the 10,000 British forces Amsbury reported was staggering.

There were some issues they did agree upon. First, in case of attack, the defense of both banks of Lake Champlain would be attempted. However, if one side had to be abandoned, the New York side should be evacuated first. Another issue mutually agreed upon was that the defenses of Mount Independence needed to be improved. This, they estimated, would take approximately six weeks for the required work to be completed. The most significant decision made was that should an attack prove to be too costly and serious, the garrison would retire before their retreat was cut off.

At this point, the fort's command was still the size of the British force, yet the prospect of defending Fort Ti still loomed as an insurmountable task. Many at the Council meeting, in fact, believed that Ticonderoga was a trap. They believed inwardly that the enormous prestige of the fort made evacuation without a fight unthinkable. In fact, except in the face of a serious assault, a retreat would make the position of the officer who ordered it impossible, evacuation of the garrison in order to save it would demand a courageous decision.

Approximately one week after the Council of Officers meeting, scouts reported that Indians had been sighted on the lake. On June 25th, more Indians were observed at Crown Point, only fifteen miles to the north. In fact, Colonel James Wilkinson, the fort's adjutant and Gates's deputy-adjutant general, reported to Gates that he had seen the sails of many large vessels on Lake Champlain. At this tine, Wilkinson also voiced his complaints about the fort's shortcomings.

The twenty-one-year-old Wilkinson tortured himself mentally about the fort's condition as he compared its half-naked, ill-disciplined, and badly-armed group of men and boys with the vastly superior body of seasoned British troops. He wondered if the garrison should fall back on Fort George at the end of the lake, then perhaps, the attempt to defend Fort Ti could lead the garrison to *lose all,* and leave the country defenseless. The enthusiastic Wilkinson, oftentimes too impetuous, had earned resentment from many of his associates. However, if it were not for his chronicles about the activities within and about Fort Ticonderoga little would be known today about the American position in the campaign against Burgoyne.

By June 30th there was undebatable proof of the British power and how they intended to use it. British troops were within three miles of Fort Ti, and within full view were two frigates, two hundred bateaux, and numerous smaller water craft sailing majestically on Lake Champlain. In spite of this visual evidence, together with Amsbury's report, St. Clair still refused to believe that the British advance was more than a feint. He still remembered that Congress in Philadelphia; it had assured him that the British would ship their army from Canada to New York by sea; the British kept their word. For the present his decision was firm. He would be patient, and wait.

⧗

On July 4, 1777, the first anniversary of the birth of the United States of America, one of Burgoyne officers, believed to have been engineer-officer Lieutenant Twiss, recognized Fort Ticonderoga's major weakness. He realized that both forts, Ti and Crown Point, were strategically positioned and towered over by a hill known as Sugar Loaf or Fort Defiance, which stood south of the creek between Lake Champlain and Lake George. By noon, British forces had already occupied the position. Twiss reported, "If we can get cannon on top of this site, we can effectively fire upon the old French fort as well as on Crown Point." "Normally, the fourteen-hundred-yard range is excessive for our cannon, but I believe that Sugar Loaf's elevation would be helpful and practical."

"Do you believe, Lieutenant Twiss that you can get cannon up that elevation?" asked Burgoyne as he looked toward Twiss and Major General Phillips.

Phillips immediately retorted, "Where a goat can go, a man can go, and where a man can go, he can drag a gun."

Burgoyne reacted promptly, "Twiss, take a fatigue party and clear a path up to the top of that mountain. General Phillips, you take a contingent of men to drag and position two light twenty-four pounders pointed right at those rebel forts."

Twiss and Phillips completed their assigned tasks without problems, but this remarkable feat was discovered too soon because of two simple and unnecessary mistakes. First, the Indians who had accompanied the British to the summit, lighted fires to cook their meals; then an even greater folly came from a gunner who prematurely fired at a vessel in the narrows, thus disclosing that not only were Indians on the summit, but that British cannon was there, too.

Hearing the cannon firing and seeing a few Redcoats roaming around the summit, General St. Clair glared frantically at the fort's adjutant, Colonel James Wilkinson, and declared "We must get away from this, for our situation has become desperate."

Immediately, St. Clair convened his Council of Officers and declared heatedly, "I believe that we have no alternative but to evacuate the fort's garrison at once." The officers, though always partial to the defeatist attitude which permeated the fort, looked somewhat astonished until St. Clair and Wilkinson informed them of their findings; then they unanimously concurred with their commanding general. "Prepare to abandon Fort Ticonderoga as soon as darkness sets in," ordered St. Clair.

One officer in an attempt to brighten the mood, said, "Let's bring good luck to the rebel cause by making this retreat the best ever." The others knowing full well that not one of them had the stomach for battle under the present conditions, stared silently toward each other and nodded agreement.

"A word of warning!" said St. Clair drawing all eyes focused toward him. "I want the decision which we have just reached here to be confined amongst you selected senior officers. At 3 P.M. this afternoon I will inform our quartermaster, but let's wait until dark before we tell the rest of the garrison."

Just before midnight, one officer asked, "Have we notified Dr. James Thatcher about our plans?"

"Oh, hell no!" was the response.

"Then get your ass to his bunk, and tell him to collect all the sick and wounded, and get his corpsmen to help him get the hospitalized aboard the boats and bateaux."

As the sun dipped in the west on July 5th, the great floating bridge to the Vermont shore became bedlam. Men poured across the lake and frantic, mostly unsuccessful attempts, were made to move cannon and supplies to the comparatively safe eastern shore. Absolute near panic prevailed everywhere, and discipline, dubious and tenuous under the best of conditions, collapsed; men and supplies struggled up the rough road over Mount Independence leading to the boat landings and the escape road to Castleton. The sick and some supplies were put on board a fleet of nearly 200 bateaux, 2 galleys, 2 schooners, and a sloop. As the heavily laden fleet prepared to depart, many able-bodied men who could have taken the Castleton road appropriated the boats, making it necessary for most of the provisions and essential supplies to be abandoned. Although a high wind was blowing making embarkation difficult, the haphazard assembly of boats successfully slipped away from shore and floated peacefully down the lake toward the initial destination, Skenesborough, the passengers and crews laughing and exulting over their crafty escape.

The retreat, despite its initial confusion, was apparently not discovered by the British until a French adventurer, Roche de Fermoy, contrary to specific orders, set a fire high up on the mount. It burned brightly and like a great torch illuminated all the surrounding area.

After the retreat had been discovered by de Fermoy, three rebel deserters slipped through to the American lines, reaching the British command post just before daylight. The deserters confirmed the Rebel retreat to Brigadier Simon Fraser. Rather awake and wait for Burgoyne, to whom he sent an army officer to inform the comfortably sleeping commander and his unpowdered mistress aboard one of the frigates, Fraser took it upon himself to pursue the rebels. His light infantry was pouring over the floating bridge, still usable although somewhat damaged by the fleeing fort garrison. The bridge was covered by several loaded cannon on the eastern Vermont shore tended by a crew of four gunners; all of whom were drunk. Somehow they had acquired a keg of Madeira and never intended wasting it. These men sober could have obeyed their orders, and thus would have been in excellent position to raise havoc with Fraser's corps and delay his light infantry. Instead, the Redcoats reached the mount just as the last of the Rebels scrambled away toward the hamlets of the Hampshire Grants.

The main American army, demoralized and disheartened as it was by the sudden loss of the *Gibraltar of the American Revolution* which Ethan Allen and Benedict Arnold had captured just over two years before, nevertheless covered their retreat expertly by effective rear-guard action and escaped safely. Confident that they had outsmarted their pursuers, the army reached the eastern shore near Skenesborough early in the afternoon, anchoring or beaching their vessels in South Bay and in Wood Creek, the small, navigable rivulet from Skenesborough to Fort Anne, some sixteen miles to the south. That first day, St. Clair led the army to Castleton, Vermont, a march of some thirty miles over a rough wagontrack. He planned to move southward to Skenesborough, not realizing the British had anticipated his move.

Despite St. Clair's orders, Colonel Seth Warner, a former Green Mountain Boy in command of the rear elements, decided to stop for the night at Hubbardton rather than continue on to Castleton, a few miles further. He had about 1,000 men in all but did not take the trouble to establish any outposts. During the night some of Burgoyne's Indian warriors, as part of their assigned function, scouted the American position and reported their findings to Burgoyne.

The Americans were fortunate during the summer of 1777; time, areas of huge rocks, caverns and cliffs, and especially the thick, impenetrable wilderness combined to slow the advance of the British troops. In fact, many of the rebel troops and the Champlain Valley inhabitants believed that only nature's obstructions could prevent an aggressive commander from occupying Albany.

Burgoyne had achieved his initial goal of capturing Fort Ticonderoga, making Lake Champlain a British lake. He believed that a celebration was in order and ordered the drum and fife to start the troops' favorite music while the commissary was ordered to break out dozens of bottles of wines and kegs of rum.

On the western front, General Schuyler sent General Herkimer further orders:

July 8, 1777

The road leading from Fort Dayton to Fort Schuyler (Stanwix) is so much incumbered with wood by the falling of trees across it, that it is rendered impassible for men or carriages: you will therefore please to order 200 of your militia to be employed in clearing it away with all the dispatch the nature of the service will admit of; each man bringing an axe with him.

Col. Gansevoort, who commands at Fort Schuyler, is very pressing for a reinforcement to carry on the necessary works at that garrison and as I have it not in my power to send up Continental troops for that purpose, I must beg you will order 200 men of your brigade to support and assistance.

❋ 1 0 ❋

IN HOT PURSUIT

NEAR FORT TICONDEROGA AND ON LAKE CHAMPLAIN

Early on the morning of July 9th, an American soldier came into Colonel John Hill's camp, located approximately one mile from Fort Anne, with a small detachment of British regulars, and told Hill that he had deserted the rebel cause. Though it was afterwards discovered that he was a spy, he also said that there were 1,000 Yankees at Fort Anne. For all of its high-sounding title, Fort Anne was no more than a squared wooden palisade, containing a few dilapidated barracks and a storehouse with almost everything constructed of wood; the soldiers at Fort Anne were in great consternation suffering under the apprehension of an imminent British attack. Immediately after the deserter's information was collected, Hill dispatched a message to Burgoyne informing him of the deserter's report, and informing him that he and his forces had advanced about eight to ten miles from the main army.

Within minutes after the deserter's information was passed to Burgoyne; and Hill had assured him that he would hold his ground and await reinforcements, the imposter disappeared from the scene. However there had been sufficient time to study the British location and its strength, which did not amount to more than 190 men including officers. Evidently, the spy's information was activated, for in less than half an hour the Americans rushed out of Fort Anne in great force. The British point-guard sentries, who were aware of the disappearing, strange intruder, were especially on guard for sudden surprises; their great courage and steadfastness forced the rebels to retreat. The rebels, however, recognizing an opportunity when they saw one, returned in force, increasing their assault so as to send the British scurrying back towards their main camp.

The victory from this minor skirmish encouraged the Ticonderoga garrison personnel. In addition, the Americans welcomed 400 New York Militia reinforcements led by Colonel Van Rensselaer who had just engaged in a successful skirmish with the British. This engagement continued for several hours during which time the Americans almost completely surrounded the British and had them near another retreat. Their ammunition supply was almost depleted when a party of Indians, with war-whoops, suddenly arrived to the cheers of their British allies. The Americans quickly withdrew to the fort with their captives, including one surgeon, the wounded Captain Montgomery, and twelve or fifteen privates.

Upon receiving Hill's message, Burgoyne ordered Hill to retire at once and despatched the remainder of the first Brigade under Brigadier General Powell to cover his retreat.

By now Hill's position had become critical to both sides, especially since the Americans had crossed the creek and the rebels were nipping at his heels. Fearing that his exposed position might be vulnerable, Hill left his wounded men and again retreated to the summit of the hill. There his force was able to forestall the American attack for two hours, until both sides had used up all of their ammunition. Suddenly, a war-whoop came ringing out of the woods to the north. All fighting stopped. Believing that the British were being reinforced, the Americans fled. Later, they learned that the war-whoops had come from a lone British officer who, deserted by his Indian scouts, had employed this strategy, hoping the enemy would believe that he headed a powerful force of Indian warriors.

This battle, a mile and one-half from Fort Anne, may have been the first occasion during which the *Stars and Strips* were flown in battle, although there are those who believe this happened at Fort Stanwix, just prior to the Battle of Oriskany. Approximately 200 casualties later, the Americans withdrew to Fort Anne, immediately set fire to that small fort, and swiftly retreated thirty miles south to Fort Edward. The British, meanwhile, marched back north to Skenesborough, leaving behind the wounded men who could not be moved and for whom Sergeant Roger Lamb, a surgeon's mate in the 9th Regiment, was ordered to be responsible. At this time, Burgoyne gave Lamb a letter, instructing him that in case he was surrounded or captured by the Americans, he was to deliver the letter to their commanding officer.

As Lamb surveyed his charges, he told one of his helpers, "This is a distressing sight to see the wounded men bleeding on the ground; and what makes it more so, the rain is pouring down like a deluge upon us."

"And what makes it even worse, sir," remarked his helper, "We have nothing to dress their wounds. The only medicine box we had filled with salve was left behind with Durgeon Shelly and Captain Montgomery when we started moving up the hill."

The injured, by now, were pleading to have their wounds dressed. Without saying a word, Lamb took off his shirt and tore it up into bandages. Immediately, his helper too, removed his shirt and a soldier's wife (the only woman who had traveled with them) removed her petticoat and each proceeded to make bandages. They tried to stop the bleeding of the wounds, distributed all the blankets they had, and tried to succor the wounded, if only with a comforting word. Eventually, they lead their charges to a small hut about two miles north, where they stayed seven days, expecting at any moment to be taken prisoner by the Americans. During those precarious seven nights, Lamb and the wounded heard their enemy cutting down trees in order to block up passage of the road and river. They were not molested by the Americans. Throughout their stay at the outpost, Lamb and his charges received most of their daily necessities from the main camp at Skenesborough. Most of the wounded, except three who had died, were ready to return to duty shortly after going back to camp.

One of the reasons Burgoyne had selected Skenesborough for his temporary main quarters was that it was a small settlement where a man named Colonel Philip Skene lived. Skene, a Loyalist leader, together with one of Burgoyne's political officers had constructed and settled in a house in the area that adopted his name.

Within five days of the seizure of Mount Defiance, Burgoyne successfully captured Fort Ticonderoga and Fort Crown Point, and chased the Americans south on Lake Champlain. Further, his men had destroyed the rebels' boats, captured their guns, and had forced them to retreat to Fort Edward. Again, this called for a celebration in the wilderness of America, after which Burgoyne ordered Fraser, with von Riedesel in support, to chase St. Clair towards Skenesborough where his army would be waiting for the Americans.

It was 5 A.M. on the morning of July 6th that General Simon Fraser, with Burgoyne's approval, led 850 elite British troops from Mount Defiance in hot pursuit of the retreating Rebel garrison. After rounding up a handful of Indians from among those who had been plundering the abandoned forts, Fraser plunged his troops into the thickly wooded hilly country, intersected by streams and dotted with ponds and lakes, allowing his men no time to eat, collect rations, or even fill their canteens. He finally called a halt at 4 P.M.

Behind Fraser's forces was General von Riedesel, also with Burgoyne's approval to act upon his own judgement. Von Riedesel lead an advance corps and a regiment of the Brunswickers, about 1,100 men in all. The plodding Germans, halting frequently to align their ranks, lagged far behind Fraser's swifter army.

Burgoyne's strategy called for Fraser's and von Riedesel's troops to chase and push St. Clair's retreating army towards Skenesborough where his main army would be waiting for them. It was an excellent plan, but one which failed to take into consideration two important factors. First, the Americans were very familiar with and accustomed to campaigning in the rough, wooded country that favored their mobile, frontier-trained troops. Second, St. Clair, having learned of Burgoyne's presence at Skenesborough, would make a wide detour, thereby drawing the pursuing British troops ever more deeply into the trackless wilderness.

Fraser knew that he would have to restrain his men before the lagging German troops fell too far behind to be any support at all. Realizing that his troops might be holding back Fraser's advance corps, von Riedesel hurried ahead and joined Fraser after he had halted his men for a *breather* in the intensely hot afternoon. As the two officers conferred, von Riedesel's superior rank made the situation awkward. The obese general did, however, lose some of his composure when his profuse sweating caused his wig to slip askew. Fraser, a special friend of Burgoyne's who from the beginning of the expedition had chosen to snub the German general and exclude him from some of the staff conferences, ignored the humorous situation, and started delicately by agreeing that Fraser's men were being held back by the slower Germans.

"I remember distinctly the orders that General Burgoyne gave to me just before we left his camp," started Fraser. "He told me to push on, and at my discretion, to attack any body of rebels that I might come up with. General, I intend to do just that!"

"I have no objections to your orders or plans," responded the experienced German cavalry officer. "In fact, I totally agree with your suggestion. My troops are moving at a much more sluggish pace through these dense woods while you and your men are more experienced in campaigning here in North America."

"I request your permission, general," suggested Fraser, "to move my troops three miles further toward the American's bivouac for the night, and attack the Americans the next day."

"Let's get our situation straight between us," replied the huge, thirty-nine-year-old general in his heavy German accent. "I have a great respect for your and General Burgoyne's military experience here in North America; I am more familiar with the European military tactics. Our German forces are here to support your efforts, not to say how and what you should do." With a wide smile and sweat rolling down his ruddy face, he continued, "In fact, I would rather be back at headquarters with my little, blue-eyed wife, Frederika, and our three tiny daughters."

"Your make me jealous," smiled Fraser, "but for now we must make war. There'll be time for other things, you can rest assured of that."

As they shook hands, they agreed that Fraser would advance his corps three miles closer toward the Americans, and that von Riedesel's slower troops would congregate in this area where they were presently meeting. At 3 A.M. the next day, the von Riedesel's troops would break camp and support Fraser's advance force. They also agreed that if Fraser found the Americans too strong for attack, he would await von Riedesel's arrival.

Immediately after parting, Fraser marched his men the three miles he and von Riedesel had agreed upon, reaching a location called

Lacey's Camp, which the Americans had left not more than an hour earlier. Foodless, except for the flesh of a cow a marksman had killed in the woods, Fraser bivouacked his men for the night.

During the night, Indian scouts captured and brought to Fraser an American sentry. From this sentry and from a few stragglers his troops had captured during the day, Fraser learned that the American rearguard was comprised of selected men under the command of one of the best American officers, Colonel Ebenezer Francis. The Fort Ti garrison, well ahead of the British, were eager to increase the distance between them. With the capture of the sentry, however, Fraser was surprised to learn that the Americans, in their haste, had assigned only one person to watch for the advancing enemy. By so doing, they denied themselves timely warning of British troop movements and remained open to surprise attacks.

St. Clair marched his retreating main army by way of the twenty-two mile wagon rutted track from Mount Defiance (Independence), which joined the old road from the eastern shore of Lake Champlain opposite Crown Point; this road ran south toward Castleton. Stimulated by the true but exaggerated report that over 500 Tories and Indians had passed that way, St. Clair did not stop at Hubbardton. Rather, he ordered his men to tramp six miles further to Castleton where the exhausted troops quickly pitched their tents.

Before leaving Hubbardton, St. Clair ordered Colonel Seth Warner together with his regiment of Green Mountain Boys, and Colonel Nathan Hale's (no relation to the Connecticut spy of that name) 2nd New Hampshire Regiment, to await the arrival of the rearguard under Colonel Francis. With positive orders, Colonel Warner, the senior officer was ordered immediately to bring all three regiments to Castleton as soon as they joined forces. Francis, and his 11th Massachusetts Regiment, caught up with Warner and Hale about four o'clock in the afternoon, and immediately all three officers promptly retired to a cabin constructed by a settler named Sellick where they discussed their next move.

The three colonels agreed that their troops were all totally exhausted after their long march and the day's sweltering heat. They were also sure their troops had outraced the sluggish main army, and so in direct opposition to St Clair's orders, they agreed to bivouac in their present locality before moving on to join St. Clair.

Hale and 360 men of the New Hampshire Regiment set stakes on Sucker Brook, a little stream that crossed the road and drained the valley, to the east of which rose the high ridge surmounted by the wagontrack leading to its junction with the old road to Castleton. Francis and the 420 men of the Massachusetts Continentals occupied the high ground around the Sellick cabin, some of which was cleared farmland. Warner and the 173 men of the Vermonters staked their claim in the woods along the ridge thus enabling him to guard the road from Crown Point and, if necessary, to act in support of Francis and Hale. Here the Americans were dominated by a towering, rocky precipitously faced hill, approximately twelve-hundreed-feet high, later named Zion Hill. Obviously, the Americans did not expect to be caught that night or even early the next day. Unfortunately, they had seriously underestimated the determination and zeal of their British pursuers.

Shortly before sunrise, after a three-mile march on July 7th, Fraser's small advance corps was joined by the 24th Regiment of Foot led by Major Grant, the Light Infantry commanded by the Earl of Balcarres, and the Grenadiers lead by Major Acland; this entire force was accompanied by the Tories, Lieutenant Colonel John Peters, and the Jessup brothers from Glens Falls. With the advance troops was von Riedesel, as he had promised, with 100 jagers and grenadiers. From the lip of the valley through which ran Sucker Brook, Fraser's forces sighted, about eight-hundred-yards away, the rebels eating their breakfast on the valley floor. Fraser gave the order to attack. Leading his men in extended order, he guided them down the wooded slope.

Caught completely off-guard, the New Hampshire soldiers shouted, "The enemy is upon us." Led by their colonel, the Rebels scattered into the woods. Warned by the sound of musket fire from Hale's dispersed troops, Warner ordered his Vermonters to take cover behind the fallen trees and shrubs in the dense forest. Besides killing twenty British soldiers, Major Grant was a causality when he exposed himself up on a tree trunk while surveying the rebels position.

Meanwhile Warner and Francis, from their Sellick cabin vantage point, received the bad news from St. Clair's courier. The British had cut the escape route to the south and, in order to reach the Hudson River, St. Clair would be forced to detour widely around the town of Rutland, Vermont. But it was already too late; the lagging rearguard had been captured and the British were advancing toward the road to Castleton.

Along the half-mile-front, the British, sweeping aside the few Vermonters who had gone to Hale's rescue, were swarming up the slope with the clear intention of cutting off the Americans' retreat. Warner and Francis's forces were trying to counterattack by forcing the British back across the wagontrack and cutting their lines of communication. The two opposing forces presented an interesting contrast. The British side was eager and aggressive because they had caught the rebels off-guard. The Americans, even though surprised while in full flight, through steadfastness and discipline, gained the higher position, had better mobility, were able to take cover, and return accurate, rapid fire. This demonstration of fire power and evasiveness led the inexperienced British Lieutenant Digby to overestimate the number of Americans. As a result, the British, with less than 1,000 men, believed they faced a rebel force over double their size.

On the crest of Monument Hill the Massachusetts Regiment, led by Francis, was behind fallen logs and a stone fence while Balcarres pushed his British forces up the hill. Realizing the danger, Francis ordered his regiment down the slope, hiding behind trees while they poured point-blank fire upon the British infantry. This unexpected counterattack halted the British assault. During the battle a musket ball grazed Balcarres's shoulder while two of his officers were killed. Colonel Francis with his right arm shattered by a bullet, ordered the Americans back to the crest of the ridge. When it became obvious that the second assault effort had also failed, Simon Fraser sent a message to von Riedesel saying that the enemy was in such strength that he was unable to withstand them unless he was speedily reinforced.

Nevertheless, not to be discouraged, Fraser launched a third assault on Monument Hill and on Francis's Massachusetts men who held the crest and the summit. Unaware of von Riedesel's proximity, Fraser ordered Balcarres and his foot soldiers to attack the hill and drive away the Rebels at bayonet point, a task that might have proved difficult, but for the timely arrival of von Riedesel. Then, from across the valley came the sounds of music, the braying of hunting horns, the screech of a hautboy (oboe), and the singing of battle hymns. These unusual sounds made the British uneasy; they feared that the American rearguard had received reinforcements from the main army and so kept up continuous musket fire. Aided by Captain Clark von Geyso's 100 jagers, and Captain Maximillian Schottelius's 800 grenadiers, the British encircled the hill, captured the crest, and marched south to trap the Americans. Francis's Massachusetts men, in disarray, retreated across the road where he was finally able to assemble them behind a log fence. Francis then ordered the men to reload their muskets and prepare for the British attack. While the British were busily preparing their ranks for the charge, Francis seized the opportunity to leap over the breastwork and to urge his men to put at least one good volley into the British ranks. This was to be his last order; a German rifle bullet crashed through Colonel Ebenezer Francis's heart. This so disheartened his troops that they quickly disappeared into the deep forest, thus thwarting the British bayonet charge and the storm of musket fire from the approaching grenadiers. It was clear to Colonel Warner that the battle was lost, so he calmly ordered his Green Mountain Boys to scatter, save themselves, and meet him at Manchester. So, they too, evaporated into the forest along with the men from Massachusetts, to live and to fight another day.

The encounter lasted only forty-five minutes. Theoretically, the British won the battle, but they failed to capture the retreating garrison. An hour later, St. Clair heard the results of the battle at Hubbardton and announced, "All is over." To his men he declared, "The only direction left for us to go, via Rutland and Manchester, and Bennington, is to Fort Edward on the Hudson where we can join forces with General Schuyler." While the British and Germans counted their losses which totaled 174 men, the former Fort Ticonderoga commandant led his garrison toward their next post. The victorious British and German troops captured 228 prisoners, including Colonel Nathan Hale, 7 captains, 10 subalterns, and 200 muskets. Hale was released on parole on July 20th, in order to respond, at his request, to the allegations of cowardice and treason that had been made against him. No charges were made and, when he was not exchanged, he gave himself up. He died on September 23, 1780, while a prisoner of war on Long Island.

The battle of Hubbardton was one of the smallest contests of the Revolutionary War, but one that taught the British soldiers that forest combat was not easy. They found, too, that they were not invincible, nor were the Americans cowardly; during the fighting in the woods the battalion's maneuvering and excellency of exercise were of little value. According to British Captain Thomas Anburey:

> During the battle (Hubbardton) the Americans were guilty of such a breach of all military rules as could not fail to exasperate our soldiers. The action was chiefly in woods, interspersed with a few open fields. Two companies of grenadiers, who were stationed in the out skirts of the woods, close to one of these fields, to watch that the enemy did not outflank the 24th Regiment, observed a number of the Americans, to the amount of near sixty, coming across the field with their arms clubbed, which is always considered to be a surrender as prisoners of war. The grenadiers were restrained from firing, commanded to stand with their arms and shew no intention of hostility; when the Americans had got within ten yards, they in an instant turned round their muskets, fired upon the grenadiers, and ran as fast as they could into the woods; their fire killed and wounded a great number of men, and those who escaped immediately pursued them and gave no quarter.

The long day ended in drenching rain and the British and German forces spent a miserable night under arms, fearful that the dastardly reinforced rebels would sneak upon them during the dark night. When the night ended with no incident, Fraser and von Riedesel marched their troops to Skenesborough, leaving the wounded to be transferred to Ticonderoga. which they reached on July 22nd.

Reporting to Lord Germain three weeks after the battle, Burgoyne, beginning to feel somewhat hopeless, instinctively complimented the American exploit in escaping the British clutches to fight another day, saying, "The New Hampshire Grants, the unconquered area on his flank now abounds [harbors] the most active and rebellious race on the Continent, and hangs like a gathering storm on my left."

⧗

"I saw it with my own eyes," Helena wept as she resumed telling the Heindricks of the horrors she had witnessed while en route with her parents to Canada. "Poor old Mrs. Cannon couldn't keep up with us. She was Mrs. Samuel Campbell's mother. She was very old and she couldn't keep up. The Indians tomahawked her. She just lay there. Her eyes were open, even after she was dead. They didn't care. I just didn't believe human beings could do such things to other humans.

"It's like a bad dream," she continued as she closed her eyes. "When we arrived at Butternut Creek, they burned all of the Buxton family's buildings."

"Lie back and rest yourself," Walter's mother, Rebecca, urged as she brought the blanket up over Helena's shoulders. Rebecca wished she could ease the pain she knew that Helena was feeling.

"Thanks, Mrs. Heindrick. This has been like a living nightmare. I had to get it out of my mind."

"How can we help?" asked Walter's father.

Walter longed to go to her, to hold her, and to let her fall asleep in his arms.

"I've got to tell you the rest of the story," Helena began, wiping the tears from her ruddy face. "After they burned the Buxton buildings, they did not kill any of the Buxtons. I don't know why, but they didn't. I guess they were in too much of a hurry to get to their Kanadaseago castle.

"I felt so sorry for Mrs. Campbell, " Helena continued. "They had killed her mother. Three of her children could walk, but she had to carry her eighteen-month-old child all the long way to Kanadaseago. When the Senecas reached their castle, we all had to watch their dance of triumph. Many scalps were paraded in front of us and the other Indians, to the rhythm of their *death-hallo*. That dance has to be the most sadistic thing I'll ever see. It is the most terrifying ritual that anyone could imagine. It certainly is beyond my imagination!"

Helena shivered, closed her eyes, and wept uncontrollably. She wrapped the blanket tighter over her shoulders and tried to escape the memories of her ordeal.

Karl went to the pantry and poured a small glass of whiskey. Holding Helen's head, he offered it to her. "Sip a little of this whiskey, Helena. It'll help you sleep."

The girl stared at Walter, then toward his mother. Both nodded agreement with what Karl had suggested. She sipped, and then lay back on the pillow. Her bloodshot, blue eyes seemed to have sunk deep into her face. The sparkle they had known had disappeared, as had the luster in her wavy, auburn hair.

The Heindricks drew the bedroom window's bright red curtains together and left the room, sadly wondering what other things Helena and her parents had experienced. "Where were her parents?" they thought as they left the room.

⧗

Fifty-three days after embarking from Montreal on July 25th, Brigadier General Barry St. Leger's expedition arrived at Oswego, located on Lake Ontario at the mouth of the Mohawk River. On that same day, Burgoyne prepared to move south from Skenesborough.

❖ 11 ❖

INTERLUDE

JULY 25, 1777

———

MOHAWK VALLEY, NEW YORK

After the successful British campaigns against Crown Point, Ticonderoga, and Hubbardton, and while Burgoyne was enjoying himself in the lap of luxury with his lady with unpowdered hair, his leader of the western expedition, Lieutenant Colonel Barry St. Leger, with his army had just arrived at Oswego, New York. Soon after St. Leger and his staff held a council of war with the Mohawk Chieftain, Joseph Brant, and a legion of 600 to 800 Iroquois warriors, which was far short of the 1,000 he had been led to believe would be recruited. St. Leger and Burgoyne agreed it was absolutely essential to capture the little fort in the wilderness, Fort Stanwix. It was located mid-way between Oswego and Albany, but they also believed that this should not demand an overwhelmingly large military force. Neither considered the fort an objective of the campaign nor a possible obstacle. Considering Burgoyne and his initial evaluation of the fort's status, together with recent scouting reports he had received, St. Leger decided that there was little need for the usual reasonable precaution of sending a scouting reconnaissance to inspect the Great Carrying Place at Wood Creek near the fort. He, therefore, left the initiative and the task to a subordinate.

On July 17th, it was eight days since St. Leger had learned of Burgoyne's capture of Fort Ticonderoga. The bounty consisted of provisions, artillery, stores, a magnitude of livestock, prisoners, and there was an advance detachment of Indians in hot pursuit of the retreating rebels. Encouraged by Burgoyne's coup, St. Leger ordered Colonel Daniel Claus and his advance guards, consisting of all officers, and eighty rank and file of the King's and 34th Regiments, along with the tribe of Missisague and Six-Nations Indians to pack and carry six-day's provisions of bread and pork, and be ready to move out from Buck Island the following morning at four o'clock. Their mission was to surprise the fort's garrison and to capture it with small arms. He reminded them of Burgoyne's explicit orders, "that the Indians were to make war only on troops, not civilians." Colonel Claus had neither sufficient arms nor vermilion, a bright red or scarlet substance used for war paint by the combined forces. Under the circumstances, he prepared his troops for battle as best he could.

While Claus was preparing for the march, Chief Brant came in his tent and told him that he needed someone to help him command the Indians. Brant was fearful that if the colonel left them at Salmon Creek, his warriors would become disgusted and disperse, which might well discourage the rest of the Six Nations from assembling. Brant believed this it would be disastrous to the entire Mohawk Valley expedition.

Claus related Brant's concern to St. Leger. The general replied that the primary reason Claus had been ordered to be alert was to quiet the Indians, who were becoming more drunk and riotous daily. St. Leger then ordered Claus to give the Indians one last quart of rum apiece.

The next day, July 25th, St. Leger arrived at Salmon Creek with the companies of the 8th and 34th Regiments and about 250 additional Indians, as well as arms and more vermilion for Brant's warriors. Immediately, Claus ordered the rest of the Six-Nations to assemble at a convenient rendezvous called Three Rivers, the junction of the Oneida, Onondaga, and Oswego Rivers, sixty miles from their destination of Fort Stanwix. On July 26, Claus, Brant, and their troops, together with the Loyalist Colonel John Butler and the Indians he had brought with him from Niagara, left Oswego and headed toward the little fort in the wilderness.

That same morning, Colonel Peter Gansevoort, the fort's senior officer, commanded 100 of the regular garrison, comprised of Continental troops, to guard the Tryon County Militia who were felling trees into Wood Creek, across the landing, and across the narrow, rutted trail leading to the fort.

Two days later, three young girls were in the fields surrounding Fort Stanwix picking raspberries, and were attacked by who were thought to be four Indians. One of the girls, with two musket balls lodged in her shoulder, managed to escape and return to the fort. Soon thereafter, rescuers from the fort found the other two girls lying on the ground, scalped and tomahawked. One had died by the time the rescuers arrived, and the other died about half an hour after being brought back to the fort.

One of the slain girls was the daughter of a former British artilleryman who had been a garrison member before the British abandoned the fort as a post. Because he was advanced in age and ill, he and his family had been granted permission to live in one of the fort's small houses and to cultivate a piece of land.

After hearing of the slaying, the fort's commander, Colonel Gansevoort, ordered the militia chopping party in the Wood Creek area to stop their work and return to the fort. He also ordered the garrisoned women and children, along with the wounded young girl and a man who had been scalped earlier, to relocate in the valley's more settled communities.

Ever since Helena had escaped from the British, Indians, and their sympathizers, she had felt unclean and like someone without a family. She felt as if she was being torn between two worlds and blamed herself for most of it. It had been her own decision to renounce her father's belief in the Crown and all it stood for; she especially hated the manner with which the British sympathizers had treated the Palatines, *those foreigners* as the Tories called them; she also abhorred their deceptive manipulation of the Indians. Conversely, she admired the spunk and determination of the Palatines and their unceasing dedicated search for freedom. The Heindricks, especially Walter's mother Rebecca, had helped to heal her loneliness and make her feel a part of their family. Still, she did dearly love her parents and missed the security with which they had cared for her. She prayed that they would return safely to their New Palatine home. Her affection for, and friendship with Rebecca and Karl's fifteen-year-old son, Walter, helped to fill much of this loneliness.

It was during the following weeks that Rebecca secretly suggested to Helena that she make a hunting shirt for Walter. Rebecca, immediately added that she would help and they could use one of Walter's old shirts as a pattern. She reminded Helena that General George Washington had given a *General Order* on July 24, 1776, that "no dress could be cheaper, nor more convenient, as the wearer may be cool in warm weather and warm in cool weather by putting on *under-cloaths* which will not change the outward dress, winter or summer, besides which it is a dress justly supposed to carry no small terror to the enemy, who think every such person is a complete marksman."

Rebecca continued, "Originally, the hunting shirt was designed as a uniform in itself. In time it was used almost exclusively around camp to save wear and tear on the uniforms; unplanned, the shirt became the favored dress when the soldiers went into battle. Indeed, it was the only sort of uniform many of them owned."

Rebecca and Helena were busily discussing the shirt's design. "All the shirts are made of the same pattern and using deer leather, home-spun wool, or linen. We'll make Walter's of deer leather," she added. "Karl and I were talking the other day about this idea," Rebecca told Helena. "He thought it was a great idea, in fact, he said he would fur-nish the deer leather if I would make a hunting shirt for him, too."

Helena beamed at Walter mother's suggestion, "That is a won-derful idea. I pray that neither one of them has to march off to bat-tle, but if they do, I would love to have them clothed in something we made especially."

"I'm delighted that you like the idea," replied the woman who was serving as her surrogate mother.

⧗

"I'm so proud that General Herkimer has asked you to be the drum-mer for the Tryon County Militia," Helena glowed as they sat alone on the bank with their bare feet in the same creek in which Walter's grandparents, Ulrich and Beth Heindrick, had roamed along and swam in while they were courting each other. "Please tell me, Walter, about the responsibilities of the drummer."

The ruddy, blond-haired, fifteen-year-old lad had constructed his own drum from pine branches and leather sides covered with white birch bark; he used narrow, leather strips to hold the leather covered top and bottom of the drum together. "First of all, they tell me that William Diamond was the first drummer who rattled out 'To Arms' for the Lexington militia," Walter proudly added.

"What do you mean when you say 'To Arms'?" asked Helena.

"You know that I'm still learning, but as I understand it, the phrase *to arms,* means that all troops should prepare themselves and take up their weapons."

"Are there other beats or sounds the drummer has to make?"

"One of the most important beats to keep constantly, I think, is the marching beat which starts and stays with the militia while it is marching," observed Walter. "Something else important to the militia is the person who plays the fife. Each militia company is led by a fife and drum. Occasionally, the fife will strike up some lively tune like 'Yankee Doodle' and the troops will all sing along," he smiled, "but a lot of them can't even carry a tune in their knapsack."

"But I bet that this kind of experience helps to keep up the troop's morale," Helena speculated.

"You're absolutely right, Helena," replied Walter. "I think our militia is very blessed to have someone like Benjamin Jefferson for its fife player. Benjamin's father, George Jefferson, is my father's blood brother. As you know Benjamin's father's parents were former slaves, and are living in Albany. When Benjamin's father learned that General Schuyler was looking for someone to play the fife for one of the general's militia, he encouraged Benjamin to volunteer for the job. He did not have a fife, so Benjamin found a small discarded hollow metal tube, about sixteen- or seventeen-inches long. He bored a hole where he needed to blow into the tube and added six holes along the tube for his fingers. After he had practiced playing a music scale and a few tunes, he marched to General Schuyler's headquarters and asked for an audition. The general was so pleased with Benjamin's performance that he told him to tell his parents that "General

Schuyler requests my presence as one of the Continental Army's fife players." His parents, of course, were overjoyed that Benjamin, as they always called him, had been personally asked by General Schuyler.

"Sometimes, Ben, uh Benjamin" Walter corrected himself, "he likes to be called Benjamin, reminds me of our Mohawk friend, White Tail, because both are such sincere, optimistic, and cheerful people with a tremendous respect for nature and life in general. They're both rather tall, slim and wiry, while I'm sorta short and stocky. It's a Heindrick characteristic," he said as an afterthought. "Another thing that White Tail and Benjamin have in common is drumming. You remember White Tail teaching us some Indian drumbeats?" quizzed Walter.

Helena nodded.

"Well, Benjamin has been teaching me various African drumbeats he had learned from his father and grandfather." Excited about his experience in the militia, Walter begged Helena, "Please come down the next time the militia drills on the New Palatine common and I'll introduce you to Benjamin. He knows the music and words to a great number of popular songs. Together, we help entertain the troops."

"I'll come down the next time you drill," promised Helena, then she quickly changed the subject altogether, still interested in the activities of the Tryon County Militia.

"I understand that the army also uses bugles for music; is that right?" asked Helena as she sensed Walter's enthusiasm for his new position and his new found friend.

"From what I have been told," Walter said, "the commands in the cavalry are usually blown on a bugle, but elsewhere in the army the fife and drums are the music makers. But of the two," he continued, looking rather sheepish, "the drummer is considered the most important, because with descriptive rattles as the flam, paradiddle, ruff, and raramacuc the drum can give commands. If there is more than one drummer, the headquarters drummer starts the beat which is repeated throughout the camp or march."

"What do you mean by a paradiddle?" frowned Helena. "That's a funny name for a drumbeat."

"I don't yet know all of these drumbeats," confessed Walter, "but I believe the paradiddle is a pattern of beats with alternate strokes of the drumsticks. I shouldn't say it, but one of my favorite drumbeats, besides the march, is the sound of reveille."

"Yes," observed Helena, "but that would mean that you would have to get out of bed before the rest of the troops."

"I know, but its great to get up early and see the sunrise. I guess I'm sorta like the rooster who wants to wake up everybody around him and tell them to have a great day."

"Do you remember last Sunday Preacher Stouffer read from the gospel of St. Matthew?"

"Sure I remember," stated Walter. He could visualize the rather stout preacher standing before the congregation carefully stroking his short-cropped, gray-speckled beard, pausing to thoughtfully select each word before he dramatically delivered his message.

"He said something about a master who was going away on a journey, and before this man left, he called his three servants and entrusted to them some of his property. I guess he called them *talents*," added Walter

"That's right," continued Helena. "He gave one servant five talents, to another two, and one to another."

"And when the master returned he approached the servants to learn how successfully they had invested their talents," added Walter.

"As you recall, Walter, the first two servants had doubled their initial number of talents, and the master rewarded them by giving them more. Then the master learned that the servant who had received only one had not invested his talent, rather he had hidden it in the ground. The master then stripped him of his one talent and gave it one of the other servants."

"I hear what you're saying, but why are you telling me a story I have already heard?" asked Walter.

"Because," she started with her flushed, dimpled cheeks smiling and the afternoon's sun bouncing bright beams through her auburn hair. She hesitated then started over again, "Because I actually believe that he was talking about you."

"How can you say that?" asked Walter.

"I know you have many talents such as farming, helping your parents with the cheese making, and hunting. But," again stopping to catch her breath, "the one talent you presently have, which no one else around here has, is playing the drum. I'm sure if you were to ask Preacher Stouffer if he was making any reference to you, he'd say yes. In his own roundabout way, he was trying to tell you that you have one exceptional God-given talent—drumming. Don't hide it; use it and you will receive additional talents."

"Alright, Helena, you have stimulated my interest in what you thought Preacher Stouffer was referring to in the gospel. The next time I see him, I'll ask him," promised Walter. "You know, Helena, I truly like him, and I have a great respect for this Valley's journeyman preacher."

After having noticed that Helena had been carrying a leather knapsack with her, Walter's curiosity was getting the best of him. He finally asked, "Please tell me, Helena, why have you been carrying that knapsack with you all day?"

"You usually carry a much smaller bag," he added.

"Well," she bashfully smiled, "I've been waiting for the appropriate time to show you and I guess that appropriate time has arrived," and she pulled out the fawn-colored, military shirt she and Walter's mother had been working on. She handed it to Walter, and proudly announced, "I made this shirt for you and your mother made one especially for your father. We're so very proud of you both, and we believe that these shirts will make you look extra good; and most important, they will be your lucky armor."

"I can't believe this," as he automatically grabbed her and kissed her for the first time. He quickly put on the hunting shirt and strutted around in a circle so Helena could see how well it fit him. "I really look military," he declared, "all I need now is my drum," as he offered Helena his hand and they started their hike back to the Heindrick homestead.

✕

On August 2nd, when Brigadier General Barry St. Leger's advance troops were first sighted near Fort Stanwix, the news vibrated throughout the Mohawk Valley like a bolt of lightning.

On August 4th, more than 800 Tryon County Militia, including Walter and his father Karl Heindrick in their new hunting shirts, reported at Fort Dayton, a small stockade fort east of New Palatine. The militia had been recruited under the May 22nd order that all 16- to 60-year-old men not presently members of the Tryon County Militia were to report to duty under the command of General Nicholas Herkimer, a square-built, forty-nine-year-old Palatine with raven hair and dancing eyes who looked more like a brick layer, a farmer, or a boatman than he resembled the veteran general that he was. Puffing on his clay pipe and looking relatively smart in his worn brown uniform, he gave the order to begin the march of approximately thirty miles west to reinforce the garrison at Fort Stanwix.

Meanwhile that same day at Fort Stanwix, the garrison celebrated the completion of the Continental flag, proudly made by the officers of the 3rd New York Regiment who had sewing skills. The warm summer breeze soon unfurled the new nation's first flag to be flown in battle, displaying its stars and stripes made of a hodgepodge of materials. A woman in the fort had contributed her red petticoat. The white stripes came from ammunition shirts. The blue for the canton served as the background for the thirteen stars, taken from a captive British officer's cloak by Captain Abraham Swartout during an earlier battle at Peekskill. It was said that no one was prouder to see the stars and stripes flying at the top of the pole than the woman who had donated her petticoat. "There's my petticoat," she exclaimed. "It looks better up there than it does on me!"

The next day, St. Leger had posted most of the Canadians, Tories, and Indians at the Lower Landing. He relegated another detachment of Tories to a position near Wood Creek, to the west of Fort Stanwix. Then he strung out small details of Indians from Wood Creek to the Lower Landing, believing that his army's circle of nearly three miles around had the fort completely surrounded except for an area on the southwest. This area was so densely wooded and extremely swampy, he believed there was no way it could be tightly held. Two days later on Wednesday, August 6th, this densely wooded and extremely swampy area would be the site of a battle which would be known as *one of the bloodiest and most bitterly fought battles of the American Revolution.*

After an approximately five-week crossing of the Atlantic, Burgoyne's messenger, Captain Henry Gardner, reached London on August 22nd to deliver the good news of the capture of Fort Ticonderoga, resulting in making Lake Champlain a British sea. All Britain rejoiced. King George III rushed in unannounced on the Queen, who was dressed only in a chemise, waving Burgoyne's dispatch before her scandalized ladies, and shouting, "I have beat them, I have beat all the Americans." Immediately, Burgoyne became the toast of the hour. Only Horace Walpole struck a sour note, "I suppose this silent, modest, humble, General Gentleman Johnny Burgoyne has not yet finished his precise description of the victorious manner in which he took possession of it." The King suggested to Lord Derby, through Germain, that the red ribbon of the Garter would be an appropriate award for his kinsman. The Earl of Derby, however, dampened the idea, due probably to some hint dropped previously by Burgoyne, who may have preferred to await the conclusion of a successful campaign; then, a peerage or an earldom would be his just reward.

Hardly anyone, in America or England could debate the fact that Burgoyne had, almost without firing a shot, assumed command of America's north country. In England, everyone expected to hear of his final achievement that would end the war, and the Loyalists immigrants in England were already chartering boats to carry them back to the states. Lord Germain anticipated Burgoyne's subsequent developments to be *rapid* and that he would win *unaided*.

In ten days, Burgoyne had captured the border forts, a flotilla of 200 vessels, 100 cannon, and an extraordinary quantity of stores, powder, and shot. The rebels were in flight, disorganized, deprived of the means of waging war, and dismayed. He had dealt them a crushing blow and had reached within seventy-five miles of his target, Albany, New York. Of those seventy-five miles, twenty-three were through the rough, swampy country that lay between his present position in Skenesborough and his next destination of Fort Edward, the post on the Hudson River, where the northern waterway commenced. For every mile advanced, the length of his supply line increased. "The next stage would require some major decisions," he mused.

❊{ 1 2 }❊

DECISIONS, DECISIONS

SPRING, 1777

———

BOSTON, MASSACHUSETTS

With quill in his hand and a quick sip of Madeira, Arnold paused, reflecting upon the weird series of events that had led to the writing of this letter. His mind raced back to that December 31, 1775, night when the lightly falling snow suddenly became a blizzard. He and Brigadier General Richard Montgomery were leaving themselves wide open to unjustified accusations, but it was a risk they must take before the end of the year; at that time many of their troops would leave for home. Thanks to the blizzard, storming a citadel like Quebec just might work. At best, the Americans would seize the city; at worst, they would fail, but no one could accuse them of not trying. He recalled marching his men through the driving snowstorm, while Montgomery's troops marched from the southwest. As both forces approached the Lower Town, a rocket cut through the air, followed by two more. This was the signal for all the church bells in Quebec to start ringing in the new year, and ring they did.

He knew there was a barricade at the street's top in which the British had placed a cannon equipped with canister shot with hunks of iron, nails, and other objects which could mow down any advancing troops much more effectively than one single cannon ball. His victory he also knew, depended on the barricade; therefore, the cannon must be captured. He saw the flash of the cannon before its debris came flying around them, but he remained untouched, and shouted to his men to follow him to the cannon. Suddenly musket fire came from all sides, from all the surrounding houses. He was almost at the barricade when a sharp pain seared his lower left leg. Thinking he might have been slightly grazed, he remembered continuing forward. But then he could go no farther and leaned against a house, shouting to his faltering troops, "Go on, God damn it, lads!" With blood oozing from the top of his boot, he ordered them to "follow Morgan and take the town!" The men followed obediently and after Colonel Daniel Morgan had captured the barricade, Arnold remembered being carried with the rest of the wounded to the Catholic convent outside the walls where his friend and surgeon, Isaac Senter, after examination discovered that part of a bullet had apparently ricocheted from a rock, entered the leg midway between knee and ankle and lodged in his heel. Dr. Senter offered him a healthy portion of rum and a musket ball to bite on, which he remembered refusing, and without the benefit of anesthesia, the surgeon continued. During recovery and convalescence, he received many messages informing him of the progress of his troops; one, sadly, stated that Montgomery had been killed and now the British were preparing to attack the field hospital and bayonet the wounded.

He remembered sitting up in his hospital bed and shouting to all within hearing distance, "Every man equip yourself with all the firearms you can muster, and defend yourself to the last." He passed his leadership to his second-in-command, Dan Morgan and quietly slipped into a delirium-racked sleep.

Upon finally recovering sufficiently to resume command, he was told that the remnant of Montgomery's army had retreated or had been captured by Sir Guy Carleton's forces. He also learned that more than 100 of his militiamen, whose enlistments were up on January 1, had headed for home, leaving fewer than 500 men in his command. By April 2, 1776, more men were attached to the tiny American outpost, and he, having been commissioned Brigadier General by Congress in recognition of his heroic march and battle, turned his command over to General David Wooster and moved down to Montreal. He was told about the letter Wooster had written to General Washington saying that Arnold had, "to his great honour, kept up the blockade with such a handful of men that the story, when told hereafter, will scarcely be credited."

Samuel Adams received a letter from Joseph Warren saying that Arnold "had made a march that may be compared to Hannibal's or Xenophon's" while Thomas Jefferson had concurred affirming that his "march and his troops is one of the greatest exploits recorded in the annals of nations." Arnold finally "paddled" away from Canada on June 18, 1776, but he knew it would not be the last the British would hear of him.

His mind came back to the present. Arnold dipped his quill, stared at the blank sheet of parchment, and took another sip of Madeira, thoughts racing in his mind until they finally reached the dreary days just before Christmas 1776. He had received Gates's orders dispatching him to New England where Washington was delighted to see him. Washington's spirits were at low tide. Like many men, Washington was subject to depression and wondered in fact whether the American cause might indeed be lost. His forces had suffered major defeats, particularly in the Battle of Long Island at Brooklyn, but had magically managed to escape the British. He knew he must share the brunt of the responsibility for defeat, but he had been plagued with incompetent lieutenants and an army that dwindled constantly as disgusted soldiers returned to their farms and mills.

Now, as Arnold entered Washington's quarters, he could feel the general's warmth which radiated throughout the room. They spent the next four days together reviewing Quebec and the other campaigns. He had always shunned excessive drinking because he had seen his father descend slowly into alcoholism when confronted with failure. He did recall, however, sipping a moderate amount of brandy and Madeira with his friend and commander-in-chief. They discussed the time when Washington had directed him to construct a fleet at Skenesboro. He had worked feverishly, getting enough skilled ship carpenters, sailmakers, riggers, and woodsmen to fell the trees needed to construct a defensive fleet. He recalled the tough battle with the British fleet and finally having to abandon his flagship, *Congress;* he was the last man to leave and had jumped ashore as she went up in flames. Then, with his men, he had rapidly retreated to Fort Ticonderoga.

What had warmed Washington more than the liquor was this visible proof of starving, unpaid soldiers held together through the hard winter in a futile blockade of Quebec. He remembered Washington saying that he possessed *magnetism and enthusiasm.* The night before he parted from Washington to leave for New England, he had spent several hours with him discussing a possible attack on the British barracks at Trenton, across the Delaware River. Arnold had been extremely excited with this idea and sensed that Washington, too, was somewhat interested in the plan. He remembered wishing he could transfuse some of his own enthusiasm and confidence into Washington's veins.

He still held the quill and the parchment remained blank as he reflected upon his triumphant reception. As he rode from city to city on the way to New Haven, Connecticut, cannon were discharged in his honor, and veterans of the long march through Maine to Quebec, who had been captured and later exchanged by the British, limped up to greet him. He fondly remembered how his friend, John Lamb, who had lost an eye while commanding the artillery at Quebec, wept as he hugged him.

After these welcoming receptions with his former New Haven neighbors and a delightful reunion with his sister, Hannah, and his three sons, he had decided to correct what he thought of as injustices incurred by his friends and fellow soldiers because of the American withdrawal from Canada.

After asking for and receiving a thousand-dollar loan from a good friend, he gave John Lamb enough money to raise a regiment of artillery. Lamb was in command as colonel and Eleazer Oswald, another friend and his secretary during the Quebec campaign, was lieutenant colonel.

Arnold had spent a week with his family and arrived in Providence, Rhode Island, on January 12, 1777, to report to General Joseph Spencer, who was, technically, his superior but Washington regarded him as merely a figurehead. There Arnold learned the British had settled into nearby Newport for their winter encampment for they believed gentlemen do make war during the winter. Arnold decided it was his time to act. He traveled to Boston in order to recruit battalions and was received with surprising warmth by the notoriously snobbish Bostonians. Two years earlier when he was a mere tradesman, he would have been snubbed in their drawing rooms, but now they could not do enough for him. He promptly became the *guest of honor* at parties where Tories and Patriots mingled freely.

Arnold continued to recruit, and according to established military custom of seniority, he was the next ranking brigadier-general candidate to be promoted to major general by Congress. True to its unpredictable fashion, he received word that Congress had decided that seniority alone was a dangerous criterion for promotion, since it established an internal military power. Congress believed strongly that this thwarted the civilian government. So the legislators in Philadelphia compromised by promoting five brigadiers to major general, based on a per-acre quota, and also on how many troops each state had sent to the Continental army.

Subsequently, he had received a letter from General George Washington explaining what had happened:

> *We have lastly had several promotions to the rank of major general and I am at a loss [as at] whether you have had a preceding appointment, as the newspapers announce, or whether you have been omitted through some mistake. Should the latter be the case, I beg you will not take any hasty steps in consequence of it; but allow time for recollection, which, I flatter myself, will remedy any error that may have been made. My endeavors to that end shall not be wanting.*

Later Arnold had learned that Washington, true to his word, had immediately written to his fellow Virginian in Congress, Richard Henry Lee:

> *non-promotion was owing to accident or design; and the cause of it. Surely a more active, a more spirited and sensible officer, fills no department in your army. Not seeing him then on the list of major generals, and no mention being made of him, has given me uneasiness, as it is not to be presumed (being the oldest brigadier) that he will continue in service under such a slight.*

Before reaching for Washington's letter, he took another sip of Madeira and dipped his quill in ink. After silently reading the complete letter two or three times, he read aloud by light of the candle that burned on his desk. He focused his eyes on Washington's words in front of him:

> *I beg you will not take any hasty steps in consequence of it, but allow time for recollection . . .*

"Recollection," he thought, "I guess that is what I have been doing for the past couple of hours." Even though Congress had made him look like a fool, he knew that his *General* recognized his value to the Continental Army, and was doing everything possible to keep him from resigning his commission.

Again he dipped his quill in ink, and began:

> *a very civil way of requesting my resignation as unqualified for the office I hold. My commission was conferred unsolicited, and received with pleasure only as a means of serving my country. With equal pleasure I resign it when I can no longer serve my country with honor. The person who, void of nice feelings of honor, will tamely condescend to give up his right and retain a commission at the expense of his reputation, I hold as a disgrace to the army and unworthy of the glorious cause in which we are engaged.*
>
> *When I entered the service of my country, my character was unimpeached. I have sacrificed my interest, ease, and happiness in her cause. It is rather a misfortune than a fault that my exertions have not been crowned with success. I am conscious of the rectitude of my intentions.*
>
> *In justice therefore, to my own character and for the satisfaction of my friends, I must request a court of inquiry into my conduct . . .*

Another dip of the quill and he signed his name

> *Respectfully yours,*
> *Benedict Arnold*

In his April 3, 1777, letter to Arnold, Washington explained the reasoning Congress had applied *as Connecticut had already two major generals, it was their full share.* He further commented, "I confess that this is a strange mode of reasoning, but it may serve to show you that the promotion which was due to your seniority was not overlooked for want of merit in you."

Washington's letter continued:

> *The point does not now admit of a doubt, and is of so delicate a nature that I will not even undertake to advise; your own feelings must be your guide.*
>
> *As no particular charge is alleged against you, I do not see upon what ground you can demand a board of inquiry. Besides, public bodies are not amenable for their actions; they place and displace at pleasure and all the satisfaction that an individual can obtain when he is overlooked is, if innocent, a consciousness that he has not deserved such treatment for his honest exertions.*
>
> *Your determination not to quit your present command while any danger to the public might ensue from your leaving it, deserves my thanks and justly entitles you to the thanks of your country.*

Immediately after hearing of the loss of Fort Ticonderoga, General Washington wasted no time in demanding the Continental Congress to transfer Major General Benedict Arnold north from Philadelphia to assist Major General Philip Schuyler. Washington believed Arnold to be one of the ablest, yet also one of the most controversial generals in the Continental Army. Washington knew Arnold very well, as if he were his own son. He knew that Arnold enjoyed the excitement of leading his men into battle, hearing the crackle of musketry and the roar of the cannon, crowding his luck and overcoming impossible odds, and outfighting the most powerful, polished army in the world. All this, Washington knew, was Arnold's sustenance and the fuel source from which the Connecticut Yankee generated his incredible energy. Washington knew that in a war, a single man could perform great feats beyond that of any whole battalion, and he had no doubts that Arnold, with all of his energy and chancy attitude, could hold back Burgoyne. He sent letters to the Connecticut and Massachusetts legislatures requesting them to immediately dispatch reinforcements to General Schuyler. In fact, he was preparing to lead his own troops when he was certain what General Sir William Howe intended to do. Yankee spies reported the concentration of British troop transports in New York harbor, they could verify their destination. It was not until July 25, 1777, that Washington deduced that Howe's objective was Philadelphia, and not the Hudson Highlands and Albany. On the previous day, Burgoyne's main body had marched from Skenesboro and camped in the burned-out ruins of Fort Anne.

On July 30, 1777, Washington was still perplexed. In his letter to General Gates he wrote, "General Howe's in a manner abandoning General Burgoyne is so unaccountable a matter, that, 'til I am fully assured it is so, I cannot help casting my eyes occasionally behind me." Unknown to Washington, on this same date, Congress, in its own unpredictable manner, had decided to replace Schuyler with Gates. Confirming Washington's belief, Howe's British fleet was preparing to sail toward to the Capes of Delaware.

When Arnold reported to Schuyler at Fort Edward, he found that the morale of the befuddled army was at an immeasurably low level. Another shock came when he learned that Colonel Barry St. Leger, with more than 1,000 troops, Tory regiments, and fierce Indian warriors led by the British educated Chief Joseph Brant, was sweeping through the Mohawk Valley from Oswego, headed for Fort Stanwix, and eventually Albany.

Schuyler himself was somewhat puzzled; he never knew from one day to another whether he or Gates commanded the Army of the North. But he knew one thing for sure; he had to send a force to relieve the siege of Fort Stanwix. Before a meeting of his brigadiers he requested a *volunteer* to lead the reinforcements to Fort Stanwix.

For a moment the silence was deafening.

Then a raspy voice yelled out, "I'll take it!"

Schuyler looked about for the individual who had volunteered to take the assignment. When he finally saw the raised hand of the man walking toward him, Schuyler realized that the volunteer was not a brigadier, but rather a major general, his second-in-command of the Army of the North, Benedict Arnold. Schuyler was so delighted he immediately issued orders for Arnold to move out as quickly as possible. With less than 1,000 men, Arnold knew he would have to recruit volunteers along the way.

When Arnold and his troops arrived at Fort Dayton, he met the rugged black Sergeant, George Jefferson, whom General Schuyler had delegated to request General Nicholas Herkimer to recruit and transfer volunteers as soon as Fort Stanwix was relieved; his need for further assistance against Burgoyne was obvious. This same Sergeant Jefferson was not only the father of Walter's fifer friend, Benjamin Jefferson, but also Walter's father's blood-brother.

⧖

Burgoyne, too, had decisions to make. His main body of troops had finally arrived at Fort Edward in July, just after Schuyler's forces had sneaked down the Hudson River to prepare a defensive maneuver four-miles north of Stillwater. Lieutenant Digby reported that, "We moved on farther to a rising ground, about a mile south of Fort Edward, and encamped on a beautiful situation, from whence you saw the most romantic aspect of the Hudson River interspersed with many small islands."

From this place Burgoyne knew that he had to decide quickly which route his troops should take to reach Albany; he believed there were two routes possible. First, the route sailing down Lake George required only a ten-mile journey over land; he believed this route the most direct and most suitable. The second choice he had identified was the route from Skenesboro, which he believed to be the less desirable due to the expected and *considerable difficulties* he would encounter.

While he sipped the last of his morning's champagne, he spoke to the empty glass, "I know the narrow parts of the river [Wood Creek] may easily be choked up and rendered impassable, and at best, a great deal of land carriage will be necessary for the artillery, provision, etc." He poured another glass of the *bubbly,* and thought, "If I know those damn Americans the way I think I do, I'd be willing to bet my old friend Charles James Fox another fifty guineas that they will unquestionably . . ." He paused. Sipped the glass. Then held the glass before his eyes and said aloud, "Those rebels will take every kind of measure to close the road from Ticonderoga to Albany by way of Skenesboro. They'll fell trees, break bridges, and construct other obvious impediments." He stared at the glass, and thought, "Those bloody bastards will do anything to thwart our advance."

After much serious consideration, he finally abandoned the water route. He reasoned that the water route would require his troops to withdraw to Ticonderoga which could conceivably damage their morale; it might even send the wrong message to the Americans. He also knew that he controlled enough boats by which to transport his army and his supplies from Ticonderoga to Fort George. He finally decided that it would be best to use both routes. He would use the water route only to transport his heavy artillery and supplies south, leaving his troops to carve their way through the woods, swamps, and lagoons from Skenesboro to Fort Edward. He did not think of one essential detail; he neglected to order an advance corps to prevent the Yankees from obstructing and destroying the route.

He had another concern on his mind. Burgoyne realized that the further his army pushed on from their major Canadian source of supplies, he was not only stretching his supply line, but had to expend troops along the way at the various captured posts. He had hoped to find that Carleton had occupied Fort Ticonderoga, but Carleton refused to staff the fort; Carlton believed that he was unauthorized by the King to do so. Therefore, Burgoyne had been compelled to leave 400 and 950 men, respectively, at Crown Point and Ticonderoga.

But Burgoyne was a determined individual and he and his troops were going to get to Albany *come hell or high water.*

⧗

Meanwhile, another general, Nicholas Herkimer commander of the Tryon County Militia, was facing a much more serious debate than one with a glass of champagne. His tent headquarters, located along the narrow rutted dirt trail called the King's Highway, seemed to absorb the morning's unpleasant and stifling heat, while threatening, black thunder clouds hovered overhead. In his headquarters, the general was facing his four regimental commanders, Colonels Ebenezer Cox, Isaac Paris, Richard Vischer, and Peter Bellinger. They wanted action! The Tryon County Militia, they believed, should be on the narrow forest trail leading from their present position, eight miles to Fort Stanwix. The militia's mission was to give relief to the fort. They all knew that last evening, General Herkimer had dispatched three messengers to the fort with orders for the commanding officer. Colonel Gansevoort was to send out sortie attacks that would keep St. Leger's attention focused on the west side of the fort. Herkimer believed this diversion would keep the British from attacking the militia's forces as it approached from the east. Once Gansevoort received the message, he was to fire three cannon shots to inform the militia of the messengers' arrival and the diversion sorties were being dispatched.

Vischer was the first to speak, "General, we think you've lost your nerve. You're too damn scared to move from this site."

Outside, the morning's heat was intolerable, but inside the tent the temperature, too, was getting increasingly feverish.

"Let's face it, you're an old man!" an officer asserted.

"I don't think you're so much scared about attacking the British. I think you're a damn Tory sympathizer. Everyone knows that your brother, Johan Jost, Jr., is a member of the King's troops under St. Leger."

"To hell with the cannon shots," declared another. "They've probably already shot their cannon and none of our sentries heard them."

"General, we have to get on the road," said the tallest officer. "We've got friends and relatives stationed at Fort Stanwix."

"Yeah, and we can't let them down," said another.

Herkimer calmly surveyed them puffing on his clay pipe, and remembered some of the times when, as a lieutenant in the French and Indian War, he was also frustrated with his commanding officers and their reluctance to do as he expected them to do. "Now, gentlemen," he announced in his thick German accent as he attempted to bring some degree of order to the group. "Let's not all talk at the same time. Please tell me what is actually on your minds and, perhaps then, we can reach a mutually agreeable decision."

"General, we've lost confidence in you," declared the first officer. "Why the hell should we wait here when we know damn well that St. Leger's men are out there pounding the hell out of the fort?"

"I agree," chimed in another. "I think we've dallied around here long enough. We've got to get on the trail and head for Fort Stanwix, whether we've heard the cannon or not."

"Gentlemen," the general began, "I have listened to you. Now it's your turn to listen to me." He calmly placed his right boot atop a hand-tooled pine chest containing his maps, clothes, and other traveling gear. He tapped his pipe on the boot heel, and proceeded to pack a fresh supply of tobacco. "You've known about the plan all along, and we all agreed upon it. Last night we dispatched Hellner and two others to deliver our message to Colonel Gansevoort. You know they're fast, seasoned messengers, and we know their reliability and capability. I truly believe that they will get through very soon—that is, if they're not already there. Then we'll hear our signal to move out of here while Gansevoort sends our requested diversionary sorties on the western front."

The officers stood with their arms folded before them, staring at the rugged, weather-beaten Palatine veteran.

"Now, as to your *insinuation* that I'm a Tory. In your minds, you believe that I am being overly cautious about moving out now, but I'm willing to wait a set amount of time. If we don't hear any reports from the fort within one hour, we'll move out on the trail at once," he reluctantly promised.

"As to this Tory business," the stubborn old Palatine continued, "I don't think that remark even deserves an acknowledgment. Only remember what I have done for this valley and the Americans here. As far as my brother, Johan Jost, Jr., is concerned, he probably is right now preparing to do battle against us with St. Leger. And, for your further information, I also have a nephew attached to Johnson's Royal Greens. That's their problem; I can live with myself and my God. I don't know whether they can or not."

Somewhat reassured, the officers all agreed to wait one hour more before any action was taken. Each officer extended his hand to the general, smiled slightly, and marched out of the tent.

✳ 13 ✳

LULL BEFORE
THE STORM

JULY 30, 1777

———

FORT EDWARD, NEW YORK

It was no small feat that Burgoyne and his troops had beaten
Schuyler's skillful delaying and scorched earth tactics and had arrived
at Fort Edward on July 30th. But all the joys of this triumphant
march were to be spoiled soon by a most unfortunate incident.

Miss Jane McCrae, the fiancée of a young Loyalist officer named
David Jones, was at Fort Edward eagerly awaiting the arrival of her
lover. Unfortunately, she was alone when some Indians, scouting
ahead of the British, found her, murdered her, and scalped her.

In reporting the incident, Captain Thomas Anburey said sorrow-
fully, "The Indians came across her by chance in the woods. At first,"
he continued, "they treated her with every mark of civility and were
bringing her back to camp, when within a mile of it, a dispute arose
between them as to whose prisoner she was. Words were growing
very loud, tempers flared, and suddenly one of them, fearful of losing
the reward for bringing her safely into camp, most inhumanly struck
his tomahawk into her skull. She died instantly."

Burgoyne was beside himself after Anburey completed his report.
He knew this kind of occurrence would serve as the propaganda tool
the Yankees very much needed; this could be the last straw to kindle
a fire of outrage and revulsion throughout the entire population,
British and Patriot alike. Burgoyne shared the horror and regret, but
knew the unfortunate affair had occurred on his watch and that in

due time, he would have to account for the incident in the House of Commons.

To make matters worse, it was Miss McCrae's fiancée, David Jones, who had rescued her scalp. The distraught Loyalist officer immediately applied for discharge and when it was refused, he deserted the British camp, and presumably returned to Canada.

As soon as he had digested the complete report, Burgoyne went immediately to the Indian camp and demanded that the murderers be delivered to him. As much as he abhorred this type of senseless savagery, Burgoyne knew he was between the proverbial *rock and hard place* if he asked for the deaths of the murderers. If, on the other hand, he exhibited indifference, he might well be accused by his American and British enemies of encouraging the Indians to continue such barbarity.

Burgoyne was dissuaded by the elderly La Corne St. Luc, a member of Carleton's Council from putting his threats into effect, but insisted that he would "rather lose every Indian in his army than connive at their enormities."

Jane McCrae's savage murder and Burgoyne's reluctance to punish those responsible for the affair was exactly the spark needed to revive among the Patriots their desire "to get them damn Redcoats and their Indian allies out the colonies." Another result of the McCrae incident and its implications was a rush of volunteers to join the local militia and the Continental Army. American General Horatio Gates went so far as to accuse Burgoyne of "hiring the savages of America to scalp Europeans and the descendants of Europeans." Gates even alleged that Burgoyne had paid a price for every scalp taken. In a letter to Burgoyne, he wrote, "Miss McCrae, a young lady lovely to the sight, of virtuous character and amiable disposition, engaged to be married to an officer in your army, was with other women and children taken out of the house near Fort Edward, carried into the woods, and there scalped and mangled in the most shocking manner." Gates concluded his letter by reminding Burgoyne that "the miserable fate of Miss McCrae was partly aggravated by her being dressed to meet her promised husband; but instead met her murderers employed by you."

Gates thoroughly enjoyed writing the letter. When his last draft was finished he showed it to Major General Benjamin Lincoln, and to James Wilkinson, his aide-de-camp.

"I can't believe, Sir, that you would consider sending such a correspondence to General Burgoyne," declared one officer. The other chimed in saying, "But, Sir, you have couched this letter in too personal terms."

"By God!" declared Gates, believing that the letter was the exact message he wanted conveyed; he wanted to hit Burgoyne where it hurt the most. He picked up the letter, turned his back to his officers, and placed the letter in a mail pouch. Saying, "I don't believe either of you can mend it," as he ushered them out of his headquarters.

Before the McCrae incident on July 22, General Washington sent a message to Schuyler as follows, "From your accounts he [Burgoyne] appears to be pursuing the line of conduct which of all others is most favorable to us; I mean acting in *detachments.*" He persuaded Schuyler to use every means to cut off and destroy one of the weaker posts. Two days later Washington reminded Schuyler of Burgoyne's increasing predicaments, "As they [the British] can never think of advancing without securing their rear by leaving garrisons in the fortresses behind, the force with which they can come against you will be greatly reduced by the detachments necessary for the purpose."

Neither Washington nor Gates could have perceived how true and prophetic this message was; Burgoyne, alone, could have and did express much concern about the supply problem being his constant nightmare:

> *How zealously so-ever a general, in such an undertaking as mine,*
> *may be served by the chiefs of departments (and much praise is due*
> *from me upon that score), for one hour he can find to contemplate*
> *how he shall fight his army, he must allot twenty to contrive how to*
> *feed it.*

On the heels of this message to Germain, Burgoyne issued a general order instructing officers to reduce their baggage; similar orders had been issued earlier but had not been obeyed. Regiments were consequently laden with baggage they could not transport once they left the lake and rivers. Only essential baggage, therefore, he ordered that all other baggage be immediately dispatched to Ticonderoga by the returning bateaux. In a July 18th letter to von Riedesel, Burgoyne stated:

> *I request you to take measures that the spirit of the order respecting the sending back officers' baggage to Ticonderoga may have due force. The baggage of the British officers is already gone, and many of them have only retained a small tent and one cloak bag. It is really for the interests of the officers, in the end, that I am pressing upon this subject.*

Apparently, Burgoyne's orders were not being followed as well as his second-in-command, General Phillips, believed they might be; he reported:

> *notwithstanding most serious and positive orders of the 16th instant that no Carts should be used for any purpose whatever, but for the Transport of Provisions, unless by particular orders from the Commander in Chief etc. as expressed in that order, there are this day about thirty Carts on the road with Baggage . . .*

Burgoyne was frustrated because of the need to stretch the supply line to garrison troops in the captured fortresses, and most of all he badly needed horses to mount von Riedesel's dragoons and to efficiently move the army. General Phillips told Burgoyne that he did not believe it was effective maneuvering when troops are ". . . unable to advance three miles without waiting about eight or ten days for our necessary supplies to be brought up." At von Riedesel's urging and being totally unaware of the storm gathering on the rebel side, especially in the New Hampshire and Vermont area, Burgoyne ordered von Riedesel to instruct Lieutenant Colonel Frederick Baum to lead an expedition that would be accompanied by Colonel Skene. When Skene heard that he was going to be assigned to this expedition, with his usual confidence, he assured Burgoyne that the country to the eastward swarmed with men who wished to take up arms for the King, and who only want the appearance of a protecting power to show themselves.

In preparation for the expedition Burgoyne and his officers marched the army down the eastern bank of the Hudson River, to Fort Miller, and he sent Simon Fraser with the advance guard to ford the river to Saratoga, thus threatening Schuyler and deterring him from sending troops eastward when he heard of Baum's expedition.

On August 11th, as Lieutenant Colonel Friederich Baum was preparing his men to march from Fort Miller, Burgoyne rode up and gave him new verbal orders that countermanded his two previous commands. He directed Baum to proceed to Bennington, Vermont, thirty miles southeast of Fort Edward, where, Burgoyne said, a Tory officer had reported a magazine of provisions and a large number of horses inadequately guarded by 300 to 400 men.

When von Riedesel heard this change of order, he said in his strong German accent, "I can't believe you would make this last minute change without some discussion with your staff officers." He glared at his superior officer with fear and astonishment and added, "this will push our foray even farther to the south, making our supply lines even longer and thinner."

Burgoyne ignored von Riedesel's concern and said there were three reasons for his change of plans:

First, it would be of great advantage to the army to gather their subsistence from the captured magazine of the enemy, until supplies could be transported to the army sufficient to last for four weeks.

Second, in case he should move with his whole army against the enemy near Stillwater, General Arnold [Schuyler was still in command] would not be able to send a strong force against Colonel Baum.

Third, that he [Burgoyne] had received intelligence that Colonel St. Leger was besieging Fort Stanwix, and that Arnold intended to send a considerable force to the relief of this place; therefore, it was of the greatest importance that a detachment of the left wing should make a move and thus intimidate the enemy, and prevent him from sending this force against St. Leger.

After Burgoyne had reviewed with von Riedesel the reasons for the change in plans, the German still had serious concerns. He said, "I have it from a fairly reliable Tory officer that the dangers of the road to Bennington are perilous. First of all, the road is not a road as we know one. Secondly and most importantly," he hesitated as he saw Burgoyne beginning to stare him down. He continued in his thick German accent, "Secondly, because the Tory officer told me he believed that at least 3,000 men would be required to capture the village and its provisions, horses, and other supplies."

Burgoyne let the German finish what he had to say. He then raised his right arm, clothed as usual in his freshly-pressed scarlet officer's jacket. He examined his jacketed left arm; saw a speck on the sleeve. He removed the black, kid-leather glove from his right hand, and meticulously proceeded to remove the speck. He replaced his glove, and said, "General von Riedesel, you and I together will parade before Lieutenant Colonel Frederick Baum and his army and order them to leave immediately."

The German general saluted his commander, and together they began their work. The two generals, astride their horses, performed a quick appraisal of the mixed force of Germans and Tories; 175 dismounted dragoons, less than 200 German infantrymen, mainly grenadiers and light troops, a squad of Hesse-Hanau artillerymen with 2 three-pounders, 50 of Fraser's marksmen, 300 Tories and Canadians, and a small number of Indians—totally about 800 men, including officers, sergeants, and musicians. Some German women were there to accompany the expedition, importantly there was also a Captain O'Connell, who was to serve as interpreter for Baum who spoke no English.

Von Riedesel had additional reservations and he wished now that he had shared these with his commander. He knew the German troops better than anyone else in Burgoyne's command. His main concern was with the composition of the attack force; it was composed primarily of Germans, who were heavily encumbered and ponderous; they would surely slow down the march. What this attack force needs, he thought to himself, is a highly mobile and speedy army especially designed for a sally into deep country. With his right hand in a salute, he smiled at the troops, and muttered a silent prayer.

There was another concern that the German general had not shared with Burgoyne, primarily because he had no hard facts; only his gut reaction warned him to be careful of Colonel Skene. He firmly believed Skene had, for his own benefit, persuaded Burgoyne to rebuild the road, which would enhance the value of his property at the very least, that lead to what could be loosely called the hamlet of Skenesboro. Burgoyne was enjoying his high living in Skenesboro's most spacious and comfortable stone house; further, Skene had given von Riedesel a *gift* of four dozen bottles of port and four of Madeira. Just the very thought of the Madeira's cheap quality made the German general nauseated and about ready to throw-up. He considered Skene sleazy, someone he distrusted, but who, unfortunately, had Burgoyne's ear and confidence.

During the first twelve hours, Baum's troops marched 16 miles from Battenkill to Cambridge. En route, the troops engaged in a skirmish with a small detail of rebels. Baum and his troops successfully drove them off after capturing eight prisoners along with several carts, wagons, and oxen. This small skirmish cost the German-led British task force many of their horses, which were killed or driven away by the Indians; Baum advised Burgoyne to pay the Indians for each horse they brought to camp. Two days later on August 13th, when Baum told Burgoyne that this information came from their prisoners, the uneasiness in camp was heightened, especially when it came from the same source. It was learned also that the magazine at Bennington was well guarded by 1,500 to 1,800 rebel troops.

Despite this disturbing news, and receiving no further instructions from Burgoyne, Baum decided to push on. In their usual manner, the Rebels kept firing from behind the bush as the British force retreated, finally bivouacking at San Coick's Mill near the confluence of Owl Kill stream and the Hoosick River, only four miles west of Bennington.

At San Coick's Mill, Baum relayed to Burgoyne the prisoners' report concerning the rebels' strength at Bennington. He added people are flocking in hourly, but want to be armed; the savages cannot be controlled; they ruin and take away anything they fancy.

To further delay Baum's march, the Yankee volunteer from Bennington, Eleazer Eggerton, stayed behind with two companions for many hours to break down the bridge on Baum's route. While completing the bridge demolition under intense enemy fire, Colonel Greg's militiamen fell back to within one mile of Bennington. As soon as Baum's forces arrived at the bridge site, repair of the bridge was the first task to be assigned.

The rebel detachment, which had engaged Baum's forces at Cambridge, immediately relayed their report of the skirmish and the number of British troops to General John Stark.

The circumstances leading to Stark's commanding position in the New Hampshire and Vermont areas were an interesting story.

Stark was appointed by the General Court of New Hampshire as the *independent commander,* which was not agreeable to Schuyler; Schuyler had already sent Major General Lincoln to take command of the Grants. The terms of Stark's commission reflected the widespread distrust which prevailed between the New Englanders and the Continentals after the evacuation of Fort Ticonderoga. When Schuyler called up the New Hampshire Militia to join his forces at Stillwater, a number of the General Court were afraid this would leave their families *prey to the enemy.* Though only in his late forties, Stark had earned a reputation as a famed Indian fighter who had marched with Roger's Rangers in the French and Indian War, rising to the rank of captain, and after serving brilliantly at Bunker Hill, he returned to his farm on the Merrimac River. He had faith in the Continental Congress and believed his services were appreciated, even when Congress had thought fit to promote junior officers over his head, a situation similar to Benedict Arnold's experience with the Congress.

Schuyler had consistently expressed concern about the British threat to the Vermont frontier though the area was not yet recognized as the fourteenth state. On July 18th, Ira Allen petitioned the General Court of New Hampshire to help "the defenseless inhabitants on the frontier who are heartily disposed to defend their liberties." In answer to the petition, Speaker John Langdon pledged; "We can raise a brigade, and our friend John Stark may be safely entrusted with the command, and we will check Burgoyne."

Stark's acceptance of an independent command was greeted with enthusiasm and rapid recruitment. Seven companies, totalling four hundred and nineteen men were recruited in the town of Concord. From July 19th to July 24th, 1,492 officers and men enlisted to fight under Stark, one-in-ten of all the New Hampshire men of voting age. After many changes of plans, Stark prevailed upon Lincoln to persuade Schuyler to revert to the original plan of threatening Burgoyne's flank. Lincoln's militia from Massachusetts, New Hampshire, and the Grants were to move north and fall at the rear of Burgoyne, while Stark and his troops were at Bennington waiting for Baum's expedition. Stark's militiamen were described by the aged veteran, Fredrick Kidder, who had survived the battle:

> To a man they wore small-clothes, coming down and fastening just below the knee, and long stockings with cowhide shoes ornamented by large buckles, while not a pair of boots graced the company. The coats and waistcoats were loose and of huge dimensions, with colours as various as the barks of oak, sumac and other trees of our hills and swamps could make them and their shirts were all made of flax and, like every other part of the dress, were homespun. On their heads was worn a large round-top and broad-brimmed hat. Their arms were as various as their costumes. Here an old soldier carried a heavy Queen's Arm, with which he had done service at the conquest of Canada twenty years previous, while by his side walked a stripling boy, with a Spanish fusee not half its weight or calibre, which his grandfather may have taken at the Havana, while not a few had old French pieces that dated back to the reduction of Louisburg. Instead of the cartridge box, a large powder horn was slung under the arm, and occasionally a bayonet might be seen bristling in the ranks. Some of the swords of the officers had been made by our Province blacksmiths, perhaps from some farming utensil; they looked serviceable, but heavy and uncouth.

Burgoyne received Baum's communiqué early that evening. In his reply, which he dispatched about seven that same evening, Burgoyne responded, "I am confident that the accounts you have sent me are very satisfactory, and I have no doubt of every part of your proceeding continuing to be the same" and advising him, "should you find the enemy too strongly posted at Bennington, and maintaining such a countenance as may make an attack imprudent, you should hold your ground, and I will either support you in force or withdraw you."

After reviewing this response with von Riedesel, Burgoyne stated, "I am not surprised to learn that the rebels at Bennington number between 1,500 and 1,800 men. However," he qualified his remark, "I did not expect such numbers, because I believed that there would be only a remnant of Colonel Seth Warner's Green Mountain Boys on that flank." Burgoyne was unaware that Warner's providential arrival toward the end of a long and exhausting day's fighting, would make the greatest contribution to one of the most significant American victories of the war.

"Do you think we should send reinforcements to Baum?" asked von Riedesel.

"Not this time of night," winked the sleepy-eyed Burgoyne who had more on his mind than Baum's position. He was thinking of his companion waiting for him with chilled champagne in his headquarters tent.

His night activities were precipitously interrupted at 6 o'clock in the morning by his aide, Sir Francis Clerke, bringing a second letter from Baum asking for reinforcements. After reading the letter, Burgoyne while pulling his pants up, instructed Clerke to fetch von Riedesel. As soon as the German general appeared, Burgoyne ordered him to immediately dispatch Lieutenant Colonel von Breymann and his advance troops to help Baum.

"Sir," he replied, "I will order von Breymann, at once, to assist Baum, but would you grant me permission to give von Breymann a few suggestions?"

By this time, Burgoyne had his scarlet jacket and his plumed hat in his hand. With his index finger on his chin, he scolded, then said, "That's a hellava good idea, my friend." While thinking to himself, I wonder what the hell that crafty old German fart is up to?

What von Riedesel did not know was that Burgoyne's orders to von Breymann had told him he was being sent out in consequence of good news received from Baum, and it was left to his judgement whether or not to attack the enemy. After joining Baum, whom he outranked, Von Breymann began his march on August 15th with 500 men and 2 six-pounder cannon, mounted on carts, which he described as follows:

> I started, therefore at 9 o'clock; and there not being any teams, I had two ammunition boxes placed upon the artillery wagons. Each soldier carried with him forty cartridges. The crossing of the Battenkill consumed considerable time, for the men had all to wade through the water. The great number of hill, the bottomless roads, and a severe and continuous rain, made the march so tedious that I could scarcely make one-half of an English mile an hour. The cannon and the ammunition wagons had to be drawn up hill one after the other. All this, of course, impeded our march very much; and I was unable to hasten it notwithstanding all of my endeavors. The carts loaded with ammunition upset, and it caused considerable trouble to right them.
>
> To this, also, was added another difficultly. The guide, whom we had, lost the way and could not find it again. At last, Major Barner found a man who put us back on the right path.
>
> All these unexpected mishaps prevented me from marching on the enemy on the 15th, as far as Cambridge, and, I, therefore, found myself obliged to encamp seven miles this side of that place.
>
> Before reaching that place, however, I wrote to Lieutenant Colonel Baum notifying him of my arrival, and sent Lieutenant Hagerman with the dispatch.

What von Breymann did not report was that as his troops sloshed through the horrendous, treacherous route, he and his officers were still requiring their men to stop frequently and dress ranks, an inherited routine of the German military fastidiousness.

While Baum and Stark were positioning their troops on the eastern front, one significant incident had already occurred, and another was about to happen in the Mohawk Valley.

❋ 14 ❋

AFTER
ORISKANY

11:00 A.M., AUGUST 17, 1777

———

THE HEIDELBERG TAVERN, NEW PALATINE

All were gathering in the front of Martha Butler's Heidelberg Tavern waiting for their minister to arrive from his earlier preaching assignment at Fort Dayton. Among the group were Harvey and Hazel Perry, the assistant manager and clerk at Wilhelm and Sarah Kerchner's, New Palatine's only general store. Presently, with the Kerchner's daughter Helena's consent, the Perry's were managing the store, since Wilhelm and Sarah had joined the Tories and emigrated to Canada except for the time when Harvey left with the Tryon County Militia to fight in the Battle of Oriskany. It was Harvey's sad responsibility to tell Helena that he had, unknowingly, fired his musket into the face of an attacker, who turned out to be her father. Filled with guilt and remorse, Harvey and his wife, with the help of Karl and Rebecca Heindrick, worked out an arrangement with Helena Kerchner. The Perrys would stay on to manage the store, and send her routine payments toward eventual partial ownership and a share of profits.

Standing with the Heindricks was George Jefferson. George had been ordered by General Schuyler to start volunteer recruitment before General Arnold arrived in the valley; included in the Heindrick group were Cal Swartz and his wife. They were Karl's neighbors and had long assisted the Heindrick family in their cheese making business; the entire valley knew that Heindrick's Limburger cheese was the one specialty for which Rebecca and Helena were completely responsible. The stubby, muscular village blacksmith, George Raab and his wife, and the village miller, Herman Swackhammer, and his wife with all of their screaming children joined the group.

All of them were startled when they heard the familiar, boisterous voice of the tavern's owner, Martha Butler. They could see that, true to form, she had everything in order. In her hands were the reins of a team of plow horses hitched to a four-wheel, buckboard wagon. Squeezed in between the buxom tavern owner and the ample-sized preacher was a beautiful, raven-haired, slender Indian woman wearing a beaded, light-colored doeskin gown.

The group stared and began whispering among themselves.

"Do you suppose that Indian woman is the preacher's wife he has always been telling us about?"

"She's not bad looking, . . . that is as Indians go," declared another, "but she looks a hellava lot older than he is."

"He probably needs an older person to keep him in tow," chuckled another.

"I've heard a lot about these Indian marriages," chimed in the first, "but, I'll bet you that me and my wife had a lot better honeymoon than they did camped out in some tepee."

"I don't know about these Indian marriages," commented another, "just look at Sir William's mistress or wife, Molly Brant, whatever you want to call her. She rules the Johnson roost. Fact is, she's the one who sent a messenger to her brother, Chief Joseph Brant, and St. Leger, warning them that Herkimer and our militia were marching down the King's Highway to relieve Fort Stanwix. If'in she hadn't sent that news, just maybe we wouldn't have had such a disastrous fight at Oriskany."

"I agree with you," said his sidekick, "them Indian women all look alike, . . . you can't trust any Indian no way."

Another expressed her opinion, "Over the past years Preacher Stouffer has been talking all about his wife." The speaker stopped a moment to collect her thoughts then asked her listeners, "What did he say her name was?"

"He used to refer to his wife as Red Bird," responded a plump woman with her apron still on. Don't sound much like a woman's name," she opinionated as she hoisted up her slipping underpants.

"I wouldn't mind having a bird like that one," snickered a scrawny farmer with a prominent adam's apple bobbing up and down.

"If she is the preacher's wife, she certainly isn't a figment of his imagination as many of us thought."

"That's the kind of figment I'd like to have nestled in my bed," commented yet another.

The congregation followed Martha Butler, Preacher Stouffer, and the Indian woman whose raven-colored hair was gathered into a single braid reaching nearly to the small of her back, into the tavern. Everyone sensed that this day was going to be different. They quietly followed the three and entered the tavern that miraculously, on every Saturday evening at midnight, became New Palatine's Dutch Reformed Church. This routine would be followed until the building they had been working on for the past year was completed, dedicated, and became their new church.

Together, Martha Butler, the preacher, and the middle-aged Indian woman walked toward the tavern's huge, stone fireplace. This time, before the preacher spoke, he stared solemnly toward the tavern owner and nodded.

In a sober and unusual serious voice, Martha Butler started, "Two weeks ago this coming Wednesday, this valley had a most horrible experience that nearly tore it apart." Some of the congregation thought they saw moisture in her eyes as she continued. "On that dark and stormy day in that dismal swamp near Oriskany, many friends and neighbors met the enemy. Some still lie out there, never to move again, while others—and you all know who, were blessed and returned to their homes. Some are whole, while others have suffered terrible injury. To all of you, we are forever deeply grateful. Bless you.

"This morning our good friend and confidant, Preacher Stouffer, together with his charming wife, Red Bird, rode in from Fort Dayton. They brought with them some good news and some bad news; no matter how we classify the news, either way it's serious," she declared, "and our friend, Preacher Stouffer, will tell us why it is important for all of us to hear it." Solemnly, she walked over to the empty, rustic maple chair near Red Bird as the circuit rider preacher, in his dusty, well-worn boots and his coarsely-woven, dark woolen suit approached the center of the hearth.

The usually jovial and cheerful preacher, with his shortly cropped, salt and pepper beard, stood in front of the tavern's huge stone fireplace, his hands clasped together as if in prayer. Some of the congregation sat on the tavern's benches and chairs while others sat on the wide-planked floor wherever they could, patiently waiting for the minister to begin.

Characteristically, Reverend Johan Stouffer covered his mouth with his ruddy right hand, and lifted his face toward the huge, rustic logs which served as the tavern's cross-beams. He crossed himself, and again clasped his hands in prayer. He picked up his well-worn, leather-bound Bible, opened it, and held it in his right hand by his side.

"Before I begin my talk, I want very proudly to introduce my lovely bride of ten years, Red Bird. I have often referred to her in my sermons. I guess many of you were wondering if I truly had a wife or it was a product of my imagination. And, if I was really married, was I ever going to allow you to see her. Again my dear friends, I am very proud of my *lady, Red Bird;* she is truly my inspiration." Before he could raise his Bible to commence his message, the congregation stood and applauded to welcome Red Bird; who stood and raised the beaded wampum she carried over her doeskin sleeve.

When the congregation had returned to their seats, their preacher closed his eyes as if praying again; then in an unusually somber tone he began.

"I'll begin with the good news, and that is, we are all here to celebrate life. The bad news is, some whom we knew are not among us.

"We never know when our time on this earth is up. Only our Lord knows that. Early this morning, I learned by messenger from our good friend Dr. Petrie, that his patient, our good and gallant leader, General Nicholas Herkimer, died last night in his sleep at home, near his and our beloved Mohawk River.

"As you remember when Dr. Petrie visited us here last Sunday, he told us the general's wounded leg might have to be amputated. Early

yesterday morning, Army Surgeon Robert Johnson elected to ampu-
tate the general's shattered leg about five to six inches below his knee
much to Dr. Petrie's misgivings. But Lieutenant Colonel Willet visited with me shortly after the surgery and told me he had found the
general sitting up in bed with a pipe in his mouth, smoking and talking, in excellent spirits. I guess we can all picture "old Honikol" puffing away on his clay pipe.

"The amputation was successful, but later on Dr. Johnson and his
assistant, Dr. Hastings, were unable to staunch the ensuing hemor-
rhaging, no matter how desperately they tried. About three hours
after the operation, the general told Dr. Johnson that his leg pained
him like the very *fires of hell,* and he asked for something to ease the
pain. Dr. Johnson then gave the general thirty drops of laudanum.
The general then surprised his doctors. He told Dr. Johnson that he
needed something stronger than medicine to ease the pain. Startled,
the doctor asked what he suggested. "Would you hand me my
[German] Bible and my spectacles from the top of the bedside table?"
asked the general. Dr. Johnson handed him his Bible and reading
glasses, and then excused himself. Remaining in the bedroom were
the general's childless wife, Maria, his close friend, Colonel John
Roff, one of his black helpers, and Assistant Surgeon Hastings, all
keeping vigil while the general, propped up against the headboard,
packed fresh tobacco in his pipe, took his tinder box, lit his pipe, and
puffed away with great composure.

"His wife told me that the general was as content as possible,
serenely smoking his pipe. Then he put on his spectacles and opened
the Bible; to her it seemed as if by providence, the book magically
opened; he never turned a page, but began reading the Thirty-eighth
Psalm. The general must have been well acquainted with that most
important of all books, the Bible, for not the most learned biblical
scholar, lay or cleric, could have selected a portion of the sacred
Scriptures more exactly appropriate to the situation of the dying
soldier.

"I want to read to you now what General Herkimer was reading
to himself and to his friends. Let's close our eyes and try to envision
what he was thinking:

> O Lord, rebuke me not in thy wrath:
>> neither chasten me in thy hot displeasure.
> For thine arrows stick fast in me, and thy hand
>> presseth me sore.
> There is no soundness in my flesh because of thine
>> anger; neither is there any rest in my bones
>> because of my sin.

The preacher paused, glanced up from his Bible, and said, "Whether we call the general's reading of this psalm an indication that he knew his Bible, or that he had a premonition of what was coming; the fact is that during this time he perceived that he needed more than medicine for his immediate peace." The preacher raised the Bible over his right hand and continued:

> For mine iniquities are gone over mine head: as an
>> heavy burden they are too heavy for me.
> My wounds stink and are corrupt because of my
>> foolishness.
> I am troubled; I am bowed down greatly; I go mourning
>> all the day long.
> For my loins are filled with a loathsome disease: and
>> there is no soundness in my flesh.

"How fitting these words are," Reverend Stouffer observed, "my loins are filled with a loathsome disease; and there is no soundness in my flesh. I'm certain that many of us, too, feel desperately lost at times. Certainly, those of you who were at Oriskany probably felt the very same fear of death, but fortunately the Lord was with you, and you are with us today." He returned to the psalm;

> I am feeble and sore broken: I have roared by reason
>> of disquietness of my heart.
> Lord, all my desire is before thee; and . . .

He stopped reading, and concluded by repeating the last line of the Psalm, "Lord, all my desire is before thee. Let us all give thanks to the Lord for bringing us this far.

"According to Dr. Petrie, the general and his wife, Maria, have agreed that if anything happened to him and he should eventually die, he desired to be buried in the family *burying ground*, a few rods from his Little Falls red brick house. Obviously, this is too soon to know when he will be buried. When I learn the date, I'll notify Martha and she will pass along the information and post it on the big maple in the common.

"We know that we need His guidance in the future, especially after you hear the rest of the news Martha Butler, Red Bird, and I brought back from Fort Dayton. But I'm going to leave that to Karl Heindrick's brother and our new found friend, Staff Sergeant George Jefferson; they will fill you in on this part," he concluded making room for the sergeant and Karl in his new *hunting shirt* on the hearth.

"Good morning, my friends," the sergeant standing erect in his blue military coat with its buff facing indicating he was part of the New York infantry began, "I share with you all the sorrow this community has experienced during the past months, especially at Oriskany. We all know that while this war may have quieted down here in the valley, on the eastern front, especially along the Lake Champlain and the New York–Vermont borders, our troops are fiercely engaging the British, Tories and Indians, commanded by General John Burgoyne; they are assisted by a number of hired German mercenaries—generals and soldiers. Our commanding officer, General Philip Schuyler, has asked me, as many of you already know, to anticipate General Benedict Arnold's arrival from Fort Dayton, expected on August 21st, by helping to recruit volunteers. We are asking some of you, once again, to pick up your musket, hatchet, and knife and join us in the Saratoga area for a period of three months. We chose this length of time because we know you must all start preparing for the harsh winter that will soon be with us in less than three months. We expect to defeat Burgoyne's forces within that time, but you know there is no guarantee; we also know that the British do not fight wars during the winter. Men, ages 16 to 60, who want to join General Benedict Arnold, General Philip Schuyler, and myself on the eastern front, please meet with me on the village common across from the tavern. Thank you for listening to me, and most of all, thank you all for making me feel welcome in New

Palatine." He bowed his head slightly and with his right hand offered his space to Preacher Stouffer.

"This has been a day none of us will ever forget," started the preacher, as in his characteristic manner, he raised his eyes toward the ceiling. He crossed himself and joined his hands in a prayer.

"We started this service with the Thirty-eighth Psalm, at General Herkimer's choosing, I might add. I think it is fitting to close the service with the reading of the five last verses of this same psalm:

> For I will declare mine inequity; I will be sorry for my sin.
>
> But mime enemies are lively, and they are strong: and
>   they that hate me wrongfully are multiplied.
> They also that render evil for good are mine adversaries;
>   because I follow the thing that good is.
> Foresake me not, O Lord: O my God, be not far from me.
> Make haste to help me, O Lord my salvation.

Crossing himself again, Preacher Stouffer concluded, "Go in peace and serve the Lord."

He went directly to Red Bird, reached for her hand, and placed it over his arm; they walked to the front door and waited outside to mingle with their friends.

Meanwhile, some of the hamlet's men were already clustering around Sergeant Jefferson. On one side of the sergeant was Walter Heindrick, who after several soul-searching conversations with his parents and Helena, had succeeded in obtaining their blessings to again volunteer as a drummerboy, but for three months only. Two things influenced this decision. First and foremost was the death of their Mohawk friend, White Tail, during the battle of Oriskany when White Tail made a vital decision to lower his tomahawk on the skull of a Tory who had his musket raised and pointed toward the wounded general. White Tail thus paid with his life for this one moment when he had sided with his blood brother and the rebels. His uncle, Chief Brant, who had witnessed White Tail's heroic act, quickly aimed a fatal shot at his nephew. Walter had witnessed this tragedy. Helena after hearing about their friend, agreed with Walter that he must avenge White Tail's death. The second issue that especially convinced

Walter's parents was George Jefferson telling his brother, Karl Heindrick, that his own son Benjamin, who was only a year older than Walter, was at Fort Dayton waiting to join him when he returned with General Arnold. Walter was also looking forward to being with Benjamin who was the fife player and, according to Benjamin's father, would probably be working with the renown Virginia rifleman, Colonel Daniel Morgan. Like Arnold, the very name of Morgan sent chills and fear among the Indians and respect among the British and Tories.

Another small group was gathering around the Heindricks and Helena Kerchner; it included Harvey and Hazel Perry. Mr. Perry was the first to speak as he approached Helena, and it was obvious that he had something serious to say. "What I have to tell you," looking directly at Helena, then moving his eyes toward all in attendance, "I think we should keep this private among ourselves; at least for the time being. It all began about a week ago when we sensed that someone had entered the general store during the night. Every morning thereafter we had the same feeling, until two days ago. Then we confirmed our suspicions; food was indeed missing. We had planted some food, hoping to trap the thief. Together with the food, a shawl and a woman's dress came up missing. We decided that it would be a good idea for me to stay in the store night before last. This I did, but I made a mistake. I was too anxious to learn who it was and I fell over a metal shovel, which made a hellava noise. I quickly got up to look out the back window."

He stopped momentarily to catch his breath, but before he could continue Rebecca Heindrick asked," Did you see whoever it was?"

"Who was it?" quizzed Karl.

"I saw a person running away from the store," Perry continued, "but I could not identify who it was. One sure thing is that the person was wearing a dress."

"How big was she?" quickly asked Helena.

"She, if it was a she," he responded, "was about average size. About the size of all you women."

"Where did she go?"

"In what direction was she headed?"

"To tell the truth I don't know where she wound up, because it was too dark. But, I believe that whoever it was headed toward the livery stable near the back of the store. I'd like to suggest that Karl and I sleep over in the store for a couple of nights," stated Harvey.

"I think that's a great idea," responded Karl as he looked toward Rebecca.

"The store is your responsibility until the Kerchners return," added Rebecca. "Hazel can stay at our home," confirming her support of Harvey's proposal.

Listening quietly, Helena began wondering if this mysterious individual was her mother. When her parents left for Canada, the townspeople of New Palatine did not treat her family as other Tory families had been treated; some had been tarred and feathered, some were driven from their homes, while many others had their property seized by the Continental government. Fortunately for Helena, when she had escaped Canada and returned to New Palatine, she learned that the Perrys had placed the entire Kerchner estate in trust for her anticipated return; they knew she was attracted to Walter Heindrick. Her mind drifted back to the identification of the secret woman.

"We'll do this for two nights," agreed Mrs. Perry, "then we'll reexamine the situation."

Everyone agreed, and began making plans to stake out the store. While they were absorbed in their plans, Martha Butler, together with Red Bird and the preacher, were headed back east toward German Flats. He was scheduled to preach there in the early evening.

⧗

The Battle of Oriskany had not quieted the western front completely. The British had dug trenches to within 150 yards of Fort Stanwix's ramparts, under which they were preparing to run a mine; the crisis of a siege was imminent. Fortunately, the Tory plot was discovered and resulted in taking several Tory prisoners, among them was a half-witted settler named John Joost Schuyler, locally known as Hon Yost; a nephew of General Herkimer's and related to General Philip Schuyler. Thanks to an ingenious plot conceived by General Benedict Arnold that capitalized upon the Indians' holy respect for Hon Yost's mental defectiveness. While George Jefferson had not been in on the actual planning process, he was fortunate to witness the Mohawks and Senecas decamping and stealing off with the liquor and clothes that they had looted from the British officers' tents and yelling that the terrible General Arnold, the *Dark Eagle,* was racing after them. The sergeant loved to tell about this important, yet humorous episode; each time George told the story, he would add some nuances to enhance the tale. He would always end his tail with the Indians retreating back to their camps. St. Leger knew that the British could no longer depend upon his Indian allies; therefore, he abandoned the siege. St. Leger ordered his troops, weighed down with their heavy packs, to retreat back through the dense forest to Oswego and Canada, thus hoping to join Burgoyne at Albany.

Benedict Arnold, at the same time, was racing toward Fort Stanwix, the British, and the Indians, but he arrived at Fort Dayton on August 21st with 950 Continentals from Brigadier General Learned's brigade. On August 23rd, Arnold and his troops had advanced as far as New Palatine, twenty miles from Fort Stanwix. While Arnold was meeting with Sergeant George Jefferson to review the status of his recruitment efforts in New Palatine and of the Oriskany veterans, he was particularly pleased to learn that the sergeant had successfully recruited a much needed drummer to join Jefferson's fifer son, Benjamin. During their session, Arnold received a message from Gansevoort thanking him for his slick idea of having Hon Yost scare the Indians to rebuke the British; St. Leger and his troops had fled the Fort Stanwix. Arnold ordered Jefferson to immediately prepare the new volunteers to join his troops when he returned from Fort Stanwix. He quickly excused himself, rallied his 950 Continentals, and headed for Fort Stanwix arriving the next day. On the 24th, Arnold led his army in pursuit of St. Leger, reaching Lake Oneida as the last British boat drew away from the shore. When he returned to the fort he temporarily assigned 700 of his troops to General Gansevoort's garrison, and marched the rest back toward New Palatine to join Sergeant Jefferson and his new recruits.

❈ 15 ❈

DOUBLE
TROUBLE

AUGUST 23, 1777

ON THE SHORES OF LAKE ONEIDA

Frustrated and disappointed after a twenty-two mile forced march from Fort Dayton, and an equally futile chase after the British to the shores of Lake Oneida in an effort to capture the forty-year-old veteran British officer, St. Leger. Arnold had hoped that if he was not able to take the retreating St. Leger, he might at least, capture some of the retreating British and Tory troops. He was totally dismayed as he and his troops watched the last of the enemy scramble from shore to board their bateaux and push-off toward open water and, he thought, probably back to Canada.

Upon returning to Fort Stanwix, Arnold received some unexpected praise from Colonel Gansevoort. Arnold knew that the Indians called him the *Dark Eagle,* the name given him by the Abenaki chief, Natanis. The Colonel chuckled as he said, "General, you will not believe it, but your very name has caused fear within the Indians and their British and Tory allies."

This was, indeed, heady praise; to hear that his name alone was enough to strike fear into the hearts of the enemy. Yet, he knew that he and his troops had to return to Albany as rapidly as possible.

After this welcomed information, Arnold arranged to leave approximately three-quarters of his own troops as reinforcements to Gansevoort's garrison. Shortly after completing the transfer, he learned of two situations requiring his prompt attention on the eastern front. First, his old friend General Horatio Gates, had been named the new commander of the Army of the North. He was not surprised to learn of Gates's promotion; some time ago General Schuyler had told him that he was not sure from day to day whether he or Gates commanded the army. It had been Schuyler, however, who had ordered Arnold to relieve Fort Stanwix and to recruit volunteers from the Mohawk Valley.

The most startling information he received was that the British advance force, under the command of Colonel Baum, had been slaughtered by the Americans, commanded by General John Stark, near Bennington, Vermont.

"Burgoyne," Gansevoort jubilantly informed Arnold, "has suffered his first major setback." Anxious to return to the battle front Arnold responded, "I agree! All the more reason I must return with haste to assist General Gates or whoever is in charge of the army."

The details of assigning Arnold's Continentals to the fort's garrison were soon completed, and Arnold then assembled the balance of his troops on the old Indian trail, now officially known as the King's Highway. Under a forced march order, they headed toward New Palatine to join Sergeant Jefferson and his new recruits.

When Arnold's army arrived in New Palatine the noonday sun was high above the hamlet's common. Dusty and exhausted he ordered his own forces to break ranks and reassemble in one hour. He was pleased to see the sergeant already starting to drill the recruits. Unlike the Continentals who wore brown uniform coats with buff facings, breeches, and stockings fastened with four buttons at the ankle and secured by a strap running under the foot in front of the heel, most of the volunteers wore the favored and familiar hunting shirt made of deer leather, homespun wool, or linen. It was this same hunting shirt design which supposedly carried no small terror to the enemy, who thought every such person a complete marksman.

The sergeant ordered the recruits to stay at ease, while he marched over to General Arnold. He saluted and reported the number of new recruits. The general commented on the good support the community had given the army and was encouraged as he noted all of the women, children, elderly, and apparently a number of wounded veterans from the Battle of Oriskany. Arnold told Jefferson to order the troops to break ranks, say their farewells to families and loved ones, and to reassemble in one hour for their march to Fort Dayton.

With sweat rolling down his brow, Arnold suggested in his raspy voice, "Let's you and I go over to that log underneath that huge maple tree; I think both of us deserve a little peace and quiet rest."

"I'll buy that idea," responded the ebony colored sergeant, glistening like a bronze statue.

While they were strolling across the common, Arnold said, "You know, Sergeant Jefferson, that I used to be a bookseller." The sergeant nodded that he had heard rumors to that effect. "I don't know why the hell a former bookseller, who loves to read all kinds of books, is here as a general." As the sergeant watched, it appeared that his general was lost in some kind of oblivion. The general continued.

"I'm fond of poetry. Especially poetry written by an old Roman poet, Horace, who admitted that he was a rotten soldier. After Horace was discharged from the Roman army, he obtained a minor bureaucratic position as a clerk, which afforded him plenty of time to write his beloved poetry."

They reached the shady area beneath the maple, sat on the log and Arnold returned to his musings. "During the past few days we've been plenty busy chasing the British, Tories, and Indians, but at night when I had a little quiet time to myself I kept thinking about what Horace said in one of my favorite poems. It goes something like this:

> Happy the man, and happy he alone,
> He, who can call today his own;
> He who, secure within, can say,
> Tomorrow do thy worst, for I have lived today.

"I guess what the old duffer was trying to tell us, is to do your best today, and then you'll be prepared to receive the worst your fate can bring you tomorrow." Still silent, the sergeant waited for the general's punch-line. "I guess I'm asking you in a roundabout way, do you believe that you have been successful in recruiting as many volunteers as possible?"

After reflecting upon his experience of living in the New Palatine community for nearly three weeks, and having been received as part of the community, especially in the Heindrick household, and Preacher Stouffer, being extremely helpful, Jefferson began, "I am pleasantly surprised that we were able to recruit this many volunteers, especially since we are right in the middle of the farmers' haying time, and the corn is about ready for harvesting. We are asking the volunteers to enlist for three months; that's a lot of time during the fall of the year for the farmers to be away from their harvesting. We all know that old man winter with his severe cold and snow will be coming very soon."

"After the news I heard yesterday about Burgoyne receiving a good licking in Bennington," replied Arnold, "perhaps we will not need three months. You know, sergeant, fighting here in the wilderness is not what these professional British and German soldiers are accustomed to. I've a feeling that Gentleman Johnny has stretched his forces too damn thinly, and extended his supply lines so much that these two issues alone give him constant nightmares." He chuckled and added, "Maybe that's why he brings along his unpowdered lady; to keep his nightmares away."

While they were talking, a man about George's age approached them wearing a hunting shirt and hobbling on a pair of homemade crutches. Quickly, George stood up and hurried over and hugged the man, returning to Arnold who was standing.

"General Benedict Arnold, I am pleased to introduce you to my newly found brother, Karl Heindrick of New Palatine. As you can see by his leg, he was one of those wounded at Oriskany; his wife, Rebecca, makes the Mohawk Valley's best Limburger cheese. They are the parents of our new recruit for drummer, Walter Heindrick. Walter, Herkimer's favorite drummer, was at the general's side when he was perched on the knoll beneath the beech tree giving orders to his troops."

If Arnold had not interrupted Jefferson's bragging about the Heindrick family, the sergeant would never have stopped. Arnold expressed pleasure in meeting Karl and learning about his patriotic and loyal family, but he knew that the day was getting short and German Flats was another ten miles away. He politely excused himself and suggested to Jefferson that he reassemble his recruits.

Arnold and his Continental troops led the way along the narrow King's Highway, it's overhanging hemlock and beech boughs forming a dark tunnel as they headed east. To add color to their march, there were hard maple trees, their leaves beginning to turn to their brilliant fall colors and for contrast, white paper birch trees sprinkled throughout the forest. Behind the Continentals were Jefferson's volunteers, many of whom were young farmhands who had never been away from their homes, strolling along as if they were on a summer's walk through the forest. Jefferson and the other volunteers who were seasoned veterans of either the French and Indian War, the recent battle at Oriskany, or both, tried vainly to get the young raw recruits in step with Walter Heindrick's drum beat so they might resemble a military force.

The importance of the Mohawk River route for trade and military purposes was established. Under the orders of General Philip Schuyler, Fort Dayton was built on the north side of the Mohawk River in July and August 1776 by the members of the Third New Jersey Regiment under the command of Colonel Elisa Dayton. In addition, the colonel had orders from Schuyler to build numerous fortifications along the river. On the morning of November 12, 1757, a raid on the north side of the river highlighted the need for forts. The French and Indians killed and captured over 100 settlers and leveled homes in the area known as German Flats that were only protected by block houses. On the following spring, similar raids against the south side of the river were not as costly. Fortunately, troops, under the command of then Colonel Nicholas Herkimer, were stationed at Fort Herkimer, a stockade erected in 1756 around the stone house built in 1740 by John Jost Herkimer, the colonel's father; these troops left the fort and met the enemy before all homes, crops, and cattle were destroyed. A nearby stone church that was not within the fort's stockade served as another stronghold in time of trouble.

The actual construction of the Fort Dayton was directed by Major Joseph Bloomfield, a 23-year-old officer, who wrote in his diary dated August 21, 1776: "The fortification ordered to be built in this place being enclosed . . . was taken up in erecting a pole on which was a flag with the name of Fort Dayton."

The fort's garrison was primarily comprised of Continental and militia troops; it also provided temporary shelter for settlers burned out by the Indians. On August 3, 1777, approximately 800 militiamen from all over the huge Tryon County area, whose southernmost point touched the northern Pennsylvania border and ran all the way north to the St. Lawrence River and the Canadian border, answered Herkimer's call to assemble at Fort Dayton; they were immediately ordered to march to the relief of Fort Stanwix. The militiamen who marched with Herkimer toward Fort Stanwix, probably did not think of their march or pending battle as an international contest; rather, they were fulfilling their resolution, adopted at the first meeting of the Palatine District Committee of Safety on August 27, 1774, that "we will unite and join with the different Districts of this County in giving whatever relief is in our power to the poor distressed inhabitants of Boston, and will join and unite with our Brethern of the Rest of this Colony in anything tending to support our Rights and Liberties."

Just twenty days later, General Benedict Arnold, leading a number of seasoned Continental troops, left Fort Dayton over the same path Herkimer led his forces. In a letter to General Horatio Gates, Arnold wrote:

> *From Mohawk River ten miles above Fort Dayton at 5:00 p.m.—*
> *this morning I marched from German Flatts for this place [Staring*
> *Creek]. The excessive bad roads and necessary precautions in*
> *marching through a thick woods retarded us so much that we have*
> *but this moment reached this place.*

The road Arnold speaks of, the King's Highway, was an impressive name for an old Indian trail only recently widened to accommodate a relief column. The frontiersmen, knowing that the experienced Indians had established the quickest and safest route of travel; widened their trail. It was late that evening when Arnold and his troops reached Fort Dayton. After thanking his men for their tough march from Fort Stanwix and New Palatine and before settling down to sleep, Arnold wrote General Gates, "There is nothing to be feared from the enemy in this quarter at the present." The next day they would advance to the American headquarters near Albany, and be ready to participate in the smashing of Gentleman Johnny and his British Northern Army.

After two fruitless nights waiting in Kerchner's General Store, Harvey Perry and Karl Heindrick decided they would spend at least one more night. During a third night they hoped fervently that the mysterious woman would return for more supplies.

After darkness had settled over the hamlet of New Palatine, the two friends silently approached the store. Each man was in his middle forties. Karl was rather muscular with a ruddy complexion acquired while managing the valley's creamery and cheese manufacturing plant and traveling throughout the valley to meet with the farmers and arrange for the collection and delivery of milk. The other, Harvey, was rather pale and stout which he had attributed to his sedentary life style working for the Kerchners. However, since the Kerchner's had gone to Canada, his responsibilities had become very demanding and he had lost about twenty pounds, making him look as trim as a farmhand in the hayfield.

As they had done on the two previous nights, the friends positioned themselves atop the sacks of grain, and nestled themselves between the bags. They arranged to take two-hour shifts. During Karl's third shift, he was alerted by a noise coming from the small window in the rear of the store. Cautiously, he maneuvered himself upon his elbows to get a better look and saw an arm reach up and pull something from the top of the window. As if by magic, the window was easily removed. Alarmed, Karl tapped Harvey on his shoulder and warned him to stay quiet. As Karl was pointing toward the window, they watched a cloaked body squeeze itself through the narrow opening and succeed in lowering itself to the floor. Quietly, the person began to move about the store, heading toward the dried fruit and the few fresh vegetables the farmers had brought to the store as barter for other wares. The intruder wandered silently about seemingly at home in the store. Meantime, the men were silently contemplating their next move. There was little doubt that the intruder was a woman, and it was apparent that she knew the location of the supplies she wanted. They waited until the woman was about to hoist her bag of booty through the window, then they grabbed both of her arms. She had a black, lace shawl drawn over her head, and as she was seized, she uttered a throaty, "Oh, no!" She dropped her booty bag and literally wilted on the floor in a sobbing heap.

Standing over her, the men knelt on either side and removed her shawl. Perry exclaimed, "Oh, Mrs. Kerchner, I'm so pleased you have returned," he hesitated a moment, then added, "home. We need you here."

With tears streaming down her cheeks, she stared blankly at her former clerk and fainted. The men quickly arranged a makeshift bed for her on a few sacks of grain. After placing her on the bed, Karl said, "Harvey, you stay here with Mrs. Kerchner and I'll rush home and get our wives and Helena. I think they'll all be pleased to learn who our mysterious woman is."

It was nearly dawn before Karl Heindrick returned with his wife and Mrs. Perry in his buckboard wagon. Ridding bareback ahead of them on one of the Heindrick's plow horses, Helena quickly covered the five miles from the Heindrick farm to the general store. She rushed through the store's front door to be met by Harvey, whispering for quiet. He hugged Helena and said, "She's still sleeping, Helena, she probably needs the sleep after what she's has been through."

"She's totally exhausted and scared," added her daughter. "I remember how frightened she was when my father hurried us all toward the Canadian border with his Tory friends. She was never political like my father and me, she sorta took things as they came and tried to adjust to the situation." She placed a light kiss on her mother's cheek, and patted her dark hair. "Mother," she said quietly to Harvey, "never entered my father's and my political discussions; father and I were always arguing who was right. He used to tell me that we have an obligation to the British king, because if it were not for the British, us Palatines would still be back in Germany *freezing our balls off*."

They moved further away from the sleeping woman and sat on a upside down wooden crate. Not losing her train of thought, Helena continued, "While father fervently supported the British, I was just as strongly in favor of the patriots; especially the Palatines who were actually British indentured servants; after all freedom was the reason they came to America in the first place.

"We did agree on one issue as far as the war was concerned," she continued. "Neither one of us completely trusted the Indians, although, I did admire Chief Joseph Brant. And you know Walter and I were very close friends with Brant's nephew, White Tail."

Harvey let the distraught young lady continue her monologue; he thought it good therapy for her.

"White Tail's tragic death was one of the main reasons Walter decided to join General Benedict Arnold and his troops."

Harvey's mind flashed back to the time when he and his friend, George Raab, were fighting almost face-to-face, eyeball-to-eyeball, with two Tories, their muskets pointed straight at them. He remembered shooting first. A split second later, George's musket fired into the other Tory's face, blowing his brains to the winds. Immediately afterwards, as they examined their victims, Harvey realized what he had done. He had killed his former boss, Helena's father.

After a soul-searching discussion of the past events that had led them to this point, Helena and Harvey heard the buckboard arrive and tie-up at the store's hitching post. Quickly, they went out of the store and greeted their families requesting that they remain quiet because Mrs. Kerchner was still sleeping. Once outside of the store, Rebecca Heindrick informed Helena there was room for her mother at their home. "In fact," Rebecca added, "she can sleep in your bed. You know that our home is your home. You're a part of our family." She stopped talking and with a smile added, "Maybe we can talk your mother in helping you and me in making the Mohawk Valley's best Limburger cheese."

They joined hands in a gesture of comradeship and family, and entered the store to tell the mystery lady what they had planned.

The sun was sending its reddish, bright morning light through the hemlocks and maples, as the little train wended its way west on the King's Highway to the Heindrick's stone farmhouse.

✻ 16 ✻

ENGAGEMENT

AUGUST 19, 1777

HEADQUARTERS CAMP OF THE NORTHERN DEPARTMENT
OF THE CONTINENTAL ARMY AT STILLWATER

It was not a friendly meeting, that August 19th when General Horatio Gates arrived at the Stillwater camp, the most recent American encampment. Stillwater was located on the Hudson River about fifteen miles above Albany, and its purpose was to relieve the beleaguered General Philip Schuyler of his post as second-in-command of the Continental Army. After a relaxed and uneventful march from Philadelphia, Gates abruptly and tactlessly, refused Schuyler's conciliatory offers and advice; Gates arbitrarily took charge. His treatment of the tried, exhausted, and patriotic Schuyler caused more ill feelings at the very moment when New York faced the worst crisis in its history. Schuyler was harried by friend and foe alike; by the British from the western and eastern fronts, and by the incessant rivalry and jealousy of their New England neighbors. Gates's promotion, it was suspected, was not necessarily gained from his proficiency on the battle field, but on his connections with Congress in Philadelphia.

Neither man knew that a tremendous power struggle was going on regarding the selection and appointment of the number-two generalship of the American Army. This power struggle was not settled by military personnel, it was, rather, fought in the back committee rooms of Independence Hall within days of the fall of Fort Ticonderoga. After Gates had refused Schuyler's request to stay in command at Fort Ti, he turned the post over to St. Clair and immediately traveled to Philadelphia. He arrived just before the long-awaited British invasion had finally come in early July.

After Gates and the New England delegates met on August 1st, Congress appointed a committee for finding a way to investigate the evacuation of Fort Ticonderoga; an alternative to a court-martial. After receiving the committee's report on August 27th, Congress appointed another committee to collect the facts and get them to General Washington with instructions to "appoint a court-martial for the total of the general officers who were in the northern department when Ticonderoga and Mount Independence were evacuated." Since Gates and Arnold had been in Philadelphia at the time of the fall of the forts, the *general officers* referred to were Schuyler and St. Clair. On August 28th, Congress appointed yet another committee comprised of John Adams, Richard Henry Lee, and Henry Laurens. This committee was charged to investigate and identify the responsibility for losing the two forts; the committee, dominated by John Adams and his fellow New Englanders, blamed Schuyler for the debacle, while at the same time, promoting Gates as Schuyler's replacement. Gates's appointment stirred up festering regional animosities between New Yorkers and New Englanders. The New Yorkers resented the ferocious attacks on their native son, Schuyler. He, along with St. Clair, was openly accused of treason by the New Englanders. Meanwhile, without any further investigation, New Englander Sam Adams wrote that the fall of Fort Ticonderoga had all the *evident marks of design.* He added that Gates was "always beloved by his soldiers because he always shared with them in fatigue and danger and he is an able and honest officer—giving spirit and vigor to our arms in the Northern Department." Four days later Congress denied Arnold's request for promotion and scrapped the Arnold-Morgan plan for an expedition to west Florida. Congressman Henry Laurens had called this venture a "vast expense of money and men, and further disgrace on our arms would be the result of so mad an enterprise."

⧗

Exhausted after another forced march from Fort Dayton east toward Albany, Arnold and his troops arrived at Stillwater. He surveyed the area, and was disappointed to see that under Schuyler, the Americans had traveled south of the Mohawk River to Stillwater after their hundred-mile retreat from Ticonderoga. He saw the danger immediately; the Americans were hopelessly exposed in open country and could be surrounded easily.

Shortly after his troops had been dispatched to their quarters, General Gates's aide informed him that the general wanted to see Arnold. Exhausted, yet flushed from his success in the Mohawk Valley, he entered the general's headquarters tent and was warmly greeted by his old friend.

"Greetings, my friend," the general said as he gave Arnold a bear hug. "What a delight and relief to see your grisly old face. You don't resemble a former bookseller, you look exactly like the person we need here to shut down Gentleman Johnny and his lobsterbacks."

"Now don't flatter me," returned Arnold, "right now my ego is just about at its apex. In fact, I learned a short time ago that my name has been presented for promotion."

"I'm delighted to hear of your success in the Valley, and hope that your promotion will be approved by Congress," Gates responded keeping secret his knowledge that Arnold's advancement had been rejected flatly by the New Englanders. Strange, he thought; Arnold himself is from Connecticut, a New Englander. "But, my friend, we have much more pressing issues here."

"You know me, sir," glowed Arnold, "you know that I'm always ready for a good fight."

"That's why we brought you here," declared Gates, "and I have just the right post for you." Looking straight at the eager general, Gates continued, "I am planning to appoint you to command our left wing, and to order you to go immediately with Colonel Thaddeus Kosciuszko to select and fortify an impregnable position. This position should, and must, command the Hudson river road leading south to Albany."

Both men knew a lot about Kos, as the officers called him. He was the impoverished son of Polish gentry who had fled from his homeland after his attempted elopement with a rich nobleman's daughter had ended unceremoniously in gunfire. Kos held a French captain's commission and had been educated at the Ecole Militaire in Paris, and at the French artillery and military engineering school at Mezieres. He was thoroughly grounded in European warfare, but he knew only from textbooks what Arnold had learned from experience.

"That sounds very exciting; although Kosciuszko and I have not as yet worked closely together, I believe that we can and will accomplish your goals."

"I have heard that he is a genius for river fortifications and has a flair for quick sketches and caricatures," added the general, "and I believe that you two will get along famously." Gates continued, "I have had the area superficially scouted. There is a high rise of land south of Stillwater known as Bemis Heights, named after a Mr. Jotham Bemis who operates a tavern at the bottom of the hill. The ridge is well fortified and, it seems to me, all that is needed is your's and Kosciuszko's blessing. You may recall the Polish colonel was employed to implement his ingenious engineering talents to strengthen Fort Ticonderoga," reminded Gates, "only to have our efforts go to waste and to the British, thanks to Schuyler," he concluded with a sneer.

Arnold chose to ignore the general's last remark; after all, he did not know how thick or thin the ice was upon which he was stepping.

Just then a young major entered the headquarters tent, and giving a crisp salute, announced, "General Gates, Sir," he said ignoring Arnold, "you are needed immediately at the commissary to review with the commissary officer the requirements needed for our next push."

Gates glared at the energetic, yet pompous youth, "Major Wilkinson, I want to introduce you to Major General Benedict Arnold, our most recent hero of the Mohawk Valley campaign." He turned to his friend, "General Arnold, my trusted aide, Major James Wilkinson."

Each gave the other a *token* hand shake, then excused themselves to their pressing duties, Gates to check in the commissary, Arnold to seek out Kosciuszko, and the twenty-year-old to shine his shoes in the general's headquarters.

Arnold was exiting the general's headquarters when he heard the arrival of Colonel Daniel Morgan and his Virginia riflemen. Before either said anything, they chuckled and slapped each other's back, agreeing that Washington had really made a very timely and well chosen match of their forces. Silently, they chose not to talk about another Arnold and Morgan expedition down the Mississippi River. They were in complete agreement on one issue: they were now ready to finish the work they had left unfinished on that snowy winter night in Quebec nearly two years earlier.

"You know, my friend," said Arnold placing his stout arm on Morgan's broad shoulders, "I think this is the first time the American forces outnumber the British, and with no snow," remembering their expedition in Canada.

"And we also know, General," Morgan smiled when he called him *general;* they were usually on a first-name basis, "with all of the forces accumulated in this area something has to pop before the godawful winter arrives. You Yankees are used to freezing your balls off, but us southerns can't take this snow shit."

"I'm glad you arrived when you did," Arnold said reflectively, "things have really changed since I was last here."

"What do you mean?" asked the Virginian, "I thought Gates was one of your best friends."

"He was, and I believe that he is still," responded the recent hero of the Mohawk Valley, "but I understand he no longer confides in his officers as he used to do. He now seems to depend on a twenty-two-year-old major named James Wilkinson, whom I hear is making it difficult for most officers to see Gates. I just left Gates's headquarters, he assigned me to a command post, and I am to work with the Polish colonel, Kosciuszko. We are to scout out a location from which to guard the river road leading south to Albany. Gates believes Burgoyne will have to cross the Hudson to get to Albany and our troops."

Morgan initially ignored Arnold's announcement, but was immediately anxious to learn if he was going to be shut off from seeing Gates, being left to dry and sway in the wind. "Is this Wilkinson the same person we used to call *Wilky* up in Canada?" asked Morgan.

"The same," declared the bemused, the recently appointed commander of the army's left wing. "He was with me for six weeks during the retreat from Canada; during that time he kept begging me to take him back as my aide before the Battle of Valcour Bay."

"I remember the little sonofabitch," proclaimed the famed rifleman. "He was a pompous, obsequious little ass with little or no loyalty. The little bastard probably sees the wind blowing in Gates's direction, and officers such as you who have been close to Schuyler, are going to be kept in deep shit."

Arnold had always admired Daniel Morgan because he told it like he truly believed it was, whether the listener liked it or not. This time they agreed to watch their asses where Wilkinson was concerned; perhaps even as far as Gates was concerned.

"Now, let's stop this bullshit," started the rugged Virginian, "tell me about your new assignment."

Arnold explained as much as he knew about the expedition Gates had assigned to him and Kosciuszko, and they agreed that together they would try to find the Polish engineer.

⧗

While Arnold and Morgan were searching for Arnold's new partner, the two old friends were getting reacquainted, catching up on their experiences.

At the same time, a stunned and amazed Sergeant George Jefferson, learned that he and Arnold were to make their reports to General Gates, not to General Schuyler. This disappointed Jefferson; Schuyler was his friend and neighbor, the person who had assigned him to Arnold to assist in the recruiting process, but he was slowly learning to adjust to many kinds of surprises since he had left his livery business in Albany. With a troubled heart, he put on a happy face and saw that his son, Benjamin, and Walter Heindrick had made acquaintances. Benjamin was seventeen, muscular and nearly six-feet tall, had been with the troops six months, and was the fife player for General Schuyler's troops. Unfortunately, the drummerboy who had accompanied Benjamin in St. Clair's retreat from Fort Ticonderoga had been killed by a British musket. When Walter heard this, he thought, maybe this is the reason why Arnold and Jefferson were so determined to have him join Schuyler. Walter was nearly half-a-head shorter than Benjamin, but was equally muscular in build. For their ages, both young men were seasoned warriors, and were expected to play intricate roles in the Northern Army's battles with Burgoyne and the British. After finishing their meal and a short gab session around the campfire, Benjamin and Walter headed for their common tent they shared with four other militiamen; fortunately, thanks to their tentmates, there was sufficient room for Walter's drum. Sergeant Jefferson, meanwhile, was discussing the politics of the Northern Army's leadership with Arnold and Morgan.

On August 15th, Baum had found Bennington more strongly garrisoned than Burgoyne had led him to believe. The Jane McCrae incident and other acts by the Indians had infuriated the Americans; many so-called Loyalists, who had joined Baum at Sancock were equally outraged and helped to swell the ranks of the American militia.

Baum received a message that Burgoyne had dispatched Lieutenant Colonel Heinrich von Breymann for reinforcement. "Where the hell is von Breymann?" he kept asking himself. In a way he was fortunate; the downpour on August 15th that prevented von Breymann's activity also delayed Stark's attack on Baum. Meanwhile, Stark and his troops established their defensive position on a hill 300-feet above the Walloomsac River, roughly midway between Sancock Mill and Bennington, that subsequently became known as *Hessian Hill.*

Baum's men, meanwhile, were busy constructing a log-and-earth redoubt to garrison Baum's dismounted dragoons. Three-hundred yards farther up the road, a bridge crossing the Walloomsac was defended by Fraser's Rangers with one three-pounder; Baum's other three-pounder was sighted in the main redoubt. Just beyond the bridge was a small elevation upon which Baum's Tories entrenched themselves; the women accompanying Baum's forces were gathered together in a wooden hut on the far bank of the Walloomsac. Everyone believed their position was as good as any in the area, and they all worked diligently throughout the wet daylight to enhance their defenses. While the soldiers were busily improving their position, parties of local farmers came and went, pausing to chat with the few Germans who could speak English. Most of these locals wore pieces of white paper in their hats, identifying them as Loyalists, they were, however, regarded with suspicion by those of their countrymen who had marched with Baum from Fort Edward. Lieutenant Colonel Ebenezer Jessup, the commander of Baum's provincial contingent, bitterly criticized his supervisor's credulity:

> He allowed people to go and come from his camp, readily believing their professions of sympathy with the Royal Cause, and imparting to them most fully and completely all information as to his strength and designs.

Baum's lack of the English language made it almost impossible for him to communicate with the locals, Loyalists or otherwise. If there was any blame, it must be placed on Skene and the other Americans and Englishmen serving under Baum. They had all underestimated the depth of outrage caused by the depredations of the Indians and, especially, the murder of Jane McCrae.

As the afternoon wore on, Baum was becoming increasingly concerned that von Breymann and his troops had not arrived. He decided to send Skene back up the road his troops had traveled to expedite von Breymann's advance. He made one mistake; he allowed Skene to take all the available horses to tow von Breymann's gun and ammunition wagons. Unfortunately, he did not realize his mistake; without the horses he was completely immobilized.

While Skene was seeking Breymann, Baum was digging trenches and erecting log palisades, and the Bennington locals were enjoying the day's novelty, as they watched Redcoats and Germans preparing for a battle. Brigadier General John Stark was having difficulty in restraining his militiamen who were eagerly clamoring to attack the hated Hessians and their despised Tory allies. Among these impetuous militiamen was Thomas Allen, a parson and leader of the Pittsfield, Connecticut contingent. Allen, arriving that night with his tired, drudging troops, went directly to Stark and demanded that they attack immediately. Rain was dripping from their tricorns and running down their noses and cheeks as Stark asked the impatient cleric, "Would you go out on this dark and stormy night?"

Before Allen could reply, Stark advised, "Rest your men, and your-self, so all might fight the better on the morrow." Stark knew he was not going to get a good sleep; he and his aide were expecting to hear news from Colonel Seth Warner who had ridden into Bennington with Warner's Green Mountain Boys. The American strength would increase to more than 2,000 troops and then the numbers and the odds would favor the Americans, but they could hardly be character-ized as an army, as described by an aged veteran of the battle:

> To a man they wore small-clothes, coming down and fastening just below the knee, and long stockings with cowhide shoes ornamented by large buckles, while not a pair of boots graced the company. The coats and waist coats were loose and of huge dimensions, with colours as various as the barks of oak, sumac and other trees of our hills and swamps could make them, and their shirts were all made of flax and, like every other part of the dress, were homespun. On their heads was worn a large round-top and broad-brimmed hat. Their arms were as various as their costume.
>
> Here an old soldier carried a heavy Queen's Arm, with which he had done service at the conquest of Canada twenty years pre-vious, while by his side walked a stripling boy, with a Spanish fusee not half its weight or calibre, which his grandfather may have taken at the Havana, while not a few had old French pieces that dated back to the reduction of Louisburg. Instead of the cartridge box, a large powder horn was slung under the arm, and occasionally a bayonet might be seen bristling in the ranks. Some of the swords of the officers had been made by our Province blacksmiths, perhaps from some farming utensil; they looked serviceable, but heavy and uncouth.

A motley collection, perhaps, but united in the determination to defend their homes, and equally determined that no damned German mercenaries and their contemptible Tory friends were going to reach Bennington.

When Arnold finally met Kosciuszko, he learned that they had friends in common. Kos, as he asked Arnold to call him, was recommended to Congress by Arnold's friend Silas Deane and had helped Benjamin Franklin lay out the river defenses at Philadelphia before joining Gates's staff. As soon as they were packed and had verified their orders from General Gates, the two new friends, set out on horseback in early September to determine the best place in which to lure the British into battle on American terms. True to his aggressive nature, Arnold suggested the Americans advance toward the enemy to provoke a British attack. By September 9th, Arnold and Kos believed that they had discovered the ideal location; upriver at present-day Saratoga.

After reporting back to Gates their selection of the site for their fortification, Gates and his staff officers, together with Arnold and Kos examined the bluff, three miles north of the Hudson's junction with the Mohawk River. From the bluff overlooking the Hudson, much to the chagrin of the younger officers in Gates's staff, Arnold outlined his plan for the battlefield. He visualized the battlefield stretching to the west, north of which high bluffs and steep hillsides dropped off into deep ravines.

Gazing outward and around the panoramic view, Arnold commented, "The British could not get around the Americans to the west or past them down the Hudson, if there were proper fortifications." He hesitated a moment, rubbed his chin, and pointed, "I believe that narrow pass would be a perfect place to build strong works and make an all-out stand." Turning to face Gates and his staff, Arnold continued, "The British would have to try to outflank our forces by attempting to circle to the west but, in the thick, hilly forests and stump-littered clearings, their artillery and dragoons, indeed all their European battle tactics, are useless. They would be forced to fight American-style and would be beaten piecemeal."

While Arnold was relating his preference for the battle strategy, Kos took paper from his portfolio and started drafting the redoubts, earthworks, bivouacs, and company streets.

When Kos had completed his sketch, Arnold took the pencil and placed Dearborn's light infantry and Morgan's rifles on the far left of the American line so as to interdict any British flanking attempt. In the center, under General Gates's personal command, he placed the best battle-hardened New England brigades of Ebenezer Learned, Enoch Poor, and John Glover forming a heavily fortified right wing. Overlooking the river and protected by the bulk of the artillery, was a scattering of Continental units to stiffen the spines of 2,000 New York and New England militia.

Gates gave his fervent endorsement of Arnold's plan, and looking at his staff officers said, "I want you and your troops to begin immediately, under Colonel Kosciuszko's and General Arnold's directions, to dig in and construct the best fortification you can build, because it will be here that you'll meet the enemy and their bloody asses. Construct this place so you can protect your own asses, and beat theirs."

❊ 17 ❊

TO ARMS

AUGUST 16, 1777

IN THE BENNINGTON, VERMONT AREA

While Gates and the Northern Department of the Continental Army were preparing for what they hoped would be the final battle of the American Revolution, Burgoyne and his forces composed of a few British regulars, Tories, but primarily German mercenaries under the command of Lieutenant Colonel Fredrich Baum, were busily positioning themselves to face Brigadier General John Stark and his approximately 2,000 New England militiamen.

The day, August 16th, had turned out to be fine and dry, and as Stark and his militiamen prepared for battle, he believed that his plan was relatively uncomplicated and would succeed. Baum's entrenched positions were outflanked by forces lead by Colonel Moses Nichols from the north and by Colonel Herrick from the south. To Stark's amazement, the Americans were frequently allowed to approach within musket range of Baum's troops in the mistaken belief that they were Tories coming to join Baum. Throwing down their disguises, Stark's *Tories* raised their muskets and shot the unsuspecting Germans. Today, local tradition relates that the first shot was fired by Jacob Ondeerkirke of Hooisick; his bullet killed a German major. The British were attacked from all sides; the flanking parties worked their way up Hessian Hill firing from behind crude breastworks. Most of the exposed soldiers threw down their arms and fled into the woods while Fraser and his rangers were pushed back from the bridge.

Starting the final confrontation, Stark led his main force down the Bennington road, where an intense battle was joined around the position manned by Baum's Loyalist contingent. Stark, meanwhile, had hitched his horse to a fence and during the fighting the horse was stolen. After the battle, he offered a twenty dollar reward for the return of his horse. True to their training, his troops swept on to attack the British main defense, while Stark was left temporarily without a horse.

The Tories, who had occupied the redoubt south of the river, were attacked by an American party led by Ebenezer Webster, the father of the famous Daniel Webster. The attacking group included Parson Allen, who, when recognizing some of the Tories as coming from his district, stood on a log and in his best pulpit manner exhorted them to defect to the American cause.

"There's Parson Allen. Let's pot him," came the cry from the redoubt.

Allen's neighbor's volley failed to harm the parson, and Webster led the rush over the breastwork. The Tory Captain Peters, takes up the story:

> A little before the Loyalists gave way, the rebels rushed with a strong party in front of the Loyalists which I commanded. As they were coming up, I observed a man fire at me, which I returned. He loaded again as he came up, and discharged again at me, crying out, "Peters, you damn Tory, I have got you." He rushed on me with his bayonet, which entered just below my left breast but was turned by my bones. By this time I was loaded and saw it was a rebel, Captain Jeremiah Post by name, an old schoolmate and playfellow, and a cousin of my wife. Though his bayonet was in my body I felt regret at being obliged to destroy him.

The Tories were forced to abandon their redoubt; the majority were taken prisoner, some succeeded in escaping down the road to join von Breymann, and others fled up the hill to throw in their lot with Baum who was by now fiercely assailed by Stark's men who had reached the summit. As their adversaries stormed in, the dragoons trudged off down the hill, running straight into Stark's reserve advancing along the road from Bennington. The battle became a confused fracas. Baum and a party of dragoons put up a stiff fight until their ammunition was exhausted. He then ordered his men to sling their carbines and fight their way out with their swords, a maneuver which gained them a little time because the Americans lacked bayonets. Baum was shot through the stomach and fell, mortally wounded, while the dragoons lumbered off into the woods hotly pursued by their light footed foes.

When Stark, who in 1759 had stood with Wolfe on the Plains of Abraham, reported to Gates about the Battle of Hessian Hill near Bennington, he stated, "The battle had lasted for two hours and it was the *hottest* I ever saw in my life. It reminded me of a continuous clap of thunder." Stark continued, "The enemy, however, was obliged to give way, and leave their field-pieces and all their baggage behind them. They were all contained within two breastworks, with their artillery, but our martial courage proved too much for them."

Gates rose from behind his field desk, walked around it, and extended his hand saying, "General Stark, you and your men are a credit to this new country and yourselves."

"Sir, I accept your congratulations for my men and myself," Stark acknowledged, "but I must tell the whole story. When the Germans were in full retreat, our troops halted to plunder the enemy's posts and several men tried to load and fire the captured cannon, but the mechanism was beyond their knowledge. When I discovered what they were doing, I advised them to discontinue their tampering before they were injured.

"Meanwhile, other squads of our troops pursued the fleeing dragoons whose heavy swords and scabbards became entangled in the trees, bringing them to a halt." Stark continued, "Then I ordered our troops to rally to secure the victory; in a few minutes, I was informed there was a large reinforcement on the march within two miles of us." Stark leaned back in his chair, and smiled, "Luckily for us," he continued, "at that moment Colonel Warner's regiment came up fresh. They marched on and began the attack anew."

Stark modestly admitted, "I ordered a hogshead of rum to be broached to refresh my exhausted men. But, would you believe it?" he asked his commander, "they were so eager to attack the enemy upon their being reinforced that they tarried not to taste it, but rushed on the enemy with an ardour perhaps unparalleled.

"You would have received a big kick from watching ole Parson Allen. He captured the German surgeon's horse, and with it a great number of large baskets filled with wine; he, then, was busily distributing it to all our wounded soldiers. He had a delightful time," Stark added as an after thought.

"That's a great way to end such a barbarous, bloody battle and, again, General Stark, I congratulate you and your troops. With this victory in Bennington, we have added one giant spike in Gentleman Johnny's coffin."

"Oh, Sir," cautioned Stark, "that's not the end. After five o'clock in the afternoon, Warner's regiment had reached the bridge captured by Skene's men and, after stopping to drink from the river, they pushed on along the bank. It was beginning to become dark and both sides were exhausted. The Germans had used all of their ammunition, many had been killed or wounded, and their artillery horses were either dead or too done-up to be useful.

"We learned that von Breymann had ordered his contingent to retreat, leaving their cannon behind. Warner's Vermonters followed, while I pushed forward as many of the men as I could to the Vermonter's assistance. This part of the battle continued obstinately on both sides till sunset. They were obliged to retreat while we pursued them in the dark. If daylight had lasted one more hour, we would have taken all of them. We did get four pieces of brass cannon, some hundred stands of arms, eight brass barrels, drums, several Hessian swords, and about 700 prisoners. We counted 207 dead on the spot but have no idea how many are wounded. The part of the enemy that escaped marched all night and we returned to our camp.

"But it was the next day, Sir, that I really screwed up," declared the New Englander.

"What do you mean, Stark," asked Gates. "Personally, I think you and the men have done a hellava job," declared the proud commander.

"Well, Sir, the next day, I learned that we had missed an opportunity to capture almost all of von Breymann's men. As darkness fell, the retreating Germans, many of whom had thrown away their arms, halted and offered to surrender, which they signified by the beat of a drum, a message that conveyed nothing to our troops. You know, Sir, we are not versed in European military etiquette. Scattering through the woods, the Germans escaped under cover of darkness and two-thirds of them reached safety at Cambridge.

"To tell the truth," confessed Stark, "at that point, I called off the pursuit; I feared that our men would end up shooting each other in the dark."

"Good idea," commented the commander.

"It is too early to give an accurate tally, General," Stark began. "As near as we can figure, Baum and von Breymann had 207 killed, and 700 captured as prisoners, who were taken to Bennington; of Baum's 375 German troops, only 9 escaped."

"What about our troops? How many did we lose?" asked the anxious commander of the Northern Department.

"Too much honour cannot be given to the brave officers and soldiers for their gallant behavior. They fought through the midst of fire and smoke, mounted two breastworks that were well fortified and supported with cannon. I can't single out any one officer because they all behaved with the greatest spirit, bravery, and honor. Colonel Warner's superior skill in action was of extraordinary help to us, and I would be happy if he and his men could be recommended to Congress.

"Sir, the sad part of this report is that our casualties numbered 30 killed and 40 wounded."

"Commendable, you and your," he stopped momentarily to correct himself, "our troops are to be complimented for their excellence in action. Just imagine, a ragtag army of rustic marksmen and backwoodsmen crushing two armies composed largely of disciplined professional soldiers and led by experienced officers; it's hard to believe. All I can say, again, is that Gentleman Johnny Burgoyne better well look out for us Yankees." He stopped, and before Stark could interrupt him, Gates warned, "But, we must not get too cocky. The war isn't over until the last shot is fired." He bowed his head and gave Stark a friendly pat on his shoulder.

Burgoyne had established his first headquarters at Fort Edward on July 14, 1777, in the Red House, a blockhouse-like building constructed some years earlier by a Doctor Smyth. The general remained there until August 14th when he moved his headquarters to the Duer House at Fort Miller, some eight miles farther down the Hudson River. It was there that he received the news of the German defeat at Bennington, and on August 20th he wrote two letters to Lord Germain. One was intended for public information, and the other was for the Secretary of State's eyes alone. Not only had he suffered a crushing defeat at Bennington, but he finally realized that it was becoming abundantly clear, as early as August 20th and probably even before, that General William Howe would not be moving his forces up the Hudson as planned; joining forces with him and St. Leger at Albany seemed improbable, if not impossible.

Burgoyne's letter intended as his official account of the Bennington catastrophe, was an unconvincing attempt to brush over the unpleasant facts. He reported that Baum and von Breymann had fought gallantly, but the former, however, had placed too much faith in the protestations of the Loyalists. Burgoyne did not wish to place blame on anyone because they had all fought so valiantly, but he did regret that "four pieces of cannon" had been lost. He admitted that about 596 men had been killed or taken prisoner, and that 26 officers had fallen into enemy hands. He added also that "men who were dispersed in the woods drop in daily." In closing his first letter, Burgoyne concluded that "a bridge of boats have been thrown across the river opposite Saratoga," and he added that "nothing within my scale of talent shall be left unattempted to fulfill his Majesty's orders."

His second letter, which was for Lord Germain's eyes only, related a somewhat dissimilar story. Burgoyne initially went out of his way to explain why he had planned and approved the Bennington campaign; it was his desperate need for horses and supplies. He also explained in detail why he had selected German rather than British troops. He severely criticized von Breymann for his slow movement; "Could General von Breymann have marched at the rate of two miles an hour during any given twelve hours out of the two and thirty, success would probably have ensued, misfortune would certainly have been avoided." Burgoyne was certain that the Prime Minister would make this clear to King Charles III.

Burgoyne realized that this was a staggering blow to his goal of defeating the Americans. The substantial losses sustained, one-seventh of the army, during the Bennington campaign not only defeated its purpose of capturing much needed horses, munitions, cannon, and other supplies for his troops, but Burgoyne's combat troops had been reduced to barely 4,500.

There were some thoughts which he had not shared with his officers, not even with his unpowdered bedmate. He chose to keep these concerns to himself and his bottle of champagne. The few reports which had been drifting back to him from St. Leger had not been encouraging. He secretly believed that Johnson's optimistic prediction about the number of Tories in the Mohawk Valley were very grossly exaggerated. Far from believing Johnson, Burgoyne had grave doubts about the Loyalists serving within his own force; about 400 of them only could be relied upon, he thought to himself as he poured another glass of champagne. He decided that Germain needed to know his true evaluation of the British situation in the upper New York area; he penned:

> *"the rest are trimmers, merely actuated by interest. The great bulk of the country is undoubtedly with the Congress, in principle and in zeal; and their measures are executed with a secrecy and dispatch that are not to be equalled.*
>
> *The Hampshire Grants in particular now abounds in the most active and most rebellious race of the continent, and hangs like a gathering storm on my left.*
>
> *Another most embarrassing circumstance is the want of communication with Sir William Howe; of the messengers I have sent, I know of two being hanged, and am ignorant whether any of the rest arrived. The same fate has probably attended those dispatched by Sir William Howe, for only one letter is come to hand, informing me that his intention is for Pennsylvania; that Washington has detached Sullivan, with 1,500 men to Albany; that Putnam is in the Highlands, with 4,000 men. That after my arrival at Albany, the movement of the enemy must guide mine; but that he wished the enemy might be driven out of the province before any operation took place against Connecticut; that Sir Henry Clinton remained in command in the neighborhood of New York, and would act as occurrences might direct.*

Burgoyne was trying desperately to maintain his optimistic attitude. Many thoughts crowded his mind as he sipped more of the sparkling, he had never envisioned that he would be required to advance through such difficult country, to confront such fierce enemy resistance without Howe's assistance. Nor had he ever contemplated being required to garrison Fort Ticonderoga, but obviously, it could not be left defenseless. He fought his despondency, to no avail. He ended his letter to Germain:

> *Wherever the king's forces point, militia to the amount of three or four thousand assemble in twenty-four hours; they bring with them their subsistence, etc., and the alarm over, they return to their farms.*
>
> *Should I succeed in forcing my way to Albany and find that country in a state to subsist my army, I shall think no more of retreat, but at the worst fortify there and await Sir W. Howe's operations.*

He reflected on an old saying he had heard years ago, "when one shoe drops, sooner or later the other one drops." He wondered when the next shoe would drop and whom it would affect. It could be Howe, St. Leger, or even himself.

When the news of Bennington reached London, Horace Walpole recorded: "General Burgoyne has had bad sport in the woods." George Washington's comment was less sarcastic, but more astute. "Now," Washington wrote on August 22nd, "let all New England turn out and crush Burgoyne."

⧗

Preacher Stouffer and his wife, Red Bird, had arrived at the Heidleberg Tavern at ten o'clock, an hour before New Palatine's church service was scheduled to begin; they had just ridden in from Fort Dayton.

He was dressed, as usual, in his homespun dark suit coat and matching pants with his well-worn leather boots touching his knee caps; all of his outer garments retained much of the forest-road's dust. Johan Stouffer, usually, traveled the church circuit alone, but this morning was special; he wanted his lady with him to share their good news with their neighbors and friends.

Red Bird, on the other hand, had a trim, slight figure for a woman about five years older than her husband's near forty years. In addition, she was almost the complete antithesis of Sir William Johnson's Mohawk wife and Chief Joseph Brant's sister, Molly, who chose to dress like the English. Red Bird, in her petite body and deer leather dress and moccasins, chose to wear her Mohawk identity with pride and to model her life after Kateri Tekakwitha. Another Mohawk and a candidate for sainthood, Kateri in 1677 had become the first Indian nun. So great was Kateri Tekakwitha's piety, it is said, that when she died a miracle occurred; smallpox scars which had disfigured her face since childhood abruptly disappeared. Whenever the Stouffers traveled together, the Palatine preacher's personality always seemed to sparkle.

They found Martha Butler, the tavern's blonde, buxom proprietor, and her handyman, the tavern's best non-paying customer, Harry Hunter, just finishing up cleaning and rearranging the tavern's chairs and benches to accommodate the church's congregation.

Abruptly, Harry disappeared out the back door into the neighboring woods to worship his own personal god who had created the tall trees, his tabernacle. Harry knew that he must sleep off the excess liquor he had consumed during the course of his work in the tavern. This morning, however, he had a few extra duties Martha had assigned before he could retreat to the woods.

Harry Hunter, too, was an interesting individual. He had continually rejected Martha Butler's and Preacher Stouffer's invitations to join in the church services. One service, however, which he had unconsciously attended, was still relatively clear in his mind. After an exhausting Saturday night of working and drinking, he had chosen a tavern table under which to sleep; he had forgotten that the next day was Sunday. During the service, he had inadvertently raised his head and hit it on the bottom of the table. His disturbance raised such a commotion; distracting Preacher Stouffer and the congregation. Harry also remembered rising, tipping his tricorn hat to Stouffer, and telling him, "Continue, Sir, with the reading of the Scripture. I was just beginning to enjoy it, but I've gotta go outside and piss." He even remembered the sermon was based on King David's Twenty-third Psalm, it said something about the Lord is my shepherd. "Hell," he decided, "I don't need this stuff, I don't raise sheep."

Martha and the Stouffers watched Harry slip out of the tavern, and hoped that he remembered his extra assignments. Stouffer, during a lull in the activity proudly announced the good news about Burgoyne's defeat at Hessian Hill near Bennington. This information had arrived at Fort Dayton just before he and Red Bird had left the fort for New Palatine. "But as you know, Martha" he said, "we have other good news which we plan to share with our congregation."

Before Preacher Stouffer could collect his thoughts, the widow Butler declared, "This news deserves a celebration," as she placed three wine glasses on the bar and poured red wine into each. Preacher Stouffer rubbed his beard, and hesitated, thinking that drinking the fruit of the vine was not the most appropriate thing to do just before commencing the church service. After reconsidering, however, "Let's bless this wine," he suggested, "our good news deserves the Lord's blessing."

Soon the residents of New Palatine and the surrounding area started straggling into the tavern, others preferred to stay outside and enjoy the crisp, cool air of the late summer morning. Some parishioners still showed evidence of their participation at Oriskany with their crutches, bandages, and missing family members. It was evident that the congregation was considerably smaller than it had been two weeks ago, because a number of militia volunteers from the hamlet were missing. When Martha Butler began to ring the cow bell to call them to worship, the people meandered into the rustic tavern, prepared to listen to their preacher. Their faces were familiar; among them were the Swartzs, Perrys, Swackhammers, Raabs, Muellers, and with the Heindricks was Helena Kerchner and a petite, frail woman with a dark shawl covering her face.

As usual, Preacher Stouffer greeted the worshippers after most had found seats with, "A hearty good morning to you," he smiled, "I have two pieces of good news to share with you this morning."

Even though he held his well worn, leather-bound Bible, today he chose to ignore the book that he knew like the palm of his hand. Standing on the hearth of the tavern's huge, stone fireplace, he cleared his throat, waited, then began, "My first good news is for all the patriots in the colonies. Just before Red Bird and I left Fort Dayton this morning to come here, we learned from the post's commander that General Johnny Burgoyne's German and Tory troops were soundly defeated at Hessian Hill near Bennington, Vermont. From what we have heard so far, this Bennington battle was a complete victory for the New England militiamen under the command of Brigadier General John Stark. Although poorly trained and equipped, Stark's troops defeated at least 1,000 well-experienced and well-equipped German mercenaries, while our forces suffered very few losses. The Germans had 207 killed and 389 taken prisoners; among them were 107 Loyalists. The battle lasted only two hours, but during those hundred and twenty minutes, men on both sides, fought bravely. Too much honor cannot be given to the brave officers and soldiers for their gallantry."

He lowered his head, folding his hands in prayer, and added, "Bless our enemies, for they, too, believe that their cause is right and just."

He raised his eyes toward his congregation again. He saw that some exhibited jubilation, others were in a daze, while still others stared at the preacher expecting to hear something more. "This morning's sermon is from the book of St. Luke, chapter fifteen." He stopped, and announced, "No, I have not forgotten about the second good news. This will come very soon." He smiled, and started reading, "This morning's lesson begins with verse 10:"

> And he said, a certain man had two sons:
> And the younger of them said to his father, Father, give me the portion of goods that falleth to me. And he divided unto them his living.
> And not many days after the younger son gathered all together, and took his journey into a far country, and there wasted his substance with riotous living.
> And when he had spent all, there arose a mighty famine in that land; and he began to be in want.

Stouffer's brow was beaded with perspiration, his hands were becoming cold and clammy. Silently he questioned himself, *should I continue reading the entire story, or should I just skip to the end?* He decided to compromise; he jumped down to the middle of verse 20:

> But when he was yet a great way off, his father saw him, and had compassion, and ran, and fell on his neck, and kissed him.
>
> And the son said unto him, Father, I have sinned against heaven, and in thy sight, and am no more worth to be called thy son.
>
> But the father said to his servants, Bring forth the best robe, put it on him; and put a ring on his hand, and shoes for his feet.
>
> And bring hither the fatted calf, and kill it; and let us eat, and be merry.
>
> For this my son was dead, and is alive again; he was lost, and is found. And they began to be merry.

"You have all probably guessed that this is the story of the prodigal son. I'm not going to interpret this scripture reading; I'll leave that up to you. Rather, I'm going to tell you a similar story to which, perhaps, we can relate.

"It seems that in our Mohawk Valley there was a small hamlet of Palatines, Dutch, Irish, Scots, English settlers, and yes, it also had a few Iroquois and black people within its boundaries. After the battles of Concord and Lexington, the settlers started debating which side they were going to support. Some preferred to be loyal to the king, while others chose to fight against him. No matter which side was chosen, only one was going to win. The winning side would win everything; the losing side would lose everything. Which ever side one chose, it was a gamble. It was a choice that was made between themselves, their conscience, and their God."

He laid his Bible on the fireplace's thick wooden mantel, and took a few steps toward the congregation so he could touch them, if he so chose. First he rubbed the beard on his round, full face, and then as he frequently did, folded his hands in prayer and looked up to the tavern's rustic rafters. He lowered his head, and continued, "In this hamlet, there was a family that chose to stay loyal to their king. Eventually, this loyalty required them to leave the Valley and, while they were gone the two political sides fought a bitter battle. During this battle, the man of this loyal family was killed, defending what he believed to be right between himself and the Lord. His family, of course, had gone with him to the north, but after learning of her husband's death, the wife chose to return to her valley home."

He smiled as he walked toward the Heindrick family, Helena Kerchner and the frail woman with the dark shawl over her head. "My friends and neighbors," he smiled, "I want all of you to welcome home our prodigal neighbor and friend, Sarah Kerchner."

With Rebecca Heindrick on one side and Helena Kerchner on the other, Sarah Kerchner very modestly stood, removed her shawl, and smiled at her long missed neighbors. Weeping quietly, she said, "I am so very happy to be home, to be with my daughter, and all my friends. The Heindricks have been so kind to Helena while I've been away, for which I'm very grateful. I hope that you can forgive me for what I have done to you, your families, and to this community." Before she could complete her thoughts, she totally fell apart emotionally, and leaned on the shoulder of her daughter. Everyone knew that Wilhelm Kerchner ruled the roost in his household; his wife and daughter always did what he told them to do, except for the time when Helena ran away from Canada and returned to New Palatine.

Preacher Stouffer tried to regain some semblance of order. "We have heard two wonderful bits of news this morning. In the gospel, St. Luke tells us that the father said *bring hither the fatted calf, and kill it; and let us eat, and be merry.*

"Thanks to our devoted friend, Martha Butler, the Heindricks, Perrys, Swartzs, and many others, we have waiting for us behind the tavern and under the apple trees, that is if Harry Hunter has done what Martha told him to do, tables set for a great thanksgiving to welcome Sarah Kerchner home. As you leave the tavern through the back door, please carry a chair or help to carry a bench with you, so we'll all have something to sit on and enjoy this festive occasion.

"Go in peace and serve the lord," the preacher said as he led the congregation out the back door finding a number of long tables packed with food and decorated with autumn leaves, dried flowers, and weeds. As they all joined hands in prayer, there was not a dry eye in the circle. Even Harry Miller had decided to join the festivities.

❋ 18 ❋

THE OTHER SHOE

SEPTEMBER 1, 1777

———

BEMIS HEIGHTS

On August 27th, General Gates appointed Colonel Daniel Morgan's Rangers to be the army's advance guard as a precautionary measure. He exercised this safeguard assignment because the long-awaited militia from New England had failed to arrive when he had expected it. Five days later, on September 1st, General Arnold returned triumphantly with 1,200 newly recruited volunteers.

For the past seven days under the direction of Colonel Kosciuszko, Walter Heindrick and Benjamin Jefferson had been given other duties in addition to those regularly assigned. They were responsible for drumming and fifing General Gates's routine calls for reveille at daybreak, and tattoo calling the soldiers to return to their tents, remaining there until reveille beating the next morning. The drummer and fife player were required to pitch in and work with the 7,000 regulars and the militia volunteers, constructing earthworks and redoubts, which spread west from the Hudson River more than a mile across a narrow flat area and then a ridge of low hills. The fortifications then turned and ran north for more than a mile to the farmhouse of John Nielson, a Loyalist who was guiding Burgoyne and would scarcely urge him to attack here. Bemis Heights, located three miles north of the Hudson River's confluence with the Mohawk, was the location selected by Arnold and Kosciuszko, and approved by Gates as the site of an engagement with the British that would perhaps be the last.

While they were resting, Walter and Benjamin realized they could see to the north how the works followed the high natural barrier of a

300-foot ravine. Mill Creek was at its bottom and there were thick, tangled woods on either side.

"Just try and imagine," began Benjamin, "if we were the British, how would you attack this site?"

"Personally, I don't know how I'd attack this place," responded the drummerboy, "but you can rest assured that foxy old goat, Burgoyne, will find a way to climb these redoubts"

"I'll place my bet on our friend, Colonel Kosciuszko, instead of Gentleman Johnny," replied Benjamin. "For the past seven days he's been right here with us, always enjoying us and, when we have time, to hear our music. His know-how and his fighting spirit really inspire me," declared the black fife player and steadfast buddy of the drummer.

Like most of the other 7,000 men, they were stripped bare down to their waists and soaked with perspiration. Glistening in the fading afternoon's sunlight their bellies reminded them that time was approaching for the evening's meal.

As Walter and Benjamin were looking toward the east, they saw Benjamin's father, Sergeant George Jefferson, approaching with General Arnold and another man they did not recognize. Unlike the general and sergeant who were dressed in the regulars' dark blue coat with buff facing, the stranger was dressed in a long, gray hunting shirt fringed at the sleeves and skirt; his homespun breeches were covered with leather fringed leggings. He was carrying a powder horn slung over each shoulder, and a knife and a small hatchet attached to his belt.

As the three men approached, Walter and Benjamin began to wonder what in the world could be the reason for these gentlemen to talk with a humble drummer and fifer.

George Jefferson chose to break the ice by greeting his son with a hug and his son's friend with a handshake, "It's about time that we call it a day, and head for the chow line. How does that sound to you?" Before the youngsters could respond, the sergeant continued, "But first, I want to introduce you to two of my good friends. You both know General Benedict Arnold."

"Yes, Sir," the youths acknowledged the general with a smart salute and a click of their heels, which was returned in a similar manner but with an added smile.

"My other friend," started the staff sergeant, "is Colonel Daniel Morgan. General Arnold and Colonel Morgan campaigned together in Canada; that's where they first met. The colonel is a legendary hero in his own right, and now, together with his Rangers, has joined our campaign against Burgoyne."

His rugged appearance may have hinted that he was a boastful, crude individual, but Morgan gracefully acknowledged the sergeant's introduction. "Thank you, Sarge, for the compliment for my Rangers and myself, but much of the credit should go to our Kentucky rifles which are vastly superior to those carried by our enemy."

"Colonel Morgan is a very demanding person," added General Arnold. "When Colonel Morgan was initially commissioned by the Continental Congress to raise a group of elite soldiers, only half of those who wanted to join were actually selected; the rest were weeded out by a shooting match to see who was most skilled with a rifle. On his way here to join us, he had started with 500 frontiersmen from Pennsylvania, Maryland, Virginia, and the Jerseys and his two trusted officers, Lieutenant Colonel Richard Butler and Major Morris."

Before the general could continue, Colonel Morgan reminded the two youngsters, "We started out from Virginia to get here. It was a hellava long, tiring march over rotten and rough so-called roads; to make matters worse the summer heat and humidity were totally stifling. When we finally arrived and reported to General Gates, we numbered only 331 tried and tough bastards who can shoot the eye out of a squirrel at one hundred yards with a Kentucky rifle, and I'm not bullshitting you either," he added with a proud grin.

"Morgan's men are extremely able and adapt easily to frontier tactics, in which they excel," exulted Arnold. "They can aim from cover and pick off the disciplined troops who have been trained for volley-firing at close range. Simply speaking, they can fight furiously and accurately and will remind you of our troops at Oriskany.

"This brings us down to the issue of why Colonel Morgan and Sergeant Jefferson and I are here with you," Arnold started his very serious discussion with the drummer and fife player. "Just in the short time you two have been in camp, both of you have made a most positive impression upon our officers and troops with your optimistic attitude and eager willingness to help wherever you can. To make it even plainer, the whole camp, from General Gates on down, have been impressed and pleased with your capabilities. So, when Colonel Morgan came to General Gates and myself telling us he needed a good drummer and fife player, we both thought of you. Before we ventured to discuss this with you, I suggested to General Gates and Colonel Morgan that I discuss the proposed new assignment first with Benjamin's father." Arnold glanced toward the proud black sergeant.

"General Arnold and I did discuss your proposed transfer from his division to Colonel Morgan's," confirmed Benjamin's father. "We both agreed that your regular duties will continue under the colonel, but knowing him, he is likely to give you a variety of other trusted and responsible duties."

"I want to emphasize the word *trusted,*" interrupted the frontiersman. "There will be times when I can't appropriately assist my officers, but I need the task done responsibly and quickly. What I'm looking for is a pair of youngsters who can do the routine drumming and fifing and possibly a hellava lot more."

The colonel stared at the youths as they leaned on their shovels, their hands aching with burst blisters. They, in turn, were staring at each other as if they could not believe what they were hearing. With smiles beaming on their faces and their eyes sparkling like fire flies, together they gave their mutual approval, "It'll be an honor to serve under you, Colonel Morgan,"

"Great, that's settled," announced Arnold, "Gentlemen, I have a chow date with General Gates; I can't keep him waiting. Why don't the four of you go and grab yourselves some grub, find a nice quiet campfire, and arrange for this transfer of duties?"

By the time the four had been served from the long chow line and were settled around a campfire, the sun had disappeared, replaced by a full, autumn moon.

Since it was customary to have six or eight soldiers as mess mates, Morgan invited his trusted officers, Butler and Morris, to join them for the evening meal. They gathered around a cast-iron kettle that hung from two forked-sticks over an open fire. It contained their daily ration of beef and some assorted vegetables received from the local farmers. While they were waiting for their stew to cook, Morgan started to tell the sergeant and his two new recruits how the much *touted* Kentucky rifle compared with the cumbersome method the Europeans still used to load and reload their rifles. "First, the European soldiers had to rap the ramrod with a little mallet in order to thrust home the bullet, which was wrapped with small pieces of greased leather and stored in the cavity of the rifle's stock. With our rifle," Morgan continued, "the rifleman just has to give the ramrod a few light taps to push the bullet against the powder to which the greased patch is adhered, securing the bullet and powder together making it grip the rifling-grooves, and he's ready to shoot again."

"One of the key differences between the two rifles besides the loading aspects," injected Lieutenant Colonel Richard Butler, "is that the Kentucky rifle has rifling-grooves, not a smooth-bore as the European rifle has. With this rifle, our Rangers can accurately hit a target at twice the range of the smooth-bore musket, which at a 100-yard range is only fifty-percent effective."

"What I think makes an enormous difference," added Major Morris, "is the reloading speed of our rifle. It's twice as fast as the time required to load a conventional rifle."

Wanting to make the meal more pleasant, rather than all business, Morris announced, "I'm starved. Let's grab our pans, scoop out our stew, and get eating before its time to beddown."

As the six waited their turn at the pot, Walter whispered to Benjamin, "Can you believe that General Arnold has assigned us to work with Colonel Morgan and his Rangers?"

"I'll tell you; it is very hard for me to believe," confided Benjamin.

After the six returned to their resting place, Benjamin's father asked, "Walter and Benjamin, how do you feel about your new assignment?"

"Great!" declared Walter, "but I don't know what you expect us to do in addition to our drumming and fifing."

"You'll be working directly with Sergeant Jefferson, who will be reporting to Lieutenant Colonel Butler," responded the colonel with the fringed leggings and jacket. "To put it bluntly, we would not have asked for you if we didn't believe that you are reliable and can do the work. I'm a tough bastard," he stopped a moment to let that statement settle, then added, "but I'm a fair bastard."

"I'll tell you how tough Morgan is," announced Butler. The startled group, including Morgan, gave Butler their complete attention. "When he was about twenty-years-old, he volunteered for service during the early days of the French and Indian War. He was assigned to General Braddock's army as a civilian wagondriver."

Before Butler could go on, Morgan interrupted, "You're aren't going to tell that damn story again, are you?"

"Hell, yes!" responded Morgan's second-in-command, "These young men have to know the kind of character they are working with." Butler continued, "He got himself in trouble; I'm not quite clear what he did. But, anyway, a British officer struck Morgan with his sword, and quicker than a rattler can strike, Morgan struck the officer back. Now remember, during those years civilians came under military law. Our friend here," he stopped a moment and smiled at his Virginian friend, "was sentenced to 500 lashes with a cat-o'-nine tails. It was a miracle he survived. He not only survived, but within two years he rose to a commissioned rank.

"In 1774 he joined the rebels in their cause against the British."

"I was pissed-off at the bloody British after the way they treated me when I was severely wounded," asserted the former farmer, noted gambler, and heavy drinker.

Butler continued, "After he had recruited about 96 frontiersmen who met his standards, they marched at the average rate of twenty-eight and one-half miles a day for some 600 miles to help relieve Boston. That's when they became known as Morgan's Rangers. After Boston, he and the Rangers joined General Arnold's to march to Quebec. There he was captured by the Redcoats, who tried to bribe him to turncoat and join them as a colonel."

"I wouldn't trust the bloody bastards as far as I could throw a Virginia mule," Morgan added.

"Naturally, he refused the British offer," proceeded Butler. "I guess the Redcoats were so frustrated with the likes of him, that they finally exchanged him with us Yanks. That's when General Washington commissioned him colonel of the riflemen. Now you've learned how tough a bastard is our beloved colonel!"

"Here's to our colonel!" declared Sergeant Jefferson as he raised his tin cup of lukewarm coffee. While the others followed suit, the modest colonel announced, "Thanks, gentlemen. It' time to bed-down. Sleep well. Tomorrow's a big day."

At Fort Edward, Burgoyne was not totally disillusioned. "I still believe that the march to Bennington was worth the hazard," he told the Secretary of State and added, "those bloody rebels did succeed in driving away cattle and removing corn that we had collected. Honestly, I believe that this misfortune could have been avoided had von Breymann marched at the rate of only two miles an hour during any given twelve hours out of two and thirty.

"Another thing," he complained to the Secretary, "I don't under-stand why we have not heard from General Howe; we sent two mes-sengers to him almost a week ago." Burgoyne would never hear from these messengers; they had been caught and hanged, probably the same fate that had befallen the messengers from Howe, from whom Burgoyne had received only one letter explaining that Howe was headed for Philadelphia.

Burgoyne experienced other disappointments. "Can you believe it?" he asked von Riedesel, "The Tories from whom we had expected substantial assistance, are reluctant to join our forces; the Indians, headed by St. Luc who escaped from Bennington, have declared their intention to go home, because they must gather their harvest.

"Just another lame-ass excuse for not wanting to fight," he added.

"I don't know what their excuse is for not wanting to fight with us as our allies but, I believe," declared the German general, "that the loss of the Sioux, Sacks, Foxes, Menominees, Winnebagos, Ottawas, and the Chippewas is very serious. We have used them very success-fully as guards at the outpost; the rebels hardly dare come near them, knowing full well that the wild men are very cunning and their eyes and ears are very acute."

Just then a group of Mohawks with their families, their villages having been laid waste by the enemy, entered the tent. These Mohawks presented to Burgoyne four scalps taken from rebels they had killed in a skirmish along the road from Fort Stanwix. Later that day, August 28th, another party led by a chief reached Fort Edward.

They had come from Oswego, traveling over one hundred miles through the wilderness, and had retreated with St. Leger.

The chief asked for the head person, the commander; he was escorted to Burgoyne. He advanced, holding out his tomahawk, which was nothing more than a small hatchet. It had either a spike or a cup for tobacco affixed opposite to the part that is intended for cutting. Tomahawks were designed for cutting and smoking; this time, the chief extended his tomahawk for the smoking of the peace pipe. Burgoyne coolly welcomed the chief, wondering why he had come to the fort and asked explicitly for him.

"I bring you ill information about your friend," paused the chief for what seemed like an hour to the general; then completed the sentence, "about General St. Leger. General, Sir," he continued, "General St. Leger was attacked by a General Herkimer near a small Indian village called Oriska. After wounding the rebel's general, St. Leger's troops were run off by a General Benedict Arnold; Indians call him the *Dark Eagle.* The last I saw, General St. Leger and most of his men were in a boat headed for Canada."

Burgoyne thought, *well the second shoe that I had anticipated would drop, has finally done so.* "Chief, I am very grateful for the news of General St. Leger but you know that I do not like it."

The chief offered Burgoyne his peace pipe, and the two entered Burgoyne's headquarters. While the chief packed tobacco and lit the pipe, Burgoyne poured two glasses of sparkling wine with which they toasted each other. They spent the balance of the afternoon toasting, and trying to forget their problems. Regretfully, Burgoyne admitted to himself that he could no longer expect any assistance from St. Leger. In fact, he decided to sever all types of communication with Canada. He knew that he could not remain stationary and appreciated that his troops, for the most part, maintained a relatively high morale. Yet, there were an increasing number of desertions, and the officers had proved reluctant to reduce their luggage as ordered. This was in direct opposition to his adjutant-general Major Kingston's orders; forbidding the use of horses and carts for private purposes. Officers were threatened with being cashiered with the utmost disgrace and, in the case of soldiers, court-martialed for theft.

He knew that it was not a good example to keep thirty carts for his personal supplies of wines, food stuffs, and other related *luxuries*. But, he was the commander of this expedition; therefore, he was privileged.

He had, however, received some good news this day. He learned that on September 3rd, 300 recruits from Canada were arriving, increasing the army to a total of 5,500 men. He had mounted the eighty remaining German dragoons and added 100 men to Fraser's marksmen to replace the Indians and to help prevent surprise attacks by American patrols, which were becoming bolder as the danger from his Indian warriors lessened.

His internal time machine told Burgoyne that it was time to meet his unpowdered mistress. But, before he could partake of this pleasure period of rest and relaxation, he had one other task that needed to be completed.

He dashed off a letter to General Gates, carried by Doctor Wood under a truce flag, denouncing the Yankees treatment of wounded prisoners, and complaining that his Tories had been refused quarter when they offered to surrender.

"There, this letter states the situation very clearly to the Yankee general," declared the frustrated Burgoyne. "Now, down to more important business." He handed the letter to Doctor Wood, excused him, looked admiringly upon his brown skinned, unpowdered companion as she presented him with a chilled bottle of champagne to open. He always looked forward to this time of day, just the two of them, except for his personal aide and manservant, who stood ready at his beck and call and guarded his privacy.

The other shoe had dropped.

❋{ 19 }❋

PREPAREDNESS

SEPTEMBER 2, 1777

THIRTEEN MILES SOUTH OF STILLWATER, NEW YORK

The late afternoon sun was beginning to descend behind the foothills of the Adirondack Mountains, its golden rays accentuating the array of fall colors. There was a slight chill in the late summer air. As General Arnold approached General Gates's field headquarters, he saw two staff escorting a stout, middle-aged man dressed in a dark, homespun suit, white shirt, and black hat customarily worn by a Quaker; they were headed toward the staff officers' tent. Arnold entered headquarters and found General Gates seated at his field desk reading some kind of document.

"Good afternoon, General," greeted Arnold. Gates, obviously upset, glanced up from his reading.

"You appear to be troubled, Sir," observed Arnold. "Is there anything I can do?"

"You may have seen a couple of our staff officers escorting Burgoyne's Tory messenger. That little, short *twit*, with the name of Doctor Wood, is our redcoat *friend* Gentleman Johnny's courier, Burgoyne needs someone to help save his ass. Doctor Wood," Gates sneered, "entered our camp under a flag of truce," his face becoming redder with each word he uttered. "Johnny had some hellava nerve to send us a damn Tory to do his dirty work!"

"Is that Burgoyne's message you're reading?"

"It is! A message should tell the reader or listener something," asserted Gates, "but all he is giving me are a lot of allegations. This letter is good only to serve as evidence when Johnny tells Lord

Germain why he lost the Battle at Bennington, and to prepare his Prime Minister for future defeats." Gates stopped a moment to quickly scan the letter, and apparently found what he wanted to read to Arnold. He began, "Listen to this; our friend, Burgoyne, objects to the way we treated his wounded prisoners. That's one thing; another is he claims we refused quarters to his Tories when they wanted to surrender. I don't know where the hell he gets his information, probably from some other lobsterback, twit like Doctor Wood."

Gates knew how the British military operated; he momentarily relaxed and briefly reviewed his experience in the British army. He could think like an Englishman. He was the son of a minor English government functionary, his mother having been housekeeper to the Duke of Leeds. In 1754 he was able to purchase a captaincy in an independent company, the ranks of which were mainly recruited from Americans. When the French and Indian War (the Seven Years' War) ended in 1762, he held the rank of major. In 1775, when he had rallied to the colonists' side, he was warmly welcomed by Washington who knew his capabilities as a staff officer. He promoted Gates to brigadier general and assigned him to his own headquarters at Cambridge. Even though General Schuyler's steadfastness of purpose and scorched-earth policy had slowed Burgoyne's advance from Ticonderoga, Washington believed in Gates's superb administrative skills.

"Is there anything I can do to help before you go and check on the 1,200 recruits I brought in from the Mohawk Valley yesterday," asked Arnold.

"I appreciate your offer," responded Gates. "All either of us needs right now is time; you take care of the recruits, and I'll write a response to Burgoyne. Good luck in your chores," Gates concluded with a pleasant smile.

"Same to you, Sir," replied Arnold, "Have a productive and happy evening."

Gates placed a clean piece of parchment before him, dipped his quill in the ink, and began his reply to Burgoyne. He began by calling Burgoyne's attention to the horrible cruelties committed by his Indians:

that the famous Lieutenant General Burgoyne, in whom the fine gentleman is united with the soldier and the scholar, should hire the savages of America to scalp Europeans and the descendants of Europeans, nay, more, that he should pay a price for every scalp so barbarously taken, is more than will be believed in England, until authenticated facts shall in every gazette convince mankind of the truth of this horrid tale.

Then he called specific attention to the scalping of Jane McCrea, whom he described as:

a country girl, of honest family in circumstances of mediocrity, without either beauty or accomplishments, who had been killed in a dispute as to the right of property in the person of the captive.

He added a closing statement and was signing his name just as Major General Benjamin Lincoln and Colonel James Wilkinson walked in. The two candles on each end of Gates's desk were burned almost to their holders, good for another half hour. He looked up and saw the two officers staring at him. "Don't just stand there, gentlemen," said the startled general who had been deep in concentration. "I've got something to read to you, then I'd like to hear your comments." After he had given the officers a briefing on the background of the letter he had just composed, be began reading.

The officers sat in the two chairs in front of the desk, they had worked with Gates previously. They knew that he was an unimaginative and cautious commander, with a warm personality; his nickname, "Granny," explained much about him. He was careful with the lives of his soldiers, devoting much of his excellent administrative ability to the improvement of their living conditions. A professional soldier, Gates knew the value of discipline, but he did not make the mistake of underrating the American militia simply because they lacked the discipline of the British Army.

When Gates finished reading, Lincoln and Wilkinson stared at each other in amazement. "Well, gentlemen, what do you think of the letter?"

Major General Lincoln was the first to answer his commander, "Don't you think it sounds a little too personal?" Colonel Wilkinson watching the eye-play between the two officers expected anything to happen.

"My God, I don't believe either of you can *mend* it." He quickly signed his name, handed it to Colonel Wilkinson, and told him to give the letter personally to Doctor Wood, who had been allowed to attend the wounded British and Tory soldiers.

Five days later, on September 8th, Gates moved his army from the mouth of the Mohawk River, marching them thirteen miles to Stillwater. Their new location had been examined for possible entrenchment by Colonel Kosciusko who had determined that the land was untenable.

⏳

Almost immediately after the battles at Concord and Lexington, Wilhelm Kerchner's attitude toward the inhabitants of New Palatine changed slowly but dramatically, toward the sympathizers who wanted their freedom from King George III. His attitude toward the newly arrived settlers, *foreigners* as he called them; expressing to them they did not appreciate all the benefits the king had given them. "You have to have authority, the King is our authority, and we must respect him," was his theme and he usually quickly added, "you can't trust those damn foreigners; they'll take our jobs and all our land."

In turn, New Palatine's residents' attitude toward the Kerchners changed; most could not tolerate Wilhelm's diatribe, while they were extremely sympathetic toward his wife and daughter.

First of all, most did not understand how the little wife could endure her marriage to Wilhelm; none could imagine what life in their home must be. Second, they understood, now, why Helena had taken up residency with the Heindricks after her return from Canada.

Over a period of months, Wilhelm went from quietly complaining about lack of respect for the king, and his resentment toward the foreigners. Gradually, he became more vocal until his neighbors would walk to the opposite side of the road whenever they saw him approaching. Unfortunately, his wife Sarah and fifteen-year-old daughter Helena were feeling the hamlet's resentment too, even if none was ever directed toward them.

Kerchner was a shrewd, clever person. He owned the hamlet's only general store. He hired Harvey Perry as his assistant manager, and Harvey's wife, Hazel, as bookkeeper. He forced his own wife and daughter to serve as clerks, yet they enjoyed their time in the store because it was an escape from his authoritarian rule. Together these four individuals not only contributed their talents, but their pleasing and considerate personalities, as well. They made it a joy for customers to shop. Wilhelm's best contribution to the running of the store was to stay as far away as possible. The shop sold everything; canned goods, bolts of cloth, sewing materials, animal feed, farm supplies, and other items that customers might desire. "Anything which can turn a profit," was Wilhelm's motto.

Everything literally exploded during a July church service in the Heidelberg Tavern after General Herkimer had directed all men, 16 to 60 years of age, to join the Tryon County Militia. Kerchner announced to the congregation that he and his family were going to Canada, immediately, to fight with the British and the Tories.

Before the battle at Oriskany, Helena escaped from Canada, had to New Palatine, and moved in with Walter Heindrick's family. During the battle, Wilhelm was killed by his former assistant manger, Harvey Perry. After the battle, Helena asked the Perrys to continue managing the store. About two weeks after the battle, Sarah Kerchner secretly returned to New Palatine only to be discovered by Karl Heindrick and Harvey. For a few weeks Mrs. Kerchner lived with the Heindricks until she and Helena returned to their home. Gradually, Sarah began working with the Perrys in the general store while Helena continued helping Rebecca Heindrick with her Limburger cheese business. No matter how exhausted she was, each night Helena would faithfully write a letter to Walter, relating the news of the community and telling him how much she missed his company and his smiling face.

The residents of New Palatine meanwhile, went out of their way to welcome Mrs. Kerchner back home. They knew how authoritarian Wilhelm had been and how he behaved regarding the war; most knew that he also exercised his inflexible rule within his family. They would whisper among themselves that Mrs. Kerchner and Helena had finally earned what all the rebels were still fighting for—*their freedom!*

In addition to their regular drumming and fifing duties, Walter Heindrick and Benjamin Jefferson continued to assist in digging a line of trenches on the steep and thickly-wooded bluff known as Bemis Heights.

"I heard one officer tell another," started Benjamin, "that General Gates asked General Stark to move his men down the Hudson river to join us here, but he refused. Stark's excuse was that he only had 800 effective soldiers and that the task was too hard for him under the present circumstances."

"I wonder what he meant by his circumstances," asked Walter.

"Well, I guess he meant that all of Burgoyne's army lay on his side of the river, figuring that Gates would have his troops go and attack Burgoyne with his brigade. Besides," Benjamin continued, "I hear Stark complained that his troops were reduced to 700 by measles and he did not have sufficient transport for them."

"Maybe," suggested Walter, "General Stark does not want to tarnish the glory he acquired at the Battle of Bennington."

"Yeah, can you imagine Burgoyne whipping-up Stark?" asked Benjamin.

"Everything's possible in love and war," responded Walter.

"Talking about love and war, have you heard from your girlfriend lately?" quizzed Benjamin.

"She's been more faithful in writing than I have," confessed Walter, "but I'm sure she knows how much I miss her. While we're talking about girlfriends, Benjamin, you have never once mentioned anything about a girlfriend or friends."

Benjamin hesitated in responding to Walter's question, then smiling he said, "I guess my real girlfriend is my mother; she's a real friend of mine. Oh, not that my father is not my friend, but he spends so much time at work."

"Well, couldn't you help your father in his work?" quizzed Walter.

"Yes," again hesitating and somewhat embarrassed, he continued, "whenever I can, I enjoy helping my mother with her baking. You see, to earn extra money, Mom has a bake shop in our home. She's the greatest baker in all of Albany! Someday I plan to have my own bake shop, and like Mom," he said proudly, "I'll be the best baker in Albany."

"That doesn't mean you can't have a girlfriend," declared Walter.

"Oh, that will come with time," Benjamin shirked off Walter's comment, "Now we have to help get this war over with."

"From what one of General Morgan's officers told me, we've got about 7,000 troops," said Walter changing the subject, "General Gates believes Burgoyne must either advance and attack us very soon, or retreat to Fort Ticonderoga before the winter snows and frost cut him off from Canada. The same officer also told me that Burgoyne left strong detachments to protect his supply line."

"According to my informant," Walter continued, "Fort Ticonderoga is very weakly held and most of the Indians have deserted the British there, making it easier for our spies to gather more precise and accurate information about the enemy's strength and intentions."

"I heard a report from one of Colonel Warner's sergeants, who had escaped from Fort Ti," added Benjamin, "that confirmed that most of the Indians have deserted."

"You remember, Walter, we saw Colonel Wilkinson set out with a reconnaissance party on September 12th. When they returned, they brought with them several prisoners, who reported that Burgoyne had abandoned his communications with Canada; he intends to pursue his march to Albany."

"I can't imagine why he would want to cut off all his communications and supplies with Canada, can you, Benjamin?"

"The only reason I can think of is that he cannot afford to wait. Remember, winter's snow comes much sooner and heavier up in Canada."

"It certainly comes quick and heavy enough down here in New York," added Walter. "I'm not looking forward to being in the battlefield trenches."

"Burgoyne probably feels the same way about winter as we do," Benjamin added standing up when he saw Colonel Morgan approaching them in his deerskin uniform, his coonskin hat's tail waving with each stride.

"Walter and Benjamin, I really appreciate the way you two have pulled double duty with your assistance on redoubling our fortifications, as well as keeping up with your regularly assigned drum and fife duties. I think you'll be pleased to learn that all of our extra work has not been in vain. With the addition of the militiamen who recently joined us, and the great number of Burgoyne's Indians still deserting him, we believe we have finally achieved superiority over the British. Plus, our surveillance informs us that Gentleman Johnny and his troops can not make a move without our knowledge nor a sound beyond his guards with safety."

"It sounds as if the strength of our armies is now completely reversed from what it was a couple of months ago," commented Walter.

"That's the way it appears to be, lads," agreed the rugged frontiersman. "Tomorrow, immediately after reveille, both of you report directly to my tent, and I will find something else for you to do besides playing music," he said as he smiled, gave them an awkward salute, and fondly remembered singing around the campfire before bedding down; Benjamin played the wooden fife he had recently made, and Walter accompanied him on the drum, as they lead the soldiers in their favorite folk songs. Frequently, Walter substituted two small pine branches in place of his drumsticks. He had discovered that using the pine branches as brushes made the drum sound better while the men were singing.

Secretly, Morgan envied the youths and their carefree, yet responsible attitude. With his hand he wagged the coontail on the back of his cap in farewell to the boys and sauntered toward General Gates's headquarters tent where he and his staff were busily bringing order into the army, checking and rechecking their defenses, and finalizing their field strategy.

⧗

The British also were putting the finishing touches on their strategy for their own battle plans. Burgoyne and his troops were busy accumulating the supplies needed to feed the troops and animals until they reached Albany. This activity took most of the latter part of August and on into the middle of September. Another detail that continually irritated Burgoyne was the British inability to determine the strength and disposition of the American forces, whereas Gates was being constantly fed a steady stream of information about the British.

Within his own ranks, Burgoyne had a keen observer who did not always agree with the manner in which he conducted the affairs in the army. It all began on August 15th when Baroness Frederika von Riedesel, age thirty-one, arrived at the British headquarters with her 3 daughters ages, five, three, and two, and 2 maids. The Baroness was grateful that Burgoyne had arranged for her to join her husband, Major General Baron Friedrich von Riedesel after a fifteen-month journey from Wolfenbuttel, Germany. The von Riedesel's were a devoted, simple, and straight-forward couple, who did not find Gentleman Johnny's sophisticated and pleasure-loving life style, to their liking. The Baroness was so intrigued with all aspects of Burgoyne's campaign that she soon began to keep a diary. She was a woman of great determination, character, and fortitude who spoke no English when she left Germany. She did not find it easy to adjust herself to the English ways; she was, however, presented to the king and queen by Lord Germain while she waited for a ship to take her, her children, and maids to Canada. The king had kissed her, inquiring kindly of her husband; later she had visited the queen on several occasions. Nevertheless, she found it difficult to accept or ignore Burgoyne's conspicuous pleasure of the *good things in life* and the unimpeded manner in which he consorted with the commissary officer's wife, Fanny. She wrote:

> *We lived in a building called the Red House . . . It was at this place that I ate Bear's flesh for the first time, and found it of capital flavor. We were often put to it to get anything to eat; not withstanding this, however, I was very happy and content, for I was with my children, and beloved by those with whom I was surrounded. There were, if I remember rightly, four or five adjutants staying with us. The evening was spent by the gentlemen in playing cards, and by myself in putting my children to bed.*
>
> *We made only small day's marches, and were very often sick; yet always contented at being allowed to follow. I still had the satisfaction of daily seeing my husband. A great part of my baggage I had sent back, and had kept only a small summer wardrobe. In the*

> *beginning all went well. We cherished the sweet hope of a sure
> victory, and of coming into the promised land; and when we passed
> the Hudson River, and General Burgoyne said, "The British never
> lose ground,"our spirits were greatly exhilarated.*

To some degree General von Riedesel shared Burgoyne's and his wife's optimism and enjoyed regarding their high spirits of certain victory, but he had a lingering concern over the absence of almost any kind of security. It was a familiar scene to see officers of low and high rank frequently within hearing distance of Tories, whose loyalty was often barely skin-deep, but after all, he rationalized, the army was on the move and heading in the right direction.

If Burgoyne had any fears, he gamely kept them to himself. His troops, which he lead across the Hudson River, consisted of 4,646 regulars, of which 2,635 were British and the rest Germans. In addition, there were about 440 Canadians and Tories, and 300 sailors, artillerymen, drivers, and bateaux men together with artillery of 35 guns and 6 mortars. Meanwhile, the number of Indians had dwindled to about 200 since they had journeyed down Lake Champlain three months earlier.

❊{ 20 }❊

THE CRISIS
IS NEAR

EARLY SEPTEMBER MORNING, 1777

OUTSIDE GENERAL GATES'S HEADQUARTERS TENT

It was a typical early September morning along the northern Hudson Valley. The evening's frost had kissed the fading green maple leaves with a blush of rouge, the dense fog was beginning to burn-off, and the sun was helping to create a new day, its rays peeping through the scattered openings in the gloomy, murky sky, reminding all those who cared that it was still up there watching.

Benjamin Jefferson and Walter Heindrick had just finished their routine assignments of sounding reveille, chow call, and the general assembly called by General Gates. After giving his staff officers and their troops his weekly report, General Gates retired to his headquarters. Benjamin and Walter had approximately two hours before they were to report to "Colonel Dan," as they fondly called Colonel Daniel Morgan. Usually, they spent this spare time near General Gates's headquarters just in case the general needed them. Over the past few weeks, they spent this *standby* time whittling and carving a set of small chessmen that could be carried in a knapsack; the chessboard was attached to the bottom of Walter's drum. They fondly remembered their early *get-to-know-each-other* times. After they had learned that they both enjoyed the game of chess, and since there were no chessmen or board available, they constructed a small, inlaid chessboard. Now, they were busily discussing who was going to whittle which color chessmen. Suddenly, Benjamin began to laugh and said, "Hell, Walter, we don't need to discuss this matter any further; you know your color, and I know mine," his chocolate colored face smiling as he slapped Walter on the back.

Walter was a little slow in catching the initial meaning of Benjamin's remark, but then understood. He realized, finally, what Benjamin was talking about when he suggested that Walter carve his chessmen out of white pine, and he would carve his out of black cherry or some other dark wood. Benjamin settled on using the wood of the cedar tree; when it was covered with an oil or bear grease it glistened a dull red. Embarrassed, Walter responded, "I must have been in some dream world; I just was not associating the chessmen with the color of our skins."

Walter needed to change the subject. "I remember my father telling me that when he and your father were about seven or eight years old, they knew they had different skin colors, but they also knew that both were living with my grandfather and your grandmother. So they decided to become brothers, Indian style. Each took his hunting knife, and cut a slash in the palm of his right hand; they then placed their slashed hands together, hugged each other, and licked the blood from their hands. From that time on they considered themselves brothers. They were always together until your grandmother took off with your father."

"I remember my father telling me about his brother, frequently, but he never ever told me his name. Nor did he ever tell me anything about this Indian-style of becoming brothers, but I really like that idea. Let's you and I do it now," suggested Benjamin.

They had become brothers about two weeks before this watch outside General Gates's tent. After the ceremony, Walter remembered one of the reasons he had agreed with Benjamin's father to volunteer for this campaign, his other blood-brother, White Tail, had been killed during the Battle of Oriskany. He didn't believe it was necessary to tell Benjamin that White Tail was killed by his uncle who was one of the Indian leaders fighting with the British. "So now," declared Benjamin, "we are really a mixture. White Tail, a Mohawk Indian with red skin. You, I don't know exactly what you are, but you have some shade of white skin after you've washed your face and hands. Me, I have nice creamy, chocolate color," he smiled.

From then on, they joked with each other about the different colored skins in their brotherhood. Most of the army had accepted seeing the youths together and hearing them call one other brother; however, some would get Walter aside and tell him it was God's will that black people should be servants to white people. When he asked them how they knew this, their response always was, "It's in the Bible." He then asked them to show him where in the Bible, and they never bothered him again.

Just as Benjamin checked Walter's queen he became aware of a rather short, stocky officer was hovering over the chessboard; it was General Benedict Arnold. "One of these days, I'd like to have you lads teach me how to play chess, but right now I have a date with General Gates," smiled Arnold.

"We'd be mighty pleased to teach you, sir," agreed Walter.

"Just tell us when, sir, and we'll be there," agreed Benjamin.

They watched Arnold enter Gates's tent. "I don't know," observed Walter, "General Arnold doesn't seem like his usual cheerful self."

"Well, I do know," replied Benjamin thoughtfully, "that each general has a different view of how a battle should be fought. I overheard General Arnold telling Colonel Dan that General Gates was too conventional. For example, Gates believes that a general's place shouldn't be at the head of his troops but rather at headquarters directing and coordinating the battle. From what I hear, Arnold believes that militarily, the soundest move is a lightening attack on an exposed flank. I don't know much about any of this stuff, I can go only by what I hear other officers and soldiers say. I would think there is some logic to both Gates's and Arnold's strategies."

"There is certainly a major difference in their respective philosophies," declared Walter. "I've heard General Arnold and others tell stories about the battle in Quebec.

"It happened on the night of December 31, 1775. The lightly falling snow had developed into a blizzard. After inspecting his troops and giving them a few of words of encouragement regarding the impending battle, Arnold promptly lead the troops into the driving snowstorm, while Brigadier General Robert Montgomery and his forces followed. As they approached Quebec's Lower Town, a rocket suddenly exploded in the air, followed by two more. Arnold and Montgomery didn't know it, but this was the signal for all the church bells in Quebec to start ringing. It was then that Arnold really displayed his leadership style. Disregarding the ringing bells, he lifted his sword high over his head, pointed it toward the Lower Town, and directed his troops to charge. He knew that his men would have to capture the British cannon before the Americans could advance upon Upper Town. His troops could see the flash of the cannon powder seconds before the explosion blasted out thousands of pieces of flying, jagged metal. Arnold shouted to his men to follow him, then musket fire suddenly poured down on them from all sides. He had almost reached the barricade when he felt a sharp pain in his lower left leg. He thought that he was only slightly wounded, either by shrapnel or something else, but he could go no further. He leaned against a building, and with blood oozing over the top of his boot, yelled to his troops, 'Go on, goddamn it, lads. Follow Morgan and take the town.'"

"I had heard that Arnold was wounded during the Battle of Quebec, but didn't know that Colonel Morgan was with him," declared Benjamin.

"Surgeon Isaac Senter, Arnold's friend, operated on him in a Catholic convent that had been designated as a field hospital. Dr. Senter offered Arnold a stiff jolt of rum and suggested he bite on a musket ball; Arnold refused both. Without any anesthesia, Dr. Senter cut Arnold's left leg between his knee and his ankle and discovered a portion of a bullet lodged there.

"Meanwhile," continued Walter's report of the Battle of Quebec, "Morgan led his men over the barricades and quickly captured a squad of British soldiers. They stormed another barricade, but were hurled back by thunderous musket and cannon fire. Morgan realized at once his only hope of survival was the immediate arrival of Montgomery's forces; with reinforcements, Morgan could storm his way into the Upper Town and victory.

"But Montgomery was not to arrive, he'd been killed. Morgan realized that he and his men were surrounded by a huge body of British troops armed with their dreaded bayonets, and that his men were throwing down their arms in surrender. With his back against a wall and tears of rage streaming from his eyes, Morgan yelled to the British, 'If you want my sword, you'll have to take it from me!'"

Benjamin was in a trance listening to Walter's story.

"Morgan stood his ground. The British threatened to shoot him, while his own troops pleaded with him to throw down his arms instead of his life. 'There'll be more battles,' they told him. As warnings and advice were called to Morgan from many directions, the tall Virginia rifleman sighted a priest in the crowd and called him forward. 'Are you a priest?' The man nodded. 'Then I give my sword to you. But not a one of these bloody cowards shall take it out of my hands.'"

Benjamin's face glowed with pride as Walter reported about Morgan's heroism. "What was Arnold doing all this time?" he inquired.

"Well, General Arnold was constantly receiving reports during his short recovery in the field hospital. Obviously, he was deeply disheartened when he learned that General Montgomery was dead and that the British were assembling their forces to attack the field hospital and bayonet the wounded. But when he finally recovered sufficiently to resume command, Arnold discovered that more than 100 militiamen, whose enlistments were up on January 1st, had returned home leaving him barely 500 men in his command. Then by April 2nd, more men were added to his force; Arnold was commissioned a Brigadier General by Congress, and he turned his command over to General David Wooster, who moved his troops to Montreal. Wooster wrote to General Washington that 'General Arnold has, to his great honor, kept up the blockade with such a handful of men that the story, when told hereafter, will be scarcely credited.'"

"Do you know, Walter," commenced Benjamin thoughtfully, "how lucky we are to be here working directly with General Arnold and Colonel Morgan?" He added, "I've heard some men who were in Quebec with Morgan and Arnold say, 'just throw them into the midst of a battle, and no matter how heavy the odds against them, their determination inevitably radiates enthusiasm and renewed vigor to their tattered troops.'"

"I agree with you, but I've been trying to figure out why Gates is so angry with Arnold," interjected Walter, "and I think I have hit upon it. There's an old adage, *there can only be one queen bee in a hive.* I'll bet he's annoyed because General Arnold has been filling his staff with former aides to Gates's nemesis, General Philip Schuyler. He especially didn't like it when Arnold selected that outspoken friend of Schuyler's, twenty-four-year-old Lieutenant Colonel Richard Varick as his secretary; remember Varick quarreled publicly with Gates.

Walter and Benjamin had lost almost all interest in their chess game; they were fascinated by their leaders' experiences and intrigues.

Suddenly, the doorflap of General Gates's tent flew open; General Arnold came storming out and nearly tripped over Benjamin, Walter, and their chessboard. They later learned from Colonel Dan that Gates had told Arnold the British were moving in three columns toward Freeman's Farm. Apparently, Arnold had expressed a desire to attack their exposed flanks, but Gates flatly refused to discuss the matter and prevented Arnold from galloping off to immediate battle. To make matters worse, Gates demanded that Arnold stay close to his side where he could keep an eagle eye on his hotheaded subordinate. Gates, however, did yield to Arnold's insistence that he send out Morgan's riflemen and several infantry regiments, under the command of Henry Dearborn, to engage Burgoyne's column, which had just arrived at the deserted Freeman log cabin.

Two days later, on September 19, 1777, Morgan and Dearborn discovered British pickets in Freeman's field immediately chased them into the woods. Benjamin and Walter accompanied Colonel Dan, but he had counseled them "to keep your drum and fife in your tent, what we need from you are your running feet and your riding skills to serve as our messengers."

Morgan and Dearborn's men had no sooner entered the woods than they ran into Burgoyne's army, which was what they had hoped. Both armies were quickly engaged, but soon afterwards Dearborn ordered his troops to retreat. Morgan's men scattered until he gave his *wild turkey call.* Hearing this familiar call, the men quickly rallied and reunited the divided command.

Burgoyne's forces were establishing their battle stations in the field, while the Americans were positioning themselves in the woods.

These maneuverings, on and near Freeman's Farm, were the beginning of what was to be known as the first engagement of the two-part Battle of Saratoga.

Benjamin and Walter spent most of that day riding back and forth between Morgan's lines and Gates's headquarters in the little red wooden house atop Bemis Heights. There Arnold was conferring with Gates. The young men would deliver their messages, then promptly return to the battlefront. Once, as Walter approached Gates, he overheard Arnold plead with Gates to let him take charge of the American field forces, but Gates was determined to keep Arnold at his side. Walter reported to Gates, "I've been informed to tell you that the battle is a stalemate, Sir." Overhearing Walter's report, Arnold sprinted to his horse, shouting, "By God, I will soon put an end to this!"

Before Gates could open his mouth, Arnold was in a cloud of dust as he spurred his horse toward the sounds of muskets and cannon. Not having completed his report, Walter sat astride his horse stunned at the turn of events. Before Walter could pull his thoughts together, Gates sent Colonel James Wilkinson, his secretary, after Arnold to bring him back. Then Gates asked Walter to conclude his report and to return immediately to the frontlines. Walter was riding back, when he saw that Wilkinson had succeeded in stopping Arnold. As he rode past the two men, he overheard Arnold reluctantly agree to obey Gates's commands and watched as Arnold furiously turned his horse around and returned to the Bemis Heights camp. Walter was beginning to believe that the conflict between Gates and Arnold was almost as intense as the one developing between the British and the Americans. He hoped, sincerely, that they would not kill each other but he kept his thoughts to himself. However, when Walter returned to Colonel Dan, whose riflemen and Dearborn's infantry were well established on the left wing, he reported what he had seen and heard at headquarters. This troubled Morgan; he trusted Walter and his observations. Now, he did not know for certain whether he was still a part of Arnold's command or should he be reporting directly to Gates. Morgan would not permit personal bias or prejudice to influence what he considered justice.

Two days earlier, on September 16th, Burgoyne's forces had heard the sound of distant drums, forewarning them that the Americans were advancing. Burgoyne, together with Generals Phillips, von Riedesel, and Simon Fraser reconnoitered the area with 2,000 of their troops and 6 cannon. The remainder of their army worked feverishly to repair the bridges destroyed by Americans. Burgoyne's detachment returned about eight o'clock in the evening without having seen the enemy. The army renewed its march the next day. They bivouacked at Swords Farm, unaware that the Americans were only four miles away. From Swords Farm a wagontrack led up the heights to the west and across the plateau which was occupied by the Americans' advance guard. The bridges' destruction made the road ahead impassible, and the army could advance no further until the bridges were repaired. On the afternoon of September 18th, General von Riedesel's scouts sighted several enemy regiments; their banners could be plainly seen. They established that three American regiments were hidden behind the hills, and two more behind the plains' woods. In addition, a warning had been given by a Yankee deserter who had reached the British camp. This report, however, was not delivered in time to prevent a sizable loss to a party of British soldiers who had roamed ahead in search of potatoes.

These soldiers were gathering potatoes in a field when they were surprised by an American scouting party that opened fire, killing and wounding about thirty men. Captain Thomas Anburey in reporting this to General Burgoyne, said "If the Yankees had exercised more caution they could have surrounded and taken the whole party prisoner." He expressed that, "such cruel and unjustifiable conduct can have no good tendency, while it serves greatly to increase hatred, and a thirst for revenge."

Burgoyne agreed with Anburey's analysis of the incident. He went to his desk at once and drafted his condemnation of the affair:

> *The Lieut. Genl. will no longer bear to lose Men, for the pitiful consideration of Potatoes, or Forage. The Life of the Soldier is the property of the King, and since neither Friendly Admonitions, repeated Injunctions, nor Corporal punishment have effect, after what has happened, the Army is now to be informed, and it is not doubted the Commanding Officers will do it solemnly, that the first Soldier caught beyond the Advanced Centennials of the Army, will be instantly Hanged.*

The incident was more than sufficient notice to Burgoyne that the enemy was not far away, and that the Americans' position known as Bemis Heights, occupied a site which dominated the road by the river. Burgoyne knew that he had to immediately learn more about their position and strength, and if possible, turn their left flank. What he would never learn until the fighting was all over, was who was commanding that left flank?

While Burgoyne and his scouts were out blindly searching the area, Gates was seated comfortably, learning from his scouts the activities of the British. He thought to himself, this is how an army's commander-in-chief should conduct a battle not as Arnold believes; he would foolishly have the leader down in the trenches and fields, in hand-to-hand contact with the enemy. Gates believed he had been fortunate when he learned from his reconnaissance on September 14th that Burgoyne intended to march to Albany. He had learned this also from three soldiers Wilkinson had captured from the British 20th Regiment, and the information was confirmed by two German deserters. On September 18th, Gates sent Arnold out to reconnoiter; that night, Colonel Colburn of the Continental army, returned from a lone reconnaissance to report that, by climbing a tree on the eastern bank of the Hudson River, he observed that Burgoyne had struck his tents and was preparing to advance. "The crisis is near," he predicted to Gates. Shortly thereafter, another scouting party, led by Colonel Benjamin Warren of the Massachusetts Militia, found the enemy in too large a number to pick a wrangle with. Gates took these reports to heart and went to bed.

When Arnold returned with Wilkinson to Gates's headquarters, another form of battle inevitably began. The two generals met in an explosion of anger on Gates's part and frustration for Arnold.

"General, what the hell was the idea of sending that devious, wimp Wilkinson after me," demanded Arnold. Hearing this, Wilkinson decided it was time for him to leave. When the general's secretary had gone, Arnold continued.

"General, you know that we can not win the battle sitting up here on top of Bemis Heights. We've got to be down there on the farm with our troops; we must lead them. I know now is the time when we can engage the British in a decisive charge, and win. Timing is every-thing here, Sir."

"Now listen here," demanded Gates, "Get off of your *know-it-all* attitude. I'm still the commanding general, and you're reporting to me. I recall that you didn't do too well up there in Quebec. If you had, Canada would now be American and not British."

One of the guards barged in and reported that he had sighted one of the messengers racing at top speed toward them. Moments later, Benjamin Jefferson reached headquarters. He leaped off his horse, handed the reins to a guard, and burst into the general's headquarters.

"I have been told to report directly to you, General Gates. Morgan's men have had to withdraw, leaving the field in the posses-sion of the British," reported the exhausted messenger with sweat and dust covering his face.

"Very well, private, return to the front immediately," ordered Gates.

On his way back to Colonel Dan, Benjamin saw a rider racing toward Bemis Heights. As the rider approached closer, he recognized Walter. He, too, was traveling at a break-neck speed. As they passed, each waved their blood-brother salute, and wondered what the mes-sage the other was carrying.

After Benjamin had left General Gates's tent, Arnold's fury and resentment continued to churn. He had been carefully fueled by those members of his staff who had served under Schuyler and who hated Gates. Meanwhile, Gates was quietly reviewing all of the anti-Arnold sentiments of Wilkinson and others on his staff who were jealous or resentful of Arnold's reputation and talents. Emotions were approaching the explosion stage.

"I hope you're happy," started Arnold, "sitting on your behind on top of this ridge out of harm's way, while our leaderless troops get their asses wiped. I know damn well, that you delight in keeping me away from our men and the action. You know that if I were down there we would have a victory. You know what, general? I do believe you don't want to win the battles if you can't have all the glory."

Gates sneered nastily and haughtily said, "Well, General Benedict Arnold as far as I know, you resigned your commission to congress and you have no right to demand a command."

"That's an outright lie. It's a pure figment of your imagination," declared the former bookseller, becoming more agitated every minute he stayed in Gates's presence.

"I expect to have your replacement, General Benjamin Lincoln of the Massachusetts Militia, reporting to me any minute," announced Gates.

Arnold thought, "And this is the fat old fart who was the militia commander promoted over me."

"If you don't like the way I am running this war," continued Gates knowing he was deliberately provoking Arnold to physical violence, "you are at liberty to leave any time you wish. This will give you an opportunity to present your case to General Washington and Congress. By the time you're through crying on their shoulders, I will have Burgoyne's own sword, as well as all of his troops' guns, cannon, and bayonets.

"In fact," Gates renewed his harangue, "General Arnold, effective as of this moment, I am detaching Morgan's riflemen and all other regiments from your command. As a general, you're as sterile as a steer calf."

Remarkably, Arnold contained his contempt and hatred for Gates. He knew that he was a better leader and soldier and that he could win a smashing victory against Burgoyne. He realized too, that Gates, who had lobbied and talked his way into this important command, was not about to have the laurels of victory seized by his gifted, impetuous subordinate. Arnold firmly replied, "If you want me out of here so you can claim all the glory, that's fine; I will leave immediately. I shall join General Washington where I know that I will be permitted to use my abilities more usefully than by merely being your lap dog on this rocky ridge, while our men get eaten up by our enemies. I'm sure you will be much more pleased with Lincoln; I understand he's an excellent yes-man, and the ring in his nose will prove to be useful for pulling him around."

Before Gates could rebuke his angry and disheartened officer, Arnold stormed out the door. In a way this exchange had been milder than many of their encounters, which had included charges, counter-charges, and insults; the voices of the men often rose to a screaming pitch, climaxing with Arnold's slamming the door and stalking out to his camp. This time he left half-heartedly fully intending to ride to General Washington's headquarters immediately.

The word of Arnold's departure spread like wildfire throughout the American camp and several officers, led by New Hampshire's General Enoch Poor, no true friend of Arnold's, circulated a petition among the general officers urging Arnold to reconsider his decision and to remain where he could do the American cause the most good. Every officer except General Lincoln and, of course, Gates, signed the petition. Amazingly Arnold did swallow his pride and agreed not to desert the army that so needed his skills and leadership.

Regardless of the signed petition, Gates completely stripped Arnold of his command. Arnold felt like a penned-up, wild dog desperately trying to leave his cage. To make matters worse, he saw lesser officers hurrying and scurrying in and out of Gates's headquarters for strategy meetings. He knew that Burgoyne had taken advantage of the American withdrawal from Freeman's Farm to erect redoubts on the slight elevations functioning as bastions from which the British could move out for a last determined effort to defeat Gates and gain access to the river road running to Albany. He also knew that Burgoyne would make the suicidal march along the river road under the cannon surmounting Bemis Heights. Arnold had concluded, therefore, that a final attack had to be made to rout the British and yearned to be included in the officers' strategy meetings. He was aware that, at times, he could become unduly stubborn and demanding. "But, hell," he thought, " I know how to fight these damn redcoats. I know I can lead our troops, and I know we'd soundly beat them."

❈ 21 ❈

DOWN ON THE
FARM

Neither Gates nor Burgoyne could have envisioned that their eventual encounter—the first of two clashes which collectively would be known as the Battle of Saratoga—on the fifteen acres of farmer Freeman's cleared fields would culminate in the demise of the traditional European style of warfare, and the introduction of the modern American or guerilla type. The only issue each commander knew was the strategy he planned to implement when he felt it was time to engage the other.

Burgoyne, a well-trained and experienced military tactician yet ever the gentleman, planned to stay with his proven successful strategy; its marching ranks and files, inevitably leading to face-to-face clubbing and bayoneting of the foe. Innovative, daring, and courageous, Burgoyne preferred to be not far from the front line of action so as to encourage and lead his troops. This strategy had worked for him in the past; he saw no reason to change.

His opposing commander-in-chief, General Horatio Gates, preferred to maintain his distance from the front lines and to depend upon his courier service to keep him informed as the battle ebbed and flowed, and then direct his troops accordingly. His second-in-command, General Benedict Arnold, on the other hand, believed in direct offensive encounters, and he never hesitated to ride into the fray at the head of his troops. So in this dual command the main difference was in the personality of the leaders. One was overly cautious while the other was, at times, too impetuous. Both were predictably unpredictable.

One thing was for sure; both sides knew that Colonel Colburn of the Continental army was correct: predicting to Gates that *the crisis is near*. The competing generals and Colburn, however, never suspected that this crisis was the first time that medieval and modern methods of warfare would clash. It would take Europeans more than a century to perceive the advantages of guerilla fighting the Americans had learned in their frontier wars against the Indians.

To reach his destination, Burgoyne knew that he would have to defeat Gates and his troops. Gates's forces blocked the only road to Albany; there was no other route except through the impenetrable, forest-clad hills to the west. Missing his Indian scouts who, in the past, had thrown an impregnable screen around his troops, Burgoyne didn't know the American strength or position. The Americans, on the other hand, knew their opponent's every move from their scouts, who in the absence of Indians, swarmed around the British camp, observing it from the tree-tops. Burgoyne was determined, and believed it imperative to probe the American position and hopefully, to turn its left wing and to drive it into the Hudson River. He was realistic enough to understand, indeed to know, that with his numerically inferior force, it was impossible to dislodge the Americans from their strong position on Bemis Heights. He knew, too, for a successful siege he would need at least three times as many men; his powerful train of siege-guns was inadequate to do the job. As it was, the marksmanship of the Yankees decimated the gunners long before the guns were within range of the rebels elevated fortifications. Arnold's scorched-earth policy, which he had experienced in Canada, was still haunting and hurting him; he had too few horses to pull his mammoth artillery and supply train, and not enough grain to feed those he had. Burgoyne estimated he had enough food left for his army for thirty days while winter was just around the corner. It was already cold in the British tents at night. Red was now seen not only in the British uniforms, but in the maple leaves, which were already dropping. Burgoyne knew, too, that he must press on to Albany or return to Quebec. He knew also there were no supplies forthcoming from Carleton in Canada, and no help from Howe in the south. Yet he moved as if he were in no hurry, as if victory was inevitable; perhaps being deceived by the Americans' quickened retreat from Fort Ticonderoga. He admitted that his intelligence was scanty, but he believed it adequate to defeat the Americans. While Burgoyne's staff officers played whist and other card games, and his troops laboriously built a highway from Canada south toward Albany on the east bank of the Hudson, Burgoyne was occupied with his unpowdered lady, Fanny Loescher, wife of his commissary officer. Their torrid love affair was alive and blooming.

Thick fog and rain on the morning of September 19th delayed Burgoyne's advance until 8 o'clock; the British and their allies moved out of camp in three columns; the right wing led by Brigadier General Simon Fraser; the center, of which Burgoyne himself was a part, was led by Brigadier General Alexander Hamilton [not the future U.S. Secretary of the Treasury]; and the left wing was led by Major General Friedrich Adolf von Riedesel, who was accompanied by the second-in-command, Major General William Phillps. Fraser's right wing was comprised of the *elite* of the British troops, the Grenadier Battalion, the Light Infantry Battalion, and the 24th Regiment, numbering in all 900 men. To these had been added Lieutenant Colonel Heindrich von Breymann's advance troops, about 500 men, and all the auxiliaries, consisting of 800 Canadians, and Tories. Four six-pounders and four three-pounders had been allotted to this column that included some of the remaining Indians.

The center column comprised four British regiments, the 9th, 21st, 62nd, and the 20th, totalling 1,100 rank and file, together with the artillerymen in charge of the six-pounders. Von Riedesel's left wing column advanced along the river road, with the three remaining German regiments and Captain Pausch's Hesse-Hanau artillery made up of six six-pounders and two three-pounders. Six companies of the British 47th Regiment and the Hesse-Hanau Regiment remained in camp to guard the baggage, bateaux, and reserve artillery. Excluding von Riedesel's column, which was intended to threaten and to hold down the American's right wing, more than 2,000 soldiers, each supplied with sixty rounds of ammunition, mounted the Heights. The two columns marched through the woods, upon reaching their positions they would advance in parallel on a signal from Burgoyne, who would order the firing of three guns.

Fraser, having the longer distance to travel marched first, making a large circle through the woods, with his objective being to gain an advantageous position to the west of the center column. Meanwhile, the center column followed the wagon-track across the plateau, turning southward where Fraser had continued westward, and after crossing the Great Ravine, again turned westward. About midday, the center column reached a position to the north of the fifteen-acre cleared patch, known as Freeman's Farm; this poor farmer's name was destined to become famous as the owner of the land upon which the battle took place that day. The clearing was on a promontory of ground between the Great Ravine and the north fork of Mill Creek, and it extended three hundred and fifty yards from north to south, sloping from east to west. To give Fraser time to reach his position, the center column halted; an assigned picket advanced to investigate the tiny cabin in the center of the clearing.

The left wing, under von Riedesel's leadership, was following the river road and advanced about two miles, halting to repair three bridges while under gun fire, finally reaching the point where a second wagon-track ran westward over the plateau.

Burgoyne was not aware that his Yankee nemeses, Benedict Arnold and his staff, had ridden north to reconnoiter the British advance. Arnold knew the British position roughly, having continually sent guerrilla parties of Morgan's riflemen to harass British work crews and to snipe at the British officers. Suddenly, Colonel Richard Varick came galloping to Arnold. He took a deep breath, and declared, "We've spotted some Redcoats on a distant hill, Sir."

Astride his black horse, Arnold, with Varick galloped to where the British had been seen. "You're absolutely right, Colonel," agreed Arnold, "They will probably reach us late tomorrow, the 19th." Arnold reined in his horse and returned to camp, disappointing Varick who had hopes of being ordered to attack with another harassment party. Instead, that night, the British camped on high ground less than two miles from the American army.

At nearly eight o'clock in the morning, General Gates first heard Colonel Colburn's memorable quote, "the crisis is near." Colburn had just returned from his lone reconnaissance where he had climbed a tree on the east bank of the river. He noted that Burgoyne's troops had struck the major portion of their tents on the plain near the river, and had already crossed the gully at the gorge of the Great Ravine. They were presently ascending the heights towards the American's left.

Upon receiving this report, the cautious Gates proposed to Arnold, "I think that we must stay right here in this fortification and let the British and their troops try to take Bemis Heights."

The impetuous and tactless Arnold jumped from his chair opposite Gates's desk, "How can you be so complacent and stupid as to say such things? You can't believe that Gentleman Johnny Burgoyne can't find a way up here. You must remember when he out-foxed us at Ticonderoga. Believe me, when it comes to fighting, Burgoyne is no gentleman," declared Arnold. "He's a fighting fool; in fact, I expect that he will personally take command of one of his columns."

"You may be correct," Gates agreed, "but I have confidence in this location as a fortress. You and Kosciuszko selected it, and Kos's ability to make it impregnable is a given. I believe we can operate from this location, and when Burgoyne attacks, our forces can just pick them off like fleas off a . . ."

Arnold did not give Gates an opportunity to complete his thought, "What if it does not work that way? What if the British overrun this fortress? What if Morgan and Dearborn are forced to retreat; where would they go if they had no camp to fall back on?" Before Gates could respond to Arnold's first question, Arnold with his face flushed red asked another question, "And if the British decide to storm our lines, and they successfully break through them, where would our retreating army take refuge?"

Again, Arnold did not give Gates a chance to reply to this projected scenario. "I'll tell you what we'll have!" declared Arnold as he faced his commanding officer, pointing his right index finger at him, "We'll have a rout! All of our efforts and the blood spilled on this site would be in vain; our army is liable to degenerate into an army of malcontents, while the volunteers would probably desert back to their farms."

Stunned, Gates pushed his chair back from the desk, and stood up to face his impetuous and brilliant, a thought he always kept to himself, second-in-command. "I'll tell you what I'll do. You know every well that I don't completely agree with you, but," he admitted, "I do think you have some good logic in your thinking; you have convinced me. You may order Colonel Daniel Morgan and his riflemen, along with Colonel Dearborn's light infantry into the woods in front of Bemis Heights to impede the British advance and to cripple them as much as possible."

Arnold performed the ritual salute to his commanding officer, and was quickly out of headquarter's confinement. He already had Gates's permission for a reconnaissance force. In addition to Morgan's riflemen and Dearborn's light infantry, he sent Benjamin Jefferson with a message to have the rest of his division prepare for immediate readiness to march out to Morgan's support. Meanwhile, Arnold had ordered Walter Heindrick, to deliver a similar message to Dearborn.

Neither Gates nor Arnold could have known, nor would never know, that the battle fought on that day, September 19th, proved conclusively that Arnold had calculated correctly. It is possible that had Gates allowed Arnold to support Morgan more energetically and take personal charge of the attack, the Americans might have gained a decisive victory. As it was, the day was just the first of two engagements; the first day, perhaps of a new history.

That night Walter and Benjamin, together with Benjamin's father, ate a very late supper around a campfire with some of Morgan's riflemen. George Franklin started the conversation, "Colonel Dan had asked me to stay at his side. So I stayed right at his side like a dog on a leash. I guess you could have called me his handyman; I was at his beck and call."

While Sergeant Jefferson was loading and lighting his pipe, Walter and Benjamin, on either side of him, were straining to hear what Ben's father was going to say. All day long the two boys had been riding back and forth between the various front lines and General Gates's headquarters. "When Morgan and his riflemen reached the southern edge of Freeman's meadow, we saw a bunch of British pickets sitting nonchalantly in the high weeds around the farmhouse. Colonel Dan ordered us to shoot just one very specific volley. That volley scattered all of the British guard into the woods on the far side, but all of the officers remained on the field. They were all dead! They couldn't run," he laughed as he looked toward one of the rifleman who seemed anxious to talk.

"We ran like the very wind in our pursuit of the fleeing soldiers," said the rifleman with the right side of his face bandaged. "Everything was going along great. We were popping those Redcoats off like sitting ducks, when all of a sudden we run smack into Gentleman Johnny's soldiers and they opened up on us with volley after volley. I'm telling you guys that Burgoyne is no sonofbitchin' gentleman. He's a fightin' fool! He had us quickly headed back across the clearing into our side of the woods."

"That's when Colonel Dan ordered me to get to General Gates's headquarters as quick as my horse could carry me and to ask for reinforcements." added Benjamin Jefferson. "For a moment, I believed that Colonel Dan thought his whole regiment had been destroyed."

"After you left," recalled Walter, "I truly believe I saw this big, old six-foot-two Virginian cry. He continued, stubbornly, to make his wild turkey call and soon his men were rallied around him."

"Why shouldn't we have come at his turkey call?" asked a bearded warrior with a scar running down the right side of his face and under his chin. Everyone knew that Colonel Dan had saved him from an Indian scalping. "Where he goes, we're right with him."

"I'll second that motion," added another tall, lean, lanky bearded rifleman with a coonskin hat. "There ain't no finer fella than Colonel Dan. I'd follow him to hell and back."

George Jefferson continued his recollections of the day, "When we retreated, we saw Burgoyne march his redcoats into the clearing and line them up by regiments. You can't imagine how impressive, trim, and orderly 3,000 redcoats, with their field artillery, can look. They had taken their battle positions. While our men were somewhat overwhelmed by their display of discipline and force, Colonel Dan and Major Dearborn passed the word to open fire on the red line before them."

"Holy hell! You guys should have seen them buggers run," declared the militiaman with the bandaged face.

"When I arrived at General Gates's headquarters and hand delivered Colonel Dan's message," started Benjamin, "General Gates just stood there, but General Arnold told Gates that this news was justification to order out Learned's and Poor's New Hampshire brigades. I rode along with them, and when we arrived we found that the riflemen had regrouped and were fighting back. Colonel Dan ordered Learned and Poor to take up their position on his left."

"That's when our entire line erupted in a volley toward the silent British line," began Sergeant George Jefferson. "We dropped plenty of Redcoats in the tall grass. They didn't even try to drag along their cannons. They turned and ran for their side of the forest. We ran after them. Our intent was to capture their cannon before they could turn it on us. We did turn their own cannon on them as best as we could, but those foolhardy British grenadiers charged us with their bayonets, driving us back across the field. For nearly four hours, charges surged back and forth until there were nearly 1,000 dead and wounded bodies in the field between the armies.

"As General Arnold ordered out each of our fresh units, seven regiments in all, he extended our battle lines farther into the woods, away from the river and curling uphill and around the British right flank. Some of our scouts reported that as our troops circled up the hill they saw British soldiers leaning on their weapons, apparently totally unaware of what was happening until their brigade was sent into the fray; confined primarily to Freeman's meadows, and . . ."

Before George could continue his explanation, the bandaged warrior inserted, ". . . and while all of us, Yanks and Brits alike, were getting beaten and some even killed, where do you think our gallant commander was?" Before anyone could respond he answered his own question, "I'll tell you where the bloody bastard was, he was up there in his safe fortress nearly two miles away, sittin' on his fat ass. The only contact he had with the front lines was what Walter, Benjamin, and other messengers brought him. What a daring bastard! Hell, you should have seen Arnold out there leading many of our charges and maneuvers. He was constantly exposed to enemy fire, preferring to lead by example more than by orders. I say, let's demand Arnold and

Colonel Dan lead us, and we'll show that pretty boy, Burgoyne, the fastest way back to England."

"I remember," began another weather-beaten, leather coated rifleman, "when Fraser's light infantry suddenly turned and skillfully fell on Arnold's right; Arnold galloped by on his big black horse, named Warren after his old mentor, up and down the line he rode, rallying all of us, shouting, 'Come on, boys. Hurry up, my brave boys!'"

"One of the proudest moments of the day," started Sergeant Jefferson, "was when I was riding along with Arnold leading, our five regiments of troops. He charged the British center, attempting to break through. Next he led a rapid countermarch through the woods on the left, trying again to break Fraser away from Burgoyne. He led us brilliantly and boldly. We are well disciplined, because we respect the man. I'll repeat, most of us would go to hell and back for him.

"As he led us down from the wooded hill, we nearly overran the British, but heavy reinforcements of Hessians stopped us. That's when Arnold ordered Walter to get back to headquarters and ask Gates to send reinforcements."

"Finally, General Arnold decided to go back to headquarters and, personally, asked Gates for more troops," stated Walter, "I was there when General Arnold was urging, entreating, and even begging General Gates for more troops. Gates gave no orders, and only once did he protest; he ordered Arnold to bring Colonel Alexander Scammel's brigade back to protect his headquarters. Arnold finally did persuade Gates to send out Learned's entire brigade from camp, and to hurry around behind the Hessians, but Gates ordered Learned not to let Arnold personally lead the counterattack; he made a point of sending only Learned and his troops. We learned later that Learned's troops got lost in the woods and stumbled into Fraser's British light infantry. When Arnold discovered this misfortune, you should have seen him fume and pace about headquarters. Anxiously, Gates and Arnold went outside and were approached by Colonel Morgan Lewis, Gates's aide. Believing that he had made a masterful decision by dispatching Learned to the field, Gates asked, 'How is the battle going now that Brigadier Learned is on the field?' 'Not well,' reported his aide, 'It's almost a stalemate, nothing decisive.' Throughout the afternoon, Arnold had couriers dispatching regiments, while pressuring Gates to attack, Finally, he could not stand Gates's defensive maneuvers any longer. He shouted, 'By God, I will put an end to it,' and he jumped astride his horse and galloped off toward the firing.

"I overheard Lewis tell Gates," continued Walter, 'You had better order him back. The action is going well. He may, by some rash act, do mischief.' Then General Gates ordered Wilkinson to bring back Arnold. That Wilkinson did! Boy! was Arnold furious, while Wilkinson beamed from ear-to-ear when they arrived back to headquarters; Arnold knew that he had no choice."

"It was a bloody shame we had to retreat into the woods, leaving the battlefield to those obnoxious Redcoats and their Hessian buddies," declared Sergeant Jefferson. "I understand that the British have experienced approximately 620 dead and wounded, while we had about 300 killed and wounded. Just think! All this blood and guts have been spilled on a measly little clearing, on a promontory of ground between the Great Ravine and the north fork of Mill Creek. Hell! That little plot of ground is no bigger than thirteen acres."

At that moment, the silence of the night was broken with faint moans from the wounded being carried back to camp, as the women from both armies stripped the dead. The eerie sounds sent chills up the backs of all who heard them, but both sides were forbidden by their commanders from giving all-out aid to the wounded for fear of touching off another round of fire.

While the American army was preparing for an uneasy sleep, General Gates was at his headquarters writing a long report to Congress, not mentioning that it was Arnold and his division who had stopped the attempted British invasion, merely alluding to 'a detachment of the army.' Meanwhile, Arnold was in his tent fuming and unable to sleep.

Walter, Benjamin, his father, and their campfire buddies were preparing to bed down, when one of them spied three figures approaching their campfire. One was easily over six-feet tall while the other two figures were dwarfed by the taller one. No one had to ask who was approaching, for everyone recognized the erect, deliberate stride of Colonel Dan. This night, the colonel had elected to make the rounds of the changing of the guards, giving each of them a word of encouragement and gratitude with either a hearty handshake or a pat on the shoulder.

After the changing of the guard, a friendly chat, and a bear hug, the three figures disappeared into the darkness.

⧗

Captain E. Wakefield attached to Dearborn's Light Infantry during the battle on Freeman's Farm is quoted:

> A persistent effort has been made from the day of the battle to rob Arnold of the glory. Being attached to Dearborn's Light Infantry, which had conspicuous part in the battle of the 19th of September and the 7th of October, I had the opportunity of witnessing the principal movement of both, and therefore speak from personal knowledge.
>
> I shall never forget the opening scene of the first day's conflict. The riflemen and light infantry were ordered to clear the woods of the Indians. Arnold rode up and, with his sword pointing to the enemy emerging from the woods into an opening partially cleared, covered with stumps and fallen timber, addressing Morgan, he said, "Colonel Morgan, you and I have seen too many redskins to be deceived by the garb of paint and feathers; they are asses in lions' skins, Canadians and Tories, let your riflemen cure them of their borrowed plumes."
>
> And so they did; for in less than fifteen minutes the "Wagon Boy," with his Virginia riflemen, sent the painted devils with a howl back to the British lines. Morgan was in his glory, catching the inspiration of Arnold, as he thrilled his men; when he hurled them against the enemy, he astonished the English and Germans with the deadly fire of his rifles.
>
> Nothing could exceed the bravery of Arnold on this day [September 19, 1777]; he seemed the very genius of war. Infuriated by the conflict and maddened by Gates's refusal to send reinforcements, which he repeatedly called for, and knowing he was meeting the brunt of the battle, he seemed inspired with the fury of a demon.

✳ 2 2 ✳

INTERLUDE

SEPTEMBER 20, 1777

———

ON AND ABOUT BEMIS HEIGHTS

Deserters were common to each side, and Burgoyne was fully informed of the raging controversy between Gates and Arnold. Burgoyne held Gates in contempt, but Arnold was a different matter. The previous year, when Arnold was Carleton's second-in-command, Burgoyne had seen the battle on Lake Champlain, and knew that the very presence of the man, who had so rattled the British navy, could be disastrous for his troops. Burgoyne knew that the time was fast approaching when he would have to strike out or starve.

The American camp was in turmoil on the morning following the battle on Freeman's meadow. The troops who had borne the brunt of the fighting were exhausted, and the whole camp was short of ammunition; down to less than forty rounds per man. Schuyler, in Albany, went around collecting lead from windows and sending it to Bemis Heights. The day dawned thick and misty, and the Americans stood behind their breastworks, expecting Burgoyne's soldiers to appear out of the mist at any moment. At about 7 o'clock in the morning, a British deserter, a corporal from the 62nd Regiment, reached the American lines. His was face blackened and discolored from uncapping cartridges with his teeth. He was brought to Colonel Wilkinson who proceeded to interrogated him. He declared:

> that he had been in the whole of the action the day before, that after night all the wounded and the women has been removed to the encampment and hospital tents near the river, and that fresh ammunition had been served to the troops who had left the

ranks not fifteen minutes before, pretending an occasion of nature; that the whole army was under arms, and orders had been given for the attack of our lines; that the mutiny act had been read at the head of each corps, and that they expected to march in ten minutes. He appeared to be much alarmed, and begged to be discharged with a pass, declaring that we should have the grenadiers at our lines on the left, in fifteen minutes.

As result of this report, Wilkinson states:

our lines were manned, and the troops exhorted, but we were badly fitted to defend works, or meet the close encounter the late hour at which the action closed the day before, the fatigue of officers and men, and the defects of our organization, had prevented the left wing from drawing ammunition, and we should not boast of more than a bayonet for every three muskets; the fog obscured every object at the short distance of twenty yards. We passed an hour of awful expectation and suspense, during which, hope, fear and anxiety played on the imagination; many could hear the movement of the enemy, and others could discern through the floating mist the advance of their column; but between dawn and nine o'clock the sun dispersed the vapor, and we had no enemy in view, the report of the deserter was discredited, and the troops dismissed, yet his information was circumstantially correct, as eventually proven.

The deserter added that he had overheard Lieutenant William Digby say, in reference to the action on September 19th, "No great advantage, honour excepted, was gained that day," and Captain Thomas Anburey stated, "It is as if we had conquered only to preserve our reputation, for we have reaped little advantage from our invincible efforts. We have gained little more by the victory than honour. Though," he added, "they remained masters of the field, the British had won a Pyrrhic victory, for they could ill afford the severe losses they had sustained."

Anburey also reported:

We heard a most tremendous firing upon our (British) left, where we were attacked in great force, and at the very first fire

Lieutenant Don of the 21st Regiment received a ball through his heart. I am sure it will never be erased from my memory, for when he was wounded, he sprang from the ground nearly as high as a man. The party that had attacked us were again driven in by our cannon, but the fire raged most furiously on our left, and the enemy were marching to turn their right flank, when they met the [our] advanced corps, posted in a wood, who repulsed them. From that time, which was about three o'clock, till after sunset, the enemy, who were continually supplied with fresh troops, most vigorously attacked the British line; the stress lay upon the 20th, 21st, and 62nd Regiments, most part of the light infantry, were at times engaged. In the conflict, the advanced corps could only act partially and occasionally, as it was deemed unadvisable to evacuate the heights where they were advantageously posted.

Sergeant Roger Lamb, a surgeon's mate attached to the 9th Regiment recorded:

The Americans being incapable from the nature of the country of perceiving the different combinations of the march, advance a strong column, with a view of turning the British line upon the right, here they met the grenadiers and light infantry, who gave them a tremendous fire. Finding that it was impossible to penetrate the line at this point, they immediately counter-marched and directed their principle effort to the centre. Here the conflict was dreadful; for four hours a constant blaze of fire was kept up, and both armies seemed to be determined on death or victory.

Men, and particularly officers, dropped every moment on each side. Several of the Americans placed themselves in high trees, and as often as they could distinguish a British officer's uniform, took him off by deliberately aiming at his person. Reinforcements successively arrived and strengthened the American line.

Lieutenant William Digby of the Shropshire Regiment, wrote:

About half past one, the fire seemed to slacken a little; but it was only to continue with double force, as between 2 and 3 p.m. the action became general on their side. From the situation of the ground, and their being perfectly acquainted with it, the whole of our troops could not be brought to engage together which was a very material disadvantage, though everything possible was tried to remedy that inconvenience, but to no effect. Such an explosion of fire I never had any idea of before, and the heavy artillery joining in concert like great peals of thunder, assisted by the echoes of the woods, almost deafened us with the noise. To an unconcerned spectator, it must have had the most awful and glorious appearance, the different battalions moving to relieve each other, some being pressed and almost broken by their superior numbers. The crash of cannon and musketry never ceased till darkness parted up, when they retired to their camp, leaving us masters of the field, but it was a dear-bought [Pyrrhic] victory if I can give it that name, as we lost many brave men. The 62nd had scarce ten men a company left, and other regiments suffered much, and no very great advantage, honour excepted, was gained by the day.

The following days, the Yankees lived in expectation of imminent enemy attack as recorded in the diaries of Colonel Henry Dearborn and Ephraim Squaire, a sergeant of the Connecticut Line. Dearborn writes that, on September 20th, he expected a general battle this day and on the 22nd he was still hourly expecting a general battle. Squaire noted:

> *20th—Today ordered to strike our tents at 3 o'clock p.m. hourly expecting the enemy to force our lines.*
> *21st—Sunday, much expecting the enemy, struck tents ready to march.*
> *22nd—We still expect the enemy.*
> *23rd—Today about 12 p.m. we are alarmed by the enemy's firing.*
> *24th—Today ordered to strike our tents.*

The Americans were receiving conflicting information. Captain Benjamin Warren reported that the British deserter from the 62nd Regiment also related that General Burgoyne had been mortally wounded, that his second-in-command had been killed on the spot, and that "most of the British regimental officers and soldiers were either killed or wounded" and he "thought it the safest way to desert to us." Captain Warren remarked "this information, hardly a picture, foreshadowed a renewal of the conflict." After a complete debriefing of the deserter, and discussing their alternative strategies, Colonel Dan and Captain Warren agreed that Warren should lead a reconnaissance team testing out the facts. Sergeant George Jefferson, his messenger son, Benjamin, together with three seasoned scouts were assigned to Warren's scouting party, while Walter Heindrick was required to stay near Colonel Dan's camp to act as his courier between headquarters and the other companies.

The reconnaissance party had been out for approximately two hours when Captain Warren dispatched Benjamin to Colonel Dan's camp requesting additional members for his scouting party. The party had found several American dead and wounded, including the body of Colonel Colburn, and they needed assistance to portage the bodies back to camp. When Captain Warren returned to camp, he reported the "loss of the enemy is very great; the field was covered with dead for about several acres." He also described the battle of the previous day as *the hottest and longest that was ever fought in America.*

That evening Sergeant George Jefferson, his son Benjamin, and their friend, Walter Heindrick, gathered around the campfire with their cronies for their supper meal; lean rations of salt pork and beef, which were as tasty as burned shoe leather. Generally, the soldiers preferred this poor offering to be fried and well done rather than broiled, as suggested by the officers. Added to these tidbits was the timeless fire cake, which was charred on the outside and raw dough inside, soldiers called this delicacy *the soldier's greatest gastronomic distress,* a dish that only the stoutest or hungriest Continental could ingest.

After enduring his supper, the sergeant, with coffee pot in hand, was making the rounds offering his cronies a second cup of coffee. While eating their meal each soldier around the camp fire was telling of his own experience during the battle on the 19th. When each had related his story, Sergeant Jefferson began, "While on a reconnaissance party this afternoon with Captain Warren, we encountered one of the most pitiful, horrific dramas." He took a long gasp of fresh air, and began again. "As we were making the rounds checking on the dead and wounded, we discovered a sixteen-year-old named British Lieutenant Hervey, of the 62nd Regiment. We learned later that he was the nephew of the British Adjutant General with the same name who had received several wounds. We learned also General Anstruthers repeatedly asked young Hervey to leave the field of battle, but the youth's heroic ardour would not allow him to quit battle while he could still stand and see his brave lads fighting beside him. While standing there with his troops, a ball struck one of his legs, making his removal absolutely necessary. While he was lying on the ground, one of the British surgeons told him to take a powerful dose of opium, to avoid seven or eight hours the of most exquisite torture; this he immediately consented to. Before he could be removed to the British hospital tent, we came upon the scene. We found the young lad badly wounded and learned that their retreating surgeon had given him the opium. Captain Warren asked him if there was anything he could do for him. In a daze, the young officer responded that as a minor, everything was already adjusted, but he had one request; with just enough life left to utter, 'Tell my uncle, I died like a soldier!'" The seasoned sergeant wiped a tear from one of his eyes and silently thanked God his own son had been spared.

The whole circle was shocked to hear George's story. The tall, bearded soldier with the coonskin hat suggested that it was time to beddown, and all followed his recommendation, wondering what the next day would bring.

The American army of regulars and volunteers was on the alert constantly for another British attack, while Morgan and his riflemen spent their time climbing trees hundred of yards from the British lines, and continuing to pick-off redcoats. But while the soldiers were fighting the British, the American commanders were fighting among themselves.

Gates, in front of his combined staff, rejected Arnold's plan to attack and then, at the height of the battle, ordered Arnold to return from the front and, instead of ordering him to deliver the *coup de grace* to the British, lead the retreat. Another annoyance that irritated

Arnold was that Gates slighted Arnold and his division by not mentioning them by name in the official dispatch to Congress. Later Arnold learned that with Gates's approval, General Lincoln, who had taken command of the New England Militia east of the Hudson, had detached Colonel John Brown to lead a raid on British supply lines between Lake Champlain and Lake George. Brown had succeeded in destroying nearly 200 British bateaux and numerous supplies; the singing of Colonel Brown's praises at Bemis Heights added to Arnold's frustration and outrage. The last strand of Arnold's self-control snapped on September 22nd when, at Wilkinson's suggestion and without consulting Arnold, Gates published orders that took Morgan's regiment of riflemen away from Arnold's division and reassigned them to his own. Morgan was to take orders only from Wilkinson. Gates made it very clear that Morgan henceforth was to make all returns and reports directly to him at headquarters. To both Arnold and Morgan this arrangement did not make sense, because riflemen were best used in the flanks as snipers, raiders, and fast-moving light infantry. By stripping Arnold of his best troops, especially those of his old comrade, Morgan, Gates publicly humiliated Arnold. Since Gates had not had the courtesy to notify him in advance, Arnold was sure it was a deliberate insult. This was the last straw! Disgraced in front of his peers and troops, Arnold wasted no time seeking out Gates and demanding an explanation.

Brushing aside Wilkinson, Arnold barged in Gates's office and demanded to hear his rationalization for Morgan's reassignment. "What the hell is going on here? I can't believe that you'd do this thing without extending me the courtesy of notifying me first. What do you take me for?" Red-faced and outraged, Arnold was about to continue, but Gates interrupted him, "I resent your arrogant tone of voice," stumbled Gates as he tried to recover from Arnold's brash entrance. The innocent viewers, Wilkinson, Gates's aide, and Brockhulst Livingston, Arnold's aide, stood by visualizing the violent hatred between the two adversaries; like bolts of lightning erupting in harsh tones and loud voices audible throughout headquarters.

"Well, if you must," Gates started, "I have been secretly dealing with Congress about you," he scoffed.

"What the hell do you mean that you have been *secretly* dealing with Congress about me?" quizzed the irate division commander.

"If you'll be quiet a minute, I'll tell you," Gates responded bluntly. "Quite frankly, I was unaware that you were still a major general."

"What ever gave you that idea?" asked Arnold. "You know damned well that I am a member of the American army as a major-general."

"That's not how I remember the situation," opined Gates in a very deliberate and controlled voice. "As I recall you submitted your resignation to Congress before coming to join the Northern Army and have suspended it since then, but not withdrawn it; I even question whether you have the right to command at all."

Startled and dumbfounded, Arnold was thoroughly upset with this information. Gates was not going to let him off that easily.

"I have another bit of news for you," said Gates glaring toward his second-in-command. "When General Lincoln arrives with reinforcements in a day or two, you will be relived of your divisional command. As far as I'm concerned, Arnold," Gates continued sneeringly, "your services are inconsequential to the army and I will be pleased to give you permission to leave here when ever you are ready."

The composure that Arnold had been able to control reasonably well was about to burst. Outraged and in a huff, Arnold decided it best to cut his losses and stalked proudly out of Gates's office. He understood that he should accept the fact that he had lost this battle; but he thought to himself *I'll be there for the final battle to win the war.*

⌛

When Arnold returned to his tent, he sat down and wrote a long letter to Gates, which he evidently intended as a memorandum of record detailing the argument for future reference. He itemized Gates's insults to him since he had returned from the Mohawk Valley:

> *For what reason I know not, as I am conscious of no offense or*
> *neglect of duty, but I have lately observed little or no offense or*
> *notice paid to any proposals I have thought it my duty to make for*

> *the public service, and when a measure I have proposed has been*
> *agreed to, it has been immediately contradicted. I have been received*
> *with the greatest coolness at headquarters, and often huffed in such a*
> *manner as must mortify a person with less pride than I have and in*
> *my station in the army.*

Aside from the lack of respect shown him, Arnold concentrated on the wording in Gates's report to Congress and on the general's order affecting Morgan's place in the chain of command. In closing, Arnold asked Gates that he and his aides be given a pass to leave camp and travel to Philadelphia where he proposed *to join General Washington.*

Arnold had an aide deliver the letter to Gates. As he was preparing for bed, he did not answer the letter that night. On the following morning, without answering Arnold's message, Gates sent Arnold a brief unsealed response for him to carry to John Hancock, President of Congress:

> *Sir,*
>
> *Major Benedict Arnold desired permission for himself and aide-de-*
> *camp to go to Philadelphia. I have granted his request. His reasons*
> *for asking to leave the Army at this time shall, with my answers, be*
> *transmitted to your excellency. I am sir.*
>
> > *HG*
> > *23d Sepr 1777*

Arnold returned the note to Gates with another letter the same day, demanding to know why he was not entitled to an answer and why Gates "did not at least condescend to acquaint me with the reasons which had induced you to treat me with affront and indignity." Even Gates's note to Hancock, Arnold said, was an *insult.* "If you have any letters for that gentleman which you think proper to send sealed, I will take charge of them."

Several hours passed while Arnold sat brooding in his tent contemplating what his next move should be, when another of Gates's aides came storming into the tent. He thrust Gates's latest written correspondence into Arnold's hand and rapidly exited. Arnold glanced over the message quickly, then sat down on his bunk and proceeded to carefully study the commander's dispatch. Quite bluntly, Gates wrote denying *insult and indignity*, and informed Arnold that he would discuss this matter no further with him in person or in writing. To add insult to injury, Gates did enclose a *common pass*.

Gates may have thought that he had Arnold off his back; that was far from the truth. The quarreling between the generals had thoroughly shaken the majority of Gates's officers. They were totally disheartened, because they could not think of going into battle against Burgoyne's regulars and Hessian allies without their most experienced and bravest general to lead them. On September 23rd, Colonel Henry Brockhulst Livingston shot-off a letter to General Philip Schuyler, Gates's predecessor and nemesis, stationed in Albany. In the letter, he updated Schuyler of the constant public quarreling and haranguing between Arnold and Gates. "Quite frankly," Livingston wrote to Schuyler, "the reason for the disagreement is that Gates hates your *guts,* and Arnold is *your friend.* The enemy is expected any hour." Adding his counsel to Schuyler, "General Arnold must not think of leaving the camp."

Schuyler's response did not smooth the waters between Gates and Arnold but it did express the thought that might be on Gates's mind. Schuyler's reply opined that it was obvious to him that Gates had precipitated the falling out because he would be indebted to Arnold "for the glory he may acquire by a victory . . . perhaps he is so very sure of success that he does not wish [Arnold] to come in for a share of it."

Finally, on September 24th, the disagreement became an open cancer throughout the camp. Colonel Livingston took matters into his own hands again, and wrote Schuyler, "General Arnold's intention to quit . . . has caused great uneasiness among the soldiers."

Brigadier General Enoch Poor, the officer who had presided over Arnold's court-martial only a year earlier, proposed generating a petition from the general officers and colonels of Arnold's division expressing their thanks to him for his services and particularly for his conduct during the recent action, hoping this testimony would serve as an incentive for Arnold to stay. Two days later, on September 26th, Livingston wrote to Gates that every line officer in the camp, except Benjamin Lincoln, had signed the petition to Arnold, "requesting him not to quit the service at this critical moment. . . . It gives me pleasure to inform you [Gates] that General Arnold intends to stay . . . though no accommodations have taken place."

In public, although it appeared that peace had been restored between the two generals; there was yet another more explosive situation about to erupt. Faced with the opposition of all but one of his senior officers on or near the eve of a battle, Gates had been working overtime behind the scenes on his idea of a *peace overture*. Through an aide, Gates suggested that Arnold make some concessions; first, would be Livingston's dismissal.

It was evident that Gates had learned of Livingston's communications with General Schuyler, "It has been several times insinuated by Gates to General Arnold that his mind has been *poisoned and prejudiced* by some of his official family, and I have been pointed out as the person who has had undue influence over him."

Upon reading Gates's request, Arnold became infuriated. At once, he sent a response to Gates telling him he would not sacrifice a friend to *please your Face of Clay*. He insisted that Livingston, as well as Varick, stay as his aides. Apparently, Livingston and Varick had inflamed Arnold's mortification and in their letters to Schuyler in Albany they gleefully and inaccurately described the unfortunate situation that should have been remedied but instead had turned into a sordid and dangerous altercation. To make matters worse, Varick quarreled with Gates during a dinner on the 19th. Varick took exception to some of Gates's comments and sprang to his feet offering his resignation as muster-master of the army. He shouted that he would sooner see Gates drawn and quartered than serve him further. Varick added, "Oh, by the way, General Arnold told me to inform you that he would cheerfully serve." After delivering Arnold's response to Gates, Livingston left of his own accord. Soon thereafter, Varick followed.

While Arnold did not directly cause Livingston's exit, Gates did accomplish the completion of his first overture from Arnold. After searching through his files, and discussing them with his lone aide,

Wilkinson, Gates found another pretext for a thundering rebuke of Arnold. He learned that Arnold had given a fifty-dollar cash reward to a soldier who had distinguished himself during the retreat from Fort Edward in July. Gates called Arnold to his headquarters and disclosed that he just learned of these rewards.

"You know, general," Gates started, "I am the only one in this army who has the right to confer such honors."

"I don't need to have you lecture to me about army protocol," responded Arnold. "As you may remember, General Schuyler was away that day and I, as his second-in-command, thought it was within my jurisdiction to make the awards."

"I'll concede your point, but I, too, can exercise my authority," Gates replied seriously, "from here on you are to be excluded from my staff meetings. In fact, the less I see of you, the better it will be for each of us." Gates closed all discussions abruptly saying, "You're dismissed!"

With Livingston and Varick gone, and Gates's order for his exclusion from staff meetings, Arnold did not sit in a corner and nurse his pride. Instead, he sought out Sergeant George Jefferson and his old friend Colonel Dan. Often, they were joined by their messengers, Benjamin and Walter. Occasionally, one of the staff officers would appear in his tent to keep him abreast of the positioning of the two armies. Morgan, one of Arnold's closest friends, was caught between a *rock and hard place.* Since the day he had been ordered to make all returns and reports directly to Gates at headquarters, Morgan and his troops seemed to have lost much of their enthusiasm and fire. During the infrequent occasions when Arnold met with Morgan and some of his riflemen, Arnold would debrief them, and ask their opinions concerning the troops and their options. What frustrated them all was that the British were gaining time while expecting their reinforcements and supplies. Periodically, Arnold would send Gates unsolicited letters of advice, unfortunately couched in terms that could only irritate the commander:

*Not withstanding I have reason to think your treatment proceeds
from a spirit of jealousy and that I have everything to fear from the
malice of my enemies and conscious of my own innocence and
integrity, I am determined to sacrifice my feelings, present peace,
and quiet to the public good and continue in the army t this critical
juncture, when my country needs my support.*

*the army are clamoring for action. The militia, who compose a great
part of the army, are already threatening to go home. Unless our
army attacks soon, I predict that four thousand men will desert, and
Burgoyne will be able to escape.*

Through various sources, Arnold learned that a British messenger
had been intercepted carrying a report that a British relief force was
moving slowly up the Hudson River. The dispatch had been hidden
in a specially-made, hollowed-out silver musket ball and swallowed
by the captured courier, who was given a powerful dose of tartar
emetic by his American captors; it produced the message before the
prisoner was hanged. In fact, Sir Henry Clinton had belatedly been
instructed to take a diversion up the Hudson to draw off American
troops from Burgoyne's army and, if necessary, relieve him. By
October 6th, the British had landed at Peekskill and captured Forts
Clinton and Montgomery at the Hudson narrows; from there they
intended to move upriver to Esopus, near present-day Kingston, and
burn the town and its important supply depots and shipyards.
Meanwhile, a fleet of sixty British ships was heading upriver from
New York City.

In addition to his many and varied resources, Arnold seemed to
have an inherent intuition, an uncanny *sixth* sense that warned him
when danger was approaching. While still fretting in his tent, he
fired-off another insolent dispatch to Gates:

*I assure you that I have no desire to command the army, I only care
for my country, by which I expect to rise or fall. . . . What I can not
understand is your idleness in the face of the enemy. I believe that
you missed the opportunity to annihilate the British at the Battle of
Freeman's Farm by not permitting me to press the attack, but that is
past.*

I remember a Puritan proverb that my mother used to lecture me when I was a schoolboy. Let me entreat you to improve the present time.

On October 1st, the smug and conceited Gates reached the end of his patience with the temperamental Arnold, whom he perceived as obsessed with his own virtues and thirsting for glory. The commander-in-chief of the Northern Army, knowing that the American army had increased to 10,000, including a band of Oneida Indians, was confident that he could operate without Arnold's assistance. Wilkinson advised him that the Indians would turn on the British the vengeance that they had prepared the Indians to inflect upon the Americans; almost daily the Oneidas brought in scalps and prisoners. Benjamin Warren recorded in his diary on September 23rd, "Indians brought in twenty-seven regulars and Hessians." Also, Warren recorded "Tories were given up to Indians to *buffet,*" by which he probably meant, "the Loyalists were made to run the gauntlet." Between September 29th and October 6th, Colonel Dearborn reported the arrival in camp at least sixty-four deserters and prisoners.

Arnold did not really want a *pass,* he had hoped that Gates would offer a *reconciliation.* A little common sense on Arnold's part might have healed the break, but Arnold's supporters, Varick and Livingston, had apparently stoked the flames of both Gates's and Arnold's resentment.

Confidently, Gates ordered Arnold stripped of his command. Gates, himself, took over as divisional commander of the left wing, while appointing General Lincoln commander of the right wing. Gates advised Arnold he could either leave Bemis Heights, or stay in his tent; stripped of his command, Arnold had no official place in the Northern Department of the Army.

❋{ 23 }❋

BEGIN THE GAME

CCTOBER 4, 1777

THE BRITISH CAMP AT FREEMAN'S FARM

Burgoyne's immediate concerns were dwindling supplies and the growing weakness of the British army due to desertions, causalities, and garrisoning captured forts. These issues worried Burgoyne but he could exercise control over them. The one issue that had him worried most was something he virtually had no control over—the weather. The past cold nights were only a foretaste of the approaching winter, when the ground would be covered with piles and drifts of snow, and the rivers and lakes frozen. Because of these obstacles, together with the growing anxiety and fatigue of the soldiers, Burgoyne became *seriously alarmed.* He was compelled to call his generals, William Phillips, Friedrich von Riedesel, and Simon Fraser to a council of war on the evening of October 4th. Everyone present knew that both armies had endeavored to reconnoitre the enemy's position. They knew also that the Americans were having greater success in this endeavor. It was imperative for the British to take the offense immediately.

Burgoyne opened the meeting, "Our provisions are becoming exhausted; winter is fast approaching; our scouts have good reason to believe that the Americans outnumber our force; and to make matters worse, we have received no word from General Sir Henry Clinton regarding his arrival with supplies and reinforcements."

The three generals nodded their knowledge of and agreement with the circumstances Burgoyne outlined; except for the news or lack of it from Clinton, his remarks did not surprise anyone.

"What is the latest news you've received from Clinton?" asked Phillps, "and when did you hear it?"

"We have not heard a word!" declared Burgoyne.

"One of our problems, Sir," injected von Riedesel, "is that the Americans have sent agents into our camp in an effort to induce our soldiers, by all kinds of representations, to desert. Our troops already know that the Americans treat their prisoners very kindly, and they are not as stern in discipline as we Europeans are; I believe the agents have found many a willing ear. Moreover, the Americans want of nothing to which the English soldier was accustomed, additionally, our arduous service only makes matters worse. These temptations added to the 800 men we have in hospital, most of whom are wounded, persuades me to agree with you, Sir, our situation is becoming dangerous." He stopped a moment, and added " If not insurmountable. I do not intend to be an alarmist, but I do agree with you, Sir, it is precarious."

After each officer had had an opportunity to appraise and to react to the known and unknown situations, Burgoyne suggested a bold plan. "I propose to leave 800 men to guard the camp and bridge, then with the remaining 4,000 men we attempt to surround the enemy's left flank."

Phillips asked, "Do you believe that 800 men would be sufficient for the task assigned to them?"

"The safety of the whole army depends upon this," observed Fraser. "If this force should be beaten and the bridges in the rear taken, then the whole army would be completely cut off; even if this detachment held its ground the position might be lost."

Before Fraser could complete his analysis, Phillips added, "It is going to require three or four days to make our way through the woods and pathless thickets, the enemy has had abundant time to mass his force on this spot. Here he would in all probability capture the offensive force and destroy the two bridges, our only means of retreat."

"I concur with all your concerns," agreed Burgoyne. "What I have proposed is a hazardous undertaking, and we must consider all options thoroughly. I propose that we inspect our fortifications and the surrounding territory very carefully, then meet again the day after tomorrow." Optimistically they adjourned.

The following day, reconnaissance was conducted seriously and in earnest, and the council met as planned. Von Riedesel was first, after Burgoyne's opening statement, to render his opinion, "Based on the knowledge I have personally gathered, as well as what I have learned from my scouts, it would be impossible to reach the enemy's rear in one day. Personally, I believe it would be better to recross the Hudson and reoccupy the old position behind the Battenkill, where communications with Canada might be regained. There, we can await news of Clinton."

Fraser agreed, "I think your suggestion deserves considerable thought, Riedesel."

Meantime Phillips was shaking his head saying, "I don't agree with you, Simon."

"Well, if you don't agree with us," asked Fraser, "what do you suggest?"

"I prefer to wait for further information before I make up my mind."

"Well, we're never going to have all the information we'll need to make a decision; there'll always be something we don't know about a situation that we'll just have to guess."

While Burgoyne's generals were discussing ideas and options he, too, had a plan. For the first time, he became impatient and announced emphatically, " I will hear of no retreat; I consider retreats to be disgraceful." Burgoyne looked at his generals and continued. "On the 7th, we will embark on another great reconnoitring expedition against the enemy's left wing. We must ascertain his position definitely and accurately so we may know if it is advisable to attack him. Should this be the case, I intend to advance on the enemy on the 8th with our entire army."

Burgoyne paused a moment, cleared his throat and went on. "If we do not think an attack advisable, then we will, on the 11th, march back to Battenkill. Meanwhile, gentlemen, let's keep watching southward, and listening for the sound of guns which will herald Clinton's approach."

One and one-half miles away, on Bemis Heights, Gates knew, as Burgoyne did not, that Clinton had advanced up the Hudson and had pierced the Highlands barrier. He had received a message from General Putnam warning Gates to *prepare for the worst.*

⧗

Madame Frederika von Riedesel, General Riedesel's wife, had just sat down for breakfast at Burgoyne's headquarters, when suddenly her husband, with the whole general staff, decamped.

In a rush, he gave her a quick love peck, and said, "Until we meet again, my dearest. We're leaving on reconnaissance," and left the building. This sudden burst of action did not surprise Madame von Riedesel, because it had happened so often. In fact, traveling with her husband on such tours, she and their three children had become accustomed to these sudden departures. Together with her children, they made their way homeward to the Smith House, meeting many Indians in war dress and armed with guns en route. She asked them, "Where are you going?" "To war! to war!" they shouted. The family had barely reached their house before they heard firing, which slowly became constantly heavier, until finally the noise became frightening.

At eleven o'clock on the morning of October 7th, Burgoyne led a division of handpicked men and ten cannon through the thick woods southwest of Freeman's Farm. This expedition's objective was to reconnoiter the enemy position which no officer had observed as yet. If an attempt to turn the American left appeared feasible, Burgoyne had decided to propose to make the attack the next day.

Lieutenant Anburey expressed concern with Burgoyne's proposal. He said, "The movement to turn the enemy's left may not be necessary to force passage and advance to dislodge the enemy. I believe, Sir," he continued, "that we could hope to accomplish both purposes without employing the greater part of the 4,500 troops."

Burgoyne pondered Anburey's observation, he agreed with Anburey that it would be very difficult to capture and occupy the small height, which was completely screened by woods. To make the situation dubious, they hardly knew much about the site; they even suspected it to be heavily fortified. Rather than attacking, Burgoyne chose to start close observation of the location. The British, continuing their surveillance, advanced beyond the two redoubts, which were named after the Earl of Balcarres and Colonel von Breymann, and reached the two small clearings that stood at the western end of the line. These clearings have also been identified as the Chatfield and Munger farms, which lay halfway between Freeman's Farm and Bemis Heights, midway between the Middle Ravine and the south fork of Mill Creek. In the meantime, Burgoyne ordered some of his troops put to work gathering the unharvested wheat, while he and his Generals Phillps, von Riedesel, and Fraser, climbed to the roofs of two small cabins in an effort view the enemy through their spyglasses; this proved to a vain attempt to discern the enemy's position. After reaching the two clearings and quickly scouting the front, Burgoyne chose not to advance; he decided, rather. to take up a defensive position by extending his troops on a frontal of one thousand yards, sending Captain Alexander Fraser [not related to Simon Fraser] with his rangers, the Tory and Canadian auxiliaries, and several Indians, to detour through the woods on the right. Next, he positioned Simon Fraser with the 24th Regiment, and the Light Infantry under the Earl of Balcarres on the right of the line. Von Riedesel, he positioned in the center with von Breymann's grenadiers and Captain Pausch's forces hauling 2 twelve-pounder guns and 2 six-pounders. Finally, he assigned Major Acland on the left with the British grenadiers and the artillery commanded by Major Griffith Williams. The flanks rested in woods, suited to shelter a lurking enemy, their right being protected by a rail fence, and the left by a small rivulet. The clearing stood on a gentle slope, and on the far right rose a densely wooded hill. According to von Riedesel, the reconnaissance force stood its ground for an hour and a half before it was attacked.

⧗

It had been reported to Gates that the British advance had been observed. Like Burgoyne and his officers, Gates had heard the advance drums beating "To Arms." At Gates's suggestion, Wilkinson mounted his horse and rode off to survey the results of the engagement. Unable to satisfy his need for knowledge at the guard post, Wilkinson proceeded from the camp, ascended a gentle incline, and observed about half a mile ahead, several enemy columns entering a field of uncut wheat. Beyond, he saw a small rivulet that he thought was probably the southern fork of Mill Creek. Even without his spyglass, he could clearly see every British movement. After about fifteen minutes of attentive observation, he felt satisfied with what he had learned, and reported back to Gates:

> After entering the field, they displayed, formed the line, and sat down in doubleranks with their arms between their legs. Foragers then proceeded to cut the wheat or standing straw, and I soon after observerd several officers, mounted on the top of a cabin, from whence with their glasses they were endeavoring to reconnoitre our left, which was concealed from their view by intervening woods.
>
> "I believe they are foraging, and endeavoring to reconnoitre our left, and I think, Sir, they offer you battle."

Initially, Gates was shocked to hear Wilkinson's first observation, that the enemy was ready to do battle. He thought for a while, then asked, "What is the nature of the ground, and what is your opinion?"

"Their front is open, and their flanks rest on woods, undercover of which they may be attacked; their right is skirted by a lofty height. I would indulge them."

"Well, then," Gates scratched his head, "order Morgan *to begin the game*. Make sure you tell Morgan to have those two young messenger lads, Benjamin and Walter, ready to ride at a moment's notice and to keep me abreast of the action. My intention is to stay in headquarters here on Bemis Heights directing the engagement." Later, he was to admit that he did not personally witness a single incident.

Wilkinson communicated Gates's orders to Colonel Morgan, who was in complete accord; the British were attacked simultaneously on the right, front, and left. While Morgan circled around through the woods to gain height on the British right, Enoch Poor fell upon their left, and Ebenezer Learned assaulted the center once the flank attack had developed. Of the 10,000 men whom, by now, he probably commanded, Gates, that afternoon, committed upwards of 9,200, some of them Continentals, some militiamen, who were from 5 different states: 4,201 from New York, 2,710 from Massachusetts, 1,408 from New Hampshire, 401 from Connecticut, and 500 from Virginia (the state from which Morgan's riflemen originated, many of whom were Irishmen). Later during the day, 3,000 Albany County Militia were also engaged, under the command of Colonel Ten Broeck, becoming a part of Patterson's brigade.

The initial engagement began between 2:30 and 3:00 P.M., according to Wilkinson. Morgan's riflemen and Dearborn's light infantry poured down on the British right wing like a torrent, attacking it on its front and rear. Morgan had been delayed by the need to sweep up Captain Fraser's auxiliaries, whom his riflemen had sent scampering through the woods. As had been planned, Poor had engaged Major Acland's grenadiers on the left, before Learned assaulted von Riedesel's troops. Within a few minutes the entire British-German line of 1,500 men was under assault by four to six times their number.

In the face of deadly volleys of musketry fire and a rapid and continuous discharge of British grapeshot, Brigadier General Enoch Poor gallantly led his brigade steadily up the slope, his men holding their fire until they reached the hill's crest on which stood the grenadiers; drawn up in line and standing shoulder-to-shoulder together with Major Griffith Williams's artillery. Into their closed ranks Poor's New Yorkers and New Hampshire soldiers poured a close-range, rapid fire, mowing down the grenadiers and decimating the gunners. Undaunted, the grenadiers fired back, taking a heavy toll of the Americans, who, excited to madness by the vexing fire of the stubborn British grenadiers, sprang to their feet and, with loud shouts, swept over the guns, killing the gunners and their horses, and rolling back the grenadiers, who were outnumbered by three to one into small, scattered groups, fought back-to-back. Lieutenant Digby, who took over command of his company after the death of Captain Wight says:

> Our cannon were surrounded and taken—the men and horses being killed—which gave them additional spirits, and they rushed on with loud shouts, when we drove them back a little

with so great a loss to ourselves, that it evidently appeared a
retreat was the only thing left for us. They still advanced under
a storm of grapeshot.

Major Acland was shot through both legs while galloping fiercely
amongst the disordered ranks shouting and encouraging them to fall
back. Seeing their leader fall, the grenadiers retreated up the slope,
leaving the ground strewn with their dead and wounded. Wilkinson,
who had joined in the attack, said that within a square of one to fifteen yards, he counted eighteen grenadiers in the agony of death, and
saw three officers propped against tree trunks, two of them mortally
wounded, bleeding and almost speechless.

By the end of the day, Digby's company, which had marched from
Canada fifty strong, was reduced to four men. Poor's troops had been
thrown back twice. Each time they would charge fiercely taking and
relinquishing one cannon five times until, in the end, the rebels carried it off in triumph. Poor's amateur soldiers had defeated the *elite* of
the British army.

As Wilkinson was carefully stepping over the dead and wounded,
he heard one cry out, "Protect me, Sir, against this boy." Turning his
eyes it was his fortune, he believed, to see a young lad, thirteen or
fourteen, taking aim at a wounded British officer who lay in the angle
of a worn fence. Inquiring his identity and rank, the wounded officer
replied, "I had the honor to command the grenadiers." His name—
Major John Dyke Acland. Wilkinson dismissed the young American
soldier. He later learned that the wounded Major Acland, seeing his
men in retreat had requested Captain Simpson of the 31st Regiment,
a close friend, to help him back to camp. Simpson, a very stout individual, carried the large and heavy Acland on his back, under heavy
fire until, closely pressed by the Americans, he was obliged to abandon him. Acland called to other retreating men, offering fifty guineas
reward to anyone who would save him. Fortunately, a large grenadier
carried until they too were overtaken by the Americans. Wilkinson
saved both their lives; dismounting from his horse, he and his servant
lifted Acland up on a horse and carried him to the American camp.

The rout of the British grenadiers, and the capture of Major
Williams's cannon, exposed the left flank to von Riedesel's

Brunswickers who, concurrently with the British grenadiers, had been under assault during the fifty-two minutes of the battle; extending along the whole line.

Meanwhile, on the right, Morgan and Dearborn fell upon the 24th Regiment, causing it to change its front to protect its rear. Though rallied frequently by their leader, Balcarres, the regiment fell back to reform behind a rail fence while under the deadly fire and gallant charges of the frontiersmen. Observing the regiment's retreat, Burgoyne sent his aide, Sir Francis Clerke, with an order to the artillery to retire and save the surviving cannon. On his way through the desperate, yet heroic, fighting, Clerke fell, severely wounded and the order was never delivered.

Balcarres's withdrawal on the right, and the demoralization of the grenadiers on the left, had severely weakened the center column, where 300 gallant Germans coolly and courageously resisted the assults of Learned's five regiments, who were supported by Ten Broeck and his 3,000 Albany County Militia. Ebeneazer Mattoon, an artillery officer in Learned's brigade, describes his part in the action against the center:

> In a few minutes, Captain Furnival's company of artillery, in which I was lieutenant, was ordered to march towards the fire, which had now opened upon our pickets in front, the picket consisting of about three hundred men. While we were marching, the whole line, up to our picket or front, was engaged. We advanced to height of ground which brought the enemy in view, and opened our fire. But the enemy's guns, eight in number, and much heavier than ours, rendered our position untenable.
>
> We then advanced into the line of infantry. Here Lieutenant M'Lane joined me. In our front there was afield of corn, in which the Hessians were secreted. On our advancing towards the corn field, a number of men rose and fired upon us. M'Lane was severely wounded. While I was removing him from the field, the firing still continued without abatement.
>
> During this time, a tremendous firing was heard on our left. We poured in upon them our canister shot as fast as possible, and the whole line, from left to right, became engaged. The smoke was very dense, and no movements could be seen; but as

it soon arose, our infantry appeared to be slowly retreating, and the Hessians slowly advancing, their officers urging them on with their hanger [swords].

The troops continuing warmly engaged, Colonel Johnson's regiment, coming up threw in a heavy fire and compelled the Hessians to retreat. Upon this we advanced with a shout of victory. At the same time Lord Auckland's corps gave way. We proceeded but a short distance before we came upon two more. Advancing a little further we were met by a fire from the British infantry, which proved vary fatal to one of Colonel Johnson's companies, in which were killed one sergeant, one corporal, fourteen privates, and about twenty were wounded.

They advanced with a quick step, firing as they came on. We returned them a brisk fire of canister shot, not allowing ourselves time even to sponge our pieces. In a short time they ceased firing and advanced upon us with trailed arms. At this juncture Arnold came up with part of Brook's regiment, and gave them a most deadly fire, which soon caused them to face about and retreat with a quicker step then they advanced.

General von Riedesel and Captain Pausch also described this stage of the battle from personal experience. Von Riedesel stated that the enemy threw their entire force on the center, which would have maintained its ground, had not Lord Balcarres fallen back on the right exposing its flank and obliging it to retreat, a move which led the regiments of Rhetz and Hesse-Hanau to form themselves into a half-circle. They retreated—or to speak more plainly—they left their positions without informing me, although I was but fifty paces from them. Each man for himself, they made for the bushes. Eventually, Pausch found himself isolated and almost completely surrounded, he retreated, making his way along the rough road to one of the cabins where he reported his two cannon, manned by four gunners and one subaltern who survived. Together, they fired three wagon-loads of ammunition until the guns became so heated that it was impossible to lay one's hands upon them. Finally, the right wing was repulsed, Pausch was forced to relinquish his position and retreat, expecting to meet the German infantry and with them to make a stand. Pausch's hopes were quickly dispelled, for the road was occupied by the Americans:

> Seeing that all was irretrievably lost, and that it was impossible
> to save anything, I ordered the remaining gunners to save them-
> selves. I was successful in carrying off one of the ammunition
> wagons, and on my way back met all the different nationalities
> of our division running pell-mell, making for our camp and
> lines.

At this critical stage of the battle, Simon Fraser spent his time riding to and fro amongst the 24th Regiment, endeavoring to halt their withdrawal under the deadly fire of Morgan's riflemen who, flushed with victory, came in with savage yells. On the left, the British grenadiers were gone, and the Germans were disintegrating. Vainly Burgoyne was trying to form a second line from the fleeing mass of men. Burgoyne's horse had been killed and shots had penetrated both his hat and waistcoat. Only Simon Fraser was left to rally any decisive maneuver in the battle, if only to ensure an orderly retreat.

⧗

That night at the officers's dinner in General Gates's headquarters, the chief point of discussion was whether the Americans should commence the attack, or receive General Burgoyne behind their breastwork at the lines should the British attempt to advance. Without surprising any one, Arnold contended for the first option saying, "The assailant has the advantage, because he can always take his own time, and choose the point of attack. And, if repulsed, he has only to retreat behind his own lines and form again."

As usual Gates believed to the contrary, "If undisciplined militia were repulsed in the open field, and the enemy pressed them again, even behind their own breastworks, if they were under a panic, they would keep on retreating even after they had passed their own lines." Besides, thought Gates, if I agree with that impetuous ex-bookseller from Connecticut, I'm afraid that the bloody bastard will probably begin firing, and bring on an engagement in the open field, contrary to his own opinion of expediency.

About one o'clock in the afternoon, Ebeneazer Mattoon, an artillery officer in Learned's brigade, reported that with Gates's permission Generals Lincoln and Arnold rode out from Bemis Heights after hearing the sound of guns that heralded the British advance. They returned after about half an hour to report, "General Gates, the firing at the river is merely a feint; their goal is our left. A strong force of 1,500 men are marching circuitously, to plant themselves on yonder height. That point must be defended, or your camp [Bemis Heights] is in danger."

Just then young Walter Heindrick came rushing into headquarters. They all glared at him, expecting to hear bad news. "General Gates, Sir, " he started, "I have good news for you. Colonel Morgan and his riflemen have almost completely defeated the British 24th Regiment. The only defense left for them is General Simon Fraser's attempt at rallying them to reform their center column. We also understand that General Burgoyne's horse has been shot from under him, and that he, too, has been shot."

"That sounds very good," smiled Gates, "Morgan, together with Dearborn's infantry, ought to be able to clean up the rest of the British." He thought a few seconds, scratched his head, and added, "Messenger Heindrick, go back and tell Colonel Morgan congratulations on his success, and tell him also that I expect him and Dearborn to completely defeat the enemy."

Walter quickly saluted the commander-in-chief, and ran out of headquarters, jumped astride his horse, and was nothing but a cloud of dust in seconds. On his way back to Morgan's line, Walter thought he recognized the dapple horse and rider coming hell-bent toward headquarters. The rider was his blood-brother, Benjamin Jefferson. Neither stopped; they knew it was important for each to carry the message to their superior, nor did they know Benjamin's message from Colonel Morgan urgently requested immediate heavy reinforcements; Morgan believed with this added strength of force his riflemen could wipe out the British.

Meanwhile, and unknown to Gates, Arnold was taking in all the reports and orders. It appeared to Arnold that Gates was casually reading the messages from the battle while lounging with his aides at headquarters. At one point, Gates seemed to look through him; incensed, Arnold could take no more. Insubordination or not, he must take part in the battle for which he had worked so long and hard for on Lake Champlain, on the Kennebec, at Quebec, and in Valcour Bay. He could not contain himself, "That is nothing, you must send a stronger force."

Glaring contemptuously at the speaker, Gates roared, "Arnold, I have nothing for you to do; you have no business here!"

Arnold responded, "General Lincoln told me he believed that we must send a strong force to support Morgan and Dearborn, at least three regiments." He stared toward Lincoln, hoping to receive confirmation of his statement. Lincoln shook his head in agreement with Arnold, but did not utter a word.

They were sitting around Gates's conference and dinner table when Colonel John Brooks entered the room reporting that the firing had increased. They all rose from the table.

"Shall I go out, and see what is the matter?" Arnold asked Gates.

Gates made no reply but, upon being pressed, said, "I am afraid to trust you, Arnold."

Arnold responded, "Pray, let me go. I will be careful, and, if our advance does not need support, I promise not to commit you."

Gates told him, "You can go and see what all this firing means."

Itching to join the fray, Arnold leaped upon his black stallion, Warren, yelling, "Victory or death," as he dug his spurs into his horse's flanks, losing no time in joining his troops who were already drawn up in ranks and impatiently asking him for orders.

At the sight of Arnold astride his horse with his war-call, Gates quickly ordered Major John Armstrong to recall Arnold. Gates's order to return Arnold to the camp was never delivered by Major Armstrong. Mysteriously, Armstrong's fast horse following a wagon trail between trees never did overtake Arnold, who was by this time far ahead.

About four o'clock in the afternoon, Arnold again plunged his spurs into the flanks of the big charger and hauled the reins until his horse cleared a sally port. Then he rode into the woods toward Morgan, Dearborn, and their men. Rounding up stragglers, he turned around and led them, cheering, toward the enemy. Then he joined with Morgan's men who were assaulting the light infantry and the 24th Regiment that Simon Fraser was endeavoring to recall and regroup. At the edge of the forest, Learned's smoke-streaked men had paused at a stream to drink. They were familiar faces, cheering men who hurried off after Arnold who called, "Come on, brave boys, come on!" His horse leaped the stream, while Arnold urged it up the exposed hillside toward the Hessians. Suddenly, as the Hessians fired, he realized that he was alone; Learned's men had broken and run back towards the woods. Wheeling his horse about, Arnold returned to the stream, rallied the men for another charge. This time the Hessians broke and ran, fleeing this madman, leaving his troops in possession of a cornfield littered with bodies.

Upon spotting a general in his brilliant uniform astride a big steel-gray mare, Arnold, according to volunteer Samuel Woodruff, recognized the military character and efficiency of that officer. He pulled up the reins of his horse, and pointing toward the officer, Arnold yelled to Morgan, "That officer upon the grey horse is of himself a host; he must be disposed of. Direct the attention of some of the sharpshooters among your riflemen to him."

Morgan nodded assent, and went over to his riflemen, and pointing to Fraser said, "That gallant officer is General Simon Fraser. I admire him, but it is necessary for him to die, do your duty!"

Legend has it that an Irishman named Tim Murphy, a famous Indian fighter and crack shot, climbed a tree and aimed at Simon Fraser. The first rifle shot cut the crupper of the horse, the next passed through its mane, a little back of the ears. An aide urged Fraser to retire and not to expose himself any longer. Murphy's third bullet penetrated Fraser's abdomen, and he fell to the ground mortally wounded.

Lieutenant Digby, the officer who had marched down from Canada, recorded that Fraser's fall helped to turn the fate of the day, and Fraser was the only wounded man the British were able to carry off. Anburey, who had stayed in camp to command the quarterguard, was present when Fraser was brought to camp on his horse supported by two officers. The scene, he says, was one the imagination must help to paint:

> The officers, all anxious and eagerly enquiring as to his wound—the downcast look and melancholy that was visible to everyone, as to his situation, and all the answer he could make

to the many enquiries was a shake of his head, expressive that it was all over with him. So much was he beloved that not only officers and soldiers but all the women flocked round, solicitous for his fate.

When Fraser had returned to his tent and was recovered a little from the faintness occasioned by the loss of blood, he told those around him that he saw the man who shot him; he was a rifleman, and up in a tree; the ball entered a little below his breast, and penetrated just below the backbone. After the Surgeon had dressed his wound, he said to him very composedly, "Tell me, Son, to the best of your skill and judgement, if you think my wound is mortal." He replied, "I am sorry, Sir, to inform you that it is, and that you cannot possibly live four and twenty hours." He then called for pen and ink, and after making his will, and distributing a few little tokens of regard to the officers of his suite, desired that he might be removed to the general hospital.

With a ball through his bowels, the dying general was taken to the house of Madame von Riedesel where her dining table had already been spread. It was cleared, and in its place they fixed a bed for the wounded Fraser. Amidst his groans, he exclaimed, "Oh, fatal ambition! Poor General Burgoyne! My poor wife!" Prayers were read to him. He then sent a message to General Burgoyne, begging that he would have him buried the following day at six o'clock in the evening, on the top of a hill, which was a sort of a redoubt. He knew no longer which way to turn. The whole entry and the other rooms were filled with the sick, who were suffering with the camp-sickness, a kind of dysentery.

After seeing Fraser fall, General Burgoyne, who had bullet holes in his collar and coat, ordered Phillips and von Riedesel to cover the retreat of the hard-pressed survivors of the ill-fated reconnaissance force. They fell back across the Middle Ravine to the fortified line where, at Freeman's Farm, the Balcarres redoubt had been constructed, and beyond which, about half a mile from it, stood the Breymann redoubt which protected its rear and prevented access to the Great Ravine, on which rested the whole of the British line. Between the two redoubts, which had been built on little knolls, there stood in a wooded hollow, two little cabins which were defended by the Canadian auxiliaries. Behind the remnants of the British light infantry, the 24th Regiment and the British and German grenadiers, came their pursuers, the regiments of Learned and Poor's brigades, and the Albany County militiamen, stout early Palatine settlers, some of whom had fought with General Nicholas Herkimer at the Battle of Oriskany. They swarmed up the slope towards the redoubt that was defended with two cannon by the Earl of Balcarres. The redoubt commanded an open space measuring about two hundred and fifty yards, and had been constructed of brushwood and logs; the Americans, with all their numerical superiority, were to find it impregnable.

When General Arnold saw the Learned brigade's situation, he galloped across the line exposing himself, as some have said, with great folly. This conduct was seen as foolish, exceedingly rash, and intemperate. Arnold galloped on flourishing his sword to encourage the troops and in a state of furious distraction, struck Captain Bell of Dearborn's infantry on the head. Bell's first impulse was, apparently, to shoot Arnold; he raised his musket and collecting himself was about to remonstrate when Arnold raced off to another part of the field, galloping again across the line of fire.

Arnold, who appeared both deranged and exhilarated, barreling downhill on his big stallion, his sword flailing, literally took command of Learned's men, many of whom were his neighbors from Connecticut. The men cheered him on for they had been balked by Lord Balcarres's stout defense and they gladly followed Arnold in attacking the two stockaded cabins, clearing out the Canadians, and exposing Breymann's redoubt to assault from the wooded hollow. Snatching up some of Morgan's riflemen, as well as Walter and Benjamin, this time with their fife and drum, Arnold joined Colonel John Brooks, who stood at the head of his Massachusetts Regiment as they began the assault on the Balcarres redoubt.

Brooks yelled, "We can't carry them."

Arnold shouted back, "Well, then, let us attack the Hessian [the Breymann redoubt] lines."

"With all my heart!" replied Brooks. He felt Arnold's energy giving spirit to the entire action.

The Breymann redoubt mounted several brass cannon. Brooks realized that instead of a breastwork, with guns mounted on three sides, it was a fort built of logs, laid horizontally between perpendicular posts, and it commanded the clearing across which the attackers must advance. The redoubt was two-hundred-yards long, had been raised on the little knoll where the ground sloped gently to the southwest, and was defended by 200 Germans.

The enemy was caught by surprise at the sudden appearance of the Americans, but did not fire except from the cannon, until the Americans reached within forty-five yards. Then the Hessians opened up a tremendous fire from the whole line, falling few attackers. Seeing that the Massachusetts infantry had taken cover at the first discharge, Arnold, rushing along the line, snatched up fifteen to twenty riflemen, including George Jefferson, and turning his horse, galloped across the clearing towards the redoubt two hundred yards away.

Riding and giving orders everywhere, Arnold and his command, with their overwhelming force, won the redoubt that otherwise might have resisted assault. Some believed that after the first attack, the Germans were so terrorized that instead of holding their lines, they looked on all as lost; after firing only one volley, they hastily abandoned the redoubt. There was some talk that the docile German infantrymen turned against the brute who commanded them; Heinrich von Breymann bore an evil and unsavory reputation as a bully and a tyrant. Seeing that his men were retreating or surrendering, he set about with his sword, striking down those who attempted to leave their posts. This was too much for one man; raising his rifle, he killed the *chivalric* von Breymann [as von Riedesel called him].

Meanwhile, a wounded German soldier, lying on the ground, seeing an American officer on a horse charging in his direction, raised his rifle and shot the horse at point blank range. The black charger rolled over, pinioning the rider, General Benedict Arnold, to the ground and breaking his left leg, the same one he had broken the previous year in Quebec. While Colonel Brooks and his men were mounting the redoubt, one of his soldiers took aim to kill the German who had felled Arnold.

Arnold called out loudly, "Don't hurt him, he is a fine fellow! He only did his duty."

Morgan, his sidekick George Jefferson, and other officers rushed toward Arnold, who waved them away. More Americans crowded into the redoubt, firing British cannon and American rifles at a British counterattack, beating it back in this last round of fighting in the last decisive Battle of Saratoga. The black sergeant directed his men to make a sling from a torn tent and ridgepoles for a litter and prepared to carry Arnold, writhing with pain, back inside the American camp. As officers asked how bad it was, Gates's aide, Major John Armstrong, who had so far failed to catch up with Arnold, bent over him and delivered Gates's order to return to headquarters. Hearing Armstrong's ridiculous remark, Arnold, in too much pain to laugh, ignored Armstrong as he was placed up on the litter.

Then Dearborn came closer. "Where are you hit?"

"In the same leg," Arnold whispered. "I wish it had been my heart."

At the British camp, Anburey watched the return of the troops who were followed by Generals Burgoyne, Phillips, and von Riedesel. He found it impossible to describe the anxiety obvious on Burgoyne's face, who came up to him inquiring if he was the officer of the quarter-guard. When Anburey replied that he was, Burgoyne sternly told him, "You must defend this post to the very last man." Meanwhile, the disgruntled British troops claimed the loss of the Breymann redoubt, the vital corner of the defense system, was due to the cowardice of the Germans; the stain of which was partially blotted out only by von Breymann's death. Conversely, Burgoyne attributed the American victory to Arnold's intervention; the loss of the redoubt had exposed the British flank, causing him to withdraw Balcarres's soldiers and to abandon the redoubt at Freeman's Farm. Burgoyne had lost half the force he had taken out that morning including a number of distinguished, brave officers. Totally disheartened, Lieutenant Colonel von Speth, with four officers and fifty men set out to retake the lost redoubt. The trusting von Speth encountered an alleged American Tory en route who offered to guide him and his troops. The man escaped in the darkness, leaving the betrayed Germans to wander about in the woods; failing to find the redoubt that Brooks's men held throughout the night.

By comparison, Wilkinson, now jealous of Arnold, told anyone who could hear him that Arnold neither rendered service, nor deserved credit on that day; adding that only Arnold's wound saved him from being overshadowed b General Gates's good fortune and popularity.

❈ 2 4 ❈

AFTERMATH

OCTOBER 8, 1777

AROUND AND ABOUT BEMIS HEIGHTS

Early in the morning following the battle, the Americans occupied the abandoned British lines; during the previous evening, Burgoyne had withdrawn his troops from north of the Great Ravine and to the Great Redoubt above the Hudson. On October 8th, the British and American armies skirmished across the Great Ravine, exchanging only aimless, random firing during which Major General Lincoln was shot in the leg, leaving Gates without an officer above the rank of brigadier general. Gates, however, had no intention to attack, he was content to play a waiting game. His best scouting reports kept him well informed, he knew that Burgoyne was running dangerously short of provisions, and that Clinton had reached the Highlands planning to advance on Albany and to attack Gates's rear. As a precaution, Gates dispatched the Albany County Militia to assist Colonel Peter Gansevoort, commander of Fort Stanwix, in strengthening his weakly garrisoned fort.

The Americans spent most of the day laying in food and other provisions while the British and the Germans were preparing to retreat. Burgoyne had decided to withdraw to Fort Ticonderoga sixty miles to the north, if that was still possible; American detachments were gathering in his rear. Burgoyne was aware, too, that the terrible North Woods winter was just around the corner.

Before October 7th, Gates had ordered Brigadier General John Fellows to march his 1,300 militiamen up the east bank of the Hudson to Battenkill, and cross to the west bank at Saratoga. Burgoyne, meantime, had sent Lieutenant Colonel Nicholas

Sutherland, with the 47th and 9th Regiments, to reconnoitre the road to Saratoga.

There remained one indispensable task that he could not delegate to anyone. Before Simon Fraser died at 8 o'clock on the morning of October 8th, he expressed the wish to be buried in the Great Redoubt. During the late afternoon on the 7th, Fraser was brought to Madame von Riedesel's house and placed on a bed at the very spot where he would have sat and partaken of a joyous evening meal, according to Madame von Riedesel, as she had invited him to dine on the day of the battle. At approximately three o'clock in the morning, Madame von Riedesel was told the general could not last much longer, nor did he. She then wrapped up her three daughters in bed coverings and went with them into the entry. The general's corpse was washed, wrapped in a sheet, and laid on a bedstead. About four o'clock on the same afternoon, Madame von Riedesel saw the new house, which had been built for her family, in flames; she knew the enemy was not far away.

At six o'clock in the evening, General Burgoyne fulfilled his vow to Simon Fraser by burying him where he had chosen. Although Fraser had requested that his funeral should be attended only by officers of his personal staff, Burgoyne, Phillips, and von Riedesel also attended. The burial service conducted at sunset by the Reverend Edward Brudenell, the chaplain of the Artillery, who, according to von Riedesel, gave a lengthy sermon. Seeing the gathering of military men at the Great Redoubt, and suspecting that it foreshadowed a military operation, the Americans opened their batteries. The shots failed to alarm the officiating chaplain who, as Burgoyne later told the House of Commons, read the service in an unfaltering voice, though frequently covered with dust that the shooting threw up on all around him. Gates said afterwards had he known the nature of the gathering, he would not have allowed any firing in that direction. General von Riedesel considered it a real military funeral—one that was unique.

While Burgoyne was busily burying their fallen hero, General Simon Fraser, another fallen hero, General Benedict Arnold, was being attended to by young Doctor James Thacher in a three-story military hospital in Albany. The Hessian's bullet had shattered Arnold's left femur. Ordinarily, the leg would have been amputated without a question, as was done to General Nicholas Herkimer after a similar wound during the Battle of Oriskany. Arnold vehemently resisted the efforts of army doctors trying to help him; perhaps he recalled Herkimer's experience. After being carried to Gates's headquarters in the makeshift litter, he was taken for an excruciatingly painful thirty-mile wagon ride, part of a long cavalcade of the wounded soldiers being transported to Albany. Upon completing the examination, the doctors insisted his leg had to come off. Arnold argued that he would rather be dead than crippled. For two days and nights, in great pain, he fought to keep his leg. At the same time he was extremely anxious that without him, Gates would let the British slip away. On October 12th, however, he was informed he was out of danger; he, in turn, demanded to be kept informed as the British retreated north, attempting to escape to Ticonderoga

Officers who brought him news found him *much weakened, in great pain, and very ill.* Dr. Thacher, who had seen Arnold recruiting his Quebec army on Cambridge Common more than two years earlier, sat up with him all night. "I watched with the celebrated General Arnold, whose leg was badly fractured by a musket ball. He is very peevish and impatient under his misfortunes, and required all my attention during the night," adding that "he was strong and seemed to recover very fast." By the 15th, Thacher reported that Arnold was in great spirits, although he had a touch of gout.

If Arnold had heard Burgoyne give him all the credit for the October 7th victory when he reported to Lord Germain in London, he probably would not have lingered so long in the hospital. Arnold would have been dismayed, however, had he learned that Gates, on the other hand, gave Arnold no credit for the victory, mentioning to Congress only that Arnold had been wounded. Rather, in his official report Gates had praised Wilkinson as a *military genius,* recommended that Congress brevet him to a brigadier-general. Samuel Adams at first resisted making the twenty-plus-year old a general. Instead, he wanted Congress to award him pair of spurs. In the end, Congress gave the boyish messenger, who brought the good news, a generalship and made him secretary of it's Board of War.

Following Fraser's funeral, when darkness had fallen and the clock was striking ten, the British, led by von Riedesel, began its retreat. The pontoon bridge across the river was broken up, and the heavily laden boats were very slowly rowed up the river against the current. The wounded had been made as comfortable as possible and were left in the hospital tents in charge of Doctor John MacNamara Hayes, the *amiable Hibernian,* as Wilkinson called him, who had elected to remain with his patients. According to Anburey, "Our retreat was made within musket shot of the enemy without a single loss, even though we were greatly encumbered with baggage. It was near eleven o'clock before the rearguard marched, and for nearly an hour, every moment we expected to be attacked, for the enemy had formed on the same spot as in the morning. We could discern this by the lanterns that the officers had in their hands, and their riding about in front of their line. Americans put their army in motion that night, but they did not pursue us in our retreat till late the next day." So as to disguise their movement from the Americans, the British were ordered to march as quietly as possible, and the watch campfires were left burning. They were successful in achieving total silence; fires were kindled in every direction and many tents were left standing, hoping the Americans would believe the camp was still active. The British traveled throughout the night until at six o'clock in the morning a halt was called, which left everyone wondering the reason. Burgoyne, strangely, ordered all the cannon ranged and counted. What did not made sense was that if they had traveled a few more miles, there would have been a much more secure place to rest. After three hours, they traveled for another hour, when another fresh halt was ordered. Meanwhile, the rain continued to come down in torrents and, after scarcely one hour, Burgoyne ordered another halt. This time, it was because 200 American troops had been reconnoitering and, according to von Riedesel, could easily have been taken prisoners by the British had not General Burgoyne lost his presence of mind.

Following the disaster on October 7th, General von Riedesel, who had become increasingly critical of Burgoyne, argued that without the delaying halts, the army could have marched all night and reached

Saratoga at daybreak. A bridge could have been started there without molestation from the enemy. "Thus," said von Riedesel, "the advantage that the army gained was completely lost by these hesitations. The enemy at once availed themselves of these delays to send as many troops as possible across the river and behind the English; thus, they not only prevented them [British] from building a bridge, but rallied the nearest townships on the opposite side, to effectively oppose the army's crossing. The Americans gathering on the eastern shore could be seen easily; while simultaneous firing on the patrols and the bateaux became constantly more frequent." Burgoyne explained later he had ordered a halt until four o'clock in the afternoon to refresh the men and to give time for the boats, which had not been able to keep pace, to catch up with the troops.

Von Riedesel, however, admitted that the chief reason for the delay was the exceedingly bad state of the roads that the incessant rain had churned into a sea of mud; the exhausted and starving teams of oxen could not pull the heavily laden wagons and carts, including the heavy cannon, which Burgoyne still wanted to drag along.

While Burgoyne was being criticized by his staff, Gates, too, came under heavy criticism for his failure to pursue the retreating army, and for leaving Fellows and his small force of militiamen alone to block the road beyond Saratoga. Fellows's camp was so ineffectively and weakly guarded that Lieutenant Colonel Autherland and his men were able to march round it without being stopped. Autherland appealed to Burgoyne to be allowed to attack Fellows; Burgoyne refused, allowing the rebel militiamen to escape across the Hudson. Thus, both Gates and Burgoyne missed excellent opportunities to capture or to elude the other.

After reaching a place called Dovecot, the retreating British army spent the entire day in a downpour. The drenched soldiers consoled themselves with the thought that if the enemy attacked, "The fate of the day,'" predicted Anburey, "would have rested solely upon the bayonet, because the heavy rain dampened the priming of firearms, and made up for American numerical superiority in that department." As Burgoyne had planned, their march resumed at 4 o'clock in the afternoon. Gates would later write to Burgoyne, that "the cruelties which mark the retreat of your army, in burning gentlemen's and farmer's houses as they pass along, is almost, among civilized nations, without precedent."

According to Madame von Riedesel, "the army spent the whole day, October 9th, in a pouring rain, ready to march at a moment's warning. The savages [the few remaining Indians] had lost their courage, and were seen going home in all directions." She added, "The slightest reverse of fortune discouraged them, especially if there was nothing to plunder."

Upon reaching Saratoga, Burgoyne proceeded to establish his headquarters in General Philip Schuyler's mansion; he remained within its warmth and comfort, while his army was camped upon the muddy ground, thoroughly soaked and hungry.

Madame von Riedesel, an avid diarist, a committed critic of Burgoyne, and an equally committed supporter of her husband, continues:

> Toward evening, we at last came to Saratoga, which was only half an hour's march from the place where we had spent the whole day. I was wet through and through by the frequent rains, and was obliged to remain in this condition the entire night, as I had no place wherever I could change my linen. I, therefore, seated myself before a fire, and undressed my children; after which, we laid ourselves down together upon some straw. I asked General Phillips who came up to where we were, why we did not continue our retreat while there was yet time, as my husband had pledged himself to cover it, and bring the army through? "Poor woman," answered he, "I am amazed at you!—completely wet through; have you still the courage to wish to go further in this weather? Would that you were only our commanding general! He halts because he is tired and intends to spend the night here and give us supper." In this latter achievement, especially, General Burgoyne was very fond of indulging. He spent half the nights in singing and drinking, and amusing himself with the wife of a commissary, who was his mistress, and who, as well as he, loved champagne.

Much latter Captain Max von Eelking sought to improve upon Madame von Riedesel's story:

While the army were suffering from cold and hunger, and everyone looking forward to the immediate future with apprehension,
Schuyler's house was illuminated, and rung with singing, laughter, and the jingling of glasses. There Burgoyne was sitting, with
some merry companions, at a dainty supper, while champagne
was flowing. Near him sat the beautiful [unpowdered] wife of an
English commissary, his mistress. Great as the calamity was, the
frivolous general still kept up his orgies. Some were of opinion
that he had made that inexcusable stand, merely for the sake of
passing a merry night. Riedesel thought it incumbent on him to
warn Burgoyne of the danger of the halt, but the latter returned
all sorts of evasive answers.

The rain had subsided leaving the American camp with nothing but
a muddy quagmire. Small campfires were scattered about with ten or
so men huddled around each one, either cooking, sitting on logs, or
in the mud eating their evening meal. Walter, Benjamin, his father,
and their cronies were drenched to the bone and shivering about the
campfire, trying to keep it going and finish cooking their evening
meal. This evening's meal was going to be a rare treat. Scouts had
gathered together three oxen which the retreating British had abandoned; whether or not they would be able to chew the meat, no one
knew, but at least the flavor would be there. Everyone's clothes were
packed with mud, thus obscuring any form of identification of rank
or grade; all were equally encased in mud. The original occupants of
their tent had been eighteen men who shared two common tents and
provided shelter for the entire group. This, too, had changed drastically during the past three or four weeks; two of their tentmates had
been killed, one was wounded and in the field hospital, and three had
chosen to return to their farms after their enlistment period had
expired. As the soldiers scooped out a portion of oxen stew and
returned to their logs, Sergeant Jefferson rose to speak. One of his
main responsibilities was to help the men keep a positive attitude, not
always an easy task. "Our skirmish on the 7th certainly set the tide of
the battle; I think we've got the redcoats on the run and they're
bogged down in the mud, to boot."

"Yeah, we've got 'em on the run, but we're in just as much mud as they are," observed a militiaman wearing a coonskin hat and with his left arm still in a sling. "I'm at the point where I'd just as soon tell them all, including old General Gates, to go to hell! I want to get back to my farm! Hell, winter's just about here, and it doesn't look like Gates is going to get off his fat ass, up there in his high and mighty fortress. Furthermore, my enlistment was over two months ago, and I know my wife can't do all the fall's harvesting by herself."

"I'll betcha," said a tall, skinny soldier wearing a tricorned hat tipped to his right, and sporting a handlebar mustache which drooped down below his mouth, "your wife has talked some of your neighbors into helping her. Never underestimate the power of women," he added, and spat out a piece of the stew he could not swallow.

"I agree with you, Jed," added Sergeant Jefferson. "Hey, listen," he continued, "whether we're on the farm or on the battlefield, we're all in this war together." Then thinking of his blood brother, Walter's father, "My brother, Karl, is back in New Palatine. I know that he is pitching in to help any and all of his neighbors with their harvesting and daily chores. The only reason he's not with us is because he was seriously wounded during the Battle of Oriskany." He looked toward Walter, and added, "He sent his son, here, in his stead."

"That's right!" agreed Walter, wiping water from his eyes which had dripped from the round brim of his hat, "Another reason I'm here is that my blood brother was killed during the same battle and I'm not going to let him die in vain."

The man with an eyepatch over his right eye said, "This war is shit, and I don't like it any better than the next person, but we're in this shooting mess and we're goin' to beat the livin' hell out of these bloody Brits before I'm leavin'. Then we all can go back to our business, whatever it is, and say to hell with the king 'cause we're goin' to be free of the bloody bastard's rule forever."

"I agree with you, Jasper," said the sergeant. "But," he cautioned, "remember there's no future if an individual's dignity is trampled upon. We've all got to stay and finish this fight so as to retain our own dignity. Then we'll all be free."

Sensing that his father wanted to end the evening on a high note, Benjamin nudged Walter, who was sitting next to him, and said, "It's time we sack-in, or before we know it, Colonel Dan will be at our sides for reveille."

Everyone took Benjamin's suggestion, and sauntered toward their shared tent or sought out a reasonably dry spot upon which to place his bedroll.

The next morning, October 10th, General Gates uncharacteristically decided to take a daring, offensive maneuver and pursue the retreating British army. He ordered Colonel Ebenezer Learned, Colonel John Nixon, and General John Glover with their brigades, accompanied by Colonel Daniel Morgan and his riflemen to cross the Fishkill Creek, and to attack the British at Saratoga, a movement that was hindered by the early morning fog, but did allow Burgoyne time to ready his army and offer battle on open ground. Following an unwary advance in the fog which might have been calamitous, the Americans retreated to the woods surrounding the village of Saratoga. Accordingly, Burgoyne withdrew his troops to the heights above, but this move forced him to abandon his comfortable headquarters in General Schuyler's mansion, which, together with several other houses, was burned to the ground. "Set on fire," wrote Madame von Riedesel, "by wicked hands." According to the general's wife, "Schuyler's beautiful house, and his mills, were burned on Burgoyne's order, to cover his retreat." The destruction of the mansion, required Burgoyne to re-establish his headquarters in the midst of his troops.

Believing that the British could still escape from the Americans, Burgoyne sent a detachment of skilled craftsmen under a strong escort consisting of Captain Alexander Frasier's marksmen and Captain McKay's Tories. Under the command of Lieutenant Colonel Sutherland, these men were instructed to open a road to Fort Edward and to repair the bridges across the creeks over which the retreat to Fort Ticonderoga would be directed. Unfortunately, delay and *too much merry-making* caused this operation to be too late; by the time Sutherland reached Fort Edward the place had been strongly garrisoned and fortified by the Americans.

Upon learning of this inexcusable error in judgement, the determined and resourceful Madame von Riedesel raced into General Burgoyne's headquarters, criticizing him to his face for failing to provide food for his officers. Several of them had come to her for sustenance, which she was able to provide, thanks to her resourceful cook who, though an *arrant knave,* was productive in all emergencies. At night, the cook had crossed small rivers in order to steal sheep, poultry, and pigs, for which he charged Madame von Riedesel a high price.

What kind of person was this woman, Burgoyne wondered? Certainly, she was not the frivolous and frolicking female he had grown accustomed to, he pathetically admitted, "I thank you, Madame, for reminding me of my duty; as you know I have been pre-occupied with many things."

"Please forgive me, Sir," she begged, "I ask your forgiveness. Fortunately, while you were busy with the march, I was able to look after other matters. When I saw brave men in want of food, it was impossible for me to keep quiet."

The embarrassed general responded, "I will give orders that the provisions be properly distributed. I want to caution you, however, Madame, that this might hinder us anew, by delaying our retreat."

That evening in the privacy with her husband, she related her encounter with Burgoyne.

"I'm afraid, my dear," General von Riedesel told his wife, "our hope of escape from the mesh which is closing in around Burgoyne and his army has already been dashed. From what I've learned from our scouts, the Americans are astride the Hudson River and circling around our camp. Simply speaking, my love," he sighed, "our situation is very precarious."

Humbly she asked her husband, "Do you think I was wrong to bring the food problem to General Burgoyne's attention?" The little blue-eyed daughter of a German general, she adored and respected the courageous father of her three daughters; at the age of thirty-nine he had distinguished himself as a more experienced and versatile soldier than Burgoyne. Accustomed though she was to travel and warfare, she longed for the day when their family could return to Germany.

He patted the back of her soft hand, "No, my dear, I just wish the general had the same feelings for his troops as you have. Unfortunately, many times he is preoccupied with other matters . . ." he stopped a moment, smiled, and continued his thought, "and other persons."

At least we're together, she thought, as she went and pushed the straw more tightly about their daughters, and snuggled close to her handsome and devoted husband.

During the whole day of October 11th, there was no rest for the British army. Its front and rear were both under constant fire from the American artillery and from marksmen who were concealed in the woods surrounding the camp rather than, as Anburey had hoped, "by giving us battle and running a chance of victory." A part of the battle was focused upon the provision boats by the river bank; they were captured and recaptured. To secure their provisions, the British were forced to land and drag the loaded boats up the hill.

As was her habit, Madame von Riedesel vividly recorded the situation:

> *The whole army clamored for a retreat, and my husband*
> *promised to make it possible, provided only that no time was lost.*
> *But, General Burgoyne, to whom an order had been promised if he*
> *brought about a junction with the army of General Howe, could not*
> *determine upon this course, and lost everything by his loitering.*
> *About two o'clock in the afternoon, the firing of cannon and small*
> *arms was again heard, and all was alarm and confusion. My*
> *husband sent me a message telling me to betake myself forthwith*
> *into a house which was not far from there. I seated myself in the*
> *calash with my children, and had scarcely driven up to the house,*
> *when I saw on the opposite side of the Hudson River, five or six*
> *men with guns, which were aimed at us. Almost involuntarily I*
> *threw the children on the bottom of the calash and myself over them.*
> *At the same time instant the churls fired, and shattered the arms of*
> *a poor English soldier behind us, who was already wounded, and*
> *was also on the point of retreating into the house.*

> *Immediately after our arrival a frightful cannonade began,
> principally directed against the house in which we had sought
> shelter, probably because the enemy believed, from seeing so many
> people flocking around it, that all the generals made it their
> headquarters. Alas! it harbored none but wounded soldiers or
> women! We were finally obliged to take refuge in a cellar, in which I
> laid down in a corner not far from the door. My children laid down
> on the earth with their heads upon my lap, and in this manner we
> passed the entire night. A horrible stench, the cries of the children,
> and yet more than all this, my own anguish, prevented me from
> closing my eyes.*

When daylight arrived and they were able to move about, and discovered that the stench they had endured throughout the night came from the carcasses of dead animals, with which the camp was strewn; in so small a place, the oxen and horses had succumbed to exhaustion and starvation.

The evening of October 11th, Burgoyne called Major Generals Phillips and von Riedesel and Brigadier General James Hamilton [the Tory Colonel Philip Skene arrived later] into a council of war during which he reviewed the situation and proposed five alternatives:

1. To wait in the present position an attack from the enemy, or the chance of favorable events.

2. To attack the enemy.

3. To retreat repairing the bridges for the artillery as the army moved, in order to force the passage of the ford.

4. To retreat by night, leaving the artillery and the baggage; and should it be found impracticable to force the passage with musketry, to attempt the upper ford, or the passage round Lake George.

5. In case the enemy, by extending to their left, leave their rear open, to march rapidly for Albany.

After serious debate, the first three and the fifth alternatives were ruled out as impracticable. Still believing that a retreat during the night was possible, General von Riedesel advocated the fourth alternative, including the abandonment of their baggage and cannon. This alternative, however, was short-lived. The scouts reported that the rebel's position on the right had so many small parties reaching out that their movement would be discovered immediately.

The American's trap was closing in on them. The attempt to break-out had been delayed too long because of Burgoyne's fatal delay in allowing Colonel Sutherland to attack Fort Edward. Falling back, on Burgoyne's order, Sutherland had been abandoned by the Tories who made their way safely to Fort Ticonderoga.

Trapped, Burgoyne's decimated and demoralized army was encircled by 16,000 Americans with cannon and rifles loaded and cocked. Staring at Skene, the Tory leader, Burgoyne bitterly spat out, "You have brought me to this pass." He paused, but continued to glare at the embarrassed Tory, "Now tell me how to get out of it." The resourceful Skene had an answer, cynical advice perhaps, but that might be worth the try. "Scatter your baggage, stores, and everything that can be spared, at proper distances," he said looking with a straight face into Burgoyne's eyes, "and the militiamen will be so busy plundering that you and the troops can clear out."

Burgoyne and the other officers looked at one another in unbelievable amazement that anyone would even dare suggest such a foolish idea. The council of war passed the evening trying to find their way out of the difficulty in which they found themselves. Madame von Riedesel, in the meantime, had her own set of problems in trying to safeguard the cellar of the house where she lodged, which had become a refuge for the women and children who were afraid to venture out while the cannonade continued. She had finished giving the cellars, which were beautifully arched, a good sweeping and fumigation, when three dangerously wounded officers were brought in, just as a fresh and terrible cannonade began. She claimed that they had no right to throw themselves against the door and come in.

Next morning, Burgoyne and his officers had vainly come to no conclusive method to resolve their dilemma. Meanwhile, Madame von Riedesel had successfully improved the condition in the cellar, where the other women made a little room in the corner by hanging curtains from the ceiling. There she and her children slept, next to the three wounded officers who assured her, upon their oaths, that in case of a hasty retreat, each would take one of her children upon his horse. One of these gentlemen, she said, could imitate very naturally the bellowing of a cow and the bleating of a calf, and if her children cried during the night, he mimicked these animals, and they at once became still. Another problem which persisted was the lack of water; every time a man approached the river for water, he would be shot. A soldier's wife finally volunteered to go to the river and bring back water. She was never molested, and they were later told she was spared because of her gender.

The officers were still deliberating their dilemma.

✳{ 2 5 }✳

NEGOTIATIONS

OCTOBER 10, 1777

—————

BRITISH HEADQUARTERS IN ALBANY, NEW YORK

On the morning of the 10th of October Burgoyne took stock of the situation; it was still raining and Gates had not made a move. Burgoyne had spent the night in Schuyler's mansion, protected by Hamilton's brigade (the 9th, 10th, 21st, and 62nd Regiments), and the artillery, whose attempts to ford the swollen stream had failed. Von Riedesel's brigade, with the rest of the army, was bivouacked north of Fishkill; his Baroness found an abandoned house, and although soaked to the skin, bedded her family down on some straw. It had been a long and depressing day. Before fording the *kill*, Hamilton set fire to Schuyler's mansion and outbuildings, because according to Burgoyne, the mansion obscured the British field of fire.

Amazingly, and most remarkable, the British troops had retained their high spirits in expectation of Clinton bringing relief from New York. One of their soldiers was heard to say, "I'm not going to stop fighting these bloody Yankees until I drop, whether that's right here or in London with King Charles at my side."

At this stage of the war there seemed to be two opinions throughout the British camp; many were convinced that relief from New York was very near. Further, a number of the British troops believed the Americans would attack, which would permit them to die gallantly or to extricate themselves with honor. It was in this somewhat confusing state of affairs that Burgoyne summoned all his officers, above the rank of captain, to another council of war.

Burgoyne opened the meeting, "We have received additional intelligence; the enemy is entrenched at Fort Edward and Fort George. Nevertheless, I am ready and willing to undertake at their head an expedition, regardless of the difficulty or hazard, should it appear to be within the compass of our strength and spirit."

Not an officer uttered a word; all seemed to be mesmerized as their commander continued, "I have reason to believe a capitulation has been contemplated by some of you, perhaps by all of you. I think most of us are very familiar with the real situation of our army. Now, if any of you have any questions regarding our situation, please speak up."

"What is the latest news about reinforcement from New York?" asked one officer.

Another was quick to respond, "I may be too optimistic, but I believe implicitly that we'll get relief very soon."

"Quite frankly," began Burgoyne, " we are very, very short of provisions. Schuyler's *scorched-earth* policy has slowed us down, giving the Americans time to gather together an army that substantially out numbers us now. Plus, the scorched-earth has virtually left little, if any, promise of collecting any food stuffs west of here."

"Approximately how many troops have we that can be placed in the field?" asked another.

"Right now we have approximately 3,500 fighting men, well provided with artillery," responded Burgoyne. "The question I have for you; can we justify placing these men before a formidable force, which out numbers us three to one, all upon the principles of national dignity and military honor?"

Before any response, Burgoyne continued, "Personally, I think it my duty to my country and to myself, to extend this council beyond its usual number; that's why I have invited all of you here. I trust that this assembly represents the army. I do not believe I can justify taking any step in such a serious matter without a concurrence of the sentiments, as should make a treaty the act of the army, as well as that of the general."

The silence was oppressive.

"Sir," said a young captain, "If you, General Burgoyne the commander-in-chief of our army, believes we have a chance to attack the enemy, I'm right here, ready, willing, and happy to follow you. To offer my life for my country."

"Nothing can be gained from such a foolhardy sacrifice," argued another.

"Wouldn't it be a much better policy to save the King's troops by a thoroughly honorable capitulation?" asked still another. "At least then we can regroup, wherever the King wants us to and give the enemy, whoever or wherever, bloody hell."

"I move" said Phillips, "that we give General Burgoyne our complete confidence and ask him to work out the best terms he can with the Americans. However, I must say I do not like the word *capitulation.*"

"I move we resolve unanimously that the present situation justifies a capitulation upon honorable terms," said the deputy adjutant-general Major Robert Kingston.

Burgoyne took a visual poll of the officers' opinion. Each favorably nodded to Kingston's motion. When the officers had left his headquarters, Burgoyne sat down and wrote to General Gates as follows:

> *After having fought you twice, Lieutenant-General Burgoyne has waited some days, in his present condition, determined to try a third conflict against any force you could bring to attack him.*
>
> *He is appraised of the superiority of your numbers, and the disposition of your troops to impede his supplies, and to render his retreat a scene of carnage on both sides. In this situation he is impelled by humanity, and thinks himself justifiable by established principles and precedents of state, and of war, to spare the lives of brave men upon honorable terms. Should Major-General Gates be inclined to trust upon that idea, General Burgoyne would propose a cessation of arms during the time necessary to communicate the preliminary terms by which, in any extremity, he and his army mean to abide.*

Burgoyne carefully folded the letter, placed it an envelope, closed the envelope, and sealed it with his wax seal. He called Major Kingston to his quarters, and solemnly handed the letter to Kingston ordering, "Under a flag of truce, take this letter and deliver it personally to

General Gates's headquarters. I suggest that you wait there for his reply."

Without a word, Kingston solemnly placed the letter in a leather bag, slung it's strap over his shoulder, saluted his commander, and quickly exited. Leaving the British headquarters near Albany, Kingston crossed the Fishkill Creek where he was met by Colonel James Wilkinson, who escorted him, blindfolded, to General Gates's headquarters. Without a word, Wilkinson walked directly to General Gates, who was sitting behind his desk, and handed him the letter; Kingston stood motionless while the blindfold was removed; neither Yankee officer acknowledged nor said a word to the British officer.

Gates opened the envelope, leaned back in his chair, propped his feet upon the desk, and proceeded to read the letter. He squinted his eyes, brushed his hair from his face, placed the letter on the desk, and apparently read the contents again. After a few minutes of thought, he nonchalantly pulled from his pocket the reply he had already written, and handed it to the astonished Wilkinson. His terms were straight forward and clearly stated:

> *General Burgoyne's army being exceedingly reduced by repeated defeats, by desertion, sickness, & their provisions exhausted, their military horses, tents, and baggage, taken or destroyed, their retreat cut off, and their camp invested, they can only be allowed to surrender as prisoners of war.*

In his initial response, Gates had decided to test Burgoyne by calling his bluff; he wanted Burgoyne to expect far more favorable terms. There was one very real threat still floating around in the back of his mind—Clinton advancing to attack his rear. Gates knew that he could not afford to waste a tremendous amount of time.

Handing his reply to Wilkinson, Gates ordered, "Give my reply to this officer. Tell him to deliver my response to his commander, General Burgoyne, and to tell the general that I am willing to accept an armistice until this day's sunset." Silently, Wilkinson handed Kingston Gates's reply, and said, "You've heard your orders, Sir, now carry them out." After saluting, Kingston was again blindfolded. He was escorted to Fishkill Creek where he solemnly boarded the craft

that had brought him to the east side and hurriedly returned to
Burgoyne's headquarters.

Burgoyne received Gates's verbal message regarding the armistice,
and immediately called another full council of officers; he read
Gates's reply calling for an unconditional surrender that the officers
unanimously rejected. Just before sunset, Kingston returned to Gates,
carrying Burgoyne's response:

> *Lieutenant-General Burgoyne's army, however reduced, will never*
> *admit that their retreat is cut off while they have arms in their*
> *hands.*

Further, Burgoyne insisted on surrender with full honors of war.
Gates extended the armistice until 10 A.M. the next day, October
15th, thereby giving himself time to reconsider his terms.

Gates sent his answer early in the morning. He accepted
Burgoyne terms, which stipulated that the *capitulation* should be
made at 3 P.M., and that the troops should lay down their arms at 5
P.M. Gates insisted on the meticulous observance of these times,
which made Burgoyne suspicious. He believed that Gates had
received news of Clinton's advance and wished to hurry the surrender.
Burgoyne played for time by objecting to the stipulation that his
troops be ordered to *ground arms* before marching out of their
encampment. He insisted that his troops must be allowed to march
out with full honors of war, before grounding their arms, and be permitted to return to England on the condition that they did not serve
again in North America during the conflict that was now raging to
the south. Before they would march disarmed from their camp,
Burgoyne relayed to Gates, "his troops will rush on the enemy determined to take no quarter." To this, Gates who had received no word
of Clinton, agreed at once. Lieutenant Colonel Sutherland and
Captain Craig, of the 47th Regiment, were ordered to cross the
Fishkill; there they were met by Wilkinson, accompanied by
Brigadier General Whipple; together and with complete authority to
act as representatives of their respective governments, they set about
drawing up the terms of capitulation, a task that occupied their entire
day.

⧖

While the negotiators were conferring, Madame von Riedesel busied herself with the wounded, for whom she made tea and coffee. She shared her food with a Canadian officer who was so weak from hunger he could scarcely stand. But not all of those who came to her cellar deserved her compassion, for some were poltroons, who she observed, were later able to take their places in the ranks. In this horrible situation, the madame and her children remained for six days; during the cessation of hostilities, her husband, General von Riedesel, was able to lie down on a bed for the first time in a long period.

Madame von Riedesel recorded the receipt of a message that did not enhance her husband's humor:

> *About one o'clock in the night, someone came and asked to speak to him. It was with the greatest reluctance that I found myself obliged to await on him. I observed that the message did not please him, as he immediately sent the man back to headquarters, and laid himself down, considerably out of humor.*

Sergeant Roger Lamb relates the following story:

> During the time of the cessation of arms, while the articles of capitulation were preparing, the soldiers of the two armies often saluted, and discoursed with each other from the opposite banks of the river (which at Saratoga was about thirty yards wide, and not very deep), a soldier of the 9th Regiment, named Maguire, came down to the bank of the river, with a number of his companions, who engaged in conversation with a party of Americans on the opposite shore. In a short time something was observed very forcibly to strike the mind of Maguire. He suddenly darted like lightning from his companions, and resolutely plunged into the stream At the very same moment, one of the American soldiers, seized with a similar impulse, resolutely dashed into the water, from the opposite shore. The wondering soldiers on both sides, beheld them eagerly swim towards the middle of the river, where they met; they hung on each others necks and wept; and the loud cries of "My brother! My dear brother!!!" which accom-

panied the transaction, soon cleared up the mystery, to the astonished spectators. They were brothers, the first had migrated from this country (England), and the other had entered the army; one was in the British and the other in the American service, totally ignorant until that hour that they were engaged in hostile combat against each other's life.

The armistice and its circulating rumors of the end of conflict created a holiday atmosphere in both camps, especially in the American camp which held many from the neighboring Mohawk Valley. In fact, Walter Heindrick and Benjamin Jefferson were instrumental in making the truce period something like a songfest, a joyous occasion. They continued to perform their fife and drum duets, and faithfully carry on their assigned courier services. As they were circulating among the troops, they discovered two other soldiers who had musical talents. One was a short, tubby, red-faced Virginian, Peter "Slim" Crockett, who had come north with Colonel Dan's riflemen with his harmonica tucked in his hip pocket. Periodically, Slim would accompany Ben and Walter in a songfest. Another late comer, Timothy O'Hare, drifted in from the Mohawk Valley to join Benedict Arnold, after hearing about his heroics. Timothy, though near the maximum age limit, firmly believed that he could assist Arnold in making "them damn Redcoats run back to their king." Unfortunately, he arrived in camp the same day Arnold was being carried off the battlefield in a litter. O'Hare was important because he was an excellent fiddler and carefully carried his fiddle in its case slung over his shoulder.

This particular day, October 15th, Walter and Benjamin hustled Slim and Timothy together and started to play some lively music. Within minutes they were surrounded by many of their fellow soldiers; while the musicians played some of their familiar tunes, soldiers were singing and dancing with each other. War was the last thing on their minds, until Colonel Dan entered the scene. The music stopped immediately, all were expecting to hear bad news, because his face was very somber as he entered the circle of his riflemen and militiamen.

"I have very good news for you who have fought with our friend Benedict Arnold. I have just received word that Arnold is strong, and is recovering very fast. In addition, there is no more talk of amputation. In fact, his doctor, James Thacher, reports that he is in great spirits, although he has a bad case of gout."

"Yeah, he's probably been drinking too much wine," yelled a whiskered rifleman, as he adjusted the tobacco cud in his mouth, and spit a brown flow of tobacco juice toward a rock.

"Let's hear a cheer for our man, General Benedict Arnold," hollered another rifleman. Before anyone could react to his suggestion, he followed up saying, "Let's hear it for Arnold! Rah! Rah! Rah! Wish you were here, Arnold!" While they were still cheering, a morose Colonel James Wilkinson entered. Everyone knew there was no love lost between Wilkinson and Arnold, nevertheless, they gave three rahs for Arnold, while Wilkinson said with scorn, "Have your fun while you can, the war's not over yet."

"What a wet-blanket that bastard is," uttered another rifleman. "He's Gates's little boy!"

"Yeah, but we better treat him right!" declared another, "Because I understand that he and Brigadier General Whipple are negotiating with two of Burgoyne's officers about terms of surrender."

"The other day I saw two Redcoat officers cross the Fishkill crik. They were met by Wilkinson and Whipple and all of them took off; went up to that shack up there on the hill," said a militiaman. "I hope the hell they hurry up and get this shitty war over so I can get back to the farm. My wife's going to be climbing the walls, if'in I'm not back soon, 'cause she knows that my enlistment time is up."

"I don't understand you Northerns," contributed Slim Crockett. "First of all, you guys up here say crik, when it should be pronounced *creek;* there's double 'e', not an 'i' in the word. I guess I can accept your peculiar pronunciation, but what really gets me confused, you guys call that stream out there 'Fish Kill Creek.' As an old time squirrel hunter, I thought I knew what the word kill meant. It means somebody or something is dead. Period. No life in it, none at all. Now up here you call that damn stream 'Fish Kill,' and I don't even see any dead fish in there."

Sergeant George Jefferson smiled, and said, "Slim, I know you're right with what you've been saying to us. This area was initially settled by the Dutch, people from the Netherlands, Holland if you prefer."

"What's the Dutch got do with what we're talking about?" asked Crockett.

"Well," responded the sergeant, "the Dutch use the word kill to mean a stream, a channel, or creek, especially when they're putting a name to something or someplace. This stream's name is only one word, *Fishkill,* not two words. Does that make any sense to you?"

"Yeah, I guess so in a way, long's you guys have to live with these screwed up names. I'll just feel more at home when I get back to Virginia, and not have to put up with a damn Dutchman's foolishness."

"Stop your beefing, we're all lucky that we're alive. Let's have some more music!" declared another.

Within seconds Walter, Ben, Slim, and Timothy had the men singing and dancing as if the surrender had already occurred. About half an hour later, the mail courier arrived, and proceeded to hand out the soldiers' mail. It did not take long for Walter and Benjamin to take theirs, and retreat to read it at their leisure.

Benjamin's mother wrote that she had seen Philip Schuyler's mansion burned to the ground. Walter learned from Helena's letter that his father no longer required crutches to walk, but occasionally used a cane. She also told him that her mother was settled in her own home, and working nearly full-time in the general store. Helena was still helping Walter's mother with the Limburger cheese business. Most important, reported Helena, the new Dutch Reformed church has been completed, and Reverend Stouffer and his wife, Red Bird, have agreed to move to New Palatine, live in the back of the church, and be the full-time minister. But, he would still have to circulate the valley until another minister could be recruited. While the young men exchanged their news, Walter said, "Benjamin, I wish you would consider moving to New Palatine."

"It would be fun if we were able to be together, but I've got to help my father with his livery, and don't forget that I still want to be a baker," solemnly responded Benjamin. "Always remember we're still brothers," he said as he crept into his sleeping bag.

"Always, brothers," agreed Walter, as he grasped Benjamin's hand. "Tomorrow's another day; let's hope Wilkinson and his cronies get that treaty finished pretty darn soon."

After an exhausting day hammering out the details of capitulation, night had arrived; Sutherland and Craig returned to Burgoyne with his copy of the draft. Burgoyne quickly perused the document, then went to his desk, placed the draft on it, and sat down to study the results of the capitulation committee's efforts.

Over fifteen minutes elapsed while Craig and Sutherland stood watching their commander-in-chief in what appeared to be a total trance. Finally, Burgoyne looked up and saw them still standing there. "Gentlemen," he acknowledged, "please forgive me, I did not realize you were still here. Please sit down, I'd like to review this document with you. First of all, I want to congratulate both of you," he hesitated and corrected himself, "all four of you for putting together a remarkably fair agreement."

Obviously pleased, they grinned and nodded acceptance, "Thank you, Sir," said Colonel Sutherland. "It was, indeed, tough negotiations. Before we started, we laid out our primary goals and their supporting objectives."

"Sorta built the skeleton of the final document, " added Captain Craig. "I think Colonel Sutherland will agree with me; the Americans, officers with the names of Wilkinson and Whipple, were fair and reasonable"

"If they weren't," said Sutherland, "we would still be over on the other side of the river."

"I don't mean to take the air out of your balloon," Burgoyne calmly said, "but, gentlemen, there is one particular word which grates on my neres. That word is *capitulation;* it literally makes my hackles rise. It must be replaced with a word that gives a more favorable—and correct impression."

Quiet thoughts were dancing about in the room; the silence was total and complete. It was Burgoyne who broke the silence, "I have it! Let's use the word *convention* instead of capitulation."

The master had spoken. Sutherland and Craig gladly agreed with his decision. At eleven o'clock that same evening, Craig wrote a letter to Wilkinson, about Burgoyne's acceptance of the treaty, with the provision that the word *capitulation* be replaced with *convention,* to which Gates readily agreed. Greatly relieved and believing that all was settled, for he had heard during the day that Clinton had passed the Highlands; Gates went to bed.

During the night, Burgoyne, too, learned of Clinton's progress from a Tory who believed that the British troops had reached Esopus and might already be at Albany. Burgoyne quickly called his council of officers to whom he put these questions:

1. May a treaty which had been definitely settled by fully empowered commissaries, even after the promise of the general to ratify all that the commissaries had agreed upon, be broken with honor?

2. Is the intelligence just received sufficiently reliable to authorize us to break so advantageous an agreement in our present situation?

3. Did the army have, indeed, a sufficient reliant spirit to defend their position to the last man?

Burgoyne had not commented at all after reading each question. After much discussion, he called the *question;* the council voted fourteen to eight that Burgoyne could *not* honorably withdraw from the treaty he had promised to sign. Even if the report of Clinton's progress was true, the distance was too great to discard the advantageous terms. Two-thirds of the officers declared their troops would not behave well if they were forced to fight on.

Burgoyne stood up and with both hands flat on his desk, declared, "I refuse to accept the council's recommendation. I'm not convinced there is no hope of relief by Clinton. To gain more time, I'm going to send another message to Gates. That old crock, wont know the difference" He dismissed the council, sat down at his desk, and began to write.

In his letter to Gates, Burgoyne accused the Americans of breaking the armistice by dispatching troops to Albany. By ordering this transfer of troops, the American numcrical superiority was reduced. This factor, alone, was the primary reason he had asked for terms. He demanded that two of his officers be allowed to inspect Gates's army. Burgoyne did not know it, but the troops he had observed leaving the American lines were a contingent of New York militia who, on the expiration of their service, had packed up and marched away without permission.

When Gates read the document of Burgoyne's charges, he was infuriated. "What in hell is that damn Burgoyne trying to do?" He responded by answering his own question, "It sounds like he wants to renew hostilities." He was trying to put two occurrences together. First this letter, and second, the news of the British burning the town of Esopus (presently known as Kingston). Eager to put an end to these games, Gates called Wilkinson, and ordered him to go to Burgoyne, and warn him that if the treaty was not immediately ratified, Gates would break off all negotiations. "And tell that bastard," Gates added, "that there have been no violations to the armistice."

"I don't give a damn what Gates says," declared Burgoyne, "I refuse to sign the treaty, and you can tell that Yankee rebel that's my final word."

Wilkinson clicked his heels, gave a crisp salute, did an about-face, and marched out the door. He leaped astride his chestnut stallion and gave the horse its reins. He had gone no further than a hundred yards before he heard someone behind him yelling, "Stop! Stop! Colonel Wilkinson, stop!" Wilkinson slowed his pace, until Major Kingston reached his side. While still astride their horses, Kingston said, "General Burgoyne instructed me to tell you, and for you in turn to inform General Gates, that he promises to give Gates his answer within two hours. Colonel, I invite you to return with me, and wait while General Burgoyne confers with his officers."

Wilkinson felt rather secure and confident with Kingston and his offer for they had been working very closely together for the past few days. "I accept your offer, Major. Thank you for your courtesy." In silence, they cantered back to the British camp.

Burgoyne began the council meeting, "Gentlemen, we're gathered here again to determine whether we should break the original treaty; I know eight of you have already expressed the opinion that we should."

One of the officers who had originally agreed with Burgoyne stood up. "Sir, all eight of us have met in caucus, and we believe that it would be wrong to break the original treaty." He immediately looked toward each of the eight officers. Silently, with an affirmative nod each agreed.

"I can't believe what I'm hearing," said Burgoyne with disgust. Irritated, he asked von Riedesel and Phillips to step outside with him. When they were alone, he said to his subordinates, "I need your confidential advice and friendly counsel."

Phillips was the first to respond, "Sir, I don't have any advice to offer you. It is a very ticklish situation we're in; we're in the proverbial position between a rock and a hard place."

"You're a lot of help," sneered Burgoyne. "If I had wanted to hear platitudes, I wouldn't have asked you out here." He stared toward von Riedesel expecting to hear something more optimistic and helpful than what he had just heard from Phillips.

Just as von Riedesel was about to offer his opinion, Brigadier General James Hamilton joined the group. Burgoyne did not appear surprised to see Hamilton and was obviously more interested to hear what von Riedesel's advice would be. "In all respect, Sir, to break the treaty at this stage of negotiations, based upon rather flimsy intelligence, would be extremely hazardous."

Stunned, Burgoyne looked at Hamilton, "What do you think?"

"I agree totally with von Riedesel," replied the newcomer. "The information we've received about Clinton and his reinforcements, is as von Riedesel says rather flimsy. So much so that I'd hesitate to stake my life on it."

"Gentlemen, I hear what all of you are telling me, but I can not accept your analysis." He stopped a moment, then instructed Phillips to tell Sutherland to inform the waiting Yankee that *the truce must end.*

Wilkinson describes his final meeting with Sutherland:

> The two hours had elapsed by a quarter, and an aide-de-camp from the General [Burgoyne] had been with me to know how matters progressed. Soon after I perceived Lieutenant-Colonel Sutherland opposite to me and beckoned him to cross the creek; on approaching me he observed: "Well, our business will be knocked on the head after all." I enquired why. He said, "The officers have got the devil in their heads and could not agree." I replied gaily: "I am sorry for it, as you will not only lose your fusee (which he had owned thirty-five years and had desired me to except from the surrendered arms and save for him as she was a favorite piece) but your whole baggage." He expressed much sorrow, but said he could not help it. At this moment I recollected the letter Captain Craig had written me the night before and taking it from my pocket I read it to the Colonel who declared he had not been privy to it; and added with evident anxiety: "will you give me that letter?" I answered in the negative and observed: "I should hold it as a testimony of the good faith of a British Commander." He hastily replied: "Spare me that letter, Sir, and I pledge you my honour I return it in fifteen minutes." I penetrated the motive and willingly handed it to him; he sprang off with it, and directing his course to the British camp, ran as far as I could see him. In the meantime I received a peremptory message from the General to break off the treaty if the Convention was not immediately ratified. I informed him by the messenger that I was doing the best I could for him and would see him in half an hour. Colonel Sutherland was punctual to his promise and returned with Captain Craig, who delivered me the Convention signed by General Burgoyne.

The contents of Captain Craig's letter to Wilkinson had irrevocably committed Burgoyne and his troops to the convention. According to

Madame von Riedesel, "the signed Convention was fortunate for us; as the Americans told to us afterwards that had the capitulation been broken we all would have been massacred; which they could have done the more easily, as we were not over four or five thousand men strong, and had given them time to bring together more than twenty thousand."

The ratified convention was most generous to the British, as it allowed the British troops to march from their camp with full honors of war and to ground their arms by the river. A free passage to England was granted, on condition of not serving again in North America. The British and German troops would march, under their own officers, to Boston, and the Canadians would be allowed to return home. Most considered that no defeated general could have wished for more generous terms.

GROUND THEIR ARMS

NEAR THE PARADE GROUNDS OF AMERICAN HEADQUARTERS

A defeat is fatal to the Army. A victory does not save it, as they have neither provisions to advance nor retreat against the enemy who by experience we know are capable of rallying at every advantageous post. And that the life and property of every provincial and dependent of this army depends upon the execution of this treaty.

—Lieutenant-General John Burgoyne

Walter and Benjamin had just finished playing reveille and were sitting around the campfire with their usual cronies enduring the troop's most distressful gastronomic substitute for breakfast, the renown *firecake*, charred on the outside and raw dough on the inside; a dish that only the stoutest or hungriest Continental could endure. As they proceeded to wash down the firecakes with strong tea, Walter looked Benjamin straight in the eye, and asked, "Did you ever think that we would see this day?"

"Oh, sure!" Benjamin responded positively with a smile. "I knew on the day my father asked me to join him and General Arnold that we would eventually defeat the British."

"I knew it," said another militiaman, "when they told me I was going to be serving with a bunch of Virginia riflemen. At first, I didn't know what to expect, but when I saw them shoot birds at a hundred yards or more, I began to believe that I was serving with a bunch of professional marksmen. To tell you the truth," adjusting his coon-skin cap and his tobacco cud, "I didn't think they knew much about military tactics."

"That's just about how I felt," agreed a tall, skinny soldier. "The way they were able to shoot, made me feel like I didn't know a damn thing about a rifle. Hell, I've been using a rifle since I was knee-high to a grasshopper, but these guys made me feel like a monkey. Except . . . ," he stopped a moment, threw the remains of his fire cake into the fire, poured another cup of black tea which could easily pass for coffee, and sauntered back to the log he had been sitting on. "Except," he repeated, "when I met their commander, Colonel Daniel Morgan. That's when I knew that I'd be willing to go to hell and back for him."

"That's how I felt when I met General Benedict Arnold," said Walter. "I honestly believed in him after my father and Sergeant Jefferson had introduced us. My father and Benjamin's father told General Arnold that they felt safe lending their sons to be members of his troops. Of, course," he smiled toward his blood-brother, "having Benjamin's father here with me helped."

All the Americans took advantage of the day. Not knowing quite what to expect, most of the troops had been given extra time for the morning meal. Along about 10 o'clock, the Americans heard drums and fifes playing in the distance and, moving toward the sound, saw the British army marching with colors flying and drums and fifes playing. It was an impressive parade, headed by Burgoyne and accompanied by General Gates's escort, Colonel James Wilkinson. Burgoyne and Wilkinson rode to the river bank, stopped, and looking toward his attendant, Burgoyne asked, "Is this river fordable?"

"Certainly, sir," Wilkinson responded, "but do you observe the people on the opposite shore?"

"Yes," replied Burgoyne, "I have seen them too damn long."

Without further discussion, Wilkinson gave the reins to his horse, entered the stream, and started to cross. He looked back toward Burgoyne, and observed, "It's safe; just don't fall in the creek because the water's cold as ice." Both laughed and proceeded across the Fishkill. They were accompanied by Major Kingston, his aides, Lord Petersham and Lieutenant Wilford, Major Generals Phillips and von Riedesel and their staffs. After reaching the opposite shore, Burgoyne and his staff, under Wilkinson's guidance, rode proudly across the meadow to the American headquarters.

Burgoyne, who had begun the day by calling his officers in council, attempted to explain his behavior since he had been given the honor of commanding their army, but he was too full of remorse to speak. According to Lieutenant William Digby, "Burgoyne dwelled too much on his orders to make the wished-for junction, and as to how the proceedings had turned out, they, he said must be the judges together with him."

It had been agreed that the convention was to be executed according to traditional eighteenth-century military decorum. Digby writes, "The British marched out, according to treaty, with drums beating and honours of war, but the drums seemed to have lost their inspiring sound, and though we beat the "Grenadiers March," which not long before was so animating, yet it seemed by its last effort, as if almost ashamed to be heard on such an occasion."

Digby looked toward Burgoyne, noticing that he was almost in tears, and realizing that had the general been alone, he undoubtedly would have allowed the tears to flow, thus venting his disappointment.

Burgoyne was resplendent in the rich, majestic royal scarlet, full-dress uniform of a British general officer as he rode up to General Gates's headquarters. The American commanding general, dressed in a plain blue frockcoat, came out of his tent to greet Burgoyne, who was leading his officers. Still on his horse, Burgoyne saluted his recent antagonist by raising his hat and bowing. "The fortunes of war, General Gates," he greeted Gates, "have made me your prisoner."

"I shall always be ready to bear testimony that it has not been through any fault of your Excellency," replied Gates most courteously.

Burgoyne dismounted, and was shortly joined by Major General William Phillips; he and Gates saluted, and shook hands with the familiarity of old acquaintances. (They had known each other when Gates served in the British army.) General Friedrich Adolf von Riedesel and the other officers were introduced in turn.

Digby, who was present, reports that he found the meeting between Burgoyne and Gates well worth watching. It seemed to him that Gates was almost as respectful as he would have been if he were the conquered; Burgoyne's noble air, though prisoner, seemed to command attention and respect from every person.

⧗

Having settled her affairs, Madame von Riedesel also attended the meeting at the American headquarters:

> Now the good woman, who had brought us water at the risk of her life, received the reward of her services. Everyone threw a whole handful of money into her apron; she received all together over twenty guineas. At such a moment, the heart seems to be specially susceptible to feelings of gratitude.
>
> At last, my husband sent to me a groom with a message that I should come to him with our children. I, therefore, again seated myself in my dear calash; and in the passage through the American camp, I observed, with great satisfaction, that no one cast at us scornful glances. On the contrary, they all greeted me, even showing compassion on their countenances at seeing a mother with her children in such a situation. I confess that I feared to come into the enemy camp, as the thing was so utterly new to me.
>
> When I approached the tents, a noble-looking man came toward me, took the children out the wagon, embraced and kissed them, and then with tears in his eyes helped me also to alight. "You tremble," he said to me; "fear nothing." "No," replied I, "for you are so kind, and have been so tender toward my children, that it has inspired me with courage."
>
> He then led me to the tent of General Gates, with whom I found Generals Burgoyne and Phillips, who were upon an extremely friendly footing with him. Burgoyne said to me, "You may now dismiss all your apprehensions, for your sufferings are at an end." I think that should certainly be acting very wrongly, to have more anxiety, when our chief had none, and especially when I saw him on such a friendly footing with General Gates.
>
> The man, who had received me so kindly, came up and said to me, "It may be embarrassing to you to dine with all these gentlemen; come now with your children into my tent, where I will give you, it is true, a frugal meal, but one that will be accompanied by the best wishes."

"You are certainly," answered I, " a husband and a father, since
you shew me so much kindness," I then learned that he was the
American general, Philip Schuyler

Only one of Gates's aides was watching as the British and German
troops paraded in the meadow to lay down their arms. Gates had
ordered that the American army be discreetly out of site. The disarmed soldiers forded the creek and marched past the headquarters
tent where Generals Gates and Burgoyne stood with their staffs.
Beyond them Gates's troops were drawn up silently, at his orders. As
the British troops marched past the American ranks a band struck up
Yankee Doodle, the American marching song.

What a spectacular site these two armies presented! First marched
the British soldiers, and then the Germans, many of whom carried or
led the pets they had acquired during the campaign: a bear, a deer,
several young foxes, and a raccoon. Behind straggled the camp followers, the wagon-drivers, the sutlers, and a number of slatternly
women, 215 belonging to the British troops and 82 to the
Germans—rather more than had been listed officially at the start of
the campaign.

After the *Convention Army* of disarmed soldiers had passed
beyond into meadow and started its 200 mile (twenty-day) march
over the Green Mountains and through the Connecticut valley to
Cambridge, Massachusetts, Burgoyne drew his sword, bowed and
offered it to Gates, who accepted it and with equal courteous, bowed
and returned it.

Madame von Riedesel and her children dined with General
Schuyler on a meal of smoked tongue, beefsteaks, potatoes, bread,
and butter. A banquet was provided for the entertainment of the general officers of both armies and their staffs that included such delica-
cies as ham, goose, beef, boiled mutton, and great platters overflowing
with so many vegetables that even the fastidious Gentleman Johnny
approved. Meanwhile, Burgoyne and Gates dined alone in Gates's
hovel, as Wilkinson called it; a rude hut, one corner of which was
occupied by the General's mattress. They ate aplenty and washed the

food down with lots of hard cider and rum; the same libations served at the banquet.

Before the convention, Burgoyne had allowed the remaining Tories to leave camp and make their way to Canada. After the Convention, Burgoyne was escorted by dragoons to Albany. Gates was extremely cautious in this venture; he and his staff had received rumors and threats from local farmers saying they planned to tar and feather the captured Burgoyne. Gates also felt obliged to provide guards for the handful of Indians and their squaws whom the farmers threatened to massacre.

While in Albany, Burgoyne stayed in General Schuyler's home. He expressed his regrets for burning his fine mansion in Saratoga. A group of Gates's soldiers replaced this mansion; the timber was cut and the house was completed within fifteen days.

The American rebels did not gloat at the discomfort of their British and Tory foes and General Gates wrote to his wife:

> *The voice of fame, ere this reaches you, will tell how greatly fortunate we have been in this department. Burgoyne and his whole army have laid down their arms and surrendered themselves to me and my Yankees. Thanks to the Giver of all victory for this triumphant success. If Old England is not by this lesson taught humility, then she is an obstinate old slut, bent upon her own ruin. Tell my dear Bob not to be too elated at this great fortune of his father. He and I have seen days adverse as well as prosperous. Let us through this life endeavor to bear both with an equal mind.*

On the next day, October 18, 1777, General Washington learned of Burgoyne's surrender. Standing proudly before his staff, he told them that his happiness had been completed, and added that Burgoyne's surrender is a "most important event which has exceeded our most sanguine expectations." A few weeks later on November 4th, Congress officially thanked Gates, Lincoln, and Arnold "for their brave and successful efforts in support of the independence of their country." Still in an Albany hospital, where he called his doctors "a set of ignorant pretenders," Arnold learned of the official recognition of the part he had played in the battle.

While Burgoyne was still in Albany, Schuyler took him to the hospital to visit his nemesis, the *real conqueror* as Burgoyne called General Benedict Arnold. Both victors and vanquished entertained great professional respect for each other, and spent about a half-day together. General Schuyler was present for a part of the time, but left the pair together while he went off to attend to private business.

Burgoyne and Arnold talked at length about the technical aspects of the battle they had fought, and as their later correspondence with one another revealed, in the privacy of Arnold's hospital room they admitted they had been the principals in the action at Saratoga, while Horatio Gates had played a very minor role in the battle. They also discussed European versus American methods of warfare, and finally wound up finding agreement on what Burgoyne called "the philosophy of war and the necessity for its avoidance."

This private visit and discussion was significant because it absorbed the attention of both the complete professional and the gifted amateur who had known nothing about waging war until his country had started its fight for independence. It was a tribute to the military acumen of Benedict Arnold that he could meet Gentleman Johnny Burgoyne as an equal. Both confessed that the patriot for whom they had the greatest respect was Philip Schuyler, whom they regarded as the most underrated general officer in the American army. General Phillips was also impressed by Schuyler, and they talked at length about the future of the war. Interestingly, Burgoyne appears to have been one of the first to realize that his defeat at Saratoga would lead to American independence, and he mentioned to Schuyler, in some detail, the possibility that the French would enter the war on the side of the Yankees. Knowing there was no reason to hang his head, Burgoyne believed sincerely that he had been defeated by a superior force simply because his fellow Englishmen had not contributed their share to his campaign. At this time, he was still completely ignorant that Lord George Germain and Sir William Howe were to blame for the rerouting of Howe's New York forces that were to junction with him in Albany.

Deeply moved by General Schuyler's magnanimity, General Burgoyne told his new found friend, "Is it to me, who have done you so much injury, that you show so much kindness!"

"That is the fate of war," replied Schuyler. "Let us say no more about it."

Three days later, Burgoyne and his entourage left Albany and traveled to Boston, en route to Cambridge. Madame von Riedesel had kept her little carriage in which she carried her baggage, and since it was late in the season and the weather was raw, she had her calash covered with coarse linen, and varnished with oil. She did not know whether it was because of the strange appearance of her wagon, but she was obliged to halt frequently; the people along the route insisted upon seeing the wife of the German general with her three children. However, she did say that the people were very friendly and particularly delighted by her ability to speak English.

According to Madame von Riedesel:

> Some of their [American] generals who accompanied us were shoemakers; and upon our halting-days they made boots for our officers, and, also, mended nicely the shoes of our soldiers. They set a great value upon our money coinage; which with them was scarce. One of our officers had worn his boots entirely into shreds. He saw that an American general had a good pair, and said to him jestingly, " will gladly give you a guinea for them." Immediately the general alighted his horse, took the guinea, gave his boots, and put on the badly worn ones of the officer, and again mounted his horse.

Watching along the road in Cambridge, Hannah Winthrop describes the disarmed captives as they march through town:

> Last Thursday, which was a stormy day, a large number of British troops came softly through the town via Watertown to Prospect Hill. On Friday we heard the Hessians were to make a procession in the same route. We thought we should have nothing to do with them, but view them as they passed. To be sure, the sight was only astonishing. I never had the least idea that the Germans produced such a sordid set of creatures in human

figure—poor, dirty, emaciated men, great number of women, who seemed to be the beasts of burden, having a bushel-basket on their back, by which they were bent double; the contents seemed to be pots and kettles, various sorts of furniture, children peeping through grid-irons and other utensils, some very young infants who were born on the road, the women bare-feet, clothed in dirty rags; such effluvia filled the air while they were passing, had not they been smoking all the time, I should have been apprehensive of being contaminated by them.

After a noble-looking advance guard, General Johnny Burgoyne headed this terrible group on horseback. The other generals, also clothed in their coats, Hessians, Anspachers, Brunswickers, etc., etc., etc., followed. The Hessian Generals gave us a polite bow as they passed. Not so the British. Their baggage wagons were drawn by poor, half-starved horses. But to bring up the rear, another fine, noble-looking guard of American brawny, victorious yeomanry, who assisted in bringing these sons of slavery to terms. Some of our wagons drawn by fat oxen, driven by joyous-looking Yankees closed the cavalcade.

The generals and other officers went to Bradish, where they are quartered at present. The privates trudged through the thick and thin to the hills, where we thought they were to be confined, but what was our surprise when in the morning we beheld an inundation of those disgraceful objects filling our streets. How mortifying it was? They in a manner demanding our houses and colleges (it had been intended to use the buildings of Harvard College to house the prisoners, but the idea was abandoned), for their genteel accommodation. Did the brave General Gates ever mean this? Did our legislature ever intend the military should prevail above the civil? Is there not a degree of unkindness in loading poor Cambridge, almost ruined before this great army seemed to be let loose upon us, and what will be the consequence time will discover.

Some polite ones say, we ought not to look on them as prisoners. They are persons of distinguished rank. Perhaps, too, we must not view them in this light of enemies. I fear this distinction will be soon lost. Surprising that our General or any of our Colonels should insist on the first university in America being disbanded for their more genteel accommodation, and we poor, oppressed people seek an asylum in the woods against a piercing winter.

General Burgoyne dined a Saturday in Boston with General Heath. He rode through the town, properly attended down Court Street and through the Main Street, and on his return walked on foot to Charlestown Ferry, followed by a great number of spectators as ever attended a pope and generously observed to an officer with him the decent and modest behaviour of the inhabitants as he passed, saying if he had been conducting prisoners through the city of London, not all the guards of Majesty could have prevented insults. He likewise acknowledges Lincoln and Arnold to be great generals.

It is said we shall have not less than seven thousand persons to feed in Cambridge and its environs, more than its inhabitants. Two hundred and fifty cords of wood will not serve them a week. Think then how we must be distressed. Wood is risen to 5.10 pounds per cord, and but there is little to be purchased. I never thought I could lie down to sleep surrounded by these enemies. But we strangely became inured to those things which appear difficult when distant.

While the British troops were quartered on Prospect Hill, and the Germans on Winter Hill, both in rough barracks, Gentleman Johnny and Phillips were forced to share a bed in a small, dirty tavern, while their staff slept on the floor. General Glover claimed that the Cambridge residents could not forget the burning of Charleston by the British earlier in the war.

Meanwhile, Madame von Riedesel had her own set of problems; even though she and her children had one room under the roof, her women servants slept on the floor along with her men servants. Although the man of the house was kind to his *guests,* his wife was one of the Madame's biggest problems. In order to revenge herself for the trouble her guests caused, every time a guest sat down to eat, the wife would set the children down at the same table and proceed to comb out their hair, which was full of vermin, thus robbing the guests of their appetites.

The conditions in Cambridge were not favorable for either the *hosts* or *guests.* The conditions for the hosts were uncomfortable, unpleasant, and extremely costly and exhausting. The prisoners, however, were barely surviving under the wretched housing conditions.

The lack of provisions, the local scarcity of fuel, their inactivity, and disappointment at not being immediately shipped home, led to trouble; brawls with guards, and *many irregularities,* as Burgoyne admitted. The soldiers flocked into the town where they were allowed to go between 8 A.M. and 3 P.M. He also acknowledged to General Heath, the commanding officer in Massachusetts, the most *enormous abuse,* including the misconduct of a number of officers at Bradish's tavern on the night of December 25th; prisoners being removed from guards, sentries abused and insulted, passes counterfeited or filled up in the *most affrontive manner,* and several highway robberies. He also agreed there had been levities, indiscretions, faults of omission and neglect, and of liquor, which he had spared no effort to correct by punishment. According to Burgoyne, the fault could not be placed on one side only, for the American Colonel Henley had stabbed a British soldier, provoked, his defenders claimed, by *haughtiness.* At his court marshall, Burgoyne alleged that wanton barbarities had been committed and a general massacre of his troops threatened.

Burgoyne was approaching the end of his patience. He was annoyed with the provisions and accommodations provided for his soldiers, for which he had been forced to personally advance £20,000 of his own money (about a quarter of million dollars by present reckoning), which placed him for some time in *a very distressed condition.* As a result, he inadvertently committed an indiscretion that was seized upon by members of congress, anxious to repudiate the convention to which Gates had tamely agreed. If the Congress believed that Burgoyne had taken unfair advantage of Gates, Burgoyne, at the present moment, was about ready to invalidate his end of the capitulation. Always the optimist, he would develop a strategy to get out of this mess!

⧗

Two mornings after the convention Walter and Benjamin were dispatched by Wilkinson to deliver messages to the various regiments. They sat huddled near the campfire nursing a second cup of boiled coffee complete with grounds and reviewing their plans for the near future. Their cronies had left to ready the supply wagons, cannon, and other equipment for the army's pending repositioning. Colonel Dan, his flowing blonde hair hanging over the back of his buckskin jacket, had just received a message from Gates to prepare his troops for *temporary leave,* thus enabling them to visit their homes before the army advanced south. His friend and assistant, Sergeant George Jefferson, was wearing his usual drape, blue jacket with its single chevron on his sleeves. "Gates is permitting the soldiers and militiamen whose homes are located near here, ten days leave," said the buckskin clad colonel as he sipped the lukewarm coffee, and spit out its grounds. "As the troops march south, wherever, he plans to permit the others to stagger their leave-time, so all will be treated fairly."

"I was hoping to hear something like this," smiled the sergeant shivering from the cold, damp fog's penetration. "As you know Benjamin's home and mine is located right here in Albany, and we've been looking forward to seeing my wife and his mother. And, for a change, to sleep in a real bed . . ."

". . . with your wife cuddled up next to you," finished his buddy and commander. Both laughed, knowing each other's thoughts and lingering to enjoy the moment of companionship.

"Now down to business," Colonel Dan changed the subject. "I'd like you to draw up a schedule to accommodate Gates's orders and fairly provide our men with leaves. Gates would like to see our schedule tomorrow morning after chow; he hopes to have the passes prepared by the end of the week."

"That sounds like a challenging project," agreed the sergeant, "I'll get right on it, and have the first draft to you after today's noon chow." Both dumped the remaining coffee and its grounds from their cups upon the campfire, and parted with a smile, each respecting the other's professionalism and friendship.

⧗

After reviewing and receiving Gates's approval of the various leave schedules, Wilkinson and his staff set about preparing passes for the individual soldiers. It was not very long before rumors started circulating throughout the camp. Leaves and passes were about the only topics of discussion, especially for those whose homes were located within close (one hundred miles or less) proximity to the camp. Others accepted the situation and understood that they would have to wait their turn. All were speculating where their next position would be. Most believed they would be traveling south to reinforce Washington. They were unaware that their victory at Saratoga would encourage the French to quickly take the advantage to get back at their old nemesis, the British, and enter the war on the side of the Americans. They all knew they were fighting to be free of England and its king's rule, but none had ever expected another country to join the Americans in this endeavor.

After the morning meal the following day, each regiment was called together while their commander supervised the distribution of the ten-day leave passes. Needless to say, those who received their passes soon began preparing for the journey home, while the less fortunate prepared themselves to pull double duty, and looked forward to their turn for leave.

During their evening meal, Walter, Benjamin, Sergeant Jefferson and their cronies were busily planning either their leaves, or contemplating their added duties. Everyone was in joyous mood, not only because of the pending leaves, but because they were part of a determined group of people who wanted to be free of the King's reign, and they had just defeated one of the best armies in the world. With dreams of victory and leave, each retreated to his own bedroll in anticipation of the following day.

⧗

Walter Heindrick, Benjamin, and his father, Sergeant George Jefferson, all rode together to the Jefferson's home in Albany, where the sergeant's wife had been doing double duty overseeing the livery operations, while maintaining her own baking business.

"Julia! Julia!" yelled the sergeant as he leaped from his horse and ran to meet his light-colored beautiful wife of twenty-five years. They almost collided as they ran toward one another; the sturdy sergeant and livery owner lifted his petite wife high and whirled her about like a toy. "Oh, how I've missed you, my love," said Julia totally oblivious to her son and his friend on their horses. "No more than I've missed you, my dearest," whispered George in her ear. While the boys were dismounting, they walked hand-in-hand toward their son and his friend. "Mother," said the jubilant son, "I love you, and have missed you as much as Dad has." "I know, my son," she acknowledged as they hugged one another.

Walter stood there appreciating the love his friends were exchanging. Wishfully he was longing to do the same with his parents and his friend, Helena. As much as he loved his parents, he was beginning to realize how much Helena meant to him; their relationship, as far as he was concerned, was fast exceeding a platonic situation.

"Walter," Benjamin broke his blood-brother's daydream trance, "I'd like to introduce you to my mother, Julia." he said proudly, "Don't you think she's the most beautiful lady this side of Boston? Mother," he continued, "this is my friend and blood-brother, Walter Heindrick, who lives in New Palatine.

The embarrassed lady extended her hand to Walter. They shook hands and then Walter hugged her and gave her a kiss on the cheek. "I feel I've known you as long as I've known Benjamin, because he is all the while talking and bragging about you, especially your bake goods"

"I've also been told a lot about you; Benjamin is proud to call you his blood-brother," stated the trim-figured, blue-eyed mother and wife. "Let's go into the house," she suggested, "perhaps I can find a sample of our baked goods, as you call them. I've really been expecting you ever since we received news of Burgoyne's surrender. So every day I have baked an extra supply of cakes and *goodies* just in case my husband and my son come calling. What a pleasant surprise to see all of you."

George started their evening meal by saying grace while all four held hands around the table. Then George explained to Julia about their leave, and its limitations. "We have ten days, my love, which I plan to stay here with you. Walter has invited Benjamin to ride along with him to New Palatine, so he can see how they live down on the farm."

'That's right!" joked Walter, "we haven't caught up yet with you city folks. Maybe someday, but I wouldn't want to count on it. Most people out our way don't like all the hustle and bustle of the city. I do think," he stopped to take another bite of pastry, "It'll be worth it to come to the city just to get another piece of your pastry. What do you call this kind? It's delicious!"

"I don't know what the cook books call them, but I call them *Julia's fingers*. See!" she said as she held out her slender brown fingers, "doesn't this pastry look my fingers?"

"The only difference I can see between the two," said her husband, "is that the pastry is filled with custard, and covered with chocolate icing." Before anyone could say another word, the sergeant added, "but, my dear, you are just as sweet." She faked a slap at his face, but quickly changed it to a hug for the grisly, rugged hunk she jealously cherished and protected.

After they had finished their evening meal, Julia broke the silence, "I suggest that you boys need a good night's sleep for your long trip tomorrow." Then shyly she said, "Benjamin, your father and I have a lot of catchin' up to do." She kissed her son and headed for the bedroom, with her husband close behind. Walter and Benjamin knew that the next few tomorrows would be long and hard days. They had calculated three days ride to New Palatine; allowing six days in the saddle, and approximately two or three days in New Palatine.

✳{ 27 }✳

HOMEWARD

MIDDLE OCTOBER, 1777

———

ALONG THE KING'S HIGHWAY FROM ALBANY

Benjamin and Walter arose from sleep just before sunrise. When they arrived in the kitchen, they found Benjamin's mother removing a pan of golden-brown cornbread from the oven.

"Good morning, gentlemen," she said, "you're just in time for some hot cornbread, ham, and eggs. A little bit of butter and maple syrup will put a fine touch on this bread," she added with a wink.

"We suspected something like that," glowed Benjamin, "because we had already smelled the aroma of the ham."

"A very pleasant way to be awakened," chimed in Walter. "I agree with you about the maple syrup on cornbread. My mother usually calls cornbread, johnny cake."

"I hope she didn't name it after Gentleman Johnny Burgoyne," laughed Benjamin.

"I don't think she did," said Walter, "Unless he had been living in Germany's Palatine most of his life. As I understand it, that's what they called cornbread over there. However," he qualified his response, "I may have misunderstood my grandparents stories of *the way it used to be.*"

Moments later, a sleepy-eyed father and sergeant entered the kitchen rubbing his eyes, and headed toward his wife. After an affectionate kiss, he said, "Good morning, my love. Oh, yes! And a good morning to you guys; I hope you slept very well because you're in for a long ride."

"Now if you gentlemen will stop your talking and set yourselves down around the kitchen table, I will see what the cook has prepared for us," said the bright-eyed, cheerful lady. As Julia approached the table with the last serving dish, George rose from his chair and assisted his wife to the table. He then suggested that everybody join hands, and proceeded to say grace, asking the Lord to be with the boys on their trip to New Palatine, and for Him to help bring a quick end to the war. After all had squeezed hands, simultaneously saying Amen, George passed the platter with the ham and eggs to their guest, Walter; all settled down to enjoy their warm, bountiful breakfast.

"I've packed a knapsack of goodies for you," announced Julia looking at her son. "Gee, I've missed you! It's been too long without you. One good thing has developed as a result of your absence, I've been introduced to your blood-brother," she smiled at Walter. "It's going to be a long three days of riding." As an after thought, she asked, "Have you sufficient bedding and clothes?"

"Mother," Benjamin said, "Walter and I brought all of our military gear, which has served us well, even though it does smell of horses."

They laughed at Julia's concern, but the men would not want it any other way. Seeing most of the coffee cups near empty, Walter went to the cast iron stove, picked up the steaming coffeepot, and proceeded to refill everyone's cup.

Not wanting to waste any of their precious time together they leisurely enjoyed breakfast. Walter silently studied the Jefferson family and their interplay. He was envious of Benjamin's family which seemed to glow with love and caring for one another; not that his family did not love each other, but Benjamin's family was more demonstrative with their feelings, constantly and shamelessly hugging and kissing. George broke the silence, "I hate to throw a wet blanket on this joyous occasion, but if you guys intend to reach New Palatine in two or three days, you better get your asses a moving."

"Now, George, you know that we do not talk that way in this house," cautioned Julia.

"Sorry, my dear," apologized George, "I've been in the army too long!"

"Regardless, of what my wife tells me," continued George, "You guys better get your butts on those horses; be off with you," he smiled, "I'll help Julia clean up the dirty dishes."

Within minutes, Benjamin and Walter were astride their army issued chestnut geldings. They weaved in and about the city's narrow streets, past office buildings, churches, private homes, apartment houses, stores, and various other buildings housing a great number of people crowded in the confining limits of a metropolitan city. After about fifteen minutes, they reached the outskirts of Albany city, and were greeted with numerous expanses of open fields. Some fields had obviously been recently harvested of their crops; corn stubble sticking up among clumps of cornstacks tied together, stacks of hay still lying in the fields. Stepping up their pace to a steady canter, they rode almost silently for about three hours, passing through the settlement of Schenectady. When the sun was directly over head, they came upon a swiftly flowing creek and stopped to rest. While Walter watered the horses in the cool stream, Benjamin set some of Julia's goodies on a flat rock near the stream. When Walter joined him, Benjamin looked up and said, "I'm beginning to like these open spaces. The cool crisp air, the birds singing, and the squirrels running and putting those hickory nuts in their mouths and then running up a tree to store the nuts in their tree hold."

Walter almost ignoring Benjamin's remarks replied, "Yeah, I'm sure you find this country life different from the city, but I'm worried that the farmers' crops wont be totally harvested this fall. The farmers are way behind the frost," observed Walter, "Those stacks of corn and hay should have been stowed away undercover by now."

"Well," began Benjamin, "just maybe the men folk have been away fighting with us. Obviously, there has been some work done. The women can't do everything while the men are away," he concluded, "maybe the neighbors have been working together and just haven't got around to completing the harvesting on these farms."

"Yeah, you're probably right," agreed Walter. "To change the subject just a little, my father told me a story his grandfather had told him about my ancestors who came over here in the very early 1700s. Even then the Iroquois Indians had gradually drifted from hunting as a means of livelihood, to agriculture. In order to create land suitable for farming, they used a method that they called *slash-and-burn*. By burning off the trees and underbrush, they'd clear land for new planting areas. When that soil was exhausted, they'd slash-and-burn more trees and bushes."

"That makes sense," declared Benjamin. "The moral of that story is never underestimate the power and the minds of Indians."

"Agreed," said Walter. "Another thing, did you ever wonder why they call this route the King's Highway?"

"Never gave it a thought," responded Benjamin. "Probably some king rode on the road, and someone suggested that we honor the king."

"If it was such an honor, don't you think they would, at least, identify the king? Like the King George III Highway."

"Why that old codger never even stepped his feet on this continent, to say nothing about riding on this road."

"I think we better get back on the road, if we're to reach New Palatine in a couple of days." Swinging into their saddles, they were soon cantering along the narrow lane leading to the King's Highway. They chose to follow the north side of the Mohawk, because some of the old timers had advised them that the north was much easier to travel. They had also been told, that just before they arrived at Fort Dayton, they would have to ford the river and then go up the south side around Little Falls.

The King's Highway was the main cart route from Albany west to Oswego. Following both sides of the Mohawk River, it usually served as each settlement's main street, as in Schenectady, Little Falls, Fort Dayton, German Flats, and New Palatine. Beyond New Palatine, the route passed through Whitestown, Oriskany, Fort Stanwix, and eventually reached Oswego and Lake Ontario. The further west one traveled, especially west of Schenectady, the road narrowed into a rutted wagon lane that wound its way through tall trees and across swamps, cut through low-lying bushes, and followed lanes that, most of the time, allowed two horses to ride abreast, occasionally coming to open clearings used as pastures for farm animals or cultivated for growing some kind crop. Most of the roads in northern New York, as well as many roads throughout the colonies, have existed since prehistoric times as simply Indian trails. These trails were usually twelve to eighteen inches wide, and depending upon the firmness of the ground worn down about six inches deep. The accuracy with which the Indians blazed these trails to save distance from point-to-point was remarkable. Indian runners were said to have been able to make the trip between Albany and the edge of Lake Erie in three days. As more people traveled the road, the paths became wider to accommodate horses and eventually wagons. Again, depending on the type of soil, or location of the route, during summer storms the road was flooded in the low areas and turned the normally rutted King's Highway into a muddy mire or even a stream. About two miles west of Oriskany, the King's Highway meandered through a forest. Towering pine trees stretched their branches to the skies, seeking sunlight, while stately oak and hickory trees competed with equally majestic maples for the few sun rays that penetrated the forest. Stubby, drooping hemlocks helped to darken the forest floor, so the highway appeared to be entering a tunnel.

On either side of the road, low bushes packed any space remaining between the tall trees. The forest floor reeked of decaying oak, beech, hickory, and maple leaves along with pine and hemlock cones and needles.

As the sun began to set, Walter and Benjamin looked for an appropriate place to camp. They selected an area covered with moss under a spruce tree, which was about ten yards from the river's edge. "This is the place," declared Benjamin, "where we're going to camp for the night."

"Agreed, I"ll water the horses while you set up camp and build the fire."

"You're on," said Benjamin as he began to gather firewood.

Julia Jefferson had packed a chunk of smoked ham, a few potatoes, and cobs of corn. In short order, Benjamin had the fire built and the potatoes and corn nestled among the hot coals. After Walter had watered and tethered the horses, he filled the canteens with cool water from the stream. They had had a long hard day of riding from Albany, through Schenectady, and were now within a half day's ride to Fort Dayton. As they sat around the campfire eating, their shadows danced among the tree branches.

Benjamin started the evening's conversation, "If I recall correctly, you told me earlier that your ancestors came to the Mohawk Valley during the very early 1700s."

"That's right," answered Walter, "I remember father telling me that his grandfather Walter, was born in 1680, and together with his wife, Kristina, reached New York City in 1709. My grandfather, Ulrich, was only nine-years-old at that time. They started out working as indentured servants for the English, tapping the evergreen trees for tar pitch in a place just north of New York City called Livingston Manor; the tar pitch was used for the British naval vessels. While my grandfather was still a youngster, he met his future wife, Elizabeth Mueller; they were married in 1720. In 1729, my grandmother died giving birth to my father, Karl, your father's blood brother."

"That's when my Grandma Georgia went to live in your grandfather's home with my father, who was only a week or two older than your father; and she served as a wet nurse for both of our fathers," commented Benjamin.

"That's right," agreed Walter. "As I understand it, our fathers were brought up as brothers, and I guess our grandparents lived very comfortably together for a little over ten years." He stopped a moment, and added, "That was until your grandfather came and took your grandmother and father back to Albany with him."

"As I remember, my father told me that those years were some of the happiest of his life," commented Benjamin.

"When my parents were married in 1755, they lived with my Grandfather Ulrich in his farmhouse; remember my Grandmother Elizabeth had died during the birth of my father. On November 12, 1757, they went into the New Palatine settlement. My father went to the smithy to have his work horse shod and a plow repaired, and my mother went shopping for some yard goods to make dresses for herself and shirts for my dad; both did some food and feed shopping, and returned to their home late in the afternoon. When they arrived, they went into total shock. Their home was burning, and on the ground in front of it was Grampa Ulrich flat on his back with an Indian spear sticking straight up in the air. The spear had been run straight through his chest; his pet dog, Fritz, lay dead near his side. Later they learned that the attackers were Canadians and Indians lead by M. de Belletre. Remember, this was during the French and Indian War. De Belletre's forces had come streaming from the mountain forests without any warning, attacking all of the Palatine settlements on the north side of the Mohawk, in and around German Flats. They made a clean sweep, burning every building; houses with or without people inside, and barns filled with harvested crops, while most of the livestock, horses, cattle, sheep, and swine were killed. In just that one day, forty Germans were scalped or burned to death; approximately sixty houses were leveled, five blockhouses destroyed, and about one hundred and fifty frightened settlers were dragged north into captivity.

"You see my grandfather and father were very loud and strong supporters of General Herkimer, the Committee of Safety, and the Tryon County Militia. That may have been one reason Grandpa Ulrich was killed and his house burned. It appeared, however, as if the attackers were determined to destroy any and all of Palatine property. I don't know! Anyway, years later came the Battle of Oriskany," he stopped a moment, "I'm sorry, Benjamin, I've talked too long and have already told you about my blood-brother, White Tail. All these things helped me decide to come along with your father and General Arnold."

"Yes, your family have suffered at lot," Benjamin agreed, "I can see why you feel so bitter toward the British, and the Indians. Thank goodness, we don't have to deal with the French these days. In fact, I've heard rumors the French may join the Americans against the British. Now, that's certainly a twist for us." He stopped to throw another log on the fire. "The story of my ancestors is not quite like yours, but there is some similarity."

"I'd love to hear about your family, and how you ended up in Albany," Walter urged.

"Your family started off as indentured servants for the British with some possibility of freedom. In 1664, my ancestors started off as slaves, with no opportunity for eventual freedom, working for the Dutch West India Company in New Amsterdam; that's what New York City used to be named. Fortunately, my ancestors were shipped up the Hudson River to Fort Orange; it's called Albany now. From there, they were transported to Schenectady. I understand that along about that time Schenectady was a stockaded trading post dealing with the Iroquois and the Canadians and had about forty houses. On February 9, 1690, at about eleven o'clock at night, there was an infamous massacre, conducted by a party of French and Indians. The ground was deep with snow, the attackers killed sixty of the inhabitants, and carried away fourteen prisoners including fifteen Negroes. My ancestors were among those Negroes. Seven years later, they escaped and returned to Schenectady; by that time the settlement included fourteen Negroes out of a population of 238. During those years, my ancestors were fortunate to be owned by the Schuylers. Mr. Schuyler recognized my grandfather's tremendous talent with his hands, especially when working with iron. So he started him off shoeing horses; eventually Herr Hans Schuyler had him make farm tools and parts for wagons. Soon the men had developed a mutual respect, and Herr Schuyler gave my grandfather his freedom; that's when he came to your father's home after my Grandma Georgia," he added. When the war came, Herr Schuyler freed all of his slaves, allowing them to join the militia if they so desired."

"That's called manumission," said Walter, "when slave owners permitted slaves their freedom if they joined the militia."

"I heard an interesting story about things in New Amsterdam," said Benjamin changing the subject. "In New Amsterdam Jews were not allowed in the militia, but colored were. Another odd thing, Jews could not own real estate, but colored could and often did. Free colored people were really free; some even owned their own indentured servants." As an added comment, Benjamin said, "I understand that Indian slavery was not uncommon during the seventeenth century."

"You must admit, Benjamin, that our families have interesting backgrounds. How fortunate we are that we live here in New York, in the United States of America, where all of us will be free when we get old King George III off our backs." He leaned back, stretched his arms, and suggested they beddown, and get some sleep before the next day's long ride. Without saying another word, they placed a few more logs on the fire, and said good night to one another. They were sound asleep, each in his bedroll while a great horned owl hooted to his mate.

⧗

Burgoyne was still fuming with dissatisfaction over his troops accommodations. He reflected upon his conqueror, General Gates, to his credit he had been a man and a soldier, doing his utmost to avoid rubbing salt into Burgoyne's and his troops' wounds. He was daydreaming, visualizing his army marching to the prearranged place on the banks of the Hudson River, close to the ruins of old Fort Hardy. It distressed him to recall his troops surrendering and piling their arms for the victors. He was grateful that Gates had been conscious of the shame Burgoyne's men must have felt; Gates had allowed only one British officer to witness the ceremony. But in spite of the good conditions about the surrender process, presently Burgoyne deeply resented the humiliation he and his troops were experiencing.

Captain Anburey reviewed the situation with Burgoyne, "It was universally understood throughout the army, that the object of our expedition was to effect a junction with the one under General Howe. You can easily conceive the astonishment it occasioned, when we were informed that General Howe's army had gone to Philadelphia. It is evident that a great error has been committed, either unintentional or designed, but where to fix it is impossible to say. Sir, I believe that *time,* that great discloser of secrets, will no doubt reveal this."

What Anburey had to say helped to soothe the wound, but it still was weeping blood.

On November 14th, Burgoyne wrote a letter to Gates outlining the deplorable condition of his troops, emphasizing that *the public faith is broke.* His irritation was taken by Congress to mean that, since the Americans had broken faith, there was no need for the British to keep faith with the Americans.

The President of Congress, Henry Laurens, claimed that Burgoyne's remark had been prompted by more than exasperation. He believed that the British intended, once their troops had been embarked, to sail the transports not across the Atlantic, but to New York City where the captive soldiers would join General Howe's army. Laurens based his opinion on British duplicity, on the inadequate tonnage of transports available, and on the scarcity of provisions for a voyage to Europe. Laurens did not know that he did possess definite *proof* against the British; the definite proof did not come to light until 1932, in a letter written by Howe to Burgoyne on November 16, 1777. The letter was marked Secret, and it directed Burgoyne after the troops had embarked upon the transports, to give his *secret directions* to the officer commanding the convoy. The officer had been instructed to follow his orders, to carry the British troops to

New York City. There they would be exchanged for an equal number of rebel prisoners, the return of whom "has been pointedly refused under the most frivolous Pretences." The foreign troops were to proceed to England.

Concluding his letter, Howe enjoined Burgoyne "to use every possible Precaution to keep the Enemy Ignorant of my Intentions, as on the least Suspicion the Troops will be infallibly stopped."

A plan for exchanging prisoners had been arranged during the previous April, but the exchange was not satisfactory for the Americans. The prisoners Howe sent "were in such a debilitated condition that many of them had died before reaching their homes," complained Washington, who refused to send healthy British prisoners in return. To rectify the balance, Howe proposed to keep the 2,202 British "convention" soldiers in New York and add them to his own army.

Whatever the rights and wrongs of these minor contentions and arguments, the stain on America's reputation was faint compared to the darker stain of the British. The British refused to treat captured American seamen as prisoners of war, and forced them to serve in the Royal Navy against their own countrymen; keeping in mind that Burgoyne wished to repudiate the lenient convention which Gates had freely agreed upon.

No wonder Burgoyne was frustrated; things just were not proceeding as he had so carefully planned.

⧗

The next morning the fog was so dense that Walter and Benjamin could not even see their horses; they did, however, hear them stirring about, and when they called the horses by name, they were answered with a gentle whinny. As on the previous night, Walter watered the horses while Benjamin built a small fire to boil some coffee. They had decided to forgo a cooked meal, instead they chewed sticks of venison jerky and ate the last of Julia's cornbread. Within an hour they were back on the road headed toward Fort Dayton.

"Have you ever been to Fort Dayton?" asked Walter.

"Right here where we are now is the farthest west I have ever been," declared Benjamin. "But from what I've seen, I know why you enjoy the area."

"At Forts Dayton and Herkimer life is centered around and about their 24 block houses," commented Walter. "Fort Dayton was the place where General Herkimer started the Tryon County Militia's march with 800 militiamen and 400 ox carts to relieve Fort Stanwix. That's the march that was ambushed at Oriskany. You've heard all about that battle."

"Yes, I've heard all about the Battle of Oriskany," agreed Benjamin. "It was just east of Fort Stanwix, I believe near the site of the battle, where my father discovered your wounded father."

"That's right, he found my father wounded and being transported back to our home. Then I met your father, and eventually he talked me into joining him and General Benedict Arnold to fight the British," joked Walter. "He didn't have to try very hard though. The toughest part in my decision was wondering what my friend Helena would say. Surprisingly, she encouraged me. Not that I don't enjoy your company, Benjamin, but I really have missed seeing her. You know what I mean, don't you?"

"Sure do!" said Benjamin. "You're fortunate to have a friend like her" he added with a slight sign of envy.

The fog was lifting enabling them to see at least thirty yards ahead, "We'd better pick up our pace if you still want to arrive at Fort Dayton early this afternoon," suggested Benjamin.

"Sorry," admitted Walter. "I guess I have been riding in a kinda daze. My head has been in the clouds the last half hour," he smiled. "I agree with you, we'd better increase our pace." They cantered along the shore, while steam was rising from the river, creating a dream-like environment.

Riding along the south shore, they came to place called Shoemaker's Tavern. "That's the place that's known as a Tory hangout," pointed Walter, "where they tried to persuade the locals to join the Royalists. If I'm correct, the place was raided, and a bunch of Tories were captured. Among the them was someone named Hon Yost Schuyler; General Arnold used Yost to scare General St. Leger and his Indians."

"The more I hear about General Arnold," said Benjamin. "The more I like him."

Quietly they rode to the place where they had been told they would have to ford the river to the south side and circle around Little Falls. "Right near here is General Herkimer's red-brick house, the place where he died," commented Walter. "Another hour, and we'll be in Fort Dayton," he added.

Their steady canter brought them to the fort known for its blockhouses, and where the Tryon County Militia held its regular weekly drills. The fort was no more than a square wooden palisade, containing a dilapidated barracks, a storage house, and a trading post. Almost everything was made of wood, and it would be hard to find more solidly constructed buildings.

Walter and Benjamin dismounted and sauntered to the trading post where a few old timers were leaning against the porch's posts; while others were sitting on the steps. They started whispering among themselves, pointing to the two young men in army uniforms.

"Where ya' from?" asked one.

"Why aren't you out there fightin' the Redcoats?"

"You guys aren't even old enough be dry behind your ears," said another.

Then a skinny, whiskered man wearing deerskin clothes came up to them, "Don't listen to those old farts, they're just jealous because the militia wouldn't accept them. Most of the time they're drunker than a hoot owl, but sure as I'm alive and right here with you, all of 'em can shoot a dove at a hundred, . . . that is one hundred yards. You young fellers look like you could use a cup of coffee and some day-old-johnny cake. Come on inside, and let me treat you to some real Yankee hospitality."

Walter and Benjamin quickly accepted his invitation. Before they knew it, they were sitting on small kegs sipping their coffee and eating the cake. "Where ya' headed for? Oh! —," before they could answer him. "My name's Herman Folkes, most people call me 'Ole Folks,' 'cause I've been around this neck of the woods so long. I even remember Johan Jost Herkimer. See, there's an old story about him and the Indians. One day he just happened to see a bunch of Indians struggling to transport a dug-out canoe. Herkimer motioned for all of them to get on one end of the canoe, and he lifted up the other end. Together they carried the canoe to the river and placed it in the water. The Indians were so impressed with his strength, they called him Kouari, Mohawk for bear, and they allowed him to build his cabin on the land that is now Fort Herkimer. Yes, Siree! Them was the times."

"He must have been quite a man," said Benjamin. "May we buy you some more coffee?"

"Don't mind if you do, ladee!"

While Benjamin was purchasing the coffee, Walter asked Ole Folks, "How much of a ride is it from here to New Palatine?"

"Oh, it's just a mite up the road; shouldn't take more than half a day," he advised, "If'n you're lucky and ride a steady pace, I suppose you could git there just after sundown. It's just beyond German Flats; north side of the river," he added.

Walter handed his friend the coffee cups and was about to say that he and Benjamin should be on the road very soon, but Ole Folks had other ideas. "Seein's you young lads are new around here, let me tell you about this wagon trail they call the King's Highway." He tipped his keg backwards, leaned against the wall, and started, "During the early days, the whole river from Schenectady to Herkimer's and German Flats was nothing but Dutch and Germans. Some claim they're Palatines, but I say if'n they talk German, they're German. Anyway, they've been on the river for better than one hundred years, and they've done little more than carve out farms along the flats. As for the highway, there were no bridges, ain't none now over the Mohawk, just crossin's. During those years most of the freight had to be boated up and down the river. The river's too shallow in places, 'specially the rifts are so bad you can't ferry more than a two-ton load at a time. A friend of mine, Sally's her name, was ten days getting herself and her baby and her furniture from Albany to Fort Stanwix; it used to be named Fort Schulyer in honor of General Philip Schulyer. They made such good time because the rains had given them seventeen inches of water at the rift narrows." As an afterthought, he said, "It took six yoke of oxen to get their bateau around the *carrying place* at Little Falls."

"That's some story!" said Walter as he stood up and motioned toward their horses tethered on the settlement commons. "I believe we've been fortunate meeting you and hearing your tales of the valley, but we must be on our way."

"I agree with Walter, Ole Folks. We'll only be two or three days in New Palatine," said Benjamin. "Let's hope that we see you on our way back to Albany. Oh, by the way, my name's Benjamin Jefferson from Albany," shaking Ole Folks's hand.

"My name is Walter Heindrick from New Palatine. It's been a pleasure meeting you, I, too, hope to see you on our way back."

They trotted to their horses, muttering about finally getting away from Ole Folks. "We did learn a lot about the valley, but I'd rather have been on the road," said Walter as he looked toward his blood-brother. Soon they were in a gentle canter, riding along the road through the forest with the tree's canopy touching above them and as the road became narrower it seemed they were entering a tunnel. It was brighter than usual because the maple trees had already shed their leaves, allowing the sunlight to drift through bare branches.

⧗

They didn't believe they would reach New Palatine before sundown, and therefore decided to camp just east of New Palatine, beside a little, quiet stream. As on the evening before, Walter watered and tethered the horses, and filled up their canteens, while Benjamin built the fire, made coffee, and pulled out the last of his mother's goodies. They were seated cross-legged on either side of the campfire eating, when Walter broke the silence, "This creek is known as Bloody Creek."

"That's a weird name for such a beautiful little stream," declared Benjamin.

"It received its name just after the Battle of Oriskany," started Walter. "At one time during the day of the battle, August 6th, the Americans were really caught off balance and were losing. Providence, however, seemed to be on the Americans' side. A thundershower came down in torrents nearly drowning the soldiers; certainly the rain washed war out of their powder and drove the British and Indians back into the woods for cover. General Herkimer took advantage of the time by instructing his men to double up behind the trees they picked for defense. He had earlier noticed that the Indians waited for a man to fire, and then as he reloaded, they would leap out from cover to shoot or knife him. By having two men behind the same tree, one could be firing while the other was reloading. That tactic really fooled the Indians, and eventually discouraged them, until finally, the Americans drove the British and Indians from the site."

Before Walter could continue, Benjamin said, "Now that's an interesting story, but it doesn't tell me how the stream came to be known as Blood Creek."

"That's what I was about to tell you," smiled Walter. "That stream swelled and overflowed with water. Dead and wounded British soldiers, Indian warriors, and American militiamen lay in the water and along the banks; their blood turned the stream red. Now you know how this creek received its name," continued Walter. "Do you still want to stay here tonight, or should we push on?"

"I don't believe there are any dead bodies lying around," began Benjamin. "Anyway all of that killing happened way west of here." He changed the subject, "While I strolled along the creek for firewood, I think I saw a few fish. If the fish like it here, I'm for staying. How about you?"

"Suits me just fine," agreed Walter. "Gee, I hope my letters reached my parents and Helena. I told them that since Burgoyne had surrendered, the rumor about camp was that some of us would be receiving short leaves. I warned them not to be surprised if I came visiting them in the near future."

"That's just about what I said to my mother when I wrote to her. I'm certain when my father wrote to Mom, he would state the time of our leave more correctly," Benjamin already missed his father and mother. The leave had been great, but it made him realize how much he loved his parents and appreciated their home. "What is New Palatine like?" he asked.

Each talked about his hometown, until the campfire needed another log. Together they searched for a few logs to throw on the fire. Shortly, they settled with their own thoughts and dreams in their bedrolls placed on top of hemlock boughs.

The next morning when Walter awoke, he did not see Benjamin. He called. Called, again. Then he heard Benjamin responding, "I'm down here, here by the creek. Come on down."

Walter crept out of his bedroll and sleepy-eyed went to the stream where he found Benjamin. He couldn't believe what he saw. Benjamin had rigged up a fishing pole and was fishing.

"See I told you last night that there were fish in this stream," holding up a string with three rainbow trout hanging on it. "I'll catch another fish if you'll take these and dress them for the frying pan."

"You're another one!" declared Walter. "I don't know how I can keep up with you. The idea of eating fried fish for breakfast really hits the spot." He took the fish, and proceeded to clean them. He had just finished placing the third fish in the frying pan, when Benjamin arrived with the fourth one.

"A feast fit for a king," said Benjamin.

"Just as long it isn't for King George III.

Soon they were astride their horses, headed on their last leg toward New Palatine.

They had traveled at a relatively steady gait for about an hour and a half when Benjamin and Walter emerged from the narrow, shadowy, wooded lane called the King's Highway into a bright clearing with open fields on both sides of the road. They felt the bright morning sunshine warm their backs as they slowed their pace to enjoy the pleasure of the pastoral scene they had entered. To their left was a field covered with cornstalk stubble and numerous pheasants in a feeding frenzy going from one unharvested corncob to the next. The other side of the road was bordered with the trail of a post-and-rail fence that disappeared into the far distance; this field served as the grazing grounds for a small herd of black and white milch cows.

"Now, my brother," declared Walter, "this is the beginning of the settlement known as New Palatine. My hometown," he proudly announced.

"I must admit you know how to pick 'em," said Benjamin. "It is so peaceful here. I love seeing the rolling hills with the brooks meandering throughout them. Oh! Look there's a small flock of white-faced sheep grazing."

"Watch out!" yelled Walter. "Those sheep are going to cross the road in front of us." The post-and-rail fence disappeared at the crest of the hill, allowing the sheep to go from one side of the road to the other at their leisure.

They stopped their horses, who had never seen such weird looking creatures with fuzzy wool all over them except on their white faces and legs. "I guess, Walter, these sheep are serving as our welcoming party."

"Now, you know that we have more sheep and cows here than we have people," said Walter. "See down the hill," he pointed, "that's the settlement of New Palatine where all the people in the surrounding area come to get their horses shod, farm tools made, purchase yards goods for clothing, corn seed, everything, including my mother's special Limburger cheese," he proudly announced. "Here the farmers and the trade stores use somewhat of a barter system."

"What do you mean by barter system?" asked Benjamin.

"Well, for example, my parents bring in their cheeses and maple syrup to Helena's mother's general store, and Mrs. Kerchner gives them credit towards the purchase of anything she has in her store. That way eliminating the necessity for a lot of cash."

"What if you don't have any goods to barter with Mrs. Kerchner?"

"Well, you could exchange services for goods. For example, your father's a blacksmith, right?" Benjamin nodded in agreement. "Your dad could either build something for the store, or he could place whatever he made on consignment in the store, and Mrs. Kerchner would sell it. There are many ways for people like your father, or anyone else who was not a farmer, to manage living around here without much money," he added as an afterthought.

Slowing down, they entered the town. Pointing to their right, Walter said, "That's George Raab's smithy shop." They saw a short, middle-aged, muscular man pounding away on an anvil. He looked toward them, recognized Walter, and yelled, "Welcome home, soldier. I thought you were still out there drumming in old Gentleman Johnny's ear."

Walter laughed and said, "We've made the British surrender back in Saratoga. Mr. Raab," he continued, "I want to introduce you to my blood brother, Benjamin Jefferson. He plays the fife, while I play the drums. We have also been assigned to serve as couriers for General Gates."

"Sounds very important. I'm mighty proud to meet you, Benjamin. Any friend of Walter's is a friend of mine. You young gentlemen better hurry up, now." He stopped and smiled, "There's a young lady up there in the general store. She's been spreading the news for the last couple of days that she was expecting your return." He extended his thick, stubby hand to Benjamin, "Mighty proud to meet you, Benjamin," While Benjamin was recovering from his nearly crushed hand, George was giving Walter's shoulder a healthy, but loving, tap. "Let's go and see what Mr. Raab is talking about."

"Is everyone here as friendly as he is?" asked Benjamin.

"Most are," declared Walter. "Personally, I believe it's the attitude we present to them that determines whether or not they are friendly to us. You're just a hellva nice person!" he said, as he leaned from his horse and patted Benjamin.

"I'll remember that, the next time you get mad at me."

By this time they were approaching the area known as the common. "That's what we refer to as the common, where in years past, residents used to bring their sheep and cows to pasture. Most recently, when General Herkimer and my father were drilling the Tryon County Militia, they use the common as their parade field. The only problem was everyone had to be pretty careful where they stepped," laughed Walter.

"That livery stable," pointed Benjamin, "looks very similar to my father's; a little smaller, I guess because father's livery is in a big settlement."

As they approached a two-story, grey field-stone building about the size of any house in Albany, Benjamin saw a weather-beaten, wooden sign hanging over its narrow, solidly built front door. Quizzically squinting and pointing toward the sign, he read Heidelberg Tavern.

"That's the Heidleberg Tavern owned by Martha Butler. Her husband was one of those Butler brothers who were Tories fighting with the British against us rebels. Martha and her husband didn't agree in each other's politics. She always encouraged the militia to assemble there; never turned away a Tory either. Her husband, Jerome Butler, would come back finding them rebels in the tavern, and try to run them out. At one time, he was the settlement's mayor, and primary supporter of the king, and was spending more and more time with Colonel John Butler and Sir Guy Johnson; the more he did, the more Martha encouraged the rebels to stay. I understand that she frequently served as an informant to the Americans. Finally, one day her husband left; she learned later that he had been killed when he participated, dressed up like an Indian, in raids upon some local houses and farms."

"Sounds like a really nice person to know," Benjamin said sarcastically. "How did she put up with him?"

"That's what all of us wondered," answered Walter. "Martha is a voluptuous lady who will not put up with any bullshit, but her heart is as big as this horse I'm riding. Plus, she is a true patriot, willing to help us all to beat the British. Very religious, too. She, in fact, lives her religion. Since there was no church in town, she made the tavern available until the community had completed that church over there on the other side of the common. Promptly at midnight on Saturdays, she would close down the bar, and overnight the tavern would be transformed into New Palatine's Dutch Reformed Mission for our residents who did not want to travel the ten miles or so east to the traditional church in German Flats. She even converted the bar area, with its fireplace as pulpit where our circuit-riding preacher, Reverend Johann Stouffer, would come and preach to us; he preferred to say that he talked with all of us. You'll have to meet him, he's a hellva nice fella."

Walter had no sooner finished the word fella when they heard someone calling at them loudly. There in the middle of the rutted, dirt road was Helena, running towards them with her arms spread out, looking like she was about to fly.

Walter tossed his horse's reins to Benjamin, "Here catch!" he yelled as he slid from his horse. There in the middle of main street they wrapped their arms around each other; they had never expressed such affection until now. They quickly separated, "Oh, Walter, I'm so glad you're back home, safe and sound. I've really missed you."

"I've dreamed of you so many times," Walter admitted. "I guess we never miss someone, until we're apart." He had almost forgotten Benjamin until he saw him walking the horses toward them. "Helena Kerchner, I'd like to introduce you to my very good friend and blood-brother, Benjamin Jefferson. He's the kind of blood-brother you and I were with White Tail."

"Does that mean that very soon I'll be your blood-sister?" she smiled. Before Benjamin could respond, Helena said, "I'm very pleased to meet you, Benjamin."

"Likewise, Miss Kerchner. Walter has frequently told me about you." Before anyone could say another word, Benjamin added, "And everything he told me was good."

Both of his friends were embarrassed; "young love" thought the year older Benjamin. Helena moved between them grabbing their hands. Benjamin still carrying the reins of both the horses, asked "Where can I hitch these horses?"

"Sorry," answered Walter and Helena simultaneously. "Bring them over to the general store, there's a place there."

Together they walked, tied up the horses, and went into the store. The first person to greet them was not Helena's mother, rather the lady who greeted them was Hazel Perry, whose husband served as assistant manager in charge of farm equipment, feed, and grains. When Helena's father decided he didn't believe in the rebel cause, he forcibly took his wife and daughter to Canada where he joined the Tory forces. The Perry's, who worked for the Kerchner's for many years, continued to keep open the settlement's only general store. They drew their regular wages and deposited the surplus into the Kerchner's bank account. When Kerchner was killed during the Battle of Oriskany, Helena's mother came back from Canada, and was so delighted with what the Perry's had done that she gave them half interest in the business.

"Welcome home, Walter! I see Helena has found you. You don't know how much she has missed you," said Mrs. Perry.

"Mrs. Perry, I'd like to introduce you to my good friend and blood-brother, Benjamin Jefferson. We were in camp together. Benjamin's parents live in Albany. We stopped off to see them, and I talked him into coming and visiting New Palatine."

She extended her hand saying, "I'm very pleased to meet any friend of Walter's. Is this the first time you have been out west here?"

"The fartherest west I've been, until I met Walter, was my hometown of Albany," smiled Benjamin. "I'm impressed with what I've seen, especially the people, they're so friendly."

"Where's mother," asked Helena?"

"She was feeling a little faint, so she decided to walk across the common to your home," answered Mrs. Perry. "By the way, did you see our new church?" she asked proudly. "We've even talked Reverend Stouffer and his wife into coming and preaching here full-time." She stopped and corrected herself, "Not really full-time until he can find a replacement for his position. The Stouffer's are going to be living for a while in the back of the church."

"I've told Benjamin about Preacher Stouffer," said Walter. "We plan to attend church tomorrow. That is, as soon as I get home to introduce Benjamin to my parents."

"I'm sorry Harvey's not here. He's my husband," Mrs. Perry said to Benjamin, "but he's been called to the Swackhammer's farm. I'm not sure what it's all about, but you can meet him tomorrow in church."

"It's been a pleasure meeting you and I look forward to meeting your husband."

"I'm going to ride out to your parents farm with you," Helena announced.

Together the three young friends mounted their horses and rode west out of town toward the setting sun and Walter's parents home.

❈ 28 ❈

AT LAST!

ON KING'S HIGHWAY

The trio were headed due west on the King's Highway from the settlement of New Palatine. Silently, each with his own thoughts, they cantered in a slow but steady gait the five miles toward Walter's home. The golden, red sun seemed to be urging them on before it finally disappeared for another 12 hours.

How strange it felt as they rode along the narrow, winding lane. First passing through a passage of over-hanging evergreens, then suddenly coming to open fields that showed signs of harvesting, or pastures with grazing livestock. The wonder of the area always seemed to put Walter into a trance. For thirty years, the Palatines had enjoyed undisputed occupancy and were unmolested; they enjoyed long periods of rest, peace, and prosperity, compared to the toils and afflictions experienced in the old country, and as a matter of fact, for fifteen years in the new country, also. His people had settled on one of the most fertile fields imaginable They had constructed sound, masonry homes and barns, especially after 1757; they had been generously rewarded for the their toil. They followed the road as it wandered down a small hill with a babbling brook at its foot; dangerous for the horses's footing. After crossing the brook, the lane continued, with stately sugar maple trees along each side. Benjamin marveled at the huge maples. Walter informed him that his grandfather, Ulrich, had planted them a few years before the 1757 massacre. He loved to see the maples trees with their brilliant colors in the fall, and anticipated that in his later years, he would be able to tap them for maple sap during the spring. Delicious, he remembered maple syrup on cornbread or German pancakes. Too bad, thought Walter, Grampa Ulrich never was able to see the how full they had grown, or enjoy the natural wonderment and the pure luscious sweetness they gave the harvesters of their sap. That was all he knew about his grandfather, except that horrible day in November 1757.

The silence was broken by Benjamin, "Look," he exclaimed, "someone has planted these trees. They look so regal, but they appear to be dead," he added.

"My Grandfather Ulrich planted those maple trees just a few years before he died," informed Walter. "They're not dead, they've lost their leaves earlier this fall; next year the leaves will reappear in all their green glory."

"That's when Walter's father taps the trees for maple sap to be boiled down into maple syrup, cream, and sugar," smiled Helena as if she could taste the sweet, rich delicacy. Thoughts went racing through her head; she could envision the men hammering the wooden spouts into the trees, hanging a wooden bucket from the spout, then wading in the snow to the next tree to repeat the process until all of the maples had been tapped. She remembered helping to drive the horse as he pulled the sled from one tree to another, while Walter's father emptied the buckets of sap into a huge barrel, then pulling the flat sled with filled barrels to the shed where a long, flat metal tray sat on top of a slow burning fire. The watery colored sap was poured into the tray and left to evaporate into syrup. Those were happy days, she thought, and hoped there would be more.

Meanwhile, Benjamin had his own thoughts. How could anyone live in such a rural, desolate country? Miles before you would see anyone. What if one became sick, how would anyone know about it? Who would be available to help? He did remember that his grandmother, Georgia, had been available to help Walter's grandfather, Ulrich, when Walter's grandmother, Elizabeth, had died in child birth. But that was a long time ago, he reasoned. Maybe they live by instinct. They do have a church. From what I've heard Walter say, most of New Palatine's residents attend church regularly. Maybe, he thought, that's the way they stay in touch with each other. He couldn't get over the distance one had to travel from one house to another; they'd have to have more than one horse. Still, he reasoned, he liked the quiet, serene setting. Who knows, he contemplated, if I ever came to live out here, I would learn to shoot something other than the British.

The maples seemed to know the direction for them to ride, beckoning them to enter a narrower, maple-lined lane to their right. The three young people entered the lane with clearings on both sides. A post-and-rail fence guided the travelers to a two-story stone farmhouse about a half-mile down the lane.

Benjamin was in awe of the building. It looked more like a fort than the farmhouse he had envisioned. The fieldstone building had what looked like loopholes placed around the first and second floors; something one would see in castles from where archers could shoot, but he had never seen a house like this in Albany. It was hard for Benjamin to realize that New Palatine was a settlement on the very western edge of New York Colony's frontier. Some Indians still marauded about the area, especially those who were fighting with the Tories and Sir John Johnson. From his horse, Benjamin could see the building's front door; it appeared to open into an entryway where the main room with a huge stone fireplace was located. The centered fireplace served to heat the entire house since there were few, if any, farmhouses and city houses built with central heating systems. He knew that such enormous fireplaces rose from a massive foundation in the house's cellar, which frequently had a dug well and a cold-root cellar to store their food stuffs. To the left of the main entrance, there was a large room, probably the master's bedroom, he thought; to the right of the main room seemed to be another one of equal size, but for what, Benjamin could not figure out. He reckoned that the kitchen probably was located to the rear of the fireplace and the two side rooms. On the second floor, there were two beautiful dormer windows located in front of the house, while traditional windows with narrow, wooden casements were conservatively placed along its front. The house was encircled with a rustic, log palisade. In front of the house, there was a huge wooden door, with iron hinges nearly two feet long and six-inches wide, serving as the entrance to the inside courtyard surrounding the house. It really is more like a fort than somebody's home here in the wilderness, mused Benjamin, with all of the farm buildings outside the palisade. He'd always heard that what the Palatines provided first was warm winter quarters for their animals. There they consumed less hay and forage for survival; and the big warm barns meant less work for the farmers during the long winter months. Obviously, thought Benjamin, this house was built to last and to ward-off intruders. It was neither Dutch, nor English. He decided to call the type of architecture classic, frontier German, built to last through Indians raids as well as icy, snowy winters, and humid, hot summers.

As soon as Walter had arrived at the huge gate-like door, he slipped from his saddle, and tied his horses's reins to the ten-feet long hitching rail that was built into the palisade. Helena and Benjamin followed suit, and trailed Walter up a flagstone walk that lead them to the house's front door. Before Walter could open the door, it burst open and he was greeted with a bear hug from a woman who was about the same age and height as Benjamin's mother, Julia. This lady, however, was slightly stouter, with hands visibly more ruddy. Her blond hair was pulled into a tight bun on top of her head. She looked as if she would be Walter's equal in a wrestling match. Her smile seemed to run from one eye to the other, and her rosy cheeks glowed like sunlight.

"My son! My son," she said, squeezing Walter. "I'm so glad you're home. Oh, Helena, there you are." Helena, too, received a huge bear hug, and a kiss right on the lips. "You were right, when you told me that Walter might be arriving today or tomorrow."

"That's right, Mother Heindrick. I just knew that he would be here very soon."

While Helena and the two Heindricks were becoming reacquainted, they had nearly forgotten Benjamin until Walter regained his senses. "Mother, this is my best friend Benjamin Jefferson. He is also my blood brother, just like White Tail and I were."

She extended her stubby hand to her son's best friend, "I'm pleased to make your acquaintance, Benjamin," she beamed. She clapped her hands together, and headed to the right of the fireplace. "Enough of all this, come on into our home. I've baked some maple-sugar cookies and your favorite, crumbcake; they're ready to be served with some hot, spiced cider. You father's still down at the cheese factory with Cal

Swartz. At times, it seems that the two of them practically live down there."

""How is father?" asked Walter, as they walked through the main room to the kitchen behind the huge fireplace, its glowing embers sending off warmth Benjamin and Walter had not experienced since leaving the Jefferson's.

"Your father has been doing remarkably well since the battle," she glanced up toward Benjamin. "He was wounded, shattering his left leg."

"Walter told me a bit about that battle; my father and I have only been engaged in the Battle of Saratoga, although that was bad enough."

"Talking about the battles," started Walter, "I was thinking about Helena, Benjamin and I taking a ride west to Fort Stanwix. I'd like to show Benjamin what this area is like. And Helena," he stopped and smiled at her, "might just like to go along for the ride and keep us company."

"That sounds great!" declared Helena with a grin. "I like the fresh air."

"How long can you boys stay?" asked Mrs. Heindrick.

"We have a total of ten days leave; we're already on our fifth day," answered Walter. "So we'll have to leave day after tomorrow."

While Mrs. Heindrick and Helena prepared the refreshments, Walter showed Benjamin about the house. The first place they visited was the cellar; the existence of the cellar itself betokened prosperity.

"After the fire in 1757," started Walter, "my father was determined to build a house that would withstand the cold winters and the Indian raids. He used the original cellar from the first house; it served for nearly six months as my parent's only home until the main house was constructed. Over here is the original cellar, now we call it the cold or root cellar. This kind of cellar is named for the type of crops usually stored in it; like carrots, parsnips, beets, potatoes, turnips, as well as squash, pumpkins, apples, pears, smoked meats, and so on. With the cellar's supply of provisions and water, the house's residents, and even our neighbors, could not be starved out in case of an enemy raid." To Benjamin, the most striking feature of the cellar was the massive supporting arch that served as the foundation of the equally massive fireplace and chimney that rose through the second story of the house.

"I guess we'd better go upstairs, or my mother is going to think that we don't want any of her cookies."

"After being down here, we're going to need something to warm our insides," commented Benjamin.

The boys walked up the slightly slanted stairs constructed of broad planks, each approximately five-feet wide. The more Benjamin had seen of Walter's home the more it confirmed his initial impression that the building was constructed to be a fortress as well as a home. When they reached the kitchen, they were greeted not by Walter's mother, but by his father, Karl.

Walter's father came to his son, patted his shoulder, and shook his hand. "Welcome, my son," he said in a strong, bass voice. His complexion and build were not what Benjamin had expected. Karl's father was tall, erect, and wiry, with eyes like a hawk. *Austere, takes no bullshit,* thought Benjamin.

"Father," started Walter, "I'm very proud to introduce you to my good friend, and blood brother, Benjamin Jefferson."

Karl Heindrick shook Benjamin's hand and said, "Any friend of Walter's is a friend of mine." He stopped to scratch his head, thought a moment, then asked, "Are you by any chance George Jefferson's son?"

"Yes, sir, I sure am," with a broad smile on his face and proudly responding, Benjamin added, "and I'm mighty proud to be."

Karl was beginning to break the coat of ice on his personality, He chuckled a bit and said, "Well, I'll be damned, we're blood-brothers-in-law. Your father, George, is my blood-brother."

"You men have been talking too much," interrupted Walter's mother. "Eat the cookies and cake while they're still warm," she said as she passed the plate.

By the time they had all managed to seat themselves around the large, oblong, wooden kitchen table Helena was pouring the hot cider from a stone pitcher into their earthenware mugs. She stopped, looked at Walter, and asked, "While you were introducing Benjamin to your father did you tell him that Benjamin was your good friend?"

"That's right," agreed Walter. "Why do you ask?

"Well, earlier today when you introduced Benjamin to Mrs. Perry, you said Benjamin was your best friend and blood-brother. You made me jealous; I thought I was your best friend. I'm glad that all understand our relationship. I suggest that tomorrow, the three of us head up to Wood Creek and perform the same ceremony we did with White Tail."

"That sounds like a great idea, Helena," agreed Walter. "You both know that you're my closest friends. That's the way it is, and that's the way it's going to be."

Walter's mother placed a full platter of cookies and cake and a pitcher of cider in the center of the table. "Here," his mother said, "from now on you help yourselves." She looked at her husband and said, "Something seems to be bothering you more than usual. Do you want to share it with us?"

"Yes, I do, and I know I should," responded Karl Heindrick. "Cal and I heard some very disturbing news."

"What is it about? The cheese business? The war? What?" his wife asked.

"A little bit about all of them." He stopped, and thought he should inform Benjamin that his wife was not just a housewife. "I don't know whether Walter has told you, Benjamin, that his mother has a business of her own. She has a special recipe for the best Limburger cheese in the Mohawk Valley. Lately, Helena has been helping with processing the cheese," he said beaming with pride.

Embarrassed, Walter's mother said, "Oh, I know you're the cheese maker in this family. I only do it, because I like to make it, and we have a great place to store and age the cheese in our root cellar. Enough about me, tell us what you and Cal heard today."

"Due to the war, all the residents in the Mohawk Valley, Palatines, Indians, and all others have been unable able to effectively complete the harvesting of our fall crops. Some of the scorched-earth tactics all of us used have added to the problems. One of the village's couriers arrived in town yesterday, and informed the Committee of Safety that Seneca Chief Sayenquerahta explained in a council at Niagara how the Fort Stanwix campaign had caused a food shortage. He is quoted as saying, 'Provision is scarce with us, owing to our having been at Fort Stanwix and by which means our Corn, which is our Chief support, was neglected.' As you all know, farming is a woman's occupation for the Indians, the war interfered drastically with Indian agriculture. For one thing, the women frequently accompanied the warriors on their expeditions and there were women along on the Fort Stanwix campaign. It was also the duty of the men to clear the fields and to enable the women to cultivate them later.

"From what Cal and I heard, the preparation and fighting of the war had cut down their 1777 planting. This crop also suffered heavily from natural causes. We understand that John Butler, that's Martha Butler's former brother-in-law," he added, "reported to Colonel Bolton the distressed situation of the Senecas and Cayugas. To quote him, 'The Indians have nothing to subsist upon but the roots and greens which they gather in the woods.' To make matters worse, although the Indians had a considerable number of cattle in the Indian country, these have been chiefly consumed by the Indians themselves. It is well known that they will not have time to raise more corn, pulse, and such edible seeds like peas, beans, lentils, and similar leguminous plants until next year; these types of food stuffs compose the principal part of the Indians' food.

"From what we heard, there are many families who have not had an ear of corn since the battle and are obliged to live, such as had them, upon their cattle; those who had no cattle are surviving upon roots. There is little likelihood of obtaining any appreciable quantity of cattle upon the frontiers because the Indians and Tories have broken up most of the settlements, and those inhabitants who have remained, such as us," he added, "are now protected by a chain of forts. If we had to," he looked about at his family, "we could exist relatively well in this house.

"The food shortage may be acute for the Indians, but food is not in an abundant supply for us settlers; this could inhibit any of our future military, defensive or offensive, operations in the Indian country. Butler also bragged that, 'If he had a prospect of being able to take any of these enemy forts, he would march against them with sufficient body for the want of provision.'

"The last most distressing bit of information came when we learned that Chief Joseph Brant is awaiting the arrival of Major John Butler with his Rangers and Sayenqueraghta with his Senecas. The warriors at Chemung are 300 strong and in high spirits. They are fully confident of repulsing the American invasion."

Karl stopped long enough to allow his family to digest this information. "Winter's almost upon us. We've already had quite a bit of snow, and it's going to get plenty worse. Starving Indians aren't friendly Indians. The Committee of Safety is going to convene in a couple of days and plan its strategy to cope with the situation. Personally, I think that this frontier is in for more killings and massacres than what General Washington may lead his soldiers through.

"Just for your information, Benjamin. Chief Joseph Brant was White Tail's uncle. He was also Sir William Johnson's protege and brother-in-law, campaigning with Johnson throughout the French and Indian War. In 1761, Sir William sent the nineteen-year-old Mohawk lad to the English-speaking Moor's Indian School, an Episcopal mission in Lebanon, Connecticut, where he improved his English and mathematics. Later, he translated the Scriptures into the Mohawk language. Thereafter, he became widely known throughout the Iroquois nation as Sir William's agent and counsel. I understand he was an invited guest of England's Queen Anne in her court. Now, Brant is known as the chief of the Mohawks. He is a realist and, above all, a Mohawk. He's a remarkable person, even if we don't necessarily agree with everything he stands for."

"I don't think the problem is totally with the Iroquois. When you stop to think about it, all the settlers who have thrown their lot in with the English, stand to lose all their life savings, property, and everything else they've worked for ever since they came from the Old Country."

"The same thing, Father," said Walter, "with people like us. We've placed all our hopes and expectations upon General Washington and his troops, believing they will be able to defeat the British. If the Tories win, we'll be desperate to find a safe place to live, to say nothing about all of our possessions."

"I hate to think that; we've placed all our hopes and prayers on gaining our freedom and independence from the king," added Mrs. Heindrick. "We've worked so hard for everything we've acquired. The very thought of losing it all, makes me sick to heart."

"Simply speaking, when two forces are in a fight," said Benjamin, "usually there's bound to be one winner and one loser. If we defeat the British, we can stay in these United States of America; if we lose, we'll either have to swear loyalty to the King or find some other place to live." He thought a moment, looked toward Helena, and said, "The loser could go to Canada much like your father did, Helena."

"That's certainly what my father did and wanted my mother and me to go along with him. Thank goodness, I was able to escape and return to New Palatine; eventually, my mother was able to return here, also," said Helena.

"This subject is so depressing," said Walter's mother. "I move that Helena and I prepare supper, while Walter finishes showing Benjamin the house and, Karl, would you please bring up some fresh corn and potatoes from the root cellar? They will be very nice with the sauerbraten I cooked this morning."

All went about their assigned tasks as if they had been given by a drill sergeant. Karl helped clean the fresh vegetables he had brought up from the cellar. He always enjoyed working in the kitchen with his wife; for him there was no *her work* and *his work*. Karl and Rebecca enjoyed sharing much of the work about their home, they realized that they could spend more time together if they didn't argue about which job was whose.

Walter led Benjamin up a flight of steep, narrow stairs that ran along the fireplace to the second floor leading into a wide hallway with two doors on either side. They went into Walter's bedroom. The interesting thing about the bed was it's construction. It was a bunk bed built along the exposed side of the fireplace chimney. Benjamin asked why there was a fixed bed against the chimney? Walter reminded him that the fireplace was the house's only source of heat. They went into the other, opposite, room and found the same configuration—a bed constructed along the fireplace chimney.

"These are bedrooms while I'm home. While I've been away, Helena has been staying here with her mother until her mother could settle down from her terrible experience with her husband and the Tories. Now, Helena only occasionally stays here when my mother gets behind on her cheese making," concluded Walter.

Outside the house, there were a few sheep grazing in what Benjamin would call a *keep*, which surrounded the entire house. He'd learned about castles, keeps, and moats while reading about medieval English history. Pointing to the sheep, "They help to keep the hay down, just in case a fire started during a raid," said Walter. "Of course, they help to keep us with meat and wool. They're something like geese; they also serve as relatively good watch dogs in case of prowlers."

"Everything your family has done with this house, appears to be in preparation for an Indian or some other kind of attack," observed Benjamin. "It's considerably different from living in Albany."

"As I have told you before," reminded Walter, "we're on the very edge of the western frontier. I'm certain that my father is more concerned about the Tories and the Indians than he shows."

They continued their walk around the compound. "That little log cabin over there," pointed Walter, "is the only building remaining after the 1757 attack. It's not much good for anything now; however, during the spring of the year we do use it for a smokehouse. Father just wants to keep it to remind us all of the atrocities that he and my mother experienced when they found out their home burnt to the ground, and his father lying with the spear through his chest. He wants us to be on guard; always."

This was all new to Benjamin. He was at a loss for words.

Early the next morning, the three young people were on their horses riding toward the site of the Battle of Oriskany. At the junction where the Heindrick property joined the King's Highway, they headed their horses west toward Wood Creek and Fort Stanwix. Few words had been exchanged among the friends; silently they appreciated the beauty of late fall which nature offered. Finally, after about two hours of riding, Benjamin broke the silence.

"What's so important about Wood Creek and Fort Stanwix that the British and Americans had such a battle there?" asked Benjamin.

"Wood Creek was one of the main arteries that the settlers used to ferry their furs and other trade goods to and from the Indians of the Lakes country," said Walter. He pulled up the reins of his horse and suggested they stop along the creek, water the horses, and see what his mother had prepared for food.

They were seated along the creek, eating more of Mrs. Heindrick's maple sugar cookies, cheese, apples, and dried fruit. "You asked about Fort Stanwix, Benjamin. What is interesting about the fort is that it has two termini in the same ocean from two different watersheds; it connects the Hudson and the Atlantic on one hand with the Great Lakes on the other. For centuries, the Indians and, in time, the white settlers boated from the west, lifted their canoes out of Wood Creek, and floated them down the Mohawk; or else they paddled up the Mohawk and floated down Wood Creek into the land of the sunset. During those early years, everything around here was deep forest, monotonous and forbidding to many travelers, since there were no intervals, no bare hills affording a vantage spot. There were hidden swamps sending forth stinking vapors, as well as stinging insects during the spring and summer; wolves howled and frogs croaked all night. Not the most welcoming areas in which to travel.

"As the volume of trade increased, the need of stations along the waterway became evident and small forts were established; as much perhaps to give shelter to the voyagers as to afford them protection against hostile or thieving Indians and others. At the carrying places, a few settlers did earn some income by assisting the boatmen in transporting their bateaux and cargoes from the Wood Creek landing place to Mohawk River landing place by using their oxen. The varying volume of water in the streams sometimes made it necessary to have two or more landing places on each end of the carry; in other words, the carry might be longer or shorter, depending upon the season. In spring the melting snow caused floods and required shorter carries.

"Wood Creek presented especial difficulties in navigation. It was extremely tortuous and subject to natural variations including huge changes in water volume. In many seasons, the boatmen were forced to construct temporary sluices to accumulate enough water to carry their craft a few rods, then the same procedure had to be repeated. My father told me he knew some artillery boats that took five days to cover four miles. I apologize for monopolizing the conversation but I really like this area, so I've studied a lot about it."

"Don't apologize," said Benjamin. "I enjoy hearing someone talking about something that he loves. You've certainly increased my interest in the area. I'm beginning to understand why your parents built their home the way they did."

"Sometimes I've seen Walter really get lost in reading books," Helena said. "Other times, just like the last few minutes, he exudes interest in something new, making his listeners want to learn more about the subject. I've thought that one day you would make an excellent teacher, Walter."

"Enough of all this stuff," said Walter. He stood up and took the reins of his horse. "Get your horses and we'll walk them over to the place where my father and I found White Tail. The lower carrying place that connected the Mohawk and Wood Creek was relatively swampy. They walked toward a high stony spot between the two streams as they came down from the north side of the road. Heading for the ridge in order to have a better view of the area, they carefully stepped with their horses on stones as they crossed the creek. Keeping their footing was extremely difficult; however, the volume of water in the creek, being lower than usual, made it easier to cross than when Walter and his father had done so just after the spring thaw.

Walter stopped, and pointed to some boulders along the creek's bank, "Do you see that big boulder that goes into the creek? Well, right near where that boulder rests in the water is tha place my father and I found White Tail."

"How did you know that he was there?" asked Helena.

"We heard a series of faint moans, followed by other rather weird sounds. We searched and were fortunate to find this young Indian lad, just about my age; he was almost drowned or frozen to death. I can remember that freezing water. He was lucky that he lived.

"When we tired to raise him from the stream, he let out a loud groan. That's when we discovered that his right foot was caught under a boulder. I placed my hands under the lad's armpits while my father tried to wrestle the boulder away from his foot. Suddenly, the boulder moved sufficiently to allow me to pull him away, but he moved too quickly. I slipped and fell, giving us both a dunking in the icy water. I guess that sudden shock gave him exactly what he needed. He opened his eyes and stared at us. We carried him over to that flat rock over there," he pointed. "Father had me go to the wagon and bring him a jug of home brew. He realized that the Indian lad had broken his leg. While I held his head, father poured a stout drink into his mouth. Then we placed his leg in a splint, and made a pair of crutches for him."

"How did you find out who he was?" asked Benjamin.

"Speaking partly in English, German, and Mohawk, we told him that his leg was broken and the splint would help the it heal. We showed him how to use the crutches and when we asked him his name, he told us White Tail and that he was a nephew of Chief Joseph Brant. We asked if he wanted us to take him home, which he did. So we packed ourselves into the wagon and headed to the Indian village of Oriska, to the west of here."

"White Tail was mighty lucky that you and your father came along at just the right time," observed Benjamin, "otherwise he would have frozen to death."

"And Walter and I would never have known him, nor his wonderful Aunt Mary," said Helena.

"Who is Aunt Mary?" asked Benjamin.

"Aunt Mary was White Tail's *aunt* by choice," stated Walter. "During a Seneca raid in Pennsylvania, she was the only one to survive. The Senecas brought her back to the Mohawk Valley to live with them. Because she was a year or two older than most of them and, perhaps because she had white skin and survived their horrendous raid, the Senecas decided to call her Aunt Mary. After living with them for a couple of years, she married White Tails's older brother, Maple Leaf. They loved each other dearly, but Maple Leaf died about three years later during a raid."

"Aunt Mary lived in the *longhouse* until Maple Leaf died," added Helena. "It is a Seneca custom for a widow to leave the longhouse and live in a separate cabin until she remarries. That's where she was living when White Tail introduced her to us. I still remember that day when we last said goodbye to them," she continued as she fondly looked at Walter. "We hugged each other goodbye. Walter and White Tail pressed their palms together bearing their blood-brother scar. We all looked forward to the next time we'd be together."

"The next time I saw White Tail," said Walter, "was when I saw him approaching me and the wounded General Herkimer."

"How far is the site of the battle from here?" asked Benjamin.

"About a good hour's ride," replied Walter. "Let's finish the food my mother prepared for us, and then we'll head that way."

They had been riding at a moderate gait, careful not to let their horses trip over the loose stones or stumble into a woodchuck hole. The meandering, narrow road lead them under towering pine trees, the branches stretching toward the sky seeking sunlight. Among them the stately oak and hickory trees competed with equally majestic maples for the rays of the sun; all with bare boughs waiting for the spring to warm their roots. The stubby, drooping hemlocks let their neighbors fight for a piece of the sky, they were content to darken the forest floor and give shelter to the rabbits, squirrel, chipmunks, and others of their four-legged friends.

The stillness seemed to penetrate the area and silenced the three young people. "It's so quiet," commented Helena, as they reached the crest of a small hill, slowed their pace, and stopped atop the small elevation. "It's almost like when we go into a church. Very humbling!"

"Haunting, you mean," said Benjamin. "Reminds me of the Twenty-third Psalm, and its *valley of the shadow of death.*"

"That's exactly what this area is, a *valley of death,*" Walter agreed. "Here's where it all happened. It really gives me chills to think of what happened here. I'll never forget it. You two, go on down there if you want to. I'll just stay up here a while."

With reins in hand, Walter pointed his horse toward a poor excuse for a bridge constructed of logs that crossed the swampy bottom of the deep semicircular ravine carved through the forest. The steep banks of the ravine were thickly covered with trees and underbrush. "General Herkimer was astride his big, white mare leading the way down this ravine. I was near him beating my drum, with my heart beating double-time. We had crossed the bridge and started up the slope on the other side. Then all hell broke loose. Yelling. Shouting. Shooting. The general immediately turned his horse and rushed back to investigate. As he rode, the general realized that both his advance and his retreat forces had been cut off. The Tories and Indians came from behind the trees and bushes, yelling, screaming, war-whooping;

their tomahawks over their heads, shooting, clubbing, and attacking the center of our troops. Fortunately, the rearguard had not started down the ravine; and therefore, was not attacked—they just beat the hell out of the area. While some of our troops were storming the hill, Herkimer's horse was wounded, then Herkimer, too, was shot in his left leg, As his horse fell over, the general untangled himself from his saddle and started to scramble free, but then he, too, fell. The bone of his leg was shattered by a musket ball, and almost immediately blood began to flow over the top of his boot.

"I really don't want to talk about it anymore," he admitted, but after a brief pause, he continued. "We carried the general, sat him on his saddle, and propped him against that low-branched beech tree over there on the knoll so he could overlook the entire battle field. That's enough," he concluded as he left his friends to stare down into the ravine and imagine the rest. Walter still heard the blood-curdling noises: the screams, groans, yells, shots, war-hoops, and he remembered helping bandage the general's wounded leg. As he again saw the Mohawk chief shoot his nephew, he went and sat under a hemlock hiding himself from the road and his friends.

"I trust that you young folks had a wonderful ride out west of here," greeted Walter's mother.

"The ride brought back many memories," Helena said. "Some were kind of sad, but what I liked about our ride was that I learned more about Benjamin, and hopefully, he learned quite a bit about what has and is happening in the Mohawk Valley. Maybe one of these days we can go and visit him and his family in Albany."

"Walter, you're very quiet. Don't you feel well? You're usually so invigorated when coming back from a ride in the forest," said his mother.

"I truly enjoyed our ride west but a couple of things brought back many sad memories. Come tomorrow, I'll be alright. Speaking about tomorrow," Walter continued, " tomorrow is the day Benjamin and I must return to camp. Maybe that's another reason why I feel so melancholy." He rose from the chair where he had been sitting, went to his mother, hugged her, and said, "I love you, mother." He then went to Helena, hugged her, and said, "I've missed you, Helena."

Benjamin stood silently watching his blood-brother getting all mushy; he knew how Walter felt. Rebecca sat watching her sixteen-year-old son display both affection and fear. She wished that she could hold him as she had when he was a baby, but no, he was a young man enrolled as a volunteer in the Tryon County Militia to fight the British. How cruel war is, tearing families apart, killing each other. All for what, she asked herself. For an intangible concept, *freedom*. She was beginning to wonder if it was worth all the killing and grief.

"Hi, Rebecca," greeted Karl as he entered the kitchen. "Hope I'm not late for dinner. The Safety Committee called an emergency meeting, the rumblings from the Indians are becoming louder."

"Karl," smiled Rebecca, "you're not late for dinner. Benjamin, Walter, and Helena were telling me about their ride to Oriskany. They also reminded me that tomorrow the boys must return so as not to be over-leave."

"Your leave has gone by so fast, but I know that most of the time you have been riding to and from our home," said Karl. "That reminds me, tomorrow is Sunday. We can ride to New Palatine's new church. We're mighty proud of the church; its taken us nearly a year to complete it. Martha Butler donated the land for the church. Mighty nice lady, Benjamin, but don't make her mad," Walter's father warned.

"We saw the church as we rode into town," replied Benjamin. "I agree with you that it is very attractive. I'm looking forward to hearing Preacher Stouffer. Walter has told me a lot about him."

After dinner, the Heindricks, Helena, and Benjamin tried to avoid talking about the war or about the Indian and Tory problems. "Let's go outside for a short walk," suggested Walter. "We all need a little fresh air, and to change the subject."

As they walked across the keep, as Benjamin chose to call the courtyard, each took deep breaths of the cold, crisp freezing air. As they exhaled, their chilled breaths resembled smoke disappearing into the dark night. Their only light was the nearby full moon as it raced across the dark, cold, starry skies. Benjamin was the first to break the silence, "Look," he pointed toward their near frozen breath as it disappeared into the darkness, "it looks like we're smoking the peace pipe. Can you just imagine the time when we'll be around in a circle smoking our peace pipes?"

"That's what we're all praying for," voiced Helena.

As they passed through the courtyard's heavy gate, consciously or unconsciously, they headed down the narrow, maple tree lined lane that eventually met the King's Highway.

"Walter," started Helena, "ever since we left the battle site, you don't seem to be with us. I don't mean this in any derogatory manner. We know that you are with us, but you are thinking of something way up there in the heavens," as she pointed up toward the clear, star-studded sky.

"I hope that you don't mind, Walter, if I add to what Helena has just said," said Benjamin. "Let's face it, you're nearly sixteen-years-old. I'm almost seventeen. Both of us have been fortunate to have survived the battles at Saratoga; many did not. But, you, Walter, went through another horrible battle at Oriskany. In a sense, we're both somewhat shell shocked. These experiences are extraordinary for adults, to say nothing about us young guys. Each of us has emerged from them relatively well. We'll probably never get completely over them, but they say that time helps to heal everything."

Walter was busily listening to his friends, but he was having trouble separating his own thoughts from what they were saying. He kicked a rock from the lane toward a maple tree, and stared toward the tree which was the recipient of the rock's impact. His thoughts reflected upon last spring when he had helped his father with the maples; tapping the trees, gathering the sap, pouring it into milk cans on a flat sledge, and eventually evaporating the sap over a fire. Then his thoughts quickly went to that day when he had watched General Benedict Arnold charge from one line to another urging his troops to go after the British. What a gallant soldier! Then there was Colonel Dan, a man's man! Then he stared at his two friends, especially Helena. I really don't want to leave her, he thought, yet I'll miss Benjamin just as much if . . .

Helena brought Walter out of his reverie. "This time tomorrow night, you and Benjamin will be on your way to Benjamin's home in Albany, then you'll be headed back to camp. Where will the army go from Albany?"

"I don't think anyone really knows except General Gates."

"Maybe we'll be directed to join General Washington in the New Jersey area."

"Perhaps your father, Benjamin, will know by the time we return," speculated Walter.

"Could be, but I wouldn't want to count on it," grinned Benjamin.

They had reached the King's Highway. A left turn would take them into the center of New Palatine; a right would take them back toward Oriskany and the western frontier. They decided to turn around and head back toward the stone farmhouse.

Finally, Walter told his friend what had been troubling him. "Ever since my father told us about the Indians and Tories and their dreadful situation, I can't help but believe that the fighting has not stopped here on the western frontier, here in the Mohawk Valley. Truthfully, I know that I must return to General Gates's army and complete my three-month enlistment. But when that's over, I don't know whether I'll stay with Gates and Morgan, or return here to serve in the Tryon County Militia."

"I suppose you could do that militia bit," suggested Benjamin. "If they want you to help General Washington, they can come after you."

Helena could stand this discussion no longer. "Earlier today, Walter, you said the three of us were going to be blood-brothers. While we're standing here in the juncture of this road, I think it's an appropriate time to seal our brotherhood."

Startled, the two boys looked at each other. "That is if you still want me as your blood-sister," said Helena.

Walter and Benjamin agreed that it was past time for this ceremony. With Walter's knife, Helena's palm was cut and each boy kissed the wound, which was then sealed by Helena's own kiss. Their embrace formed a tight circle to symbolize their brotherhood. They inhaled deeply; their warm breath turning into Benjamin's version of smoking a peace pipe. Without saying a word, hand-in-hand the young trio solemnly and reverently retraced their path back to the fortress that served as Walter's family home. As they approached, the fortress cast an awesome shadow, with smoke slowly rising from the huge stone chimney.

"I see my parents have kept the fire ablaze for us. What say we have some hot cider and some of my mother's maple-sugar cookies."

The only answer he received was the low, bleat of the sheep grazing in the farmhouse's keep. All seemed to like Walter's suggestion.

❋{ 29 }❋

THE PARTING

HEINDRICK'S FARMHOUSE IN NEW PALATINE

Rebecca Heindrick had risen early to build up the heat in the fire-place, and prepare her family's breakfast. This morning would be the last time her family would be all together before . . . ? While the corn-bread was baking in the stone hearth and the coffee brewing in an iron kettle hanging on the fireplace bracket, she cut thick slices from a slab of home-smoked bacon and laid them in a baking pan, along with some sliced potatoes left over from the previous night's dinner. This she placed in the stone hearth along with the pan of cornbread. She would wait until the family arrived before she prepared the eggs.

Karl was first to arrive. "Rebecca, my dear, I wish that you had awakened me, so I could help with the cooking. You know that I like to help you in preparing breakfast; I think it's the most important meal of the day," he concluded.

"I agree with you," commented his wife, "if we get the day started well, it's bound to be a good day." Rebecca gave Karl a big hug and reminded him, "This is a very special day; the last time we'll be together as a family for a long time. At least we're going to church together this morning, and hopefully, God will be with our boys and our troops."

Just then Helena entered the kitchen and gave her prospective mother-in-law a kiss on the cheek. Ever since Helena had escaped from the Tories in Canada and returned to New Palatine, Rebecca had adopted Helena as her surrogate daughter.

Shortly, Walter and Benjamin arrived dressed in their army uni-form, and leaving their packed dufflebags near the front door. Walter gave his mother a loving kiss, while she was busily placing the food on the table. Karl motioned them all to the table, and lead the family in saying grace.

"This is a very special morning," began Rebecca. "We are celebrating our new friend and blood-brother into our family, but we're also celebrating the day when Karl is walking without either a crutch or a cane. Karl's leg is totally healed; I've begged him to stay here and help with the cheese factory and farm."

"You know, my dear, that is not difficult to do," responded Karl as he patted his wife's hand. "However, I'm still very concerned about a the rumblings and rumors I hear about the Indians and their Tory friends. I"m afraid that the war is not over here in the valley."

"That's all the more reason it is necessary for you to stay around here," concluded Rebecca.

Helena, wanting to change the subject, asked Benjamin, "How many days is it going to take you and Walter to return to the army camp?"

"That depends upon when we leave New Palatine," responded Benjamin. "We're planning to stop at my parent's home in Albany; my father's joining us there. If everything goes well, we should be in camp within three days."

"Talking about your father, Benjamin, how has he been standing up in this war? " quizzed Karl.

"We're all thankful because most of the time we have been working directly with Colonel Daniel Morgan. My father and Colonel Dan get along real well. They act like bosom buddies."

"Father," said Walter, "Colonel Dan and General Arnold have made serving in the army almost a pleasure, but General Gates and his cronies, especially Major Wilkinson, are something else," he concluded with a slight question in his eye, as he placed another piece of bacon and cornbread on his plate.

As Rebecca filled their mugs with coffee, she suggested, "We'd better leave for church within the hour. While you men are packing and hitching up the wagon, Helena and I will pack a picnic lunch for us to have after church."

"Would you please pack some food for Benjamin and me for our trip to Albany?" asked Walter.

"I've already done that, my son. You see you're always on my mind," smiled his mother. "I want you and Benjamin to remember there's always an open door for you two."

Just before they excused themselves from the table, Karl held out his arms; one to his wife, the other to Benjamin. "Let's all give thanks to the Lord for His blessings," he started, "and bring us all, including Benjamin's parents, around this table in the very near future." With a squeeze of hands, they said Amen, and set about the chores Rebecca had assigned.

After they had ridden nearly an hour east along the familiar King's Highway with its tree-lined narrow wagon trail, occasional post-and-rail fences, cleared, fallow fields awaiting spring's planting, they turned right into a still narrower wagon path filled with standing, dead grass. The lane directly opposite the settlement's common, the Heidelberg Tavern, and Kerchner's general store, lead them to New Palatine's new church; a story-and-half high was constructed almost entirely of fieldstone. Near the front of the church, Karl helped Rebecca and Helena off the wagon; afterwards, the Hendrick men tendered their horses and wagon in a long livery stable at the distant end of the church.

When the men returned to the front of the church, there was the Reverend Johann Stouffer, along with his wife Red Bird, ushering his parishioners into the church in the same manner Walter and his father used to corral their sheep into a pen to await spring shearing.

The preacher stood on the ground near the first step of the church wearing his familiar thread-bare, dark wool jacket and matching pants, with a huge smile on his bearded face, his rotund, six-foot body jiggling with joy as he saw the Heindrick men approaching. At the preacher's side stood Red Bird, looking every bit the Mohawk Indian princess she was; dressed in a long, soft, light-colored, doeskin tunic and pants, handsomely decorated with little strings of multi-colored beads. Her moccasins, with attached strings of beads, looked as if she had just finished making them, unlike the men who almost always were wearing dusty or muddy shoes.

"Gentlemen," the preacher said gleefully to the Heindrick men as they walked up the few steps leading into the church. Ignoring Karl, he said, "Welcome back home, Walter, it's great to see you looking so well. Who is this young lad with you?" he asked as he stared at the colored youth dressed in a military uniform. Before Walter could reply, the preacher gave Karl a hearty handshake welcoming him along with the young men.

"Reverend Stouffer, this is my good friend, and blood-brother, Benjamin Jefferson," Walter proudly announced.

"You remember meeting my blood-brother, George Jefferson from Albany," chimed-in Karl. "Well, Benjamin is George's son. He and Walter have been serving with Generals Gates and Arnold, and Colonel Dan Morgan on the eastern front near Saratoga."

Extending his hand toward the preacher, Benjamin said, "I'm mighty proud to meet you, Sir. The Heindricks have told me about the many good things you have done throughout this valley, especially here in New Palatine."

"Don't believe everything you hear about me," the embarrassed Reverend warned him. "I want you to meet my better half, Red Bird," he said looking towards his wife and beaming like a child that had just received a stick of candy. "She's the one who inspires me." Red Bird and Benjamin cordially shook hands, as she suggested, "We'd better enter the church before the sermon begins." She added, "We wouldn't want to miss the preacher's sermon, would we?" Joyfully, she lead her husband and the Heindrick clan into the church's vestibule where Rebecca and Helena were waiting. Here the Stouffers and Heindricks separated. The Reverend waited in the vestibule to prepare himself, while Red Bird and the Heindricks entered the church's sanctuary with its vaulted ceiling, rough hewed beams, and pews crowded with parishioners. Walking down the central aisle, they located their empty pew and asked the preacher's wife to join them.

Everyone throughout the valley knew the Reverend Stouffer's first love after Red Bird and the Lord, was theatrics. Peeking through the door into the sanctuary, he saw that the moment for his entrance had arrived. Gad! How he missed the tavern's huge fireplace and its hearth; it served as his stage from which he could easily stroll among the congregation. He really appreciated the townspeople constructing this house of God, but he thoroughly disliked having to walk up those two or three steps to the pulpit; it's elevated position made him feel so uneasy. He disliked being the *high and mighty*, staring down upon his congregation. I'm just a simple country preacher, he thought, they're going to have to take me as I am while I talk from ground-level, and walk among my flock.

The congregation was quietly waiting and just before it grew restless he made his *entrance*. He quietly opened the door into the sanctuary, strolled down the middle aisle with his well-worn, black leather Bible placed above his heart, and headed toward the church's pulpit. The congregation politely watched him. When he reached the *rail*, he walked through its opened gate and stepped onto the raised platform behind the rail. "This platform is going to be my fireplace hearth," he thought. Instead of the fireplace behind him, there was a huge window with plain glass that allowed light into the sanctuary There also three strategically placed narrow, casement windows on each side of the church.

With the Bible still above his heart, the preacher reverently turned and faced the congregation. He bowed his head, and silently asked for *guidance*. This was the second time he would speak in this church. It was his church. He had worked right along with the settlers to help construct it.

"Good morning," he cheerfully said.

"Good morning," the congregation responded in a loud unison.

"Before we begin our service," the reverend began, "I want you all to welcome home Karl and Rebecca Heindrick's son, Walter, and his young friend and blood-brother Benjamin Jefferson. They are home on leave from the eastern front near Saratoga, where they assisted General Gates in defeating General Burgoyne and the British. Gentlemen, would you please rise so all of your friends and neighbors can see you?"

The congregation started looking about the sanctuary, finally their eyes fixed on two young men standing near the rear of the church in their military uniforms. "Let's give these young men a hearty welcome home," said the preacher as he began clapping his hands. All clapped; some more politely than vigorously. The preacher was wondering what some of the more conservative members thought when he had announced that these two were blood-brothers. Oh! Jeepers, he thought, this is the way the world is, we're all God's children.

"For this morning's sermon, I am going to refer to a number of passages from the Bible. The first comes from II Samuel, 22, verses 2 and 3:

> And he said, "The Lord is my rock and my fortress and my deliverer;
>
> The God of my strength, in whom I will trust; my shield and the horn of my salvation, my stronghold and my refuge; my Savior, You save me from violence.

The second passage also comes from II Samuel, 1, verses 25 and 27:

> How the mighty have fallen in the midst of the battle!
> How the mighty have fallen, and the weapons of war perished!

Still standing on the raised platform behind the rail, he paused a moment, and held his worn Bible before him. "When I heard that Walter and his friend, Benjamin, were home, and would be attending this service, I searched through the Bible trying to find a passage that I thought would be appropriate. With the eastern front in mind, and what has happened there—our American troops with their rag-tag uniforms and lack of military training defeated one of the mightiest armies in the world. Oh! how the mighty have fallen in the midst of battle. And yes, the weapons have perished. Unfortunately, this war is far from over. It may last only a few more months or perhaps it may drag on a few more years. Only our Lord knows how long it's going to last." He carefully stepped down from the platform onto the main floor of the church.

Gently he rubbed his close-cropped beard, and thoughtfully surveyed the rustic ceiling of the church, lowered his head, and said, "We have nothing to fear; as Samuel tells us, *the Lord is my fortress and my salvation, and my deliverer.* This does not mean that we don't have to help the Lord; we can not just sit down and wait for the final defeat. Like many of you who have gallantly served during the Battle of Oriskany, and as Walter and Benjamin are now serving, we must all do our share." He bowed his head as he walked down the center aisle. "With God's help and His shield, the mighty will fall."

Before he said another word, he strolled from one side of the church to the other, then back to the center aisle, and facing his captivated audience said, "What I fear most is not that the British will defeat us; I sincerely believe that we will win. But what concerns me most is that we will want *security* instead of *freedom*. That we will want a comfortable, secure life. Initially, when we started this war, we asscrted that we were fighting for our freedom from the king's rule."

With his hand still holding the Bible, again he rubbed his beard, and said, "The Bible gives us reassurance that God will be with us during the battle, but we'll need Him as much after the war as we need Him during the war.

"Most of you know that I am very much interested in drama and Greek history," renewing his monologue. "I'd want to leave you with one thought; let us pray history does not repeat itself. I want you to remember; after the Greeks had gained their freedom; they wanted a comfortable and secure life. What eventually brought the powerful Greek civilization down was that they did not want to give to society, instead, they wanted society to give to them. With the freedom they had fought so valiantly to earn, the Greeks began to want, to demand freedom from *responsibility*. It was then that the Greeks lost their freedom! Let us all keep this historical fact in mind. When we finally defeat the mighty British, and have gained our freedom from the English king, we must not forget the dangers still on our own western frontier. Yes, my dear friends, with freedom our new treasure, comes new responsibilities," he said as he surveyed the congregation. He concluded, "Let's all pray to the Lord to help us to accept these responsibilities in order to preserve our long sought freedom."

Returning to the center of the raised platform, and making the sign of the cross, Reverend Stouffer said, "Go in peace to love and serve the Lord." Momentarily, he bowed his head and solemnly walked down the center aisle, giving friendly acknowledgements to those he passed. As he passed Red Bird, he stretched out his hand, joined it with hers, and together they walked to the front of the church. Knowing and calling everyone by name, the preacher and his wife greeted each and every parishioner with a personal message as they exited. When Martha Butler met the Reverend, he whispered in her ear, "I surely miss your tavern with its huge fireplace and *my hearth.*" She smiled knowingly and said, "Anytime you need a stage, you know where you can find one."

The Heindricks shared the picnic lunch, which Rebecca and Helena had packed, with some of their feathered friends, the chickadees, sparrows, the demanding blue jays, as well as with a few mischievous chipmunks and grey squirrels on the community's common. Sharing the meal with the birds and animals helped to take their minds off the inevitable parting. Finally, it was time for the tearful, yet joyous farewell. All were thankful to have had Walter and Benjamin with the family. As the young soldiers prepared to leave New Palatine they had to muster up internal fortitude to hold back tears.

"Men aren't supposed to cry," Walter kept saying to himself. He took a side-long glance at Benjamin and saw a few tears roll down his cheeks. "I guess it's alright for some men to cry," he thought; giving his mother a big kiss and hug. He met his father in a bear hug, and said, "I love you, father."

"I love you, too, my son, and may God be with you."

While Walter and Helena were saying goodbye in their own intimate manner, Benjamin was the recipient of one of Rebecca's loving kisses and Karl's bear hugs. He quickly mounted his horse as Walter assisted Helena into the Heindrick's wagon. Soon the young warriors were headed east toward Albany with the sun casting their shadows ahead of them. The Heindrick wagon was traveling into the sunset toward their home on the western frontier.

That afternoon Walter and Benjamin rode until they lost sight of the sun through the tall trees bordering the King's Highway. Each knew his routine by now; Walter watered the horses, while Benjamin built a campfire and unpacked the goodies. The next day they would ride for at least twelve hours; if they were lucky they would arrive at Benjamin's Albany home late that evening.

During the boys' leave, General Burgoyne and 20 of his officers were guests in the home of General Philip Schuyler, his wife and daughters, who showed them the most hospitable courtesy. When Burgoyne apologized for the destruction of Schuyler's mansion in Saratoga, Schuyler replied, "That's the fate of war—let us say no more about it." Schuyler's reply did not make Burgoyne feel any better about himself or the result of the conflict. He was beaten and depressed; believing that Generals Howe and Clinton had let him down. However, Burgoyne believed Lord George Germain was the real *culprit* for the unsuccessful campaign and his misfortunes; Germain had not allowed sufficient latitude in the orders he had drafted. What worried Burgoyne most was that the ministers would probably close ranks to defend themselves; leaving him struggling to justify his own actions.

While staying at the Schuyler's home, Burgoyne sent out numerous letters to rally support in London. On October 20, 1777, he sent a letter to Lord George Germain officially informing him of the Saratoga convention. He intended to take his stand on the inflexibility of his orders, which gave him no option but to force a passage to Albany. His private letter to Germain, accompanied his official dispatch:

> *I rest my confidence, in the justice of the King and his councils, to*
> *support the General they thought proper to appoint to as arduous an*
> *understanding, and under as positive a direction, as perhaps a*
> *cabinet ever framed. It will, I am sure, be remembered, my Lord,*
> *that a preference of exertions was the only latitude given to me, and*
> *that to force a junction with Sir William Howe, or at least a*
> *passage to Albany, was the principle, the letter, and the spirit of my*
> *orders.*
>
> *The expediency of advancing being admitted, the consequences*
> *have been honourable misfortunes. The British have persevered in a*
> *strenuous bloody progress. Had the force been all British, perhaps the*
> *perseverance had been longer. But as it was, will it be said, my*
> *Lord, that in the exhausted situation described, and in the jaws of*
> *famine, and invested by quadruple numbers, a treaty which saves*
> *the army to the state, for the next campaign, was not more than*

could have been expected? I call it saving the army, because if sent home, the state is thereby enabled to send forth the troops now destined for her internal defence; if exchanged, they become a force to Sir William Howe, as effectually, as if any other junction had been made.

The conclusion of his letter to Lord Germain, contained a favorable report on General Gates and the American army:

The standing corps which I have seen, are disciplined. I do not hazard the term, but apply it to the great fundamental points of military institution, sobriety, subordination, regularity and courage. The militia are inferior in method and movement; but not a jot less serviceable in woods. My conjectures were very different after the affair of Ticonderoga, but I am convinced they were delusive; and it is a duty to the state to confess it.

In regard to myself, I am sunk in mind and body, but while I have a faculty of either, it shall be exerted for the King's service.

In a letter to his personal friend, Colonel Richard Philipson, who was on the King's equerries, Burgoyne confirmed his distressed situation:

As to myself, I am exhausted in mind and Body, the agitation of the One, and the Fatigues of the other are too much for me. An American Winter, should that be my Fate, will be decisive of my Health, possibly of my life—To the last moment beassured of the inviolable affection of Dear Philipson.

Yours,

J. Burgoyne.

In most of his letters, Burgoyne clearly displayed his mental distress at the time. He omitted, however, the fact that he could have declined command of the expedition; but he did illustrate the lines along which he contemplated designing his defense *in absentia*. The blame for failure lay not with Burgoyne, but with others; he and his troops had performed at their best.

Sergeant George Jefferson, his son, Benjamin, and Walter Heindrick returned to General Gates's headquarters on the last day of their leave, reporting directly to Colonel Dan. "I hope you gentlemen had a relaxing and peaceful leave," Morgan greeted them, "but now it's back to war and all of its ramifications. For starters, General Gates has called a special assembly of each division; he's meeting with our division this afternoon, just before evening chow."

"Do you have any idea what its all about?" asked Sergeant Jefferson.

"Sergeant, you know better than to ask such questions; we all know that General Gates is predictably unpredictable. One thing for sure," smiled Colonel Dan, " he's not going to have us chase Burgoyne with all his Redcoats and their Hessian hired-hands."

Colonel Dan Morgan's division turned out in full military array, except for the veteran members of Morgan's Rangers, who were dressed, as usual in their deerskin military shirts and leggings with the customary fringes along the neckline, sleeves, and leggings to facilitate the dripping of rain from their clothing. In contrast, General Gates presented a very imposing figure dressed in his full military regalia. There was, however, something not visible to the casual observer. Colonel Dan was probably one of the most admired and respected officers present; General Gates, on the other hand, craved such respect, but had not the faintest idea how to gain a fraction of the admiration Morgan and Arnold had achieved. Nevertheless, Gates was the commanding officer of the American Army in the North.

"Gentlemen," Gates addressed the division from a wooden box high enough for him to see the back row of the troops. "First of all, troops at ease," he commanded. Immediately, there was a rustle of uniforms rubbing against each other, and the sound of rifles being placed on the ground. Smiling, he said, "I want to welcome back those of you who have returned from leave; I do hope you are sufficiently rested, and prepared for your next assignment." There was much turning of heads, and silent wondering what the general was about to announce.

"I have some good news and some bad news to share with you. First, I am pleased to tell you that General George Washington has informed me that our battle at Saratoga may be one of the most decisive battles of the American Revolution. It certainly is the most important planned military engagement since Lexington and Oriskany. Our success has instilled new confidence in all America, and helped in attracting many fresh recruits to the American Army. In short, our victory at Saratoga has been useful in knitting the colonies more firmly together into a closer union. Internationally, our victory has attracted the attention of many foreign nations, especially the French, who are seriously considering assisting us in driving the British out of the United States of America. I am proud to say that the British have evacuated Forts Ticonderoga and Crown Point and have given up all hope of using the Hudson-Champlain route. In addition, Clinton, who had started up the Hudson River to join Burgoyne, has hastened back to New York City. By the end of this year, 1777, the British will be holding only New York City, Philadelphia, and Newport.

"As your commanding officer, I do not want to claim the Saratoga victory all to myself. I believe that much of the leadership credit goes to Colonel Daniel Morgan, who superbly wrecked Burgoyne's attempts to break through the two battles at Freeman's Farm, which have since become known as the Battle of Saratoga. I owe a debt of gratitude to my able assistant, Lieutenant Colonel James Wilkinson; without him, we could very easily still be fighting the British. On the evening of October 16th, while I was seriously considering reopening hostilities with the British, Colonel Wilkinson came into my tent carrying with him the convention signed by Burgoyne, dated Camp at Saratoga, October 16, 1777. Lastly, I owe each and everyone of you a depth of gratitude for your steadfast resilience, and your daring resistance over the experienced and professional British and German military forces. I just wish I could shake each of your hands."

"Oh, stop this bullshit!" thought George Jefferson. "If you were Colonel Dan, you'd say our names when you shook hands with us. And what about General Benedict Arnold? You make it sound as if he wasn't even with us at Freeman's Farm. Hell, without Arnold, you would have been chased off your Bemis Heights fortress." Still boiling, George dragged his attention back to what General Gates was saying.

"The other news that I want to share with you is not entirely bad news, especially for those of you who have completed your tenure of enlistment. Although General Washington tells me his enlistment campaign has improved substantially since our victory at Saratoga, he says he needs more troops."

"I can't imagine Washington talking to Gates," thought Sergeant Jefferson. "If anything, Washington probably sent Gates the same routine letter he sent to all his commanders, requesting them to quickly ship as many troops as available. Gates loves to pour on his importance by name dropping. Talking to Washington," he thought contemptuously, "next he'll be telling us he's been talking to God."

"Washington has directed me to immediately move troop reinforcements south. As I have already told you, New York City, Philadelphia, and Newport are still held by the British. This cannot be! The British must be removed from these cities; Washington needs our assistance. I order each of you to give Washington's request serious thought; keeping in mind that I will need to maintain a military force here to stabilize this area. For those of you who have nearly completed your enlistment tenure, I encourage you to keep these two options in mind before you deciding to return to your homes and farms. In three days, you are hereby ordered to report to Colonel Morgan with your decision. One—go with Washington, two—stay here or, three—go home. You are dismissed!"

The troops broke ranks, seeking out their own group of cronies to prepare their evening meal and discuss their options.

⧗

While stoking up the campfire and preparing supper, Sergeant George Jefferson was still fuming over what he heard General Gates tell his troops. "The audacity of the man," he though, "totally ignoring General Arnold's contribution to the battles at Freeman's Farm." The more he brooded, the angrier he became. By the time everyone received the evening's meal ration, George was ready to express his resentment. Fortunately, the mouth-watering meal helped smooth his ire. Whenever the army was lucky enough to be camped near a city, the men were supplied with such niceties as corned beef, pork, fresh beef, and fish, as well as rice, Indian meal, hog's lard, potatoes, peas, beans, onions, turnips, and fresh or hard bread. Occasionally, there were so few fresh vegetables available that greens found around the camp, such as watercress and lamb's quarter were used in soups that helped disguise this fact; these meals were generally disliked by the average soldier. "Tonight's meal must have been designed by General Gates," thought the sergeant, for the menu was outstanding; starting off with a camp luxury, freshly baked bread. The corned beef had been boiled with the root vegetables—potatoes, cabbage, and carrots.

"I guess the old fart is trying to make us feel good tonight," said a tall, skinny soldier dressed in coonskin hat, deerskin hunting shirt, and leggings.

"I wish they'd feed us this way every day," said a rather rotund member of the group.

"Hell, you weigh enough," declared another. "If you weighed any more, we'd have to carry you about in a wheelbarrow. You'd be a piss-poor fighting machine shooting from a wheelbarrow."

"You know damn well that I'm a better marksman with one hand tied behind my back than you are with both of you'rn arms."

Walter and Benjamin enjoyed the meal. Not quite as good as their mother's cooking, but much better than the usual army chow.

"Okay, Okay!" interrupted Sergeant Jefferson. "Now that we don't have the British to demand our attention, all you guys seem able to do is find fault with the food. I suggest that we eat up and appreciate what they're feeding us tonight, because I betcha we'll be on a march south to join General Washington's forces within a week or so."

"No, sir," declared the rotund soldier with a gleam in his eyes. "I've already sent a letter to my wife to bring our horse and wagon right to the camp gate as soon as my enlistment tenure is finished; just seven more days. Eat your heart out, my friends, and when I," he quickly corrected himself, "when we get home, I'm goin' to settle down and hibernate with my little chicken for the long, cold winter's nap. Don't expect to see me until spring arrives; then you're goin' to hav'ta hunt damn hard to find me."

"I can't believe what I hear you saying," said Skinny, "I can't imagine any woman wanting to keep company with you all winter. I always say, the closer to the bone, the sweeter the meat."

"Cool your talk," demanded the sergeant, "we have two young men here. We have more serious things to consider. Remember that

General Gates wants you to report to Colonel Dan within three days telling him which of the three options you intend to choose. I think we already know what our chubby friend is going to do," he concluded.

"I'm goin' to follow'r Colonel Dan Morgan from here to kingdom come," declared the skinny soldier with the coonskin cap. "He's my kind'a man! Some different than our beloved leader, General Gates," as he wrinkled up his nose, spat out a piece of fat on the ground, and wiped the grease from his chin with his deerskin sleeve.

The sergeant surveyed the ten men huddled around the campfire; three had declared their intention to march south and join Washington's forces. Three said they didn't want to leave the area, only intending to stay with General Gates until their enlistment terminated. One said he intended to go wherever Colonel Dan went.

"You've asked us what we're gonna do," said the rotund lover. "Now, let's hear what you, Benjamin, and Walter are gonna do."

"Whatever you youngsters decide to do," declared the skinny one, who played the fiddle, "I've really enjoyed making music with you. We sure helped make this army life more pleasant for many." He looked around the campfire, "Wherever all you guys go, you're gonna miss our music."

"There's no argument about that," all agreed. "But, we haven't heard what the sergeant is going to do."

"To tell you the truth," the sergeant replied, "I don't know. While we were on leave, Walter, Benjamin, and I found out something that really disturbs us—me in particular."

Skinny leaned over, placed his elbows on his boney knees, and asked, "What are you talking about?"

"I going to defer your question to Walter, because it was his father who informed him and Benjamin of the situation."

"It seems that the war here in New York Colony, especially along the Mohawk Valley, has deprived the Indians and Tories of much of their fall harvest crops," Walter began, "and you know the winters here are usually very severe. What the Tryon County Committee of Safety has found out that the Tories are trying to stir up the Indians into a frenzy against us rebels. They've even started by burning a number of remote farm homes and out buildings. They have often succeeded in taking some of the farmers' harvest storage and then burn the remaining harvest and buildings. My father believes the Indians are being encouraged, lead, and financially supported by the British through their Tory activists. If this is true, he believes the battles at Oriskany and Saratoga will be mild compared to the warfare that will probably spread like wild-fire throughout the valley."

"On the way back from New Palatine," added Benjamin, "Walter and I discussed what we had learned about the situation in New Palatine and westward toward Oswego. The Mohawk Valley is actually either in or on the very edge of the western frontier with Indians running about scared skinny that we white folk," he stopped, and corrected himself, "we white and black folk are slowly but steadily beginning to take over much of their property. Personally, I understand their resentment," he concluded.

"What do you black folks know about freedom?" asked one of the cronies. "Hell, you've been slaves all your lives."

"Let me answer that question," injected Sergeant Jefferson. "My parents were slaves brought over here from Africa by the Dutch. Fortunately, they were blessed to have been owned by the Schuyler family in Albany. Mr. Schuyler taught my father the blacksmith craft; when I came along, they taught me the trade, too. As you may remember, manumission was an incentive for blacks to join the state's militia. Mr. Schuyler encouraged me to take advantage of that opportunity and eventually, Mr. Schuyler gave my father the opportunity to earn ownership in his livery and blacksmith business. Now, we're equal partners with three livery and blacksmith shops in the city of Albany."

"What you gettin' at?" asked one.

"What I'm getting at," answered the black sergeant, "is that I just pray that we Americans will give the Indians as much chance at freedom as we black folks have received."

"None of you guys have told us what option you're gonna to choose," declared an impatient rifleman. "Personally, I think that you're just lookin' for a chance to stay home."

"I suppose you'll just have to wait a couple of more days, before you learn what we plan to do," said the sergeant. "I can promise one thing, we'll do what is right for our families and for our country," he concluded with a smile and a wink at his son and Walter.

EPILOGUE

> Political language . . . is designed to make lies sound truthful and murder [war] respectable, and to give an appearance of solidity to pure wind.
>
> — George Orwell

When General George Washington heard on October 18, 1777 of Burgoyne's convention at Saratoga, he called the surrender a *most important event which exceeded our most sanguine expectations.* On November 4th, Congress officially thanked Generals Gates, Lincoln and Arnold *for their brave and successful efforts in the support of the independence of their country.* The American victories at Oriskany, and especially, at Saratoga did rid the New York and the New England colonies of formal British military threat. In fact, by the end of 1777, the British held only Philadelphia and Newport. Six months later the British would abandon Philadelphia; the center of organized conflict shifted toward the South. Informal military conflict continued for years to plague the Mohawk Valley with guerrilla raids staged by the Indians and Tories.

The Americans had won a prodigious victory, far greater than any of the participants could ever have imagined. The threat to divide the colonies had been defeated, but most importantly, the Americans had gained far more than local success. When the news of Burgoyne's defeat reached Paris on December 5, 1777, the very next day King Louis XVI declared his recognition of the United States of America. On February 6, 1778, he signed the formal Treaty of Alliance that turned the family quarrel into a world-wide conflict and in which France bankrupted herself in a vain attempt to avenge the defeats of the previous French and Indian Wars. Interestingly, by signing the treaty, King Louis XVI signed his own death-warrant, for the ideas of liberty carried back across the Atlantic by the French soldiers and sailors hastened the French Revolution that broke out in 1792.

It would be nearly three years later, on November 25, 1781, in London at 10 Downing Street, that British Prime Minister Lord North learned of the British defeat at Yorktown. Throwing up his arms, as though hit in the breast by a musket ball, he cried, "O God it is all over!" But it took more than a year-and-a-half longer to formally end the American Revolutionary War. It had spread to almost every part of the world, and now Britain was fighting not only the United States of America, but also France, Spain, and the Netherlands.

Formal peace negotiations began at Paris in April 1782, between Benjamin Franklin and Richard Oswald, a liberal Scots merchant sent over by the Earl of Shelborne. When John Jay arrived on June 23rd, he raised objections to the wording of Oswald's commission, "To treat with the Thirteen Colonies . . . or any parts thereof." He insisted on Oswald's obtaining a new commission to treat with "The United States of America." The preliminary treaty of peace was signed on November 30, 1782, more than thirteen months after Cornwallis's surrender at Yorktown. News of the preliminary treaty did not reach America until March 12, 1783. The definitive treaty was dated February 3, 1783, and General Sir Guy Carleton, now British commander in New York City, completed the evacuation of his garrison on November 25, 1783. General Washington marched in, his ill-clad troops a stark contrast to the smart, scarlet-uniformed regulars who departed. But as a spectator remarked, "They were *our* troops . . . and I admired and gloried in them the more, because they were weatherbeaten and forlorn."

At the Franunces Tavern on December 4, 1783, Commander-in-Chief Washington and the few remaining officers of the British army dined together for the last time. Filling a wine glass, Washington held it up and said, "With a heart full of love and gratitude, I now take my leave of you. I most devoutly wish that your later days may be as prosperous and happy as your former ones have been glorious and honorable." With tears in his eyes, Washington invited each officer to come forward and shake his hand. Later, he mounted a horse to ride south and resign his commission to congress.

General Horatio Gates—Gates's success at Saratoga gave him courage to scheme against Washington, whose commission he coveted. A small group of his co-conspirators failed to oust the commander-in-chief, and Gates was forced to content himself with command of the Army in the south replacing Benjamin Lincoln. There in 1780, his blunders lost the battle of Camden. He galloped two hundred miles, ostensibly to bring help, but more likely in panic. After selling his Virginia estate Traveler's Rest in 1790, Gates called his slaves together and announced to them that they were free men. Subsequently, he moved to New York City where he purchased an estate called Rose Hill Farm. He became a Jeffersonian Republican and served a single term in congress from 1800 to 1801. On April 10, 1806, and at the age of seventy-eight, Gates died at Rose Hill Farm.

Colonel James Wilkinson—Colonel Wilkinson experienced a fall out with General Gates, and retired from the army absolutely devoid of combat experience. He rejoined it in 1791, becoming Commander-in-Chief and serving with distinction in the War of 1812, before he was finally court-martialed for conspiring to commit treason with Aaron Burr. He died in 1825.

Major General Philip Schuyler—Burgoyne had the greatest of respect for General Philip Schuyler, whom he regarded as the most underrated general officer on the American side. Burgoyne's aide-de-camp, Major General William Phillips, also had been impressed by Schuyler, and the trio, while staying in General Schuyler's mansion in Albany, talked at length about the future of the war. It was during these sessions that Burgoyne predicted that his defeat at Saratoga would lead to American independence, and he mentioned to Schuyler, in some detail, the possibility that the French would enter the war on the side of the rebels.

After the war, Schuyler held numerous state and national offices; he represented New York State in the first senate of the United States supporting his son-in-law, Alexander Hamilton's financial program. After a short term, he was defeated for re-election by Aaron Burr in 1791. Six years later he defeated Burr for the same seat, but was forced to resign because of ill-health in January, 1798. His loyal friend

George Washington died. Alexander Hamilton was killed by Aaron Burr in a duel. His loving wife, Catherine died of apoplexy in 1803, hastening his own death on November 18,1804.

Major General Benjamin Lincoln—Fat, lame, and undramatic, Benjamin Lincoln possessed all the traditional virtues of a New Englander: reliability, sobriety, and common sense. In his limping stride, he participated in the victories at Saratoga and Yorktown, and between them, had the dubious distinction of surrendering the Southern Army at Charleston. After the war, Lincoln served in Washington's administration as commissioner plenipotentiary to negotiate a peace with the Indians of the South, and, in 1793, to establish a treaty with the Western Indians at Sanducky. In 1809, he resigned his office of collector while under political fire, and on May 9, 1810, he died in the Hingham, Massachusetts house in which he was born.

General Benedict Arnold—Arnold whose services were lauded by almost everyone except General Gates, became disgruntled by the failure of congress to recognize his merits, and encouraged by his Tory wife, changed sides in 1780. His attempt to betray the fort at West Point, where he commanded, was foiled, and he joined the British army, in which he was given the rank of major general. While living in General Schuyler's mansion in Albany, Burgoyne was taken by Schuyler to the hospital to visit his real conqueror, as Burgoyne referred to Arnold. Some of Arnold's critics claim that the seed for his defection was planted by Burgoyne during their private meetings while Arnold was hospitalized. Not only was Arnold not thinking of treason at the time, but Gentleman Johnny would not tolerate any such talk. In fact, no one was more shocked than Burgoyne when Arnold tried to sell out the garrison at West Point. Arnold campaigned in the south against his former friends, and at the end of the war retired in England. Several years later while Arnold was living on the half-pay of a retired British brigadier, the two men came face-to-face in a London club. Gentleman Johnny turned on his heel and stalked off without speaking. Arnold applied for a French commission, but was denied a command when the war with revolutionary

France broke out. Denied a chance at another military career, he traded with the West Indies, where he was well thought of, and invested in privateering ventures that turned out badly. Rejected once again in his request for military service, he died in 1801, forlorn and almost forgotten in Britain; was buried, at his request, in the uniform of the nation whose independence he had helped to achieve. His wife, Peggy Shippen Arnold, who three years later wrote to her father, "General Arnold's affection for me is unbounded. He is the best of husbands." She experienced the satisfaction of seeing her children started in respectable careers in which they were to attain reasonable fame; none has achieved such military importance as their ancestor, the tireless and deadly Dark Eagle as the Indians called him, none has put self-interest or injured pride before honor.

Major Henry Dearborn—Dearborn witnessed Cornwallis's surrender at Yorktown, and served two terms in Congress and as Secretary of War to President Thomas Jefferson. He became a major general and served in the 1812 war against Britain, dying in 1829.

Colonel Thaddeus Kosciuszko—Kosciuszko (Washington misspelled his name eleven different ways) was the mastermind and designer of many of the fortifications and defenses at West Point, as well as, Bemis Heights.

Colonel Daniel Morgan—After the Revolutionary War, Morgan set his combative sights on the politics of the 1790s. He was a fervent believer in Washington's Federalist policies, and convinced that Jeffersonian Republicans were trying to destroy the Constitution. In 1797, he ran on the Federalist ticket and won a seat in the House of Representatives where he could do battle in the Halls of Congress with the Republicans. Advancing age reduced his once mighty frame to near helplessness, but he remained mentally alert. Shortly before his death on July 6, 1802, he told his doctor, "If I could be the man I was when I was twenty-one years of age, I would be willing to be stripped stark naked on the top of the Allegheny Mountain, to run for my life with a pack of dogs a my heel." Truly, Morgan symbolized Crevecoeur's image of the American—a wholly new man.

Lieutenant General "Gentleman Johnny" Burgoyne—To Burgoyne himself, the Continental Congress granted parole pardon, so he could return to England to defend himself from aspirations after an intricate and unsuccessful campaign. He was allowed to sail to Britain on March 3, 1778, but only after he had paid in coin all the bills owed by his army.

The British government, as part of its scheme to silence Burgoyne, ordered him to return to America, which he refused to do, pleading ill health. The Americans did not ask him to relinquish his parole and, on February 2, 1782, he was exchanged for 1,047 enlisted men and minor officers that Edmund Burke called *taking a quantity of silver in exchange for gold*.

Burgoyne was in no physical condition to fight anymore. He had left his sickbed too soon and suffered a relapse, but he refused to take the rest his physicians said he needed. It was far more important, he felt, to visit his troops daily, listen to their complaints, and pass along their requests for improved housing and better food to Major General William Heath, who was responsible for the prisoners. Burgoyne believed he would have been derelict in his duty had he neglected his subordinates and, even as a prisoner of war, Burgoyne's sense of honor was his primary consideration. Burgoyne's officers, British and German, were paroled and allowed to return to their homes. The soldiers were not so fortunate. In November 1778, they were marched, during the depths of winter, from Massachusetts to Virginia and few, if any, reached Europe. They disappeared, assimilated into the American population. Burgoyne spent much of the year recovering his health and spirits at Bath, England, preparing his case against Germain and paying court to a young singer, Susan Caulfield. He could afford to wait while the aggrieved Howe took up the cudgels against Germain. The government had failed to make Burgoyne the scapegoat for Saratoga and most people thought him more sinned against than sinner. Germain, therefore, switched his attack against Howe, claiming he had botched the operation by failing to support Burgoyne as Germain had directed him to do.

Eventually, Burgoyne resigned all his official appointments, wrote a comedy (play), begat four children by Susan Caulfield, whom he did not marry. He was crippled by gout and died at age sixty-nine on

August 4, 1792, soon after returning home from attending the play at the Little Theatyre in the Haymarket. The end came swiftly with Susan Caulfield at his bedside. He was buried in Westminster Abbey.

In 1799 a bill was introduced in Parliament authorizing the expenditure of funds to erect a statue in honor of Lieutenant General John Burgoyne. But the wars with Napoleon caused the House of Commons to devote itself to more pressing matters, and the measure was forgotten as new generals, few of them members of parliament and none of them playwrights, seized centerstage, and captured the hearts and imagination of the public. The last of the eighteenth century's renaissance men was virtually forgotten after his death. There is not one statute of Burgoyne to be found in a monument-filled London, nor one theater plaque to commemorate his literary achievements. It remained for an Irishman, George Bernard Shaw, to make Burgoyne immortal. "Gentleman Johnny," as G.B.S. refers to him, steals the show in one of Shaw's most popular plays, *The Devil's Disciple*. In his notes about the play Shaw renders a judgment on his characters that will last as long as men can read: "Burgoyne fell a victim."

Felix and Fanny Loescher—Felix Loescher served as Burgoyne's commissary-general on one condition, that his wife Fanny, who was less than half his age, part Indian, and rumored to be a flighty girl, would not be left behind, as she might get into trouble. Therefore, he would accompany the expedition only if he could bring her with him. Burgoyne, always with an eye for female beauty, consented; especially for one who did not powder her blue-black tresses. It became evident that Fanny Loescher was endowed with a quality, probably with her husband's understanding, that set her apart; she was amenable, which the other ladies were not. Unfortunately, the latest reference found about the two Loeschers was that riding apart from the rest was Mrs. Fanny Loescher, who was given quarters of her own and who did not go to the tent of the commanding officer until evening. Nothing has been found about Felix, but it can be assumed that he completed his tour of duty as well as his wife did.

General Friedrich Adolf and Madam Frederika von Riedesel— The von Riedesels accompanied the British troops to Virginia. They returned to Canada, where their fourth daughter was born and appropriately named America, and in 1783 they went home to Brunswick, Germany, where the general died in 1800. American historians owe Madam von Riedesel a huge debt of gratitude for her detailed diary accounts of her experience during the war.

General Sir Henry Clinton—Clinton seemed to be immune to criticism. With a small force under his command, he attempted to create a diversionary tactic to assist Burgoyne, and by this he had helped himself to secure favorable cooperation with Burgoyne, who, accordingly, influenced Germain and Howe. Clinton became commander-in-chief when, in 1778, Howe resigned and returned to England, to defend himself against his critics.

General Sir William Howe—Eventually, General Howe appeared before the House of Commons where he criticized Lord George Germain (Sackville) for not giving positive orders. There was a lasting stigma attached to Howe, who, it was believed, had left Burgoyne in the lurch. He either disobeyed orders, or more probably, Germain had muddled the plans for the campaign, or he had, at least in Sir Guy Carleton's opinion, pretended to direct operations of the war three thousand miles distant. All three men survived the blow to their reputations. Germain distorted the truth by telling partial truths. Burgoyne insisted that the orders that he force his way to Albany had been inflexible. Howe's candor shocked rather than appeased those who believed that he had shown lack of military judgement. Howe, eventually, became a full general and died in 1814.

It was on Christmas Day, 1776, when Gentleman Johnny Burgoyne huddled with his friend, Charles James Fox, in London's fashionable Brook's Club and made the wager that he would be home victorious from America by Christmas 1777. They made the wager official when Burgoyne dictated to the clerk the club's first entry, which still stands (if the betting book survived the Second World War):

> John Burgoyne wages Charles (James) Fox one pony (fifty
> guineas) that he will be home victorious from America by
> Christmas 1777.

That day few doubted that the genial and gregarious lieutenant general would collect. As they parted, Fox leaned over his dapper friend's shoulder and whispered, "A bit of warning to you, Burgoyne; be not overly sanguine in your expectations. I believe when next you return to England you will be a prisoner on parole."

In December, 1778, Charles James Fox had not been scheduled to make an address before the House of Commons, but he leaped to his feet as soon as Edmund Burke had finished speaking about "Ignorance stamped every step during the course of the expedition, but it was the ignorance of the Minister (Lord Germain) for the American department, not to be imputed to General Burgoyne, of whose good conduct, bravery and skill I do not entertain the shadow of doubt." Fox, even more contemptuous of Germain, stated:

> An army of ten thousand men destroyed through the ignorance,
> the obstinate, wilful ignorance and incapacity of the noble lord,
> calls loudly for vengeance. A gallant General sent like a victim
> to be slaughtered, where his own skill and personal bravery
> would have won him laurels, if he had not been under the direc-
> tion of a blunderer, which circumstance alone was the cause of
> his disgrace, is too shocking a sight for humanity to bear
> unmoved. The General was imposed upon and deceived; this
> House has been imposed upon and deceived! Burgoyne's orders
> were to make his way to Albany, there to wait the orders of Sir
> William Howe and cooperate with him. But General Howe
> could have known nothing of this matter, for he was gone to a
> different country, and left the unhappy Burgoyne and his troops
> to make the best terms for themselves! If the Minister pursues
> the end of American independence, let him make peace terms
> with the Americans! Let him not sacrifice a great General and
> his courageous troops! Let him not make of this House and this
> nation a laughing-stock for the whole world to mock and
> deride!"

The defenseless Germain, unable to admit he had *totally forgotten* to send Howe's orders to him, took temporary refuge behind a barrier of "military necessity". It has been said that Germain was never one to let someone else's honor stand in the path of his own aims.

⧗

The Battle of Saratoga was the turning point of America's war for independence. General Gates, as commander-in-chief, received credit that both Americans and British believed should have been given to General Benedict Arnold, who now began to think that his talents would be better appreciated by King Charles III than by the Continental Congress.

REFERENCES, RESOURCES, AND READINGS

For those interested in reading more about the Mohawk Valley, its settlement, its defense, and the Battles of Oriskany and Saratoga, these are among the readings that served the author of this book

Billias, George Athan. *George Washington's Generals.* New York: William Morrow and Company, 1964.

Boylan, Brian Richard. *Benedict Arnold: The Dark Eagle.* New York: W. W. Norton & Company, Inc., 1973.

Division of Archives and History. *The American Revolution in New York: Its Political, Social and Economic Significance.* Albany: The State University of New York, 1926.

Dixon, Nancy Wagner. *Palatine Roots.* Camden, Massachsetts: Picton Press, 1994.

Ellis, David, *The Saratoga Campaign,* New York: McGraw-Hill Book Company, 1969.

Furneaux, Rupert. *The Battle of Saratoga.* New York: Stein and Day Publishers, 1971.

Graymont, Barbara. *The Iroquois in the American Revolution.* Syracuse: Syracuse University Press, 1972.

Hamilton, Edward P. *Fort Ticonderoga: Key to a Continent.* Boston: Little, Brown and Company, 1964.

Herkimer, Gil. *Roads to Oriskany: A Saga about the Settlement and Defense of New York's Mohawk Valley during the 1700s,* Corpus Chrisiti: Alfa Publishers, 1996.

Hislop, Codman. *The Mohawk.* New York: Rinehart & Company, Inc., 1948.

Kimball, Sterling O. *The Mohawk Valley Starings and Allied Famlies.* Herkimer, New York: Herkimer County Historical Society, 1998.

Lewis, Paul, *The Man Who Lost America: A Biography of Gentleman Johnny Burgoyne.* New York: Dial Press, 1973.

Lunt, James. *John Burgoyne of Saratoga.* New York: Harcourt Brace Jovanovich, 1975.

Mackesy, Piers. *The War for America: 1775-1783.* Lincoln, Nebraska: University of Nebraska Press, 1993.

Morison, Samuel Eliot. *The Oxford History of the American People, Volume one, Prehistory to 1789.* New York: Oxford University Press, Inc., 1965.

Oneida County. *History of Oneida County, New York.* Oneida: Utica Public Library.

Patrick, Hazel, Jane Spellman, and William Watkins. *The Mohawk Valley Herkimers and Allied Families.* Herkimer, New York: Herkimer County Historical Society, 1989.

Randall, Willard Sterne. *Benedict Arnold: Patriot and Traitor.* New York: William Morrow and Company, Inc., 1990

Watkins, William H. *Slavery in Herkimer County.* Herkimer, New York: Herkimer County Historical Society, *LEGACY*, no. 3, 1990.

Wilbur, C. Keith. *The Revolutionary Soldier, 1775-1783.* Old Saybrook, Connecticut: The Globe Pequot Press, 1969.